THE PENGUIN BOOK OF

ENGLISH PASTORAL VERSE

INTRODUCED AND

EDITED BY

JOHN BARRELL AND JOHN BULL

ALLEN LANE

First published in 1974

Allen Lane
A Division of Penguin Books Ltd
21 John Street, London WC1N 2BT

ISBN 0 7139 0610 3

Printed in Great Britain by
Cox & Wyman Ltd
London, Fakenham and Reading

Set in Monotype Bembo

For
Tom Raworth
and
Tim Clark

CONTENTS

The wisdom of a learned man cometh by opportunity of leisure: and he that hath little business shall become wise.

How can he get wisdom that holdeth the plough, and that glorieth in the goad, that driveth oxen, and is occupied in their labours, and whose talk is of bullocks?

He giveth his mind to make furrows; and is diligent to give the kine fodder.

[*Ecclesiasticus*, 38, vv. 24–6]

M. JOURDAIN: *But why shepherds again? It always seems to be shepherds.*

MUSIC MASTER: *Because, if you are to have people discoursing in song, you must for verisimilitude conform to the pastoral convention. Singing has always been associated with shepherds. It would not seem natural for princes, or ordinary folk for that matter, to be indulging their passions in song.*

M. JOURDAIN: *Very well. Let's hear them.*

[Molière, *Le Bourgeois Gentilhomme*, 1670]

ACKNOWLEDGEMENTS

For permission to reprint the poems in this anthology, acknowledgement is made to the following:

For John Clare's 'Shepherd's Calendar', 'Winter Fields' and 'The Mores', to Professor Eric Robinson and the Clarendon Press, Oxford; for Thomas Hardy's 'In Time of "The Breaking of Nations"', to the Trustees of the Hardy Estate, the Macmillan Company of London and Basingstoke, the Macmillan Company of Canada Ltd, and the Macmillan Company of New York; for Rochester's 'As Chloris full of harmless thought ...' and 'Fair Chloris in a pigsty lay ...', to Yale University Press; and for W. B. Yeats's 'Ancestral Houses', to the Macmillan Company of London and Basingstoke, the Macmillan Company of Canada Ltd, and the Macmillan Company of New York.

We would like to thank Professor Philip Edwards, Tim Clark, Noella Smith and Jania Miller for their assistance of various kinds; Marjorie McGlashan for her help in typing the Introduction; and Margaret Hine for tracking down the text of one of the more obscure poems and Matthew Barreli for help with the index. We would also like to thank Mrs Anne Tibble for providing the text of John Clare's 'The Lament of Swordy Well'.

INTRODUCTION

What is for us the best-known account of the origins of Man opens with a lengthy description of the creation of his environment: 'In the beginning God created the heaven and the earth', we are told in the *Book of Genesis*, and it is not for a further twenty-five verses, until the earth is fully formed and 'God saw that it was good', that the author first turns his attention to Man. The order of events is perfectly appropriate. One of the major themes of Man's recorded thought has been a recurrent attempt to make sense of his relationship to the world he finds himself in. It is as impossible to conceive of Man in a void as it has become to think of him outside society, a solitary animal in a featureless landscape; and of course the two contexts – the geographical and the social – are inextricably linked. The setting which the *Genesis*-author creates for his lone, unfallen man is a suitably unthreatening, harmonious one, a garden free of all social conflict where 'the man' is nursed in a world ready-populated with animal and vegetable life that just waits to be utilized:

> And the LORD God planted a garden eastward in Eden
> and there he put the man whom he had formed.
>
> And out of the ground made the LORD God to grow
> every tree that is pleasant to the sight, and
> good for food . . .

Now, a view of the world as a garden existing only to shelter and provide for 'the man' does not really square with 'Man-in-society's' later historical experience of Nature as either hostile and threatening or, at the least, as raw material to be disciplined and exploited. Outside the garden there is another world, a place of 'thorns also and thistles', where the conflicting demands of separate individuals must be reconciled and the ground tilled and worked for food. And even within the garden, we learn, all is not as it first appears, for the original harmony is something that 'the man' will have to labour at to maintain:

> And the LORD God took the man, and put him into the garden of Eden to dress it and to keep it.

The strict pastoral simplicity of Eden is then very fragile – in the *Genesis* story, the episode in the garden is little more than a brief interlude before the long account of Man's first struggles as a social animal – and the garden contains within itself the seeds of its own destruction, of civilization, the fruit of the Tree of Knowledge. And yet, in the face of all his experience to the contrary, it is this image of Nature as Paradise that has continued to haunt the imagination of Man, and it is this paradox that gives rise to most of the poetry in this anthology.

Towards the end of Cervantes's novel, Don Quixote, finally compelled to relinquish his heroic aspirations, considers the possibility of a pastoral life, spurred on by having observed some ladies and gentlemen of the court at play:

> This is the field where we met the gay shepherdesses and gallant shepherds, who here proposed to revive another pastoral Arcadia. The project was both new and ingenious, and if you think well of it, Sancho, we will follow their example and turn shepherds . . . I will buy some sheep and everything needful for the pastoral vocation . . . and we will wander through the mountains, woods and meadows, singing here, lamenting there, drinking of the liquid crystals of the springs, or of the limpid streams, or the mighty rivers. The oaks shall give us of their sweetest fruit with generous hands; the trunks of the hard cork-trees shall offer us seats; the willows, shade; the roses, perfume; the broad meadows, carpets of a thousand blended colours.*

Cervantes here mocks the pastoral dream of his hero, a dream as misbegotten as Quixote's attempts to revive a feudal code of chivalry.

*Cervantes, *Don Quixote,* translated by J. M. Cohen, Penguin Books, 1950, p. 902.

What is mistaken, and to the reader comic, about both endeavours is that they display a completely mistaken view of the organization of man in society, and of man in his natural surroundings. Quixote seeks to re-establish a world of past values which conflict directly with those of the age he finds himself in – a world, furthermore, which may never have had more than an imagined existence. The terms of the world Quixote conjures with are very like those of the Garden of Eden. For Quixote's courtiers, Nature will organize itself and provide its fruits, without the effort of either noble or labourer. Now it is clear that Cervantes wishes his reader to see that this view of Nature is a false one – to understand that this is not how Quixote or the courtiers in fact come by their daily bread – but what is equally clear is that there are two different kinds of false vision involved here, that of Quixote and that of the courtiers. In the idealized landscape that Quixote describes, the actual complex organization of the countryside is quite invisible, and for the courtiers it is appropriate that it should be so. Their pastoral game, their playing at shepherds, is a ritual celebration of their freedom from economic struggle. Thus, although as an account of the harvest it is distinctly unreliable, it is in keeping with their role in society; it is *as if* Nature were providing for them in the way that Quixote believes. Since the courtiers are, as it were, *unable* to see the labourers in the field, the rural setting serves easily as location for all those more primitive virtues – honesty, peace, innocence, etc. – that are felt to have been irretrievably lost in the sophisticated world of the court. But for Quixote, there is not even this tenuous link with reality. His chivalric pose had anyway been a way of escaping from the, for him, impossible demands of the contemporary world, a retreat to a world of past chivalric virtues more properly the domain of the courtiers. So that the dream that he would act on is not only a false one, but its falsity is not even related to his own situation – he is a usurper of the pastoral role as he had been of the chivalric, a man dreaming above, not below, his station.

This passage comes close to the essential nature of the Pastoral; the way of life that is here presented satirically will more usually be offered by the poets in this anthology in the expectation of a quite serious response from the reader. It is obvious that this view of the countryside is from the perspective of the town or court – and it is a view which suggests a particular kind of relationship between the town, where the writer and his readers would normally live, and the country. The originator of the Pastoral, Theocritus (*c.* 310–250 B.C.), had adapted in his *Idylls* the popular songs and ballads of a Sicilian peasant culture for a sophisticated and literate urban public, so that the Pastoral had been from the outset an urban interpretation of rural matters; and, although in comparison with what was to follow, the *Idylls* do exhibit something of an original, non-urban simplicity, the countryside evoked by Theocritus already allows a distinction between the 'real' and the literary, and the Pastoral is already in the process of becoming a way of *not* looking at the country, at least as much as a way of looking at it. For the pastoral vision is, at base, a false vision, positing a simplistic, unhistorical relationship between the ruling, landowning class – the poet's patrons and often the poet himself – and the workers on the land; as such its function is to mystify and to obscure the harshness of actual social and economic organization. The elements of Quixote's dream are not drawn from any observation of life in the country, but from the stock of an aristocratic culture – just as his aspirations to chivalry had been awakened by the reading of romance literature. At the outset, the Pastoral is a *mythical* view of the relationship of men in society, at the service of those who control the political, economic, and cultural strings of society.

One of the strongest components of the myth is the idea of a Golden Age (in the Arcadia that Quixote was to revive), of an era of pastoral simplicity. The Pastoral was supposed to be the first state of civilized man once he left behind him the solitary activities of hunting and fruit-collecting, and entered society as a shepherd or herdsman; and the first manifestation of art was thought to have been the pastoral songs and ballads produced by the shepherd. A Golden Age suggests a sense of permanence, a world in which values are secure and the social order stable, and where the function of the artist is not threatened by social change. The invocation of a Golden Age will be evidence of a present uncertainty about the stability of society; the pastoral poet becomes the type of the unspoilt shepherd in an idealized form of modern society, one which reflects its structure without its complexities. What the Golden Age represents will vary according to historical circumstances. To the Renaissance poet, the myth offered a conveniently nostalgic view of a feudal past where a harmonious pre-urban community was still felt to exist; while for poets in the period of industrial revolution it was still available in altered form, as a view of *their* immediate past. The availability of the pastoral myth, to describe quite different sorts of changes in social organization, is one of the most important reasons for its perpetuation long after the passing of the particular circumstances which had first called it into existence.

As a supposed historical location, the Golden Age was looked for in both the past and the future, as a setting for man when he first put on the clothing of civilization, or as the future Paradise – the Utopia, the New Jerusalem – he aspired towards. It is a part of a Classical sense of history (which was revived in the Renaissance) as a cyclical process, in which civilizations reach a state of perfection and then *inevitably* decline. This is to replace a feudal notion of history as static and unchanging, with one of endlessly repeated patterns in which the idea of a Golden Age offers hope as well as nostalgia; a notion which is itself threatened in the eighteenth and again in the nineteenth centuries by one of history as continual improvement, a change which has further repercussions on the pastoral tradition. In addition, the Golden Age could be located in the present, most usually as a celebration of court life (as in the Elizabethan period), or as indicative of a literary renaissance (as in the 'Augustan' periods of Roman and English history). The possibility of three different historical locations for a pastoral age gives rise to what is a central ambiguity in the myth. To look back despairingly to an earlier form of society which is seen to have changed irreparably is in flat contradiction to either a celebration of contemporary pastoral life or a looking-forward to a future in which social change will have brought about a new era. The Pastoral allows for a direct opposition to social change, a reactionary clinging to a static present, and an often desperate belief in future improvement. Nor are we able to say that these represent subsequent stages in the development of a pastoral tradition. The Golden Age frequently allowed of two or three interpretations at the same point in time; so that when the Pastoral enters England by way of Italy at the time of the Renaissance, it is both as a way of dealing nostalgically with the complexities of a post-feudal world, and as a vehicle for the celebration of a supposed new Golden Age at the court of Elizabeth. An imagined historical past vies with an imagined historical present.

But the most frequent invocation of the Pastoral is not historical at all. It is as an imaginary society, an alternative to the real world that the poet inhabits, that it finds its most common form. The Pastoral afforded a way of attacking contemporary abuses obliquely, by reference to an idealized vision of what life in the country was like. This strain was not present at all in Theocritus, and originates with Virgil, whose *Eclogues* are the chief model for early English efforts in the genre. It is this critical, ahistorical feature of Pastoral which becomes most ingrained in the literary culture, and which insists on appearing in what are apparently the most unpastoral places. For instance, when Duke Ferdinand, in the *Duchess of Malfi*, wishes to lecture his sister on her behaviour, he turns naturally to a pastoral allusion, before getting to his main point, his fears for the loss of her reputation:

> Death told them, they should find him in great battles,
> Or cities plagu'd with plagues: Love gives them counsel
> To inquire for him 'mongst unambitious shepherds,
> Where dowries were not talk'd of.

Ferdinand, as the prime symbol of court corruption in the play, calls on that tradition which is most directly critical of him in order to preach to his sister on the need for social hypocrisy! The pastoral assumptions serve as a dramatic shorthand, further alerting the audience to the unarcadian nature of the court, and indicating the positive alternative offered by the Duchess's marriage with Antonio, who is, like the 'unambitious shepherds' conjured up by Ferdinand, considerably her social inferior. The alternative world is one which counters the corruption of town and court with rural honesty and simplicity, and in which *divisions* by rank and class have small place, although social distinctions are recognized and acknowledged. This mingling of aristocratic and plebeian is to be found in Theocritus, and is fundamental to the form and content of the Pastoral. In the Pastoral, a primitive egalitarianism flourishes (again as an idealized and 'untrue' account of social organization), but it is an egalitarianism that can occur only within agreed literary conventions.

Now it would be absurd to believe that the writers of Pastoral somehow conspired together to produce this world of myth. It is not sufficient to think of the pastoral world simply as one of convenient fantasy to be opposed to a 'real' world – although, in the later development of the Pastoral, there were many poets who did believe this. George Puttenham, in his *Arte of English Poesie* (1589), is insistent on this point: 'the Poet devised the *Eglogue* long after the other *drammatick* poems, not of purpose to counterfait or represent the rusticall manner of loves and communication: but under the vaile of homely persons and in rude speeches to insinuate and glaunce at greater matters.' The Pastoral, as Puttenham rightly says, was a 'devised' form, but it did provide the poet with a way of talking about *his* world and its values. But it follows none the less that there was always liable to be a tension between the mythical and the naturalistic components of the form, and it is really the history of this tension that we shall be tracing out in this anthology. As the possibility of social mobility and of economic progress increases, so the pastoral tradition, which had originally rested on a separation of social worlds, is first threatened and finally almost fades away.

★

The main problem which confronts anyone attempting to make an anthology such as this is one of definition. To subsume the poetry of, say, Spenser and Goldsmith under the same general heading is to invite immediate difficulties. What is called 'Pastoral' in 1580 is not at first sight much like what is called 'Pastoral' in 1770, and yet the reader is left with a firm impression of a shared tradition, of a common body of material being worked over. But it is not sufficient to point to the subject-matter which these two versions of Pastoral have in common, the description of life in the country, for by no means all the poems about life in the country justify the name of Pastoral, or would have been thought to do so when they were written. One thing that concerns us in this anthology is to show how the same word came to be applied to courtly Elizabethan eclogues and to, for example, certain sorts of late-eighteenth-century descriptive poems, without any apparent break in the tradition, without any point where we could say that one sort of Pastoral ends, and an entirely new sort begins. For this reason our general method has been a chronological ordering of the material divided into convenient sections, each section prefaced by a short account of significant developments within the period. We have, however, felt free to deviate from this chronological order where it seemed useful to do so – the placing of Stephen Duck's *The Thresher's Labour* with the other versions of 'Anti-Pastoral', for instance, rather than with the Augustan poetry that should strictly surround it.

We have not attempted – and indeed could not attempt – anything like a complete coverage of the field. We have been more interested to suggest the range and the persistence of the Pastoral, and our main interest has been the relationship between the conventions of Pastoral and the actuality of rural life. A good deal of Pastoral – especially seventeenth-century Pastoral – is hardly at all an attempt to describe life in the English countryside, but is almost entirely preoccupied with the meaning of its own conventions. We believe, however, that the history of the pastoral tradition is first and foremost a product of the changing relationship between the mythical and the actual, the ideal and the real; and that only in a study of this relationship can the unity of the tradition – the reason for including such diverse poems from periods so different in character – be understood. To keep the size of the anthology within manageable proportions, two restricting factors have operated. Although there are notable exceptions – Burns,

Beattie and such expatriates as James Thomson – we have concentrated on the *English* pastoral tradition. Secondly, and even more regretfully, we had early to take a decision not to include any examples of what is a fundamental part of the tradition, the translations and 'English'd' versions of Theocritus, Virgil, etc., or of the contemporary French and Italian writers who provided between them a model for many of the early versions of the English Pastoral.

We have normally printed the earliest reliable texts of the poems chosen. The date beneath each poem is usually the date of first publication in any form, although it has not always proved possible to check whether the dates of supposed first publication were not in fact preceded by publication in anthology or magazine form. Pastoral poetry raises problems peculiar to itself over whether or not to modernize the text, and it is a problem that we have largely allowed to solve itself. Many of the early pastoral poems are written in a language archaic not only to our eyes, but to those of its contemporary audience – frequently the poet relies heavily on such archaism. Thus it would be unwise to tinker unnecessarily with the text – beyond, for example, replacing the ancient with the modern *s*; and notes have been provided only where it seems absolutely necessary. Towards the end of the seventeenth-century section of the anthology it will become apparent that the text is increasingly regularizing itself, as the archaisms dwindle in importance and as the written language is reduced to the order that we are used to. For similar reasons, in the poetry of the eighteenth century onwards we have occasionally adopted a more settled version of the text than the first edition, since by that time the poet himself often revised the text in later editions.

GLOSSARY OF PASTORAL TERMS

BUCOLIC: Pastoral (from the Greek βουκόλος, a herdsman).

DORIC: Rustic, usually with reference to the use of a rough rural dialect, such as that spoken in Classical times in the Peloponnese and in the Greek cities of Sicily and Southern Italy.

ECLOGUE: *Also* EGLOG, EGLOGUE etc. A short poem, usually a pastoral dialogue (from ἐκλογή, a selection).

ELEGY: A pastoral lament for the death of a fellow-shepherd (from ἔλεγος, a mournful poem); in later centuries the term comes to be applied to the nostalgic evocation of an Arcadian ideal in which the sense of the past-ness, the irrecoverability of that ideal, predominates; contrast IDYLL.

GEORGIC: A didactic version of Pastoral, in which the intention is to idealize country life, but as a life of industry, not idleness, and to impart practical knowledge about agriculture etc. (from γεωργικός, pertaining to agriculture).

IDYLL: A short descriptive sketch of an idealized country scene; the term comes to describe optimistic evocations of pastoral life, which suggest that the Arcadian ideal is (almost) attainable (from εἰδύλλιον).

THE ELIZABETHAN PASTORAL

During the Dark and Early Middle ages, the Pastoral all but disappeared in Europe. It did find some form of expression in the troubadour *pastourelles* in France, poems which reflect the transition from a popular ballad tradition to a sophisticated court culture – and thus have as their dominant theme the conflict between the two worlds in the attempted seduction of a peasant girl by a courtly knight. But feudal society was too stratified, too static, to allow a proper consideration of pastoral matters. Interest in the Pastoral revives in the Renaissance when the feudal idea of community is first seriously threatened. But the Pastoral offered more than a nostalgic myth. It is the *Eclogues* of Virgil that are taken as a model, with the possibilities that they afforded for a greater sophistication, for didacticism, and even for religious satire; an apparently humble cloak for dangerous thought. As the Bible became available in the sixteenth century in the vernacular, so the links between the Pastoral and Christ the shepherd-king were strengthened, with an emphasis on the nativity and its associations with the pastoral theme of regeneration and the coming of the new Golden Age. These strands were most highly developed in Italy – particularly by Petrarch and by Mantuan, to whom Spenser's *The Shepheardes Calendar* acknowledges a debt – and it is by way of Italy that the mainstream of the Pastoral reaches England.

Apart from a few translations, and the 'eglogs' of Barnabe Googe, the first important attempt to write an English Pastoral is *The Shepheardes Calendar* (1579), a poem in which the conventions established by a number of pastoral poets – Theocritus, Virgil, Sannazaro, Mantuan, Marot – are assimilated and 'English'd' with remarkable success. Spenser's shepherds – Colin Clout, Hobbinol, Cuddie and the rest – have almost all been identified with members of Spenser's circle and correspondence – Colin is Spenser himself – and most of them reveal a sophistication, a delicacy, and a learning which a number of critics have thought so uncharacteristic of shepherds as almost to break in on the 'kind', to be not at all the proper language of the genre. But these shepherds, at least as courtly as their European predecessors, are equally capable of the bucolic roughness we find in Theocritus, and Spenser's problem in this poem, and his success, was a matter of finding a form in which the sophisticated and the bucolic could coexist. The essence of this sort of Pastoral, as William Empson has put it, is the belief that 'you can say everything about complex people by a complete consideration of simple people'; but, however you disguise the fact, this is bound to involve making shepherds more complex than shepherds are expected to be; so that we can suspend our disbelief only in proportion as we can be made to feel that these are credible shepherds talking.

Unlike Italy and France, England had still to develop a secure and protected literary language when Spenser began writing, and even the poets most determinedly devoted to a separation of genres, of 'kinds', by language as well as by subject-matter, were liable to find their poems being invaded by words obviously inappropriate to the type of poem they were writing. A properly written eclogue requires an infusion of dialect – Theocritus' peasants had spoken in Doric, and Spenser half-invented an archaic provincial dialect to put in the mouths of his shepherds, too. In Italy and France, where the theory of kinds was well established, the use of dialect was understood easily for what it was – the conventional attribute of shepherds and of the kind appropriate to them. It was not the best language, but the *proper* language of the kind, so that the 'low' words didn't so much point to the low things they described, as make a general point about the humble status of Pastoral. In England we find Spenser trying to make the same point, with the help of cumbersome glosses, but in *The Shepheardes Calendar*, and in the Pastorals of many of his successors, this language has a quite different effect from the one officially intended. The dialect-words or the low-life words used by Spenser, or by Drayton for example, are by no means as unusual as they ought to seem, because they are parts of a language quite proper in other types of English writing. They will not let us see them as literary curios, or simply as signs of the kind being used – they point firmly to the things they denote. When Spenser refers to a 'galage', or when Drayton mentions 'start-ups', we recognize that this is a possible version of English Doric, but we visualize also with disarming clarity the rude action of the rustic pulling on his boots. The artificial roughness so carefully cultivated by the pastoral poet gives way for a moment to a genuine roughness which the Pastoral had previously no less carefully excluded; and as the language points to an image of a contemporary and a recognizable reality, it suggests the possibility that the Pastoral might be used to describe rural life not only in Arcadia, but in the England of 1580.

It can hardly be said that Colin, Cuddie and the rest are made to be particularly knowledgeable about sheep – they know rather more than a well-read townsman of the twentieth century might be expected to know, but not a great deal more; it doesn't seem, either, that their credibility is much to do with the archaisms that Spenser finds for them to speak. But apart from Colin himself, Spenser's shepherds are capable of speaking with a cheerfully colloquial tone, and a robustness of expression, which represent a far more serious attempt to find an English Doric than do the intrusive and well-researched words from provincial and Middle English. This tone is not the invariable one of Hobbinol and the others – it disappears and reappears during the course of each eclogue, and alternates with a far more courtly tone; so that an eclogue will often be introduced by some talk about sheep and some raillery between the participants in the dialogue, which gives way to a lyrical complaint, or to a more sententious passage written partly in a 'higher' language, in turn succeeded by a particularly broad piece of shepherd's talk. This causes some strange disjunctions of level: the roughness of the shepherds' language invites us to believe in them as real shepherds; but when we do, it is their politeness we are asked to admire, so that we cannot help noticing that these are not shepherd-poets, but sometimes shepherds and sometimes poets; that when they make their complaints, they have to employ a different language from that of their usual banter.

In this way the poem obliges us to recognize a variety of social possibilities and identities: we have to distinguish between a set of low-life characters speaking a fairly plausible version of colloquial, rural English; the friends of Spenser masquerading as these shepherds; Colin himself, masquerading as a more conventional shepherd-poet, who because he is unhappy in love has the excuse never to descend from the polite language into the language of his friends; and those friends again, disguising themselves for a second time, this time as more conventional Arcadian shepherds on Colin's level, whenever they have something of real importance to say. The disjunctions, the different levels, the artifices by which Spenser should be able to lead us away from any contemporary reality, instead keep leading us back to it, and invite us to ask what sort of natural simplicity, what sort of Arcadia, could be the product of so much necessary confusion and artifice.

The idea that the Pastoral is masquerade, that the 'shepherd's weeds' are not the natural attributes of the poet, but are perhaps too self-consciously assumed by him, was much exploited by Shakespeare and by other writers who sometimes chose to be satirical at the Pastoral's expense, but it is never far away from Spenser either. It becomes explicit in the passage from the sixth book of *The Faerie Queene*, included in this anthology. Sir Calidore, staying among the shepherds of Arcadia and finding fair Pastorella unimpressed by his 'courteous guize', assumes the dress of a shepherd and then easily wins her love. But in becoming a shepherd he does not cease to be a chivalrous knight; and when Pastorella finds that she does finally prefer Sir Calidore to the shepherd Corydon, it is because his knightly qualities, so unusual and so becoming in a 'shepherd', strike an answering chord in her heart. For she too, although she does not know it, is not really of shepherd-stock, but of altogether higher degree. Sir Calidore has traditionally been identified with Sir Philip Sidney, and whether or not this was Spenser's intention, the figure of the knight dressed as a shepherd is very close to the hardly less fictitious character attributed to Sir Philip by many Elizabethan writers and nostalgic Jacobeans. The mythological Sir Philip embodied all the values of one kind of pastoral vision: he was the most learned and the most chivalrous courtier, at once the most brilliant individual and the most faceless, the most anonymously perfect knight. He was also the shepherd-poet Astrophel, and author of the *Arcadia*, a model Pastoral in prose and verse; and while in the title of Spenser's 'Astrophel', a pastoral elegy on his death, Sidney is described as 'the most noble and valorous knight', in the poem itself he is 'a *gentle* shepherd borne in Arcady'; that is to say, a shepherd, but an exceptionally well-born one.

The court is of course conventionally opposed in Pastoral to the country, but in the figures of Sir Calidore and Sir Philip courtier and shepherd coexist so harmoniously that it becomes hard to distinguish between them, and in this version of Pastoral both combine in their distrust of the court. We can see fairly clearly here the Golden Age being relocated in the myth of a recent feudal past: the courtier or poet represents himself as estranged from the hurly-burly of the Renaissance court, the world of individualism, the struggles for preferment, so that he becomes an old-fashioned courtly poet, or valorous knight, in a court that has left him behind. This first act of masquerade is followed by a second, as the courtier disguises himself next as a shepherd. The world thus created – in *The Faerie Queene*, and in the poems from the *Arcadia* – has far more to do with the dream of an old social order than with that of a pre-historic Golden Age. It is a world in which a 'natural' chivalry and a 'natural' simplicity replace the artful and the politic, and in which such classes of people as the poem admits can meet in an apparently natural social order, accepted by everyone; so that knights can become shepherds, and knights again, just because there is no question of these transformations reflecting any actual social mobility. The shepherds in Spenser's later Pastoral, and in the *Arcadia*, are far more courtly than were those in the more homely passages of *The Shepheardes Calendar*; one could never imagine Sir Philip as Cuddie, complaining that his shoe was stuck to his foot by the cold.

The prevailing tone of this higher kind of Pastoral is nostalgic, and although nostalgia is a permanent conventional feature of earlier

Pastoral, it reappears in Sidney's poems particularly as the malaise of the Renaissance, 'wanhope' or 'accidie'. In Sidney's 'Disprayse of a Courtly life', a courtier presents himself as having been, formerly, a shepherd, who tended his sheep with the other shepherds 'lovingly like friends'; but now he lives in the 'servile Court', where pride and intrigue make him long for the artlessness of the country; he prays that Pan might restore him to his former state; and the poem ends with the moral that 'the meane estate is best'. But this version of pastoral-courtly 'accidie' is more complex than at first appears, for Sidney's nostalgia is implicitly recognized by him as being for an ideal literary world, and not for any real or possible alternative way of life. As such it carries with it the assurance that no return is possible, that there is nothing to return to.

The nostalgia of Sidney becomes still more problematic when we find it expressed by those already inhabiting his Arcadia. A very large number of the poems from the *Arcadia* itself are laments, some to do with disappointments in love but all expressing a generalized despair which sees no chance of a return or a release. The process by which this final refinement of pastoral nostalgia has been reached is complicated enough: the poet, who first imagines himself as a poet or courtier from an earlier time, then imagines himself as a shepherd in a classical Arcadia; but his nostalgia is not removed by these two movements back in time – it stays with him, so that he finds himself still looking back to the Golden Age he apparently already inhabits, or to a Golden Age before the Golden Age. The hopelessness, the impossibility of Arcadia becomes clearer with each fresh artifice and masquerade – the poets of the generation after Sidney look back to the arguably less artificial *Shepheardes Calendar* to discover how the Pastoral might still be written.

Apart from the dramatists, the most remarkable poet of this next generation is Michael Drayton, who in *The Shepheardes Garland* (1593) is clearly impatient with masquerades and searches for Arcadia. There is in Drayton's Pastoral no simple or formal nostalgia for the Golden Age – his shepherds are old, their time has past, they live on to mock the pastoral pretensions of those around them. The few youthful shepherds in these eclogues are quickly relieved of their lyricism and their hopes by their much-lived elders. *The Shepheardes Garland* is centred on the ageing Rowland (presumably the poet) who looks back to a time when life was better, a time before urbanization and the first processes of the manufacturing industries, before the trees were ripped up to reveal the mineral earth beneath them. There is no suggestion of a recoverable pastoral age, for 'the golden age is gone' and 'wishes may not revoke that which is past'. The tone is one of almost unrelieved pessimism. In the final eclogue, Rowland, after half a night lamenting the hopelessness of his past aspirations, retires to bed, 'never a man alive so hard bested'. The future has nothing to offer, and the contemplation of the past brings only despair.

Drayton never really fitted into the court circle to which he looked so unsuccessfully for patronage. In the fourth eclogue, Wynkin bemoans the loss of Sir Philip Sidney, in the shape of Elphin, 'the God of Poesie', and we see not only the pessimistic awareness of the growth of a new kind of urban, not courtly, culture, but an acute sense of the significance for poetry of this change. Drayton's Pastoral, for all its freshness and its brilliance of detail, is a self-conscious turning-back not to some imaginary idealized Arcadia but to a time immediately before he was writing, the great period of Spenser and Sidney; the world those poets had turned away from has become an Arcadia for Drayton. And his despair is the stronger precisely because he can no longer locate the Golden Age in a mythical and a feudal past. In the first eclogue, Rowland, surrounded by all the traditional emblems of a pastoral Spring, remains as an aged shepherd outside the tradition that has produced him, a creature of Winter:

> The heavens with their glorious starry frame,
> Preparde to crowne the sable-vayled night:
> When *Rowland* from this time-consumed stock,
> With stone-colde hart now stalketh towards his flock.

The final line – and especially that sudden change of tense – removes Rowland's despair from the well-rehearsed lines of conventional complaint, and introduces a personal tone that is predominant throughout the rest of the eclogues.

In the eighth eclogue we have the deliberate archaism of Motto's 'worthy rhyme' of Dowsabell, which seems to exist only to indicate its irrelevance in a changed society. The story, with its heavy echoes of Chaucer – and so with the suggestion of an earlier literary 'pastoral' age when it was possible for the poet to prosper – delights the reader with its simple expression of reciprocated love, only to return him inevitably to the sad and unfulfilled reality of the present; just as elsewhere, the love poetry of the young Rowland can be recalled, but only ironically. There was no possibility of a resurrection of an Elphin, for the Elizabethan Golden Age (that of Betta in the third eclogue) had ended. The courtly shepherd with his elaborate series of masks has been replaced in Drayton by the figure of the poet no longer able to rely on court patronage. For the first time in the development of the English Pastoral the poet finds himself quite shut out of his courtly Arcadia. The sense of despair is even stronger in the revised version of the eclogues, produced after the accession of James I, when 'malice denies mee entrance with my sheepe'. In the revised ninth eclogue (which becomes the tenth in the second version) Drayton, in an image which recalls the end of the original first eclogue, brings Rowland no longer to a restless sleep, but to death; as one who 'as a stone, alreadie seemed dead'.

Some be of opinion . . . that the pastorall Poesie . . . should be first of any other, and before the Satyre comedie or tragedie, because . . . the shepheards and haywards assemblies and meetings when they kept their cattell and heards in the common fields and forests, was the first familiar conversation . . . But for all this, I do deny that the Eglogue *should be the first and most auncient forme of artificiall Poesie, being perswaded that the Poet devised the* Eglogue *long after the other* drammatick *poems, not of purpose to counterfait or represent the rusticall manner of loves and communication: but under the vaile of homely persons and in rude speeches to insinuate and glaunce at greater matters.*

[George Puttenham, *Arte of English Poesie*, 1589]

Is it then the Pastorall Poeme *which is misliked? (For perchance where the hedge is lowest they will soonest leape over) is the poore pipe disdained, which somtimes out of* Mœlibeus *mouth, can shewe the miserie of people, under hard Lords and ravening souldiers? And again by* Titerus, *what blessednesse is derived, to them that lie lowest, from the goodnesse of them that sit highest? Sometimes under the prettie tales of Woolves and sheepe, can enclude the whole considerations of wrong doing and patience; sometimes shew that contentions for trifles, can get but a trifling victory, wher perchance a man may see, that even* Alexander & Darius, *when they strave who should be Cocke of this worldes dunghill, the benefit they got, was, that the afterlivers may say,* Hæc memini et victum frustra contendere Thirsim. Ex illo Coridon, Coridon est tempore nobis.*

[Sir Philip Sidney, *The Defence of Poesie*, 1598]

* Virgil, *Eclogues*, VII, 69–70. 'These things I remember, and that Thyrsis strove in vain and was vanquished; from that time Corydon, Corydon alone, has been our poet.'

BARNABE GOOGE

Egloga Tertia

MENALCAS CORIDON

A pleasaunt wether *Coridon*,
  and fytte to kepe the fyelde,
This moone hath brought, hearst you the birds
  what joyfull tunes they yeld?
Loe: how the lustie lambes do course,
  whom spring time heate doth pricke
Beholde againe, the aged Yewes,
  with bouncinge leapes do kicke,
Amongst them all, what ayles thy ramme,
  to halte so muche behynde,
Some sore mischaunce, hath him befaln
  or els some griefe of minde,
For wonte he was, of stomacke stoute
  and courage hye to be,
And looked proude, amongst ye flocke,
  and none so stout as he.

CORIDON

A great mishap, and griefe of mynde,
  is him befalne of late,
Which causeth him, against his wyll,
  to lose his olde estate.
A lustie flocke hath *Titirus*,
  that him *Dametas* gave,
Dametas he, that Martir died,
  whose soule the heave[n]s have,
And in this flocke, full many Yewes
  of pleasaunte forme do goe,
with them a mighty Ramme doth ronne,
  that workes all Woers woe.

My Ramme, when he the pleasaunt dames
 had vewed rounde aboute,
Chose grounde of battayle, with his foe
 and thought to fyght it oute.
But all to weake, (alas) he was,
 althoughe his harte was good,
For when his enemye him espied,
 he ranne with cruell moode.
And with his croked weapon smote,
 hym sore upon the syde,
A blowe of force, that stayde not there
 but to the legges dyd glyde.
And almoste laamd the woer quyte.
 (suche happes in love there be:)
This is the cause, of all his griefe
 and waylynge that you se.

MENALCAS

Well *Coridon* let hym go halte,
 and let us both go lye,
In yonder busshe of Juniper,
 the Beasts shall fede hereby.
A pleasaunt place here is to talke:
 good *Coridon* begyn,
And let us knowe the Townes estate,
 that thou remaynest in.

CORIDON

The Townes estate? *Menalcas* oh
 thou makste my harte to grone,
For Vice hath every place posseste,
 and Vertue thence is flowne.
Pryde beares her selfe, as Goddesse chiefe
 and boastes above ye Skye,
And Lowlynes an abjecte lyes,
 with Gentlenes her bye,

Wyt is not joynde with Symplenes,
  as she was wont to be,
But sekes the ayde of Arrogance,
  and craftye Polycie.
Nobylitie begyns to fade,
  and Carters up do sprynge,
Then whiche, no greater plague can hap,
  nor more pernicious thynge.
Menalcas I have knowen my selfe,
  within this thyrtye yeare,
Of Lordes and Auncient Gentelmen
  a hundreth dwellynge theare,
Of whom we Shephardes had reliefe
  suche Gentlenes of mynde,
Was placed in theyr noble Hartes,
  as none is nowe to fynde.
But Hawtynes and proude Disdayne
  hath nowe the chiefe Estate,
For syr John Straw, and syr John Cur,
  wyll not degenerate.
And yet, they dare account them selves
  to be of Noble bludde.
But Fisshe bred up, in durtye Pooles,
  wyll ever stynke of mudde.
I promyse the *Menalcas* here,
  I wolde not them envye.
Yf any spot of Gentlenes
  in them I myght espye.
For yf theyr Natures gentell be,
  thoughe byrth be never so base,
Of Gentelmen (for mete it is)
  they ought have name and place:
But when by byrth, they base are bred,
  and churlisshe harte retaine,

Though place of gentlemen thei have
  yet churles they do remayne.
A proverbe olde, hath ofte ben harde
  and now full true is tryed:
An Ape, wyll ever be an Ape,
  thoughe purple garments hyde.
For seldom, wyll the mastye[1] course, [1] mastiff
  the Hare or els the Deare:
But styll, accordynge to his kynde.
  wyll holde, the hogge by th'eare.
Unfitte are dunghill knights to serve
  the towne with Speare in fielde:
Nor strange it semes, (a sudain Chop)
  to leape from whyp, to shielde.
The chiefest man, in all our towne,
  that beares the greatest swaye,
Is *Coridon* no kynne to me,
  a Neteherd[2] th'other daye. [2] cowherd
This *Coridon* come from the Carte,
  In honour chiefe doth sytte,
And governes us: because he hath
  a Crabbed, Clownish wytte.
Nowe se the Churlysh Crueltye,
  that in hys harte remayns.
The selye Sheape yat Shephards good,
  have fosterd up wyth Paynes,
And browght awaye, from Stynkyng dales
  on pleasant Hylles to feade:
O Cruell Clownish Coridon
  O cursed Carlish Seade:
The simple Shepe, constrayned he,
  theyr Pasture swete to leave,
And to theyr old corrupted Grasse,
  enforceth them to cleave.

Such Shepe, as would not them obaye
  but in theyr Pasture byde,
with cruell flames, they did consume
  and vex on every syde.
And with the shepe, ye Shephardes good,
  (O hate full Hounds of Hell,)
They did torment, and dryve them out,
  in Places farre to dwell.
There dyed *Daphnes* for his Shepe,
  the chiefest of them all.
And fayre *Alexis* flamde in Fyre,
  who never perysshe shall.
O Shephards wayle, for *Daphnes* deth.
  Alexis hap lament,
And curs the force of cruell hartes,
  that them to death have sent.
I, synce I sawe suche synfull syghts,
  dyd never lyke the Towne,
But thought it best to take my sheepe,
  and dwell upon the downe.
Wheras I lyve, a pleasaunt lyfe,
  and free from cruell handes,
I wolde not leave, the pleasaunt fyelde
  for all the Townysh Landes.
For syth that Pryde, is placed thus,
  and Vice set up so hye:
And Crueltie doth rage so sore,
  and men lyve all awrye:
Thynkste you? yat God, will long forbere,
  his scourge, and plague to sende?
To suche as hym do styll despyse,
  and never seke to mende?
Let them be sure he wyll revenge,
  when they thynke leaste upon.

But looke a stormy showre doth ryse,
  whiche wyll fall heare anone,
Menalcas best we nowe departe,
  my Cottage us shall keepe,
For there is rowme for the, and me,
  and eke for all our sheepe:
Som Chestnuts have I there in store
  with Cheese and pleasaunt whaye,
God sends me Vittayles for my nede,
  and I synge Care awaye.

[1563]

EDMUND SPENSER

The Shepheardes Calendar
February

CUDDIE THENOT

Ah for pittie, wil rancke Winters rage,
These bitter blasts never ginne tasswage?
The kene cold blowes through my beaten hyde,
All as I were through the body gryde[1].
My ragged rontes[2] all shiver and shake,
As doen high Towers in an earthquake:
They wont in the wind wagge their wrigle tailes,
Perke as Peacock: but nowe it avales.

[1] pierced
[2] bullocks

THENOT

Lewdly complainest thou laesie ladde,
Of Winters wracke, for making thee sadde.
Must not the world wend in his commun course
From good to badd, and from badde to worse,

From worse unto that is worst of all,
And then returne to his former fall?
Who will not suffer the stormy time,
Where will he live tyll the lusty prime?
Selfe have I worne out thrise threttie yeares,
Some in much joy, many in many teares:
Yet never complained of cold nor heate,
Of Sommers flame, nor of Winters threat:
Ne ever was to Fortune foeman,
But gentle tooke, that ungently came.
And ever my flocke was my chiefe care,
Winter or Sommer they mought well fare.

CUDDIE

No marveile *Thenot*, if thou can beare
Cherefully the Winters wrathfull cheare:
For Age and Winter accord full nie,
This chill, that cold, this crooked, that wrye.
And as the lowring Wether lookes downe,
So semest thou like good fryday to frowne.
But my flowring youth is foe to frost,
My shippe unwont in stormes to be tost.

THENOT

The soveraigne of seas he blames in vaine,
That once seabeate, will to sea againe.
So loytring live you little heardgroomes,
Keeping your beastes in the budded broomes:
And when the shining sunne laugheth once,
You deemen, the Spring is come attonce.
Tho gynne you, fond flyes, the cold to scorne,
And crowing in pypes made of greene corne,
You thinken to be Lords of the yeare.
But eft, when ye count you freed from feare,
Comes the breme[3] winter with chamfred[4] browes,
Full of wrinckles and frostie furrowes:

[3] cold
[4] chopped

Drerily shooting his stormy darte,
Which cruddles the blood, and pricks the harte.
Then is your carelesse corage accoied[5], [5] daunted
Your carefull heards with cold bene annoied.
Then paye you the price of your surquedrie[6], [6] pride
With weeping, and wayling, and misery.

CUDDIE

Ah foolish old man, I scorne thy skill.
That wouldest me, my springing youngth to spill
I deeme, thy braine emperished bee
Through rusty elde, that hath rotted thee:
Or sicker thy head veray tottie[7] is, [7] wavering
So on thy corbe[8] shoulder it leanes amisse. [8] crooked
Now thy selfe hast lost both lopp and topp,
Als my budding braunch thou wouldest cropp:
But were thy yeares greene, as now bene myne,
To other delights they would encline.
Tho wouldest thou learne to caroll of Love,
And hery[9] with hymnes thy lasses glove. [9] worship
Tho wouldest thou pype of *Phyllis* prayse:
But *Phyllis* is myne for many dayes:
I wonne her with a gyrdle of gelt,
Embost with buegle about the belt.
Such an one shepeheards woulde make full faine:
Such an one would make thee younge againe.

THENOT

Thou art a fon[10], of thy love to boste, [10] fool
All that is lent to love, wyll be lost.

CUDDIE

Seest, howe brag yond Bullocke beares,
So smirke, so smoothe, his pricked eares?
His hornes bene as broade, as Rainebowe bent,
His dewelap as lythe[11], as lasse of Kent. [11] soft

See howe he venteth[12] into the wynd. [12] sniffs
Weenest of love is not his mynd?
Seemeth thy flocke thy counsell can,
So lustlesse bene they, so weake so wan,
Clothed with cold, and hoary wyth frost.
Thy flocks father his corage hath lost:
Thy Ewes, that wont to have blowen bags,
Like wailefull widdowes hangen their crags[13]. [13] necks
The rather Lambes bene starved with cold,
All for their Maister is lustlesse and old.

THENOT

Cuddie, I wote thou kenst little good,
So vainely tadvaunce thy headlesse hood.
For Youngth is a bubble blown up with breath,
Whose witt is weakenesse, whose wage is death.
Whose way is wildernesse, whose ynne Penaunce,
And stoopegallaunt Age the hoste of Greevaunce.
But shall I tel thee a tale of truth,
Which I cond of *Tityrus*[14] in my youth, [14] i.e. Chaucer
Keeping his sheepe on the hils of Kent?

CUDDIE

To nought more *Thenot*, my mind is bent,
Then to heare novells of his devise:
They bene so well thewed, and so wise,
What ever that good old man bespake.

THENOT

Many meete tales of youth did he make,
And some of love, and some of chevalrie:
But none fitter then this to applie.
Now listen a while, and hearken the end.

There grewe an aged Tree on the greene,
A goodly Oake sometime had it bene,

With armes full strong and largely displayd,
But of their leaves they were disarayde:
The bodie bigge, and mightely pight[15],
Throughly rooted, and of wonderous hight:
Whilome had bene the King of the field,
And mochell mast to the husband did yielde,
And with his nuts larded many swine.
But now the gray mosse marred his rine[16],
His bared boughes were beaten with stormes,
His toppe was bald, and wasted with wormes,
His honor decayed, his braunches sere.
  Hard by his side grewe a bragging brere,
Which proudly thrust into Thelement,
And seemed to threat the Firmament.
Yt was embellisht with blossomes fayre,
And thereto aye wonned to repayre
The shepheards daughters, to gather flowres,
To peinct their girlonds with his colowres.
And in his small bushes used to shrowde
The sweete Nightingale singing so lowde:
Which made this foolish Brere wexe so bold,
That on a time he cast him to scold,
And snebbe the good Oake, for he was old.
  Why standst there (quoth he) thou brutish blocke?
Nor for fruict, nor for shadowe serves thy stocke:
Seest, how fresh my flowers bene spredde,
Dyed in Lilly white, and Cremsin redde,
With Leaves engrained in lusty greene,
Colours meete to clothe a mayden Queene.
Thy wast bignes but combers the grownd,
And dirks the beauty of my blossomes rownd.
The mouldie mosse, which thee accloieth[17]
My Sinamon smell too much annoieth.
Wherefore soone I rede thee, hence remove,
Least thou the price of my displeasure prove.

[15] pitched into the ground

[16] bark

[17] encumbers

So spake this bold brere with great disdaine:
Little him answered the Oake againe,
But yielded, with shame and greefe adawed[18],
That of a weede he was overcrawed.
  Yt chaunced after upon a day,
The Hus-bandman selfe to come that way,
Of custome for to servewe his ground,
And his trees of state in compasse rownd.
Him when the spitefull brere had espyed,
Causeless complained, and lowdly cryed
Unto his Lord, stirring up sterne strife:
O my liege Lord, the God of my life,
Pleaseth you ponder your Suppliants plaint,
Caused of wrong, and cruell constraint,
Which I your poore Vassall dayly endure.
And but your goodnes the same recure,
Am like for desperate doole[19] to dye,
Through felonous force of mine enemie.
  Greatly aghast with this piteous plea,
Him rested the goodman on the lea,
And badde the Brere in his plaint proceede.
With painted words tho gan this proude weede,
(As most usen Ambitious folke:)
His colowred crime with craft to cloke.
  Ah my soveraigne, Lord of creatures all,
Thou placer of plants both humble and tall,
Was not I planted of thine owne hand,
To be the primrose of all thy land,
With flowring blossomes, to furnish the prime,
And scarlot berries in Sommer time?
How falls it then, that this faded Oake,
Whose bodie is sere, whose braunches broke,
Whose naked Armes stretch unto the fyre,
Unto such tyrannie doth aspire:
Hindering with his shade my lonely light,

[18] confounded

[19] grief

And robbing me of the swete sonnes sight?
So beate his old boughes my tender side,
That oft the bloud springeth from woundes wyde:
Untimely my flowres forced to fall,
That bene the honour of your Coronall.
And oft he lets his cancker wormes light
Upon my braunches, to worke me more spight:
And oft his hoarie locks downe doth cast,
Where with my fresh flowretts bene defast.
For this, and many more such outrage,
Crawing your goodlihead to aswage
The ranckorous rigour of his might,
Nought aske I, but onely to hold my right:
Submitting me to your good sufferance,
And praying to be garded from greevance.
  To this the Oake cast him to replie
Well as he couth: but his enemie
Had kindled such coles of displeasure,
That the good man noulde stay his leasure,
But home him hasted with furious heate,
Encreasing his wrath with many a threate.
His harmefull Hatchet he hent in hand,
(Alas, that it so ready should stand)
And to the field alone he speedeth,
(Ay little helpe to harme there needeth)
Anger nould let him speake to the tree,
Enaunter his rage mought cooled bee:
But to the roote bent his sturdy stroke,
And made many wounds in the wast Oake
The Axes edge did oft turne againe,
As halfe unwilling to cutte the graine:
Semed, the senceless yron dyd feare,
Or to wring holy eld did forbeare.
For it had bene an auncient tree,
Sacred with many a mysteree,

And often crost with the priestes crewe[20]
And often halowed with holy water dewe.
But sike fancies weren foolerie,
And broughten this Oake to this miserye.
For nought mought they quitten him from decay:
For fiercely the good man at him did laye.
The blocke oft groned under the blow,
And sighed to see his neare overthrow.
In fine the steele had pierced his pitth,
Tho downe to the earth he fell forthwith:
His wonderous weight made the grounde to quake,
Thearth shronke under him, and seemed to shake.
There lyeth the Oake, pitied of none.
Now stand the Brere like a Lord alone,
Puffed up with pryde and vaine pleasaunce:
But all this glee had no continuaunce.
For eftsones Winter gan to approche,
The blustring Boreas did encroche,
And beate upon the solitarie Brere:
For nowe no succoure was seene him nere.
Now gan he repent his pryde to late:
For naked left and disconsolate,
The byting frost nipt his stalke dead,
The watrie wette weighed downe his head,
And heaped snowe burdned him so sore,
That nowe upright he can stand no more:
And being downe, is trodde in the durt
Of cattell, and brouzed, and sorely hurt.
Such was thend of this Ambitious brere,
For scorning Eld

[20] holy water vessel. The whole episode is an anti-clerical satire.

CUDDIE

Now I pray thee shepheard, tel it not forth:
Here is a long tale, and little worth.
So long have I listened to thy speche,

That graffed to the ground is my breche:
My hartblood is welnigh frorne I feele,
And my galage[21] growne fast to my heele:
But little ease of thy lewd tale I tasted.
Hye thee home shepheard, the day is nigh wasted.

[21] boot

Thenots Embleme:
Iddio perche e vecchio,
Fa suoi al suo essempio.
Cuddies Embleme:
Niuno vecchio,
Spaventa Iddio.

From *May*

PIERS

The time was once, and may againe retorne,
(For ought may happen, that hath bene beforne)
When shepeheards had none inheritaunce,
Ne of land, nor fee in sufferaunce:
But what might arise of the bare sheepe,
(Were it more or lesse) which they did keepe.
Well ywis was it with shepheards thoe:
Nought having, nought feared they to forgoe.
For *Pan* himselfe was their inheritaunce,
And little them served for their mayntenaunce.
The shepheards God so wel them guided,
That of nought they were unprovided,
Butter enough, honye, milke, and whay,
And their flockes fleeces, them to araye.
But tract of time, and long prosperitie:
That nource of vice, this of insolencie,
Lulled the shepheards in such securitie,

That not content with loyall obeysaunce,
Some gan to gape for greedie governaunce,
And match them selfe with mighty potentates,
Lovers of Lordship and troublers of states:
Tho gan shepheards swaines to looke a loft,
And leave to live hard, and learne to ligge[1] soft: [1] lie
Tho under colour of shepeheards, somewhile
There crept in Wolves, ful of fraude and guile,
That often devoured their owne sheepe,
And often the shepheards, that did hem keepe.
This was the first sourse of shepheards sorowe,
That now nill be quitt with baile, nor borrowe.

[1579]

SIR PHILIP SIDNEY

Four poems from the *Arcadia*

Dorus

Come shepheard's weedes, become your master's minde:
Yeld outward shew, what inward change he tryes:
Nor be abasht, since such a guest you finde,
Whose strongest hope in your weake comfort lyes.

Come shepheard's weedes, attend my woefull cryes:
Disuse your selves from sweete *Menalcas*' voice:
For other be those tunes which sorrow tyes,
From those cleere notes which freely may rejoyce.
  Then power out plaint, and in one word say this:
  Helples his plaint, who spoyles himselfe of blisse.

Dorus

My sheepe are thoughts, which I both guide and serve:
Their pasture is faire hilles of fruitless Love:
On barren sweetes they feede, and feeding sterve:
I waile their lotte, but will not other prove.
My sheepehooke is wanne hope, which all upholdes:
My weedes, Desire, cut out in endlesse foldes.
  What wooll my sheepe shall beare, whyle thus they live,
  In you it is, you must the judgement give.

Dorus

Feede on my sheepe, my chardge my comforte feede,
With sonne's approche your pasture fertill growes,
O only sonne that suche a fruite can breede.

Feede on my sheepe, your fayer sweete feeding flowes,
Eache flower eache herbe dothe to your service yeeld,
O blessed sonne whence all this blessing goes.

Feede on my sheepe, possesse your fruitefull fyeld,
No woolves dare howle, no murrayne can prevaile,
And from the stormes our sweeteste sonne will shield.

Feede on my sheepe, sorrow hathe stricken sayle,
Enjoye my joyes, as you dyd taste my payne,
While our sonne shynes no clowdie greeves assaile.
  Feede on my sheepe, your Native joyes mayntayne,
  Your woll is riche: no tonge can tell my gayne.

Philisides

Leave of my sheepe: it is no tyme to feede,
My sonne is gon, your pasture barrein growes,
O cruell sonne thy hate this harme dothe breede.

Leave of my sheepe, my shower of teeres oreflowes,
Your sweetest flowers, your herbes, no service yeeld,
My sonne alas from me for ever goes.

Leave of my sheepe, my sighes burne up your filde,
My plaintes call wolves, my plagues in you prevaile,
My sun is gon, from stormes what shall us sheelde?

Leave of my sheepe, sorrowe hathe hoysed sayle,
Wayle in my woes, taste of your master's payne,
My sun is gon, Nowe clowdie greeves assayle.
  Leave off my sheep my mourninge to maintayne,
  You beare no woll, and losse is all my gayne.

[1590]

Ninth Song

From *Astrophil and Stella*

Go my flocke, go get you hence,
Seeke a better place of feeding,
Where you may have some defence
From the stormes in my breast breeding,
And showers from mine eyes proceeding.

Leave a wretch, in whom all wo
Can abide to keepe no measure,
Merry flocke, such one forgo,
Unto whom mirth is displeasure,
Only rich in mischiefe's treasure.

Yet alas before you go,
Heare your wofull maister's story,
Which to stones I els would show:

Sorrow onely then hath glory,
When tis excellently sory.

Stella fiercest shepherdesse,
Fiercest but yet fairest ever;
Stella whom ô heavens do blesse,
Tho against me shee persever,
Tho I blisse enherit never.

Stella hath refused me,
Stella who more love hath proved,
In this caitife hart to be,
Then can in good eawes be moved
Toward *Lamkins* best beloved.

Stella hath refused me,
Astrophil that so wel served,
In this pleasant spring must see
While in pride flowers be preserved,
Himselfe onely winter-sterved.

Why alas doth she then sweare,
That she loveth me so dearely,
Seing me so long to beare
Coles of love that burne so clearely;
And yet leave me helplesse meerely?

Is that love? forsooth I trow,
If I saw my good dog grieved,
And a helpe for him did know,
My love should not be beleeved,
But he were by me releeved.

No, she hates me, wellaway,
Faining love, somewhat to please me:

For she knowes, if she display
All her hate, death soone would seaze me,
And of hideous torments ease me.

Then adieu, deere flocke adieu:
But alas, if in your straying
Heavenly *Stella* meete with you,
Tell her in your piteous blaying,
Her poore slave's unjust decaying.

[1591]

Disprayse of a Courtly life

Walking in bright *Phœbus*' blaze
Where with heate oppreste I was,
I got to a shady wood,
Where greene leaves did newly bud.
And of grasse was plenty dwelling,
Deckt with pyde flowers sweetely smelling.

In this wood a man I met,
On lamenting wholy set:
Rewing change of wonted state,
Whence he was transformed late,
Once to Shepheard's God retayning,
Now in servile Court remayning.

There he wandring malecontent,
Up and downe perplexed went,
Daring not to tell to mee,
Spake unto a sencelesse tree,
One among the rest electing
These same words, or this effecting:

'My old mates I grieve to see,
Voyde of me in field to bee,
Where we once our lovely sheepe,
Lovingly like friends did keepe,
Oft each other's friendship proving,
Never striving, but in loving.

'But may Love abiding bee
In poore shepheard's base degree?
It belongs to such alone
To whom arte of Love is knowne:
Seely shepheards are not witting
What in art of Love is fitting.

'Nay, what neede the Arte to those,
To whom we our love disclose?
It is to be used then,
When we doe but flatter men:
Friendship true in hart assured,
Is by nature's giftes procured.

'Therefore shepheardes wanting skill,
Can Love's duties best fulfill:
Since they know not how to faine,
Nor with Love to cloake Disdaine,
Like the wiser sorte, whose learning,
Hides their inward will of harming.

'Well was I, while under shade
Oten Reedes me musicke made,
Striving with my Mates in Song,
Mixing mirth our Songs among,
Greater was that shepheard's treasure,
Then this false, fine, Courtly pleasure.

'Where, how many Creatures be,
So many pufft in minde I see,
Like to *Junoe's* birdes of pride,
Scarce each other can abide,
Friends like to blacke Swannes appearing,
Sooner these than those in hearing.

'Therefore *Pan*, if thou mayst be
Made to listen unto me,
Grant, I say (if seely man
May make treaty to god *Pan*)
That I, without thy denying,
May be still to thee relying.

'Only for my two loves' sake,
In whose love I pleasure take,
Only two do me delight
With their ever-pleasing sight,
Of all men to thee retaining,
Grant me with those two remaining.

'So shall I to thee alwayes,
With my reedes, sound mighty praise;
And first Lambe that shall befall,
Yearely decke thine Altar shall:
If it please thee be reflected,
And I from thee not rejected.'

So I left him in that place,
Taking pitty on his case,
Learning this among the rest,
That the meane estate is best,
Better filled with contenting,
Voyde of wishing and repenting.

[1611]

EDMUND SPENSER

From *Astrophel*

A Pastorall Elegie upon the death of the most Noble and valorous Knight, Sir Philip Sidney

Shepheards that wont on pipes of oaten reed,
Oft times to plaine your loves concealed smart:
And with your piteous layes have learned to breed
Compassion in a countrey lasses hart.
Hearken ye gentle shepheards to my song,
And place my dolefull plaint your plaints emong.

To you alone I sing this mournfull verse,
The mournfulst verse that ever man heard tell:
To you whose softened hearts it may empierse,
With dolours dart for death of Astrophel.
To you I sing and to none other wight[1]*,* — [1] man
For well I wot my rymes bene rudely dight[2]*,* — [2] made

Yet as they been, if any nycer wit
Shall hap to heare, or covet them to read:
Thinke he, that such are for such ones most fit,
Made not to please the living but the dead.
And if in him found pity ever place,
Let him be moov'd to pity such a case.

A Gentle Shepheard borne in *Arcady*,
Of gentlest race that ever shepheard bore:
About the grassie bancks of *Hæmony*,
Did keepe his sheep, his litle stock and store.
Full carefully he kept them day and night,
In fairest fields, and *Astrophel* he hight[3]. — [3] was called

Young *Astrophel* the pride of shepheards praise,
Young *Astrophel* the rusticke lasses love:
Far passing all the pastors of his daies,
In all that seemly shepheard might behove.
In one thing onely fayling of the best,
That he was not so happie as the rest.

For from the time that first the Nymph his mother
Him forth did bring, and taught her lambs to feed,
A sclender swaine excelling far each other,
In comely shape, like her that did him breed,
He grew up fast in goodnesse and in grace,
And doubly faire wox both in mynd and face.

Which daily more and more he did augment,
With gentle usage and demeanure myld:
That all mens hearts with secret ravishment
He stole away, and weetingly beguyld.
Ne spight it selfe that all good things doth spill,
Found ought in him, that she could say was ill.

His sports were faire, his joyance innocent,
Sweet without sowre, and honny without gall:
And he himselfe seemd made for meriment,
Merily masking both in bowre and hall.
There was no pleasure nor delightfull play,
When *Astrophel* so ever was away.

For he could pipe and daunce, and caroll sweet,
Emongst the shepheards in their shearing feast:
As Somers larke that with her song doth greet
The dawning day forth comming from the East.
And layes of love he also could compose.
Thrice happie she, whom he to praise did chose.

Full many Maydens often did him woo,
Them to vouchsafe emongst his rimes to name,
Or make for them as he was wont to doo,
For her that did his heart with love inflame.
For which they promised to dight, for him,
Gay chaplets of flowers and gyrlonds trim.

And many a Nymph both of the wood and brooke,
Soone as his oaten pipe began to shrill:
Both christall wells and shadie groves forsooke,
To heare the charmes of his enchanting skill.
And brought him presents, flowers if it were prime,
Or mellow fruit if it were harvest time.

But he for none of them did care a whit,
Yet wood Gods for them often sighed sore:
Ne for their gifts unworthie of his wit,
Yet not unworthie of the countries store.
For one alone he cared, for one he sight,
His lifes desire, and his deare loves delight.

Stella the faire, the fairest star in skie,
As faire as *Venus* or the fairest faire:
A fairer star saw never living eie,
Shot her sharp pointed beames through purest aire.
Her he did love, her he alone did honor,
His thoughts, his rimes, his songs were all upon her.

To her he vowd the service of his daies,
On her he spent the riches of his wit:
For her he made hymnes of immortall praise,
Of onely her he sung, he thought, he writ,
Her, and but her, of love he worthie deemed,
For all the rest but litle he esteemed.

Ne her with ydle words alone he vowed,
And verses vaine (yet verses are not vaine)
But with brave deeds to her sole service vowed,
And bold atchievements her did entertaine.
For both in deeds and words he nourtred was,
Both wise and hardie (too hardie alas).

In wrestling nimble, and in renning swift,
In shooting steddie, and in swimming strong:
Well made to strike, to throw, to leape to lift,
And all the sports that shepheards are emong.
In every one he vanquisht every one,
He vanquisht all, and vanquisht was of none.

Besides, in hunting, such felicitie,
Or rather infelicitie he found:
That every field and forest far away,
He sought, where salvage beasts do most abound.
No beast so salvage but he could it kill,
No chace so hard, but he therein had skill.

Such skill matcht with such courage as he had,
Did prick him foorth with proud desire of praise:
To seek abroad, of daunger nought y'drad,
His mistresse name, and his owne fame to raise.
What needeth perill to be sought abroad,
Since round about us, it doth make aboad?

It fortuned, as he that perilous game
In forreine soyle pursued far away:
Into a forest wide and waste he came
Where store he heard to be of salvage pray.
So wide a forest and so waste as this,
Nor famous *Ardeyn*, nor fowle *Arlo* is.

There his welwoven toyles and subtil traines
He laid, the brutish nation to enwrap:
So well he wrought with practice and with paines,
That he of them great troups did soone entrap.
Full happie man (misweening much) was hee,
So rich a spoile within his power to see.

Eftsoones all heedlesse of his dearest hale,
Full greedily into the heard he thrust:
To slaughter them, and worke their finall bale,
Least that his toyle should of their troups be brust.
Wide wounds emongst them many one he made,
Now with his sharp borespear, now with his blade.

His care was all how he them all might kill,
That none might scape (so partiall unto none)
Ill mynd so much to mynd anothers ill,
As to become unmyndfull of his owne.
But pardon that unto the cruell skies,
That from himselfe to them withdrew his eies.

So as he rag'd emongst that beastly rout,
A cruell beast of most accursed brood
Upon him turnd (despeyre makes cowards stout)
And with fell tooth accustomed to blood,
Launched his thigh with so mischievous might,
That it both bone and muscles ryved quight.

So deadly was the dint and deep the wound,
And so huge streames of blood thereout did flow,
That he endured not the direfull stound,
But on the cold deare earth himselfe did throw.
The whiles the captive heard his nets did rend,
And having none to let, to wood did wend.

Ah where were ye this while his shepheard peares,
To whom alive was nought so deare as hee:
And ye faire Mayds the matches of his yeares,
Which in his grace did boast you most to bee?
Ah where were ye, when he of you had need,
To stop his wound that wondrously did bleed?

Ah wretched boy the shape of dreryhead,
And sad ensample of mans suddein end:
Full litle faileth but thou shalt be dead,
Unpitied, unplaynd, of foe or frend.
Whilest none is nigh, thine eylids up to close,
And kisse thy lips like faded leaves of rose.

A sort of shepheards sewing of the chace,
As they the forest raunged on a day:
By fate or fortune came unto the place,
Where as the lucklesse boy yet bleeding lay.
Yet bleeding lay, and yet would still have bled,
Had not good hap those shepheards thether led.

They stopt his wound (too late to stop it was)
And in their armes then softly did him reare:
Tho (as he wild) unto his loved lasse,
His dearest love him dolefully did beare.
The dolefulst beare that ever man did see,
Was *Astrophel*, but dearest unto mee.

She when she saw her love in such a plight,
With crudled blood and filthie gore deformed:
That wont to be with flowers and gyrlonds dight,
And her deare favours dearly well adorned,
Her face, the fairest face, that eye mote see,
She likewise did deforme like him to bee.

Her yellow locks that shone so bright and long,
As Sunny beames in fairest somers day
She fiersly tore, and with outragious wrong
From her red cheeks the roses rent away.
And her faire brest the threasury of joy,
She spoyld thereof, and filled with annoy.

His palled face impictured with death,
She bathed oft with teares and dried oft:
And with sweet kisses suckt the wasting breath,
Out of his lips like lillies pale and soft.
And oft she cald to him, who answerd nought,
But onely by his lookes did tell his thought.

The rest of her impatient regret,
And piteous mone the which she for him made,
No toong can tell, nor any forth can set,
But he whose heart like sorrow did invade.
At last when paine his vitall powres had spent,
His wasted life her weary lodge forwent.

Which when she saw, she staied not a whit,
But after him did make untimely haste:
Forth with her ghost out of her corps did flit,
And followed her make like Turtle chaste.
To prove that death their hearts cannot divide,
Which living were in love so firmly tide.

The Gods which all things see, this same beheld,
And pittying this paire of lovers trew,
Transformed them there lying on the field,
Into one flowre that is both red and blew.
It first growes red, and then to blew doth fade,
Like *Astrophel*, which thereinto was made.

And in the midst thereof a star appeares,
As fairly formd as any star in skyes:
Resembling *Stella* in her freshest yeares,
Forth darting beames of beautie from her eyes,
And all the day it standeth full of deow,
Which is the teares, that from her eyes did flow.

That hearbe of some, Starlight is cald by name,
Of others *Penthia*, though not so well
But thou where ever thou doest finde the same,
From this day forth do call it *Astrophel*.
And when so ever thou it up doest take,
Do pluck it softly for that shepheards sake.

Hereof when tydings far abroad did passe,
The shepheards all which loved him full deare,
And sure full deare of all he loved was,
Did thether flock to see what they did heare.
And when that pitteous spectacle they vewed,
The same with bitter teares they all bedewed.

And every one did make exceeding mone,
With inward anguish and great griefe opprest:
And every one did weep and waile, and mone,
And meanes deviz'd to shew his sorrow best.
That from that houre since first on grassie greene
Shepheards kept sheep, was not like mourning seen.

[1586]

The Faerie Queene
Book VI, Canto IX

Calidore hostes with *Melibœ*,
 And loves fayre *Pastorell:*
Coridon envies him, yet he
 For ill rewards him well.

I

Now turne againe my teme, thou jolly swayne,
Backe to the furrow which I lately left.
I lately left a furrow, one or twayne,
Unplough'd, the which my coulter hath not cleft;
Yet seem'd the soyle both fayre and frutefull eft,
As I it past: that were too great a shame,
That so rich frute should be from us bereft;
Besides the great dishonour and defame,
Which should befall to *Calidores* immortall name.

II

Great travell hath the gentle *Calidore*
And toyle endured, sith I left him last
Sewing the *Blatant Beast*,* which I forbore
To finish then, for other present hast.
Full many pathes and perils he hath past,
Through hils, through dales, through forests, and through plaines,
In that same quest which fortune on him cast,
Which he atchieved to his owne great gaines,
Reaping eternall glorie of his restlesse paines.

* The allegorical figure of scandal.

III

So sharply he the Monster did pursew,
That day nor night he suffred him to rest,
Ne rested he himselfe, but natures dew,
For dread of daunger not to be redrest,
If he for slouth forslackt so famous quest.
Him first from court he to the citties coursed,
And from the citties to the townes him prest,
And from the townes into the countrie forsed,
And from the country back to private farmes he scorsed.[1]

[1] chased

IV

From thence into the open fields he fled,
Whereas the Heardes were keeping of their neat,
And shepherds singing to their flockes (that fed)
Layes of sweete love and youthes delightfull heat:
Him thether eke, for all his fearefull threat.
He followed fast, and chaced him so nie,
That to the folds, where sheepe at night doe seat,
And to the litle cots, where shepherds lie
In winters wrathfull time, he forced him to flie.

V

There on a day, as he pursew'd the chace,
He chaunst to spy a sort of shepheard groomes,
Playing on pipes and caroling apace,
The whyles their beasts there in the budded broomes
Beside them fed, and nipt the tender bloomes;
For other worldly wealth they cared nought.
To whom Sir *Calidore* yet sweating comes,
And them to tell him courteously besought,
If such a beast they saw, which he had thether brought.

VI

They answer'd him that no such beast they saw,
Nor any wicked feend that mote offend

Their happie flockes, nor daunger to them draw;
But if that such there were (as none they kend)
They prayd high God them farre from them to send.
Then one of them, him seeing so to sweat,
After his rusticke wise, that well he weend,
Offred him drinke to quench his thirstie heat,
And, if he hungry were, him offred eke to eat.

VII

The knight was nothing nice, where was no need,
And tooke their gentle offer: so adowne
They prayd him sit, and gave him for to feed
Such homely what as serves the simple clowne,
That doth despise the dainties of the towne.
Tho, having fed his fill, he there besyde
Saw a faire damzell, which did weare a crowne
Of sundry flowres with silken ribbands tyde,
Yclad in home-made greene that her owne hands had dyde.

VIII

Upon a litle hillocke she was placed
Higher then all the rest, and round about
Environ'd with a girland, goodly graced,
Of lovely lasses; and them all without
The lustie shepheard swaynes sate in a rout,
The which did pipe and sing her prayses dew,
And oft rejoyce, and oft for wonder shout,
As if some miracle of heavenly hew
Were downe to them descended in that earthly vew.

IX

And soothly sure she was full fayre of face,
And perfectly well shapt in every lim,
Which she did more augment with modest grace

And comely carriage of her count'nance trim,
That all the rest like lesser lamps did dim:
Who, her admiring as some heavenly wight,
Did for their soveraine goddesse her esteeme,
And, caroling her name both day and night,
The fayrest *Pastorella* her by name did hight.

X

Ne was there heard, ne was there shepheards swayne,
But her did honour; and eke many a one
Burnt in her love, and with sweet pleasing payne
Full many a night for her did sigh and grone:
But most of all the shepheard *Coridon*
For her did languish, and his deare life spend;
Yet neither she for him nor other none
Did care a whit, ne any liking lend:
Though meane her lot, yet higher did her mind ascend.

XI

Her whyles Sir *Calidore* there vewed well,
And markt her rare demeanure, which him seemed
So farre the meane of shepheards to excell,
As that he in his mind her worthy deemed
To be a Princes Paragone esteemed,
He was unwares surprisd in subtile bands
Of the blynd boy; ne thence could be redeemed
By any skill out of his cruell hands;
Caught like the bird which gazing still on others stands.

XII

So stood he still long gazing thereupon,
Ne any will had thence to move away,
Although his quest were farre afore him gon:
But after he had fed, yet did he stay

And sate there still, untill the flying day
Was farre forth spent, discoursing diversly
Of sundry things as fell, to worke delay;
And evermore his speach he did apply
To th' heards, but meant them to the damzels fantazy.

XIII

By this the moystie night approching fast
Her deawy humour gan on th' earth to shed,
That warn'd the shepheards to their homes to hast
Their tender flocks, now being fully fed,
For feare of wetting them before their bed.
Then came to them a good old aged syre,
Whose silver lockes bedeckt his beard and hed,
With shepheards hooke in hand, and fit attyre,
That wild the damzell rise; the day did now expyre.

XIV

He was, to weet, by common voice esteemed
The father of the fayrest *Pastorell*,
And of her selfe in very deede so deemed;
Yet was not so; but, as old stories tell,
Found her by fortune, which to him befell,
In th' open fields an Infant left alone;
And, taking up, brought home and noursed well
As his owne chyld; for other he had none;
That she in tract of time accompted was his owne.

XV

She at his bidding meekely did arise,
And streight unto her litle flocke did fare:
Then all the rest about her rose likewise,
And each his sundrie sheepe with severall care
Gathered together, and them homeward bare:

Whylest everie one with helping hands did strive,
Amongst themselves, and did their labours share,
To help faire *Pastorella* home to drive
Her fleecie flocke; but *Coridon* most helpe did give.

XVI

But *Melibœe* (so hight that good old man)
Now seeing *Calidore* left all alone,
And night arrived hard at hand, began
Him to invite unto his simple home:
Which though it were a cottage clad with lome,
And all things therein meane, yet better so
To lodge then in the salvage fields to rome.
The knight full gladly soone agreed thereto,
(Being his harts owne wish,) and home with him did go.

XVII

There he was welcom'd of that honest syre
And of his aged Beldame homely well;
Who him besought himselfe to disattyre,
And rest himself till supper time befell;
By which home came the fayrest Pastorell,
After her flocke she in their fold had tyde:
And supper readie dight they to it fell
With small adoe, and nature satisfyde,
The which doth litle crave contented to abyde.

XVIII

Tho when they had their hunger slaked well,
And the fayre mayd the table ta'ne away,
The gentle knight, as he that did excell
In courtesie and well could doe and say,
For so great kindnesse as he found that day
Gan greatly thanke his host and his good wife;
And drawing thence his speach another way,

Gan highly to commend the happie life
Which Shepheards lead, without debate or bitter strife.

XIX

'How much' (sayd he) 'more happie is the state
In which ye, father, here doe dwell at ease,
Leading a life so free and fortunate
From all the tempests of these worldly seas,
Which tosse the rest in daungerous disease;
Where warres, and wreckes, and wicked enmitie
Doe them afflict, which no man can appease;
That certes I your happinesse envie,
And wish my lot were plast in such felicitie.'

XX

'Surely, my sonne,' (then answer'd he againe)
'If happie, then it is in this intent,
That having small yet doe I not complaine
Of want, ne wish for more it to augment,
But doe my selfe with that I have content;
So taught of nature, which doth litle need
Of forreine helpes to lifes due nourishment:
The fields my foode, my flocke my rayment breed;
No better doe I weare, no better doe I feed.

XXI

'Therefore I doe not any one envy,
Nor am envyde of any one therefore:
They, that have much, feare much to loose thereby,
And store of cares doth follow riches store.
The litle that I have growes dayly more
Without my care, but onely to attend it;
My lambes doe every yeare increase their score,
And my flockes father daily doth amend it.
What have I, but to praise th' Almighty that doth send it!

XXII

'To them that list the worlds gay showes I leave,
And to great ones such follies doe forgive;
Which oft through pride do their owne perill weave,
And through ambition downe themselves doe drive
To sad decay, that might contented live.
Me no such cares nor combrous thoughts offend,
Ne once my minds unmoved quiet grieve;
But all the night in silver sleepe I spend,
And all the day to what I list I doe attend.

XXIII

'Sometimes I hunt the Fox, the vowed foe
Unto my Lambes, and him dislodge away;
Sometime the fawne I practise from the Doe,
Or from the Goat her kidde, how to convay:
Another while I baytes and nets display
The birds to catch, or fishes to beguyle;
And when I wearie am, I downe doe lay
My limbes in every shade to rest from toyle,
And drinke of every brooke when thirst my throte doth boyle.

XXIV

'The time was once, in my first prime of yeares,
When pride of youth forth pricked my desire,
That I disdain'd amongst mine equall peares
To follow sheepe and shepheards base attire:
For further fortune then I would inquire;
And, leaving home, to roiall court I sought,
Where I did sell my selfe for yearely hire,
And in the Princes gardin daily wrought:
There I beheld such vainenesse as I never thought.

XXV

'With sight whereof soone cloyd, and long deluded
With idle hopes which them doe entertaine,

After I had ten yeares my selfe excluded
From native home, and spent my youth in vaine,
I gan my follies to my selfe to plaine,
And this sweet peace, whose lacke did then appeare:
Tho, backe returning to my sheepe againe,
I from thenceforth have learn'd to love more deare
This lowly quiet life which I inherite here.'

XXVI

Whylest thus he talkt, the knight with greedy eare
Hong still upon his melting mouth attent;
Whose sensefull words empierst his hart so neare,
That he was rapt with double ravishment,
Both of his speach, that wrought him great content,
And also of the object of his vew,
On which his hungry eye was alwayes bent;
That twixt his pleasing tongue, and her faire hew,
He lost himselfe, and like one halfe entraunced grew.

XXVII

Yet to occasion meanes to worke his mind,
And to insinuate his harts desire,
He thus replyde: 'Now surely, syre, I find,
That all this worlds gay showes, which we admire,
Be but vaine shadowes to this safe retyre
Of life, which here in lowlinesse ye lead,
Fearlesse of foes, or fortunes wrackfull yre
Which tosseth states, and under foot doth tread
The mightie ones, affrayd of every chaunges dread.

XXVIII

'That even I, which daily doe behold
The glorie of the great mongst whom I won,
And now have prov'd what happinesse ye hold
In this small plot of your dominion,

Now loath great Lordship and ambition;
And wish th' heavens so much had graced mee,
As graunt me live in like condition;
Or that my fortunes might transposed bee
From pitch of higher place unto this low degree.'

XXIX

'In vaine' (said then old *Melibœ*) 'doe men
The heavens of their fortunes fault accuse,
Sith they know best what is the best for them;
For they to each such fortune doe diffuse,
As they doe know each can most aptly use:
For not that which men covet most is best,
Nor that thing worst which men do most refuse;
But fittest is, that all contented rest
With that they hold: each hath his fortune in his brest.

XXX

'It is the mynd that maketh good or ill,
That maketh wretch or happie, rich or poore;
For some, that hath abundance at his will,
Hath not enough, but wants in greatest store,
And other, that hath litle, askes no more,
But in that litle is both rich and wise;
For wisedome is most riches: fooles therefore
They are which fortunes doe by vowes devize,
Sith each unto himselfe his life may fortunize.'

XXXI

'Since then in each mans self' (said *Calidore*)
'It is to fashion his owne lyfes estate,
Give leave awhyle, good father, in this shore
To rest my barcke, which hath bene beaten late
With stormes of fortune and tempestuous fate
In seas of troubles and of toylesome paine;

That, whether quite from them for to retrate
I shall resolve, or backe to turne againe,
I may here with your selfe some small repose obtaine.

XXXII

'Not that the burden of so bold a guest
Shall chargefull be, or chaunge to you at all;
For your meane food shall be my daily feast,
And this your cabin both my bowre and hall:
Besides, for recompence hereof I shall
You well reward, and golden guerdon give,
That may perhaps you better much withall,
And in this quiet make you safer live.'
So forth he drew much gold, and toward him it drive.

XXXIII

But the good man, nought tempted with the offer
Of his rich mould, did thrust it farre away,
And thus bespake: 'Sir knight, your bounteous proffer
Be farre fro me, to whom ye ill display
That mucky masse, the cause of mens decay,
That mote empaire my peace with daungers dread;
But, if ye algates covet to assay
This simple sort of life that shepheards lead,
Be it your owne: our rudenesse to your selfe aread[2].'

[2] take

XXXIV

So there that night Sir *Calidore* did dwell,
And long while after, whilest him list remaine,
Dayly beholding the faire *Pastorell,*
And feeding on the bayt of his owne bane:
During which time he did her entertaine
With all kind courtesies he could invent;
And every day, her companie to gaine,

When to the field she went he with her went:
So for to quench his fire he did it more augment.

XXXV

But she that never had acquainted beene
With such queint usage, fit for Queenes and Kings,
Ne ever had such knightly service seene,
But, being bred under base shepheards wings,
Had ever learn'd to love the lowly things,
Did litle whit regard his courteous guize,
But cared more for *Colins* carolings
Then all that he could doe, or ever devize:
His layes, his loves, his lookes, she did them all despize.

XXXVI

Which *Calidore* perceiving, thought it best
To chaunge the manner of his loftie looke;
And doffing his bright armes himselfe addrest
In shepheards weed; and in his hand he tooke,
Instead of steele-head speare, a shepheards hooke;
That who had seene him then, would have bethought
On *Phrygian Paris* by Plexippus brooke,
When he the love of fayre *Oenone* sought,
What time the golden apple was unto him brought.

XXXVII

So being clad unto the fields he went
With the faire *Pastorella* every day,
And kept her sheepe with diligent attent,
Watching to drive the ravenous Wolfe away,
The whylest at pleasure she mote sport and play;
And every evening helping them to fold:
And otherwhiles, for need, he did assay
In his strong hand their rugged teats to hold,
And out of them to presse the milke: love so much could.

XXXVIII

Which seeing *Coridon*, who her likewise
Long time had lov'd, and hop'd her love to gaine,
He much was troubled at that straungers guize,
And many gealous thoughts conceiv'd in vaine,
That this of all his labour and long paine
Should reap the harvest ere it ripened were:
That made him scoule, and pout, and oft complaine
Of *Pastorell* to all the shepheards there,
That she did love a stranger swayne then him more dere.

XXXIX

And ever, when he came in companie
Where *Calidore* was present, he would loure
And byte his lip, and even for gealousie
Was readie oft his owne heart to devoure,
Impatient of any paramoure:
Who, on the other side, did seeme so farre
From malicing, or grudging his good houre,
That all he could he graced him with her,
Ne ever shewed signe of rancour or of jarre.

XL

And oft, when *Coridon* unto her brought
Or litle sparrowes stolen from their nest,
Or wanton squirrels in the woods farre sought,
Or other daintie thing for her addrest,
He would commend his guift, and make the best;
Yet she no whit his presents did regard,
Ne him could find to fancie in her brest:
This new-come shepheard had his market mard.
Old love is litle worth when new is more prefard.

XLI

One day, when as the shepheard swaynes together
Were met to make their sports and merrie glee,

As they were wont in faire sunshynie weather,
The whiles their flockes in shadowes shrouded bee,
They fell to daunce: then did they all agree
That *Colin Clout* should pipe, as one most fit;
And *Calidore* should lead the ring, as hee
That most in *Pastorellaes* grace did sit:
Therat frown'd *Coridon*, and his lip closely bit.

XLII

But *Calidore*, of courteous inclination,
Tooke *Coridon* and set him in his place,
That he should lead the daunce, as was his fashion;
For *Coridon* could daunce, and trimly trace:
And when as *Pastorella*, him to grace,
Her flowry garlond tooke from her owne head,
And plast on his, he did it soone displace,
And did it put on *Coridons* instead:
Then *Coridon* woxe frollicke, that earst seemed dead.

XLIII

Another time, when as they did dispose
To practise games and maisteries to try,
They for their Judge did *Pastorella* chose;
A garland was the meed of victory:
There *Coridon* forth stepping openly
Did chalenge *Calidore* to wrestling game;
For he, through long and perfect industry,
Therein well practisd was, and in the same
Thought sure t' avenge his grudge, and worke his foe great shame.

XLIV

But *Calidore* he greatly did mistake,
For he was strong and mightily stiffe pight,
That with one fall his necke he almost brake;

And had he not upon him fallen light,
His dearest joynt he sure had broken quight.
Then was the oaken crowne by *Pastorell*
Given to *Calidore* as his due right;
But he, that did in courtesie excell,
Gave it to *Coridon*, and said he wonne it well.

XLV

Thus did the gentle knight himselfe abeare
Amongst that rusticke rout in all his deeds,
That even they, the which his rivals were,
Could not maligne him, but commend him needs;
For courtesie amongst the rudest breeds
Good will and favour. So it surely wrought
With this faire Mayd, and in her mynde the seeds
Of perfect love did sow, that last forth brought
The fruite of joy and blisse, though long time dearely bought.

XLVI

Thus *Calidore* continu'd there long time
To winne the love of the faire *Pastorell*,
Which having got, he used without crime
Or blameful blot; but menaged so well,
That he, of all the rest which there did dwell,
Was favoured and to her grace commended.
But what straunge fortunes unto him befell,
Ere he attain'd the point by him intended,
Shall more conveniently in other place be ended.

[1595]

NICHOLAS BRETON

A sweete Pastorall

Good Muse rock me a sleepe,
with some sweet Harmonie:
This wearie eye is not to keepe
thy warie companie.

Sweete Love be gone a while,
thou knowest my heavines:
Beauty is borne but to beguile,
my hart of happines.

See how my little flocke
that lov'd to feede on hie:
Doo headlong tumble downe the Rocke,
and in the Vallie die.

The bushes and the trees
that were so fresh and greene:
Doo all their dainty colour leese,
and not a leafe is seene.

The Black-bird and the Thrush,
that made the woods to ring:
With all the rest, are now at hush,
and not a noate they sing.

Sweete *Philomele* the bird,
that hath the heavenly throate,
Dooth now alas not once affoord
recording of a noate.

The flowers have had a frost,
each hearbe hath lost her savour:
And *Phillida* the faire hath lost,
the comfort of her favour.

Now all these careful sights,
so kill me in conceite:
That how to hope upon delights
it is but meere deceite.

And therefore my sweete Muse
that knowest what helpe is best,
Doo now thy heavenly cunning use,
to set my hart at rest.

And in a dreame bewray
what fate shall be my friend:
Whether my life shall still decay,
or when my sorrow end.

A Sheepheards dreame

A silly Sheepheard lately sate
among a flock of Sheepe:
Where musing long on this and that,
at last he fell a sleepe.
And in the slumber as he lay,
he gave a pitteous groane:
He thought his sheepe were runne away,
and he was left alone.
He whoopt, he whistled, and he call'd,
but not a sheepe came neere him:
Which made the Sheepheard sore appall'd,
to see that none would heare him.

But as the Swaine amazed stood,
in this most solemne vaine:
Came *Phillida* foorth of the wood,
and stoode before the Swaine.
Whom when the Sheepheard did behold,
he straite began to weepe:
And at the hart he grew a cold,
to thinke upon his sheepe.
For well he knew, where came the Queene,
the Sheepheard durst not stay:
And where that he durst not be seene,
the sheepe must needes away.
To aske her if she saw his flock,
might happen pacience moove:
And have an aunswere with a mock,
that such demaunders proove.
Yet for because he saw her come
alone out of the wood:
He thought he would not stand as dombe,
when speach might doo him good.
And therefore falling on his knees,
to aske but for his sheepe:
He did awake, and so did leese
the honour of his sleepe.

[1591]

'SHEPHERD TONIE' (ANTHONY MUNDAY?)

The Wood-mans walke

Through a faire Forrest as I went
upon a Sommers day,
I met a Wood-man queint and gent,
yet in a strange aray.
I mervail'd much at his disguise,
whom I did know so well:
But thus in tearmes both grave and wise,
his minde he gan to tell.
Friend, muse not at this fond aray,
but list a while to me:
For it hath holpe me to survay
what I shall shew to thee.
Long liv'd I in this Forrest faire,
till wearie of my weale:
Abroade in walks I would repaire,
as now I will reveale.
My first dayes walke was to the Court,
where Beautie fed mine eyes:
Yet found I that the Courtly sport,
did maske in slie disguise.
For falshood sate in fairest lookes,
and friend to friend was coy:
Court-favour fill'd but empty bookes,
and there I found no joy.
Desert went naked in the cold,
when crouching craft was fed:
Sweet words were cheapely bought and sold,
but none that stood in sted,

Wit was imployed for each mans owne,
plaine meaning came too short:
All these devises seene and knowne,
made me forsake the Court.
Unto the Citty next I went,
in hope of better hap:
Where liberally I launch'd and spent,
as set on Fortunes lap.
The little stock I had in store,
me thought would nere be done:
Friends flockt about me more and more,
as quickly lost as wone.
For when I spent, they then were kinde,
but when my purse did faile:
The formost man came last behinde,
thus love with wealth doth quaile.
Once more for footing yet I strove,
although the world did frowne:
But they before that held me up,
together troad me downe.
And least once more I should arise,
they sought my quite decay:
Then got I into this disguise,
and thence I stole away.
And in my minde (me thought) I saide,
Lord blesse me from the Cittie:
Where simplenes is thus betraide,
and no remorce or pittie.
Yet would I not give over so,
but once more trie my fate:
And to the Country then I goe,
to live in quiet state.
There did appeare no subtile showes,
but yea and nay went smoothly:

But Lord how Country-folks can glose,
 when they speake most soothly.
More craft was in a buttond cap,
 and in an old wives rayle:
Then in my life it was my hap,
 to see on Downe or Dale.
There was no open forgerie,
 but under-handed gleaning:
Which they call Country pollicie,
 but hath a worser meaning.
Some good bold-face beares out the wrong,
 because he gaines thereby:
The poore mans back is crackt ere long,
 yet there he lets him lye.
And no degree among them all,
 but had such close intending:
That I upon my knees did fall,
 and prayed for their amending.
Back to the woods I got againe,
 in minde perplexed sore:
Where I found ease of all this paine,
 and meane to stray no more.
There, Citty, Court, nor Country too,
 can any way annoy me:
But as a wood-man ought to doo,
 I freely may imploy me.
There live I quietly alone,
 and none to trip my talke:
Wherefore when I am dead and gone,
 think on the Wood-mans walke.

[1600]

Olde Damons *Pastorall*

From Fortunes frownes and change remov'd,
wend silly Flocks in blessed feeding:
None of *Damon* more belov'd,
feede gentle Lambs while I sit reading.

Carelesse worldlings, outrage quelleth
all the pride and pompe of Cittie:
But true peace with Sheepheards dwelleth,
(Sheepheards who delight in pittie.)
Whether grace of heaven betideth,
on our humble minds such pleasure:
Perfect peace with Swaines abideth,
love and faith is Sheepheards treasure.
On the lower Plaines the thunder
little thrives, and nought prevaileth:
Yet in Citties breedeth wonder,
and the highest hills assaileth.

Envie of a forraigne Tyrant
threatneth Kings, not Sheepheards humble:
Age makes silly Swaines delirant[1], [1] mad
thirst of rule garres[2] great men stumble. [2] causes
What to other seemeth sorrie,
abject state and humble biding:
Is our joy and Country glorie,
highest states have worse betiding.
Golden cups doo harbour poyson,
and the greatest pompe, dissembling:
Court of seasoned words hath foyson[3], [3] plenty
treason haunts in most assembling.

Homely breasts doo harbour quiet,
  little feare, and mickle solace:
States suspect their bed and diet,
  feare and craft doo haunt the Pallace.
Little would I, little want I,
  where the mind and store agreeth,
Smallest comfort is not scantie,
  least he longs that little seeth.
Time hath beene that I have longed,
  foolish I, to like of follie:
To converse where honour thronged,
  to my pleasures linked wholy.

Now I see, and seeing sorrow
  that the day consum'd, returnes not:
Who dare trust upon tomorrow,
  when nor time, not life sojournes not?

[1600]

ROBERT GREENE

From *Menaphon*

Dorons *Eclogue joynd with* Carmelas

Sit downe *Carmela* here are cubbs for kings,
Slowes blacke as jeat, or like my Christmas shooes,
Sweete Sidar which my leathren bottle brings:
Sit downe *Carmela* let me kisse thy toes.

CARMELA:

Ah *Doron*, ah my heart, thou art as white,
As is my mothers Calfe or brinded Cow,
Thine eyes are like the slow wormes in the night,
Thine haires resemble thickest of the snow.

The lines within thy face are deepe and cleere
Like to the furrowes of my fathers waine,
Thy sweate upon thy face dooth oft appeare
Like to my mothers fat and Kitchin gaine.

Ah leave my toe and kisse my lippes my love,
My lippes and thine, for I have given it thee:
Within thy cap tis thou shalt weare my glove,
At foote ball sport thou shalt my champion be.

DORON:

Carmela deare, even as the golden ball
That *Venus* got, such are thy goodly eyes,
When cherries juice is jumbled therewithall,
Thy breath is like the steeme of apple pies.

Thy lippes resemble two Cowcumbers faire,
Thy teeth like to the tuskes of fattest swine,
Thy speach is like the thunder in the aire:
Would God thy toes, thy lips and all were mine.

CARMELA:

Doron what thing dooth moove this wishing griefe.

DORON:

Tis Love *Carmela* ah tis cruell Love.
That like a slave, and caitiffe villaine thiefe,
Hath cut my throate of joy for thy behove.

CARMELA:

Where was he borne?

DORON:

In faith I know not where.
But I have had much talking of his dart.
Ay me poore man, with manie a trampling teare,
I feele him wound the forehearse of my heart,

What doo I love? O no, I doo but talke.
What shall I die for love? O no, not so.
What am I dead? O no my tongue dooth walke.
Come kisse *Carmela*, and confound my woe.

CARMELA:

Even with this kisse, as once my father did,
I seale the sweete indentures of delight:
Before I breake my vowe the Gods forbid,
No not by day, nor yet by darkesome night.

DORON:

Even with this garland made of Holly-hocks
I crosse thy browes from everie shepheards kisse.
Heigh hoe how glad am I to touch thy lockes,
My frolicke heart even now a free man is.

CARMELA:

I thanke you *Doron*, and will thinke on you,
I love you *Doron*, and will winke on you.
I seale your charter pattent with my thummes,
Come kisse and part for feare my mother comes.

[1589]

CHRISTOPHER MARLOWE

The passionate Sheepheard to his love

Come live with mee, and be my love,
And we will all the pleasures prove,
That Vallies, groves, hills and fieldes,
Woods, or steepie mountaine yeeles.

And wee will sit upon the Rocks,
Seeing the Sheepheards feede theyr flocks,
By shallow Rivers, to whose falls,
Melodious byrds sings Madrigalls.

And I will make thee beds of Roses,
And a thousand fragrant poesies,
A cap of flowers, and a kirtle,
Imbroydred all with leaves of Mirtle.

A gowne made of the finest wooll,
Which from our pretty Lambes we pull,
Fayre lined slippers for the cold:
With buckles of the purest gold.

A belt of straw, and Ivie buds,
With Corall clasps and Amber studs,
And if these pleasures may thee move,
Come live with mee, and be my love.

The Sheepheards Swaines shall daunce and
  sing,
For thy delight each May-morning,
If these delights thy minde may move;
Then live with mee, and be my love.

[1600]

*The Nimphs reply to the Sheepheard**

If all the world and love were young,
And truth in every Sheepheards tongue,
These pretty pleasures might me move,
To live with thee, and be thy love.

Time drives the flocks from field to fold,
When Rivers rage, and Rocks grow cold,
And Philomell becommeth dombe,
The rest complaines of cares to come.

The flowers doe fade, and wanton fieldes,
To wayward winter reckoning yeeldes,
A honny tongue, a hart of gall,
Is fancies spring, but sorrowes fall.

Thy gownes, thy shooes, thy beds of Roses,
Thy cap, thy kirtle, and thy poesies,
Soone breake, soone wither, soone forgotten:
In follie ripe, in reason rotten.

Thy belt of straw and Ivie buddes,
Thy Corall claspes and Amber studdes,
All these in mee no meanes can move,
To come to thee, and be thy love.

But could youth last, and love still breede,
Had joyes no date, nor age no neede,
Then these delights my minde might move,
To live with thee, and be thy love.

[1600]

* See also 'The Baite', p. 149.

From the 11th Book of *The Ocean to Scinthia*

Shee is gonn, Shee is lost! Shee is found, shee is ever faire!
Sorrow drawes weakly, wher love drawes not too.
Woes cries, sound nothinge, butt only in loves eare.
Do then by Diinge, what life cannot doo . . .

Unfolde thy flockes, and leve them to the feilds
To feed on hylls, or dales, wher likes them best,
Of what the summer, or the springe tyme yeildes,
For love, and tyme, hath geven thee leve to rest.

Thy hart, which was their folde, now in decay
By often stormes, and winters many blasts
All torne and rent, becumes misfortunes pray,
Falce hope, my shepherds staff, now age hath brast.

My pipe, which loves own hand, gave my desire
To singe her prayses, and my wo uppon,
Dispaire hath often threatned to the fier,
As vayne to keipe now all the rest ar gonn.

Thus home I draw, as deaths longe night drawes onn.
Yet every foot, olde thoughts turne back myne eyes.
Constraynt mee guides as old age drawes a stonn
Agaynst the hill, which over wayghty lyes

For feebell armes, or wasted strenght to move.
My steapps are backwarde, gasinge on my loss,
My minds affection, and my sowles sole love,
Not mixte with fancies chafe, or fortunes dross.

To God I leve it, who first gave it me,
And I her gave, and she returned agayne,
As it was herrs. So lett his mercies bee,

Of my last cumforts, the essentiall meane.
  But be it so, or not, th' effects, ar past.
  Her love hath end; my woe must ever last.

[*c.* 1592]

RICHARD BARNFIELD

The Shepherds Content
or
The happines of a harmless life

Of all the kindes of common Countrey life,
Me thinkes a Shepheards life is most Content;
His State is quiet Peace, devoyd of strife;
His thoughts are pure from all impure intent,
His Pleasures rate sits at an easie rent:
  He beares no mallice in his harmless hart,
  Malicious meaning hath in him no part.

He is not troubled with th'afflicted minde,
His cares are onely over silly Sheepe;
He is not unto Jealozie inclinde,
(Thrice happie Man) he knowes not how to weepe;
Whil'st I the Treble in deepe sorrowes keepe;
  I cannot keepe the Meane; for why (alas)
  Griefes have no meane, though I for meane doe passe.

No Briefes nor Semi-Briefes are in my Songs,
Because (alas) my griefe is seldome short;

My Prick-Song's alwayes full of Largues and Longs,[1]
(Because I never can obtaine the Port
Of my desires: Hope is a happie Fort.)
  Prick-song (indeed) because it pricks my hart;
  And Song, because sometimes I ease my smart.

[1] i.e., my written music is always full of the longest (and so, saddest) notes

The mightie Monarch of a royal Realme,
Swaying his Scepter with a Princely pompe;
Of his desires cannot so steare the Healme,
But sometime falls into a deadly dumpe,
When as he heares the shrilly-sounding Trumpe
  Of Forren Enemies, or home-bred Foes;
  His minde of griefe, his hart is full of woes.

Or when bad subjects gainst their Soveraigne
(Like hollow harts) unnaturally rebell,
How carefull is he to suppresse againe
Their desperate forces, and their powers to quell
With loyall harts, till all (againe) be well:
  When (being subdu'd) his care is rather more
  To keepe them under, than it was before.

Thus is he never full of sweete Content,
But either this or that his joy debars:
Now Noble-men gainst Noble-men are bent,
Now Gentlemen and others fall at jarrs:
Thus is his Countrey full of civill warrs;
  He still in danger sits, still fearing Death:
  For Traitors seeke to stop their Princes breath.

The whylst the other hath no enemie,
Without it be the Wolfe and cruell Fates
(Which no man spare): when as his disagree
He with his sheep-hooke knaps them on the pates,
Schooling his tender Lambs from wanton gates:

Beasts are more kinde then Men, Sheepe seeke not blood
But countrey caytives kill their Countreyes good.

The Courtier he fawn's for his Princes favour,
In hope to get a Princely ritch Reward;
His tongue is tipt with honey for to glaver[2];
Pride deales the Deck whilst Chance doth choose the Card,
Then comes another and his Game hath mard;
Sitting betwixt him, and the morning Sun:
Thus Night is come before the Day is done.

[2] flatter

Some Courtiers carefull of their Princes health,
Attends his Person with all dilligence
Whose hand's their hart; whose welfare is their wealth,
Whose safe Protection is their sure Defence,
For pure affection, not for hope of pence:
Such is the faithfull hart, such is the minde,
Of him that is to Vertue still inclinde.

The skilfull Scholler, and brave man at Armes,
First plies his Booke, last fights for Countries Peace;
Th'one feares Oblivion, th'other fresh Alarmes;
His paines nere ende, his travailes never cease;
His with the Day, his with the Night increase;
He studies how to get eternall Fame;
The Souldier fights to win a glorious Name.

The Knight, the Squire, the Gentleman, the Clowne,
Are full of crosses and calamities;
Lest fickle Fortune should begin to frowne,
And turne their mirth to extreame miseries:
Nothing more certaine than incertainties;
Fortune is full of fresh varietie:
Constant in nothing but inconstancie.

The wealthie Merchant that doth crosse the Seas,
To *Denmarke, Poland, Spaine,* and *Barbarie*;
For all his ritches, lives not still at ease;
Sometimes he feares ship-spoyling Pyracie,
Another while deceipt and treacherie
  Of his owne Factors in a forren Land;
  Thus doth he still in dread and danger stand.

Well is he tearmd a Merchant-Venturer,
Since he doth venter lands, and goods, and all:
When he doth travell for his Traffique far,
Little he knowes what fortune may befall,
Or rather what mis-fortune happen shall:
  Sometimes he splits his Ship against a rocke;
  Loosing his men, his goods, his wealth, his stocke.

And if he so escape with life away,
He counts himselfe a man most fortunate,
Because the waves their rigorous rage did stay,
(When being within their cruell powers of late,
The Seas did seeme to pittie his estate)
  But yet he never can recover health,
  Because his joy was drowned with his wealth.

The painfull Plough-swaine, and the Husband-man
Rise up each morning by the breake of day,
Taking what toyle and drudging paines they can,
And all is for to get a little stay;
And yet they cannot put their care away:
  When Night is come, their cares begin afresh,
  Thinking upon their Morrowes busines.

Thus everie man is troubled with unrest,
From rich to poore, from high to low degree:
Therefore I thinke that man is truly blest,

That neither cares for wealth nor povertie,
But laughs at Fortune and her foolerie;
  That gives rich Churles great store of golde and fee,
  And lets poore Schollers live in miserie,

O fading Branches of decaying Bayes
Who now will water your dry-wither'd Armes?
Or where is he that sung the lovely Layes
Of simple Shepheards in their Countrey-Farmes?
Ah he is dead, the cause of all our harmes:
  And with him dide my joy and sweete delight;
  And cleare to Clowdes, the Day is turnd to Night.

SYDNEY. The Syren of this latter Age;
SYDNEY. The Blasing-starre of England's glory;
SYDNEY. The Wonder of wise and sage;
SYDNEY. The Subject of true Vertues story;
  This Syren, Starre, this Wonder, and this Subject;
  In dumbe, dim, gone, and mard by Fortunes Object.

And thou my sweete *Amintas* vertuous minde,
Should I forget thy Learning or thy Love;
Well might I be accounted but unkinde,
Whose pure affection I so oft did prove:
Might my poore Plaints hard stones to pitty move;
  His losse should be lamented of each Creature,
  So great his Name, so gentle was his Nature.

But sleepe his soule in sweet Elysium,
(The happy Haven of eternall rest:)
And let me to my former matter come,
Proving by Reason, Shepheard's life is best,
Because he harbours Vertue in his Brest;
  And is content (the chiefest thing of all)
  With any fortune that shall him befall.

He sits all Day lowd-piping on a Hill,
The whilst his flocke about him daunce apace,
His hart with joy, his eares with Musique fill:
Anon a bleating Weather beares the Bace,
A Lambe the Treble; and to his disgrace
  Another answers like a middle Meane:
  Thus every one to beare a Part are faine.

Like a great King he rules a little Land,
Still making Statutes, and ordayning Lawes;
Which if they breake, he beates them with his Wand
He doth defend them from the greedy Jawes
Of rav'ning Woolves, and Lyons bloudy Pawes.
  His Field, his Realme; his Subjects are his Sheepe
  Which he doth still in due obedience keepe.

First he ordaines by Act of Parlament,
(Holden by custome in each Countrey Towne),
That if a sheepe (with any bad intent)
Presume to breake the neighbour Hedges downe,
Or haunt strange Pastures that be not his owne;
  He shall be pounded for his lustines,
  Untill his Master finde out some redres.

Also if any prove a Strageller
From his owne fellowes in a forraine field,
He shall be taken for a wanderer,
And forc'd himselfe immediatly to yeeld,
Or with a wyde-mouth'd Mastive Curre be kild.
  And if not claimd within a twelve-month's space,
  He shall remaine with Land-lord of the place.

Or if one stray to feede far from the rest,
He shall be pincht by his swift pye-bald Curre;
If any by his fellowes be opprest,

The wronger (for he doth all wrong abhorre)
Shall be well bangd so long as he can sturre.
  Because he did annoy his harmeles Brother,
  That meant not harme to him nor any other.

And last of all, if any wanton Weather,
With briers and brambles teare his fleece in twaine,
He shall be forc'd t'abide cold frosty weather,
And powring showres of ratling stormes of raine,
Till his new fleece begins to grow againe:
  And for his rashnes he is doom'd to goe
  Without a new Coate all the Winter throw.

Thus doth he keepe them, still in awfull feare,
And yet allowes them liberty inough;
So deare to him their welfare doth appeare,
That when their fleeces gin to waxen rough,
He combs and trims them with a Rampicke bough,
  Washing them in the streames of silver *Ladon*,
  To cleanse their skinnes from all corruption.

Another while he wooes his Country Wench,
(With Chaplets crownd, and gaudy girlonds dight)
Whose burning Lust her modest eye doth quench,
Standing amazed at her heavenly sight,
(Beauty doth ravish Sense with sweet Delight)
  Clearing *Arcadia* with a smoothed Browe
  When Sun-bright smiles melts flakes of driven snowe.

Thus doth he frollicke it each day by day,
And when Night comes drawes homeward to his Coate,
Singing a Jigge or merry Roundelay;
(For who sings commonly so merry a Noate,
As he that cannot chop or change a groate)

And in the winter Nights (his chiefe desire)
He turns a Crabbe or Cracknell in the fire.

He leads his Wench a Country Horn-pipe Round,
About a May-pole on a Holy-day;
Kissing his lovely Lasse (with Garlands Crownd)
With whoopping heigh-ho singing Care away;
Thus doth he passe the merry month of May:
And all th'yere after in delight and joy,
(Scorning a King) he cares for no annoy.

Thus have I showed in my Countrey vaine
The sweet Content that Shepheards still injoy;
The mickle pleasure, and the little paine
That ever doth awayte the Shepheards Boy:
His hart is never troubled with annoy.
He is a King, for he commands his Sheepe;
He knowes no woe, for he doth seldome weepe.

He is a Courtier, for he courts his Love:
He is a Scholler, for he sings sweet Ditties:
He is a Souldier, for he wounds doth prove;
He is the fame of Townes, the shame of Citties;
He scornes false Fortune, but true Vertue pitties.
He is a Gentleman, because his nature
Is kinde and affable to everie Creature.

Who would not then a simple Shepheard bee,
Rather than be a mightie Monarch made?
Since he injoyes such perfect libertie,
As never can decay, nor never fade:
He seldome sits in dolefull Cypresse shade,
But lives in hope, in joy, in peace, in blisse:
Joying all joy with this content of his.

But now good-fortune lands my little Boate
Upon the shoare of his desired rest:
Now I must leave (awhile) my rurall noate,
To thinke on him whom my soule loveth best;
He that can make the most unhappie blest:
  In whose sweete lap Ile lay me downe to sleepe,
  And never wake till Marble-stones shall weepe.

[1594]

MICHAEL DRAYTON

The subject of Pastorals, as the language of it ought to be poor, silly, & of the coursest Woofe in appearance. Neverthelesse, the most High, and most Noble Matters of the World may bee shaddowed in them, and for certaine sometimes are: but he who hath almost nothing Pastorall in his Pastorals, but the name (which is my Case) deales more plainly, because detracto velamine, *he speakes of most weightie things . . . The chiefe Law of Pastorals is the same which is of all Poesie, and of all wise carriage, to wit,* DECORUM, *and that not to be exceeded without leave, or without at least faire warning. For so did* VIRGIL, *when he wrote,*

– Paulò maiora canamus.

Master EDMUND SPENSER *had done enough for the immortalitie of his Name, had he only given us his* Shepheards Kalender, *a Master-piece if any. The* Colin Clout *of* SKOGAN, *under King* HENRY *the Seventh, is prettie: but* BARKLEY's Ship of Fooles *hath twentie wiser in it.* SPENSER *is the prime* Pastoralist *of* England. *My Pastorals bold upon a new straine, must speake for themselves, and the Taber striking up, if thou hast in thee any Country-Quicksilver, thou hadst rather be at the sport, then heare thereof. Farewell.*

[*To the Reader of his Pastorals,* 1619]

The First Eglog

From *Idea, The Shepheardes Garland*

When as the joyfull spring brings in
  the Summers sweete reliefe:
Poore *Rowland* malcontent bewayles
  the winter of his griefe.

Now *Phœbus* from the equinoctiall Zone,
Had task'd his teame unto the higher spheare,
And from the brightnes of his glorious throne,
Sends forth his Beames to light the lower ayre,
The cheerfull welkin, comen this long look'd hower,
Distils adowne full many a silver shower.

Fayre *Philomel* night-musicke of the spring,
Sweetly recordes her tunefull harmony,
And with deepe sobbes, and dolefull sorrowing,
Before fayre *Cinthya* actes her Tragedy:
The Throstlecock, by breaking of the day,
Chants to his sweete, full many a lovely lay.

The crawling snake, against the morning sunne,
Now streaks him in his rayn-bow coloured cote:
The darkesome shades, as loathsome he doth shunne,
Inchanted with the Birds sweete silvan note:
The Buck forsakes the launds where he hath fed,
And scornes the hunt should view his velvet head.

Through all the partes, dispersed is the blood,
The lustie spring, in flower of all her pride,
Man, bird, and beast, and fish, in pleasant flood,
Rejoycing all in this most joyfull tide:

Save *Rowland* leaning on a Ranpick tree,
O'r growne with age, forlorne with woe was he.

Oh blessed *Pan*, thou shepheards god sayth he,
O thou Creator of the starrie light,
Whose wonderous workes shew thy divinitie,
Thou wise inventor of the day and night,
Refreshing nature with the lovely spring,
Quite blemisht erst, with stormy winters sting.

O thou strong builder of the firmament,
Who placedst *Phœbus* in his fierie Carre,
And by thy mighty Godhead didst invent,
The planets mansions that they should not jarre,
Ordeyning *Phebe*, mistresse of the night,
From *Tytans* flame to steale her forked light.

Even from the cleerest christall shining throne,
Under whose feete the heavens are low abased,
Commaunding in thy majestie alone,
Whereas the fiery Cherubines are placed:
Receive my vowes as incense unto thee,
My tribute due to thy eternitie.

O shepheards soveraigne, yea receive in gree,
The gushing teares, from never-resting eyes,
And let those prayers which I shall make to thee,
Be in thy sight perfumed sacrifice:
Let smokie sighes be pledges of contrition,
For follies past to make my soules submission.

Submission makes amends for all my misse,
Contrition a refined life begins,
Then sacred sighes, what thing more precious is?

And prayers be oblations for my sinnes,
Repentant teares, from heaven-beholding eyes,
Ascend the ayre, and penetrate the skies.

My sorowes waxe, my joyes are in the wayning,
My hope decayes, and my despayre is springing,
My love hath losse, and my disgrace hath gayning,
Wrong rules, desert with teares her hands sits wringing:
Sorrow, despayre, disgrace, and wrong, doe thwart
My Joy, my love, my hope, and my desert.

Devouring time shall swallow up my sorrowes,
And strong beliefe shall torture black despaire,
Death shall orewhelme disgrace, in deepest furrowes,
And Justice laie my wrongs upon the Beere:
Thus Justice, death, beleefe, and time, ere long,
Shall end my woes, despayre, disgrace, and wrong.

Yet time shall be expir'd and lose his date,
And full assurance cancell strongest trust,
Eternitie shall trample on deathes pate,
And Justice shall surcease when all be just:
Thus time, beleefe, death, Justice, shall surcease,
By date, assurance, eternity, and peace.

Thus breathing from the Center of his soule,
The tragick accents of his extasie,
His sun-set eyes gan here and there to roule,
Like one surprisde with sodaine lunacie:
And being rouzde out of melancholly,
Flye whirle-winde thoughts unto the heavens quoth he.

Now in the Ocean *Tytan* quencht his flame,
And summond *Cinthya* to set up her light,
The heavens with their glorious starry frame,

Preparde to crowne the sable-vayled night:
When *Rowland* from this time-consumed stock,
With stone-colde hart now stalketh towards his flock.

[1593]

Pastoralls

The Fourth Eglogue

MOTTO:

Shepheard, why creepe we in this lowly vaine,
As though our store no better us affords?
And in this season when the stirring Swaine
Makes the wide fields sound with great thundring words?

Not as 'twas wont, now rurall be our Rimes,
Shepheards of late are waxed wondrous neate.
Though they were richer in the former Times,
We be inraged with more kindly heate.

The with'red Laurell freshly growes againe,
Which simply shaddow'd the *Pierian* Spring,
Which oft invites the solitary Swaine,
Thither, to heare those sacred Virgins sing:

Then if thy Muse have spent her wonted zeale,
With with'red twists thy fore-head shall be bound:
But if with these shee dare advance her Saile,
Amongst the best then may shee bee renown'd.

GORBO:

Shepheard, these Men at mightie things doe ayme,
And therefore presse into the learned Troope,
With filed Phraze to dignifie their Name,
Else with the World shut in this shamefull Coope.

But such a Subject ill beseemeth me,
For I must Pipe amongst the lowly sort,
Those silly Heard-groomes who have laught to see,
When I by Moone-shine made the *Fayries* sport.

Who of the toyles of *Hercules* will treat,
And put his Hand to an eternall Pen,
In such high Labours it behooves he sweat,
To soare beyond the usuall pitch of Men:

Such Monster-tamers who would take in Hand,
As have tyde up the Triple-headed Hound,
Or of those Gyants which 'gainst Heaven durst stand,
Whose strength the Gods it troubled to confound:

Who listeth with so mightie things to mell,
And dares a taske so great to undertake,
Should rayse the blacke inhabitants of Hell,
And stirre a Tempest on the Stygian Lake.

He that to Worlds Pyramides will Build
On those great Heroes got by heavenly Powers,
Should have a Pen most plentifully fill'd
In the full Streames of Learned *Maro's* Showres.

Who will foretell Mutations, and of Men,
Of Future things and wisely will inquire,
Before should slumber in that Shadie Den,
That often did with prophesie inspire,

South-saying *Sybils* sleepen long agone,
We have their Reed, but few have cond their Art,
And the *Welsh* Wisard* cleaveth to a Stone,
No Oracles more Wonders shall impart.

* Merlin.

When him this Round that neerest over-ran,
His labouring Mother to this light did bring,
The sweat that then from *Orpheus* Statue ran,
Foretold the Prophets had whereon to sing.

When Vertue had allotted her a Prize,
The Oaken Garland, and the Lawrell Crowne,
Fame then resum'd her lofty wings to rise,
And Plumes were honour'd with the purple Gowne.

When first Religion with a golden Chayne,
Men unto fayre Civilitie did draw,
Who sent from Heaven, brought Justice forth againe,
To Keepe the Good, the viler sort to awe.

That simple Age as simply sung of Love,
Till thirst of Empire and of Earthly swayes,
Drew the good Shepheard from his Lasses Glove,
To sing of slaughter, and tumultuous frayes.

Then *Joves* Love-theft was privily descry'd,
How he plaid false play in *Amphitrio*'s Bed,
And young *Apollo* in the Mount of *Ide*,
Gave *Oenon* Physicke for her Mayden-head:

The tender Grasse was then the softest Bed:
The pleasant'st Shades esteem'd the statelyest Halls,
No Belly-Churle with *Bacchus* banqueted,
Nor painted Rags then covered rotten Walls:

Then simple Love, by simple Vertue way'd,
Flowres the favours, which true Faith revealed,
Kindnesse againe with kindnesse was repayd,
And with sweet Kisses, Covenants were sealed.

And Beauties selfe by her selfe beautified,
Scorn'd Paintings Pergit[1], and the borrowed Haire,
Nor monstrous Formes deformities did hide,
The Foule to varnish with compounded Faire.

[1] decoration

The purest Fleece then covered the pure Skin:
For pride as then with *Lucifer* remayn'd;
Ill-favoured Fashions then were to begin,
Nor wholesome Cloathes with poysoned Liquor stayn'd.

But when the Bowels of the Earth were sought,
Whose golden Entrailes Mortalls did espie,
Into the World all mischiefe then was brought,
This fram'd the Mint, that coyn'd our miserie.

The loftie Pines were presently hew'd downe,
And Men, Sea-Monsters, swam the bracky Flood,
In Wainscote Tubs to seeke out Worlds unknowne,
For certayne Ill, to leave assured Good.

The Steed was tamde and fitted to the Field,
That serves a Subject to the Riders Lawes,
He that before ranne in the Pastures wyld,
Felt the stiffe curbe controule his angrie Jawes.

The *Cyclops* then stood sweating to the Fire,
The use thereof in softning Metals found,
That did streight Limbs in stubborne Steele attire,
Forging sharpe Tooles the tender flesh to wound.

The Citie-builder, then intrencht his Towres,
And laid his Wealth within the walled Towne,
Which afterward in rough and stormie Stowres,
Kindled the fire that burnt his Bulwarkes downe.

This was the sad beginning of our woe,
That was from Hell on wretched mortals hurl'd,
And from this Fount did all those Mischiefes flow,
Whose inundation drowneth all the World.

MOTTO:

Well, Shepheard, well, the golden Age is gone,
Wishes no way revoke that which is past:
Small wit there were to make two griefes of one;
And our complaints we vainly should but waste.

Listen to me then, lovely Shepheards Lad,
And thou shalt heare, attentive if thou be,
A prettie Tale I of my Grandame had,
One Winters Night when there were none but we.

GORBO:

Shepheard, say on, so may we passe the time,
There is no doubt, it is some worthy Rime.

MOTTO:

Farre in the country of *Arden*,
There won'd a Knight, hight *Cassamen*,
  As bold as *Isenbras*:
Fell was he and eager bent,
In Battaile and in Tournament,
  As was the good Sir *Topas*.
He had as antike Stories tell,
A Daughter cleaped *Dowsabel*,
  A Mayden faire and free.
And for she was her Fathers Heire,
Full well she was ycond the leire[2],
  Of mickle courtesie.
The Silke well couth she twist and twine,
And make the fine March-pine,
  And with the Needle-worke:

[2] well conned in knowledge

And she couth helpe the Priest to say
His Mattens on a Holy-day,
  And sing a Psalme in Kirke.
She ware a Frock of frollick Greene,
Might well become a Mayden Queene,
  Which seemly was to see;
A Hood to that so neat and fine,
In colour like the Columbine,
  Iwrought full featuously[3].
Her features all as fresh above,
As is the Grasse that growes by *Dove*,
  And lythe as Lasse of *Kent*.
Her skin as soft as *Lemster* Wooll,
As white as Snow, on *Peakish* Hull,
  Or Swan that swims in *Trent*.
This Mayden in a Morne betime,
Went forth when *May* was in the prime,
  To get sweet Setywall,
The Honey-suckle, the Harlocke,
The Lilly, and the Lady-smocke,
  To decke her Summer Hall.
Thus as she wandred here and there,
And picked of the bloomie Bryer,
  She chanced to espy
A Shepheard sitting on a Banke,
Like Chanti-cleere he crowed cranke,
  And pip'd full merrily.
He learn'd his Sheep, as he him list,
When he would whistle in his fist,
  To feed about him round.
Whilst he full many a Carroll sang,
Untill the Fields and Medowes rang,
  And that the Woods did sound.
In favour this same Shepheard Swaine,
Was like the Bedlam *Tamberlaine*,

[3] elegantly

Which held proud Kings in awe.
But meeke as any Lambe mought bee,
And innocent of ill as he,
Whom his lewd Brother slaw.
This Shepheard ware a Sheepe-gray Cloke,
Which was of the finest loke,
That could be cut with sheere.
His Mittens were of Bauzons[4] skin,
His Cockers[5] were of Cordiwin[6],
His Hood of Miniveere[7].
His Aule and Lingell[8] in a Thong,
His Tar-box[9] on his broad Belt hung,
His Breech of *Cointree* Blue.
Full crispe and curled were his Lockes,
His Browes as white as *Albion* Rockes,
So like a Lover true,
And piping still he spent the day,
So merry as the Popinjay,
Which liked *Dowsabell*.
That would she ought, or would she nought,
This Lad would never from her thought,
She in love-longing fell.
At length she tucked up her Frocke,
White as the Lilly was her Smocke,
She drew the Shepheard nie:
But then the Shepheard pip'd a good,
That all his Sheepe forsooke their food,
To heare his Melodie.
Thy Sheepe, quoth shee, cannot be leane,
That have a jolly Shepheards Swaine,
The which can pipe so well:
Yea but (saith he) their Shepheard may,
If piping thus he pine away,
In love of *Dowsabell*.

[4] badger's
[5] leggings [6] corduroy
[7] white fur
[8] knife
[9] i.e., as a 'cure-all' for sheep ailments

Of love, fond Boy, take thou no keepe,
Quoth she, looke well unto thy sheepe,
  Lest they should hap to stray.
Quoth he, So had I done full well,
Had I not seene faire *Dowsabell*
  Come forth to gather May.
With that she 'gan to vaile her head,
Her Cheekes were like the Roses red,
  But not a word she said,
With that the Shepheard 'gan to frowne,
He threw his prettie Pipes adowne,
  And on the ground him laid.
Saith she, I may not stay till Night,
And leave my Summer Hall undight,
  And all for love of thee.
My Coat, saith he, nor yet my Fold,
Shall neither Sheepe nor Shepheard hold,
  Except thou favour mee.
Saith she, Yet lever I were dead,
Then I should lose my Maiden-head,
  And all for love of men.
Sai'th he, Yet are you too unkind,
If in your heart you cannot find,
  To love us now and then.
And I to thee will be as kind,
As *Colin* was to *Rosalind*,
  Of courtesie the flowre.
Then will I be as true, quoth she,
As ever Maiden yet might be
  Unto her Paramour.
With that she bent her Snow-white knee,
Downe by the Shepheard kneeled shee,
  And him she sweetly kist.
With that the Shepheard whoop'd for joy,

Quoth he, there's never Shepheards Boy,
That ever was so blist.

GORBO:

Now by my Sheephooke, here's a Tale alone,
Learne me the same, and I will give thee hire,
This were as good as Curds for our *Jone*,
When at a Night we sitten by the fire.

MOTTO:

Why gentle *Gorbo*, ile not sticke for that,
When we shall meet upon some merrie day:
But see, whilst we have set us downe to chat,
Yon Tykes of mine begin to steale away.

And if thou please to come unto our Greene,
On *Lammas* day, when as we have our Feast,
Thou shalt sit next unto the Shepheards Queene,
And there shalt be the only welcome Ghest.

The Tenth Eglogue

What time the wearie weather-beaten Sheepe,
To get them Fodder, hie them to the Fold,
And the poore Heards that lately did them keepe,
Shuddred with keenenesse of the Winters cold:
The Groves of their late Summer pride forlorne,
In mossie Mantles sadly seem'd to mourne.

That silent time, about the upper World,
Phœbus had forc'd his fierie-footed Teame,
And downe againe the steepe *Olympus* whurld,
To wash his Chariot in the Westrene streame,
In Nights blacke shade, when *Rowland* all alone,
Thus him complaines his fellow Shepheard's gone.

You flames, quoth he, wherewith thou Heaven art dight,
That me (alive) the wofull'st Creature view,
You, whose aspects have wrought me this despight,
And me with hate, yet ceaslesly pursue,
  For whom too long I tarryed for reliefe,
  Now aske but Death, that onely ends my griefe.

Yearly my Vowes, O Heavens, have I not paid,
Of the best Fruits, and Firstlings of my Flock?
And oftentimes have bitterly invayde,
'Gainst them that you prophanely dar'd to mock?
  O, who shall ever give what is your due,
  If mortall man be uprighter then you?

If the deepe sighes of an afflicted brest,
O'rwhelm'd with sorrow, or th'erected eyes
(Of a poore Wretch with miseries opprest)
For whose complaints, teares never could suffice,
  Have not the power your Deities to move,
  Who shall e'r looke for succour from above?

O Night, how still obsequious have I beene
To thy slow silence whispering in thine eare,
That thy pale Soveraigne often hath beene seene,
Stay to behold me sadly from her Spheare,
  Whilst the slow minutes duly I have told,
  With watchfull eyes attending on my Fold.

How oft by thee the solitary Swayne,
Breathing his passion to the early spring,
Hath left to heare the Nightingale complaine,
Pleasing his thoughts alone, to heare me sing!
  The Nymphes forsooke their places of abode,
  To heare the sounds that from my Musicke flow'd.

To purge their Springs and sanctifie their Grounds,
The simple Shepheards learned I the meane,
And Soveraine simples to their use I found,
Their teeming Eawes to helpe when they did yeane[1]:
  Which when againe in summer time they share,
  Their wealthy Fleece my cunning did declare.

[1] give birth

In their warme Coates whilst they have soundly slept,
And pass'd the Night in many a pleasant Bowre,
On the Bleake Mountaines I their Flocks have kept,
And bid the Brunt of many a cruell showre,
  Warring with Beasts in safety mine to keepe;
  So true was I, and carefull of my Sheepe.

Fortune and Time, why tempted you me forth,
With those your flattering promises of Grace,
Fickle, so falsly to abuse my worth,
And now to flie me, whom I did imbrace?
  Both that at first incourag'd my desire,
  Lastly against me lewdly doe conspire.

Or Nature, didst thou prodigally waste
Thy gifts on me infortunatest Swayne,
Only thereby to have thy selfe disgrac'd?
Vertue in me why was thou plac'd in vaine?
  If to the World predestined a prey,
  Thou wert too good to have beene cast away.

Ther's not a Grove that wondreth not my wo,
Nor not a River weepes not at my tale,
I heare the Eccho's (wandring to and fro)
Resound my griefe through every Hill and Dale,
  The Birds and Beasts yet in their simple kinde
  Lament for me, no pittie else that finde.

None else there is gives comfort to my griefe,
Nor my mis-haps amended with my mone,
When Heaven and Earth have shut up all reliefe,
Nor care availes what curelesse now is growne:
  And teares I finde doe bring no other good,
  But as new Showres increase the rising Floud.

When on an old Tree, under which ere now,
He many a merry Roundelay had sung,
Upon a leavelesse Canker-eaten Bow,
His well-tun'd Bag-pipe carelesly he hung:
  And by the same, his Sheepe-Hooke, once of price,
  That had beene carv'd with many a rare device.

He call'd his Dog, (that sometime had the prayse)
Whitefoote, well knowne to all that kept the Playne,
That many a Wolfe had werried in his dayes,
A better Curre, there never followed Swayne:
  Which, though as he his Masters sorrowes knew,
  Wag'd his cut Taile, his wretched plight to rue.

Poore Curre, quoth he, and him therewith did stroke,
Goe, to our Cote, and there thy selfe repose,
Thou with thine Age, my Heart with sorrow broke:
Be gone, ere Death my restlesse Eyes doe close,
  The Time is come, thou must thy Master leave,
  Whom the vile World shall never more deceave.

With folded Armes thus hanging downe his Head,
He gave a grone, his Heart in sunder cleft,
And as a Stone, alreadie seemed dead,
Before his Breath was fully him bereft:
  The faithfull Swayne, here lastly made an end,
  Whom all good Shepheards ever shall defend.

[1616]

THE PASTORAL DRAMA

The reaction against the aristocratic Arcadia of Spenser and Sidney was led by the Elizabethan and Jacobean dramatists, and in particular by Shakespeare. Sidney and Spenser were eloquent adherents to a European tradition which saw poetry in terms of different 'kinds' with different subjects appropriate to them; so that kings, lords, military leaders could properly appear only in the Heroic kind, or the Tragic, while Pastoral was concerned with a polite version of low life as it was lived by shepherds. But when Pastoral began to be written in England, there was already a native tradition directly inimical to such a hierarchical idea of literature. Other poets, in other countries of Europe, had achieved in the Pastoral kind a fairly unproblematic synthesis of elements in their native literatures, whether peasant songs or pastoral ballads, with the conventions they had inherited from the ancients; but only in England had a popular drama developed, during the Middle Ages, in which it was not at all unusual for members of the highest and the lowest ranks of society to be represented together on the stage. An example of an English comedy in which courtly and low-life characters are brought together in a version of Pastoral – *Sir Clyomon and Clamydes* – is included in this anthology, and the culmination of the tradition can be seen, of course, in Shakespeare, and perhaps particularly in the relationship between Prince Hal and the riff-raff of the Boar's Head. It is not that social distinctions are done away with in this English tradition; they preoccupy Shakespeare considerably, and their importance is continually reaffirmed by him; but in English drama, and to an extent in the Elizabethan novel, these distinctions can be explored by figures from the nobility and from low-life together. This tradition had begun with the medieval Christian drama, in which differences of rank had receded into unimportance before the long perspectives of purgatory and damnation; and it was well equipped to deal with the social confusions of England in the second half of Elizabeth's reign in a way which the pure Pastoral – with its commitment to deal only with low-life characters, or with courtiers masquerading as shepherds – was not.

In Shakespeare's *As You Like It*, the pretensions of the Pastoral to provide a possible alternative to the struggles of the courtly life are deflated, at the same time as we are still invited to enjoy those pretensions for what they are worth. Shakespeare's technique in this play is to bring together two sorts of shepherd from two literary traditions: Corin and Audrey belong to a native English tradition, the impossibly earthy rustics who had been made fun of in *Sir Clyomon and Clamydes*; Silvius and Phebe are a refined and delicate shepherd and shepherdess from the pages of the *Arcadia*. When the courtly characters Rosalind, Celia and Touchstone first arrive in the forest of Arden, they seem to expect from Corin something of the welcome that Sir Calidore found among the shepherds of *The Faerie Queene*; Corin replies that he wishes he could be of more help, but he is 'shepherd to another man', who is not given to deeds of hospitality. This intrusion of economic realities into the English Arcadia invites us to expect that Shakespeare will go out of his way to point the contrast between Corin and the anachronistic lovers Silvius and Phebe; but in fact almost all the weight of Shakespeare's satire is brought to bear against the genuinely low-life shepherds. For Touchstone, in his conversations with Corin and with Audrey, keeps insisting, and reasonably enough, that if theirs is the pastoral life it is really not more attractive than life at court; the simplicity of the one hardly compensates for the loss of comfort in leaving the other. And this insistence, that there is a pastoral life which is both real and difficult, creates the context in which we can evaluate the pastoral tradition inhabited by Silvius and Phebe, and indeed the pastoral elements in the play as a whole. We are invited to enjoy this courtly Pastoral, but for what it obviously is – a masquerade, a game for the amusement of bored courtiers and not a conceivable alternative to the uncongenial and disorderly reality of life in Elizabeth's court.

In contrast, *The Winter's Tale*, which dates from late in Shakespeare's career, does seem to offer the pastoral life as a serious alternative to that of the court. The play divides naturally into three sections: the court where jealousy and tyranny prevail; the countryside of Bohemia which displays all the virtues of the simple rural life in a naturalistic setting; and finally the court again, improved and softened by its contact with the country. Shakespeare has altered his main source (Greene's *Pandosto*, 1592) in ways which emphasize the *positive* qualities of the pastoral alternative. The old Shepherd who finds the abandoned Perdita thinks naturally of caring for the child before he discovers the treasure left with her, whereas in Greene the baby and the wealth are discovered simultaneously and covetousness is the prime instigation of the action of the shepherd and his wife. Furthermore, Shakespeare's presentation of the lives of the shepherds is much more vivid (as is evident from the extract in this anthology), and the detailed celebration of the natural life has no counterpart either in Greene or in the forest in *As You Like It.* The sheep-shearing feast-scene was frequently played as a separate piece throughout the late eighteenth century, and the removal of this scene from its courtly setting is a fair indication of the nature of its appeal.

However, in spite of the presentation of a court life ameliorated by that of the country, it is evident that the strength of *The Winter's Tale* is essentially that of myth. The court may be infused with the virtues of the country, but there is never a formal fusion. The possibility of an actual, as opposed to a mythic, social mobility, is mocked when (V, 2) the old Shepherd and the Clown are rewarded for their fostering of the King's daughter by being made Gentlemen, and yet still continue to act the role of naïve and gullible rustics. The two finest ornaments of the rural scene are (of course) disguised aristocrats; Perdita is always seen to be as different from her fellow shepherds as was Pastorella in *The Faerie Queene*; and the Prince Florizel has no difficulty in recognizing her aristocratic qualities through her 'unusual weeds'. Indeed her part as Queen of the Feast is a recognition of her implied majesty. Perdita gives to Camillo and the disguised Polixenes flowers worthy of their age, hybrid carnations and gillyflowers, 'which some call Natures bastards', thus affording Polixenes opportunity to discourse on the benefits of a cross-breeding of the 'baser kind' and the 'nobler race', precisely that process which, as it appears, will occur if he consents to the marriage of his son Florizel to the base Perdita. Ironically, it is Perdita who argues against the marriage of the high and the low, court and country. The world of *The Winter's Tale* is ultimately that of the 'Whitsun Pastorals', where, for a short while, the illusion of social mobility can appear, but where in the end the old harmony and the old order will prevail. Shakespeare's court audience always knows that the beautiful and virtuous shepherdess is Perdita, the heir to the throne of Sicily. *The Winter's Tale* may preach on the surface a gospel of cross-breeding, but the final effect is a celebration not of the rural life but, albeit often ambiguously, of that of the court; thus the play both proclaims and precludes the alternative.

Shakespeare's success in the dramatic Pastoral had much to do with his willingness to bring together the conventions of the 'right Pastoral' and those of English low-life comedy; in *As You Like It* he was concerned to distinguish between these two traditions, in *The Winter's Tale* to join them together in a fiction of the pastoral life at once delightful and credible. Ben Jonson, in his play *The Sad Shepherd* (*c.* 1612), appears to be trying to write as conventional and proper a Pastoral as he can, but one dealing with English and not Arcadian shepherds; the result is a sort of epitaph on the first phase of conventional English Pastoral. Like Corin in *As You Like It*, the shepherds in Jonson's play are quite conscious of the economic realities which have stopped Sherwood Forest from being an English Arcadia. The exchange of speeches on pages 133–5 is an eloquent account of the appearance in Sherwood of a new sort of sheep-farmer, more acquisitive than the old, and puritanical in attitude to the traditional feasts and sports of English shepherds. This theme, or a version of it, will be heard again from time to time throughout the history of the Pastoral in England; and yet it comes more strangely from the mouths of Jonson's shepherds than it had from Shakespeare's Corin. The language Jonson invents for the shepherds in his play has a delightful simplicity which nevertheless belongs quite clearly to the formal, the courtly Pastoral, far more than to the English comic tradition. They complain of their fate in a homelier version of the same sophisticated Arcadian despair we saw in Sidney; and, like Sidney's shepherds, their tone reveals a quite fatalistic acceptance of their obsolescence. And in this way the sense of an old style of shepherd unequipped to deal with the demands of a changing style of agriculture is matched precisely by our sense of the inadequacy of the old pastoral conventions to deal with this sort of intrusion of reality. These shepherds are automata, wound up years ago but still stumbling around the changed landscape; they are trapped by an anachronistic tradition, by the fact that Jonson is not prepared to admit any very thorough mixture of kinds; so that the shepherds can never become genuinely comic in a way that might re-animate them, and make us feel their disappearance is less than inevitable.

ANONYMOUS

From *Sir Clyomon and Clamydes*

[*Enter* CORIN *a Shepheard*]

CORIN: Gos bones, turne in that sheep there and you be good fellowes,
Jesu how cham beraide;
Chave a cur here, an a were my vellow, cha must him conswade,
And yet an cha should kisse, looke you of the arse, cha must run my selfe, an chil,
An cha should entreat him with my cap in my hand ha wad stand stil.
But tis a worlde to zee what mery lives we shepheards lead,
Why we're Gentlemen and we get once a thorne bush over our head,
We may sleep with our vaces against the zone[1], an we were hogs,
Bath our selves, stretch out our legs an't were a kennell of dogs:
And then at night when maides come to milkin, the games begin,
But I may zay to you my nabor *Hogs* maid had a clap; wel let them laugh that win.
Chave but one daughter, but chould not vor vorty pence she were zo sped,
Cha may zay to you, she lookes every night to go to bed:
But tis no matter, the whores be so whiskish[2] when thare under a bush,
That thare never satisfied, til their bellies be flush.
Well cha must abroad about my flocks, least the fengeance wolves catch a lambe:

[1] sun

[2] skittish

Vor by my cursen zoule, thale steale an cha stand by, there not averd of the dam.

NERO: Wel, to scape the pursute of the king, of this same shepheard here,
Suspition wholly to avoyd, for service ile enquire:
Wel met good father! for your use a servant do you lacke?

CORIN: What, you wil not flout an old man, you court nod Jacke?[3]

[3] courtly fellow

NERO: No truly father, I flout you not; what I aske I would have.

CORIN: Gos bones they leest, serve a shepheard an be zo brave?[4]

[4] smartly dressed

You courtnoll crackropes wod be hangd, you do nothin now and then
But come up and downe the country, thus to flout poore men.
Go too, goodman boy, chave no zervis vor no zuch flouting Jacks as you be.

NERO: Father I thinke as I speake, upon my faith and troth beleeve me
I wil willingly serve you, if in case you wil take me.

CORIN: Doest not mocke?

NERO: No truly father.

CORIN: Then come with me, by gos bones chil never vorsake thee.
Whow, bones of my zoule, thowilt be the bravest shepherds boy in our town,
Thous go to church in this coate, bevore Madge a Sonday in her gray gown.
Good lord, how our church-wardens wil looke upon thee, bones of god zeest,
There will be more looking at thee, then our Sir John the parish preest.
Why, everybody wil aske whose boy thart, an cha can tel thee this by the way,

Thou shalt have al the varest wenches of our town in the
veelds vor to play.
Theres nabour *Nychols* daughter, a jolly smug whore with
vat cheekes,
And nabour *Hodges* maide, meddle not with her, she hath
eaten set leekes.
But theres *Frumptons* wench in the freese
scake,[5] it will do thee good to see
What canvosing[6] is at the milking time
betweene her and mee.

[5] woollen cape
[6] frolicking

[Written 1570–90, published 1599]

WILLIAM SHAKESPEARE

From *As You Like It*

Act II, Scene I

[*Enter* DUKE SENIOR: AMYENS, *and two or three Lords like Forresters.*]

DUKE SENIOR: Now my Coe-mates, and brothers in exile
Hath not old custome made this life more sweete
Then that of painted pompe? Are not these woods
More free from perill then the envious Court?
Heere feele we not the penaltie of *Adam*,
The seasons difference, as the Icie phange
And churlish chiding of the winters winde,
Which when it bites and blowes upon my body
Even till I shrinke with cold, I smile, and say
This is no flattery: these are counsellors
That feelingly perswade me what I am:

Sweet are the uses of adversitie
Which like the toad, ougly and venemous,
Weares yet a precious Jewell in his head:
And this our life exempt from publike haunt,
Findes tongues in trees, bookes in the running brookes,
Sermons in stones, and good in every thing.

AMIENS: I would not change it, happy is your Grace
That can translate the stubbornesse of fortune
Into so quiet and so sweet a stile.

DUKE SENIOR: Come, shall we goe and kill us venison?
And yet it irkes me the poore dapled fooles
Being native Burgers of this desert City,
Should in their owne confines with forked heads
Have their round hanches goard.

FIRST LORD: Indeed my Lord
The melancholy *Jaques* grieves at that.
And in that kinde sweares you doe more usurpe
Then doth your brother that hath banish'd you:
To day my Lord of *Amiens*, and my selfe,
Did steale behinde him as he lay along
Under an oake, whose anticke roote peepes out
Upon the brooke that brawles along this wood,
To the which place a poore sequestred Stag
That from the Hunters aime had tane a hurt,
Did come to languish; and indeed my Lord
The wretched annimall heav'd forth such groanes
That their discharge did stretch his leatherne coat
Almost to bursting, and the big round teares
Cours'd one another downe his innocent nose
In pitteous chase: and thus the hairie foole,
Much marked of the melancholie *Jaques*,
Stood on th'extremest verge of the swift brooke,
Augmenting it with teares.

DUKE SENIOR: But what said *Jaques*?
Did he not moralize this spectacle?

FIRST LORD: O yes, into a thousand similies.
First, for his weeping into the needlesse streame;
Poore Deere quoth he, thou mak'st a testament
As worldlings doe, giving thy sum of more
To that which had too must: then being there alone,
Left and abandoned of his velvet friend[1];
'Tis right quoth he, thus miserie doth part
The Fluxe of companie: anon a carelesse Heard
Full of the pasture, jumps along by him
And never staies to greet him: I quoth *Jaques*,
Sweepe on you fat and greazie Citizens,
'Tis just the fashion; wherefore doe you looke
Upon that poore and broken bankrupt there?
Thus most invectively he pierceth through
The body of Countrie, Citie, Court,
Yea, and of this our life, swearing that we
Are meere usurpers, tyrants, and whats worse
To fright the Annimals, and to kill them up
In their assign'd and native dwelling place.
DUKE SENIOR: And did you leave him in this contemplation?
SECOND LORD: We did my Lord, weeping and commenting
Upon the sobbing Deere.
DUKE SENIOR: Show me the place,
I love to cope him in these sullen fits,
For then he's full of matter.
FIRST LORD: Ile bring you to him strait.

[*Exeunt*]

[First performed *c.* 1598]

[1] i.e., the deer

From *The Winter's Tale*

Act IV, Scene 4

[*Enter* FLORIZELL, PERDITA, SHEPHERD, CLOWNE, POLIXENES, CAMILLO, MOPSA, DORCAS, SERVANTS, AUTOLICUS.]

FLORIZELL: These your unusuall weeds, to each part of you
Do's give a life: no Shepherdesse, but *Flora*
Peering in Aprils front. This your sheepe-shearing,
Is as a meeting of the petty Gods,
And you the Queene on't.

PERDITA: Sir: my gracious Lord,
To chide at your extreames, it not becomes me:
(Oh pardon, that I name them:) your high selfe
The gracious marke o'th'Land, you have obscur'd
With a Swaines wearing: and me (poore lowly Maide)
Most Goddesse-like prank'd up: But that our Feasts
In every Messe, have folly; and the Feeders
Digest with a Custome, I should blush
To see you so attyr'd: sworne I thinke,
To shew my selfe a glasse.

FLORIZELL: I blesse the time
When my good Falcon, made her flight a-crosse
Thy Fathers ground.

PERDITA: Now Jove affoord you cause:
To me the difference forges dread (your Greatnesse
Hath not been us'd to feare:) even now I tremble
To thinke your Father, by some accident
Should passe this way, as you did: Oh the Fates,
How would he looke, to see his worke, so noble,
Vildely[1] bound up? What would he say? Or how
Should I (in these my borrowed Flaunts) behold
The sternnesse of his presence?

FLORIZELL: Apprehend
Nothing but jollity: the Goddes themselves
(Humbling their Deities to love) have taken

[1] vilely

The shapes of Beasts upon them. Jupiter,
Became a Bull, and bellow'd: the greene Neptune
A Ram, and bleated: and the Fire-roab'd-God
Golden Apollo, a poore humble Swaine,
As I seeme now. Their transformations,
Were never for a peece of beauty, rarer,
Nor in a way so chaste: since my desires
Run not before mine honor: nor my Lusts
Burne hotter then my Faith.

PERDITA: O but Sir,
Your resolution cannot hold, when 'tis
Oppos'd (as it must be) by th'powre of the King:
One of these two must be necessities,
Which then will speake, that you must change this purpose,
Or I my life.

FLORIZELL: Thou deer'st *Perdita*,
With these forc'd thoughts, I prethee darken not
The Mirth o'th'Feast: Or Ile be thine (my Faire)
Or not my Fathers. For I cannot be
Mine owne, nor any thing to any, if
I be not thine. To this I am most constant,
Though destiny say no. Be merry (Gentle)
Strangle such thoughts as these, with any thing
That you behold the while. Your guests are comming:
Lift up your countenance, as it were the day
Of celebration of that nuptiall, which
We two have sworne shall come.

PERDITA: O Lady Fortune,
Stand you auspicious.

FLORIZELL: See, your Guests approach,
Addresse your selfe to entertaine them sprightly,
And let's be red with mirth.

SHEPHERD: Fy (daughter) when my old wife liv'd: upon
This day, she was both Pantler, Butler, Cooke,
Both Dame and Servant: Welcom'd all: serv'd all,

Would sing her song, and dance her turne: now heere
At upper end o'th Table; now, i'th middle:
On his shoulder, and his: her face o'fire
With labour, and the thing she tooke to quench it
She would to each one sip. You are retyred,
As if you were a feasted one; and not
The Hostesse of the meeting: Pray you bid
These unknowne friends to's welcome, for it is
A way to make us better Friends, more knowne.
Come, quench your blushes, and present your selfe
That which you are, Mistris o'th'Feast. Come on,
And bid us welcome to your sheepe-shearing,
As your good flocke shall prosper.

PERDITA: Sir, welcome:
It is my Fathers will, I should take on mee
The Hostesseship o'th'day: you're welcome sir.
Give me those Flowres there (*Dorcas.*) Reverend Sirs,
For you, there's Rosemary, and Rue, these keepe
Seeming, and savour all the Winter long:
Grace, and Remembrance be to you both,
And welcome to our Shearing.

POLIXENES: Shepherdesse,
(A faire one are you:) well you fit our ages
With flowres of Winter.

PERDITA: Sir, the yeare growing ancient,
Not yet on summers death, nor on the birth
Of trembling winter, the fayrest flowres o'th season
Are our Carnations, and streak'd Gilly-vors,
(Which some call Natures bastards) of that kind
Our rusticke Gardens barren, and I care not
To get slips of them.

POLIXENES: Wherefore (gentle Maiden)
Do you neglect them.

PERDITA: For I have heard it said,

There is an Art, which in their pidenesse shares
With great creating-Nature.

POLIXENES: Say there be:
Yet nature is made better by no meane,
But Nature makes that Meane: so over that Art,
(Which you say addes to Nature) is an Art
That Nature makes: you see (sweet Maid) we marry
A gentler Sien, to the wildest Stocke,
And make conceyve a barke of baser kinde
By bud of Nobler race. This is an Art
Which do's mend Nature: change it rather, but
The Art it selfe, is Nature.

PERDITA: So it is.

POLIXENES: Then make you Garden rich in Gilly'vors
And do not call them bastards.

PERDITA: Ile not put
The Dible in earth, to set one slip of them:
No more then were I painted, I would wish
This youth should say 'twer well: and onely therefore
Desire to breed by me.

*

PERDITA: Come, take your flours,
Me thinkes I play as I have seene them do
In Whitson-Pastorals: Sure this Robe of mine
Do's change my disposition:

FLORIZELL: What you do,
Still betters what is done. When you speake (Sweet)
I'ld have you do it ever: When you sing,
I'ld have you buy, and sell so: so give Almes,
Pray so: and for the ord'ring your Affayres,
To sing them too. When you do dance, I wish you
A wave o'th Sea, that you might ever do
Nothing but that: move still, still so:
And owne no other Function. Each your doing,

(So singular, in each particular)
Crownes what you are doing, in the present deeds,
That all your Actes, are Queenes.

PERDITA: O *Doricles**,
Your praises are too large: but that your youth
And the true blood which peepes fairely through't,
Do plainly give you out an unstain'd Shepherd
With wisedome, I might feare (my *Doricles*)
You woo'd me the false way.

FLORIZELL: I thinke you have
As little skill to feare, as I have purpose
To put you to't. But come, our dance I pray,
Your hand (my *Perdita*:) to Turtles paire
That never meane to part.

PERDITA: Ile sweare for 'em.

POLIXENES: This is the prettiest Low-borne Lasse, that ever
Ran on the greene-sord: Nothing she do's, or seemes
But smackes of something greater then her selfe,
Too Noble for this place.

CAMILLO: He tels her something
That makes her blood looke on't: Good sooth she is
The Queene of Curds and Creame.

CLOWN: Come on: strike up.

DORCAS: *Mopsa* must be your Mistris: marry Garlick to mend her kissing with.

MOPSA: Now in good time.

CLOWN: Not a word, a word, we stand upon our manners,
Come strike up.

[*Heere a Daunce of Shepheards and Shephearddesses.*]

★

[*Enter Servant*]

SERVANT: O Master: if you did but heare the Pedler at the

★ Florizell, the son of the King of Bohemia, Polixenes, is disguised as Doricles, a shepherd.

doore, you would never dance againe after a Tabor and Pipe: no, the Bag-pipe could not move you: hee singes severall Tunes, faster then you'l tell money: hee utters them as he had eaten ballads, and all mens eares grew to his Tunes.

CLOWN: He could never come better: hee shall come in: I love a ballad but even too well, if it be dolefull matter merrily set downe: or a very pleasant thing indeede, and sung lamentably.

SERVANT: He hath songs for man, or woman, of all sizes: No Milliner can so fit his customers with Gloves: he has the prettiest Love-songs for Maids, so without bawdrie (which is strange,) with such delicate burthens of Dildo's and Fadings: Jump-her, and thump-her; and where some stretch-mouth'd Rascall, would (as it were) meane mischeefe, and breake a fowle gap into the Matter, hee makes the maid to answere, *Whoop, doe me no harme good man*: put's him off, slights him, with *Whoop, doe mee no harme good man.*

POLIXENES: This is a brave fellow.

CLOWN: Beleeve mee, thou talkest of an admirable conceited fellow, has he any unbraided Wares?

SERVANT: Hee hath Ribbons of all the colours i'th Rainebow; Points, more then all the Lawyers in *Bohemia*, can learnedly handle, though they come to him by th'grosse: Inckles, Caddysses, Cambrickes, Lawnes[2]: why he sings em over, as they were Gods, or Goddesses: you would thinke a Smocke were a shee-Angell, he so chauntes to the sleevehand, and the worke about the square on't.

[2] tapes and fine linens

CLOWN: Pre'thee bring him in, and let him approach singing.

PERDITA: Forewarne him, that he use no scurrilous words in's tunes.

CLOWN: You have of these Pedlers, that have more in them, then youl'd thinke (Sister.)

PERDITA: I, good brother, or go about to thinke.

[*Enter* AUTOLICUS *singing:*]

Lawne as white as driven Snow,
Cypresse blacke as ere was Crow,
Gloves as sweete as Damaske Roses,
Maskes for faces, and for noses:
Bugle-bracelet, Necke-lace Amber,
Perfume for a Ladies Chamber:
Golden Quoifes, and Stomachers
For my Lads, to give their deers:
Pins, and poaking-stickes[3] of steele.
What Maids lacke from head to heele:
Come buy of me, come: come buy, come buy,
Buy Lads, or else your Lasses cry: Come buy.

[3] used for stiffening plaits of ruffs

[First performed *c.* 1609]

From *The Tempest*
Act II, Scene I

GONZALO, ANTONIO, SEBASTIAN

GONZALO: Had I plantation of this Isle my Lord.
ANTONIO: Hee'd sow't with Nettle-seed.
SEBASTIAN: Or dockes, or Mallowes.
GONZALO: And were the King on't, what would I do?
SEBASTIAN: Scape being drunke, for want of Wine.
GONZALO: I'th' Commonwealth I would (by contraries)
Execute all things: For no kinde of Trafficke
Would I admit: No name of Magistrate:
Letters should not be knowne: Riches, poverty,
And use of service, none: Contract, Succession,
Borne, bound of Land, Tilth, Vineyard none:
No use of Mettall, Corne, or Wine, or Oyle:
No occupation, all men idle, all:
And Women too, but innocent and pure:
No Soveraignty.
SEBASTIAN: Yet he would be King on't.

ANTONIO: The latter end of his Common-wealth forgets the beginning.
GONZALO: All things in common Nature should produce
Without sweat or endevour: Treason, fellony,
Sword, Pike, Knife, Gun, or neede of any Engine
Would I not have: but Nature should bring forth
Of it owne kinde, all foyzon, all abundance
To feed my innocent people.
SEBASTIAN: No marrying 'mong his subjects?
ANTONIO: None (man) all idle; Whores and knaves.
GONZALO: I would with such perfection governe Sir:
T'Excell the Golden Age.

[First performed *c.* 1611]

SAMUEL DANIEL

From *The Queenes Arcadia*

Act I, Scene I

ERGASTUS, MELIBŒUS

ERGASTUS: How is it *Melibœus* that we finde
Our Country, faire *Arcadia*, so much chang'd
From what it was; that was thou knowst of late,
The gentle region of plaine honesty,
The modest seat of undisguised truth,
Inhabited with simple innocence:
And now, I know not how, as if it were
Unhallowed, and divested of that grace,
Hath put off that faire nature which it had,
And growes like ruder countries, or more bad.
MELIBŒUS: Indeed *Ergastus* I have never knowne
So universall a distemperature,
In all parts of the body of our state,

As now there is; nor ever have we heard
So much complaining of disloyalty,
Among'st your yonger Nymphes, nor ever found
Our heardsmen so deluded in their loves,
As if there were no faith on either side.
We never had in any age before
So many spotlesse Nymphes, so much distain'd
With blacke report, and wrongfull infamy;
That few escape the tongue of malice free.

ERGASTUS: And me thinkes too, our very aire is chang'd,
Our wholesome climate growne more maladive;
The fogges, and the Syrene offends us more
(Or we made thinke so), then they did before.
The windes of Autumne, now are sayd to bring
More noysomnesse, then those do of the Spring:
And all of us feele new infirmities,
New Fevers, new Catarres, oppresse our powers;
The milke wherewith we cur'd all maladies,
Hath either lost the nature, or we ours.

MELIBŒUS: And we that never were accustomed
To quarrell for our bounds, how do we see
Montanus and *Acrysius* interstrive
How farre their severall Sheep-walkes should extend,
And cannot be agreed do what we can:
As if some underworking hand strake fire,
To th'apt inkindling tinder of debate,
And fostred their contention and their hate.

ERGASTUS: And me thinkes too, the beauty of our Nymphes
Is not the same, as it was wont to be.
That Rosie hew, the glory of the Cheeke,
Is either stolne, or else they have forgot,
To blush with shame, or to be pale with feare:
Or else their shame doth make them alwayes blush;
For alwayes doth their beauties beare one hew,
And either Nature's false, or that untrue.

MELIBŒUS: Besides their various habits grow so strange,
As that although their faces certaine are,
Their bodies are uncertaine every day,
And alwayes differing from themselves so farre,
As if they skorn'd to be the same they are.
And all of us are so transform'd, that we
Discerne not an *Arcadian* by th'attyre;
Our ancient Pastorall habits are despis'd,
And all is strange, hearts, clothes, and all disguis'd.
ERGASTUS: Indeed unto our griefe we may perceive,
The whole complection of *Arcadia* chang'd,
Yet cannot finde the occasion of this change:
But let us with more wary eye observe
Whence the contagion of these customes rise,
That have infected thus our honest plaines,
With cunning discord, idle vanity,
Deceiptfull wrong, and causlesse infamy;
That by th'assistance of our graver Swaines,
We now at first, may labour to prevent
The further course of mischiefes, and restore
Our late cleane woods, to what they were before.
MELIBŒUS: Content *Ergastus*, and even here will be
A place convenient for so fit a worke:
For here our Nymphs, and heardsmen on this Greene,
Do usually resort, and in this Grove
We may observe them best, and be unseene.

Act II, Scene 2

CLORIS, TECHNE

CLORIS: What, is this creature then you praise, a man?
TECHNE: A man? yes *Cloris*, what should he be else?
CLORIS: Nought else, it is enough he be a man.
TECHNE: Yea and so rare a man as ever yet

Arcadia bred, that may be proud she bred
A person of so admirable parts;
A man that knowes the world, hath seene abrod,
Brings those perfections that doe truly move;
A gallant spirit, an understanding love.
O if you did but know how sweet it were,
To come unto the bed of worthinesse,
O knowledge, of conceits, – where strange delights
With strange discourses still shall entertaine
Your pleased thoughts with fresh varietie, –
Ah you would loath to have your youth confin'de,
For ever more betweene the unskilfull armes
Of one of these rude unconceiving Swaines,
Who would but seeme a trunke without a minde;
As one that never saw but these poore plaines,
Knowes but to keepe his sheepe, and set his fold,
Pipe on an Oaten Reede some Rundelayes,
And daunce a Morrice on the holy dayes.
And so should you be alwayes sweetly sped
With ignorance, and two fooles in a bed.
But with this other gallant spirit you should
Be sure to overpasse that tediousnesse,
And that saciety which cloyes this life,
With such a variable cheerefulnesse,
As you will blesse the time t'have beene his wife.

[1606]

JOHN FLETCHER

From *The Faithful Shepherdess*

Act III, Scene I

[*Enter* PERIGOT *and* AMARILLIS *in the shape of* AMORET.]

SULLEN SHEPHEARD: But these fancies must be quite forgot,
I must lye close heere comes younge *Perigot*,
With subtill Amarillis in the shape,
Of *Amorit*, pray love hee may not scape.
AMORET: Beloved Perigot, show me some place,
Where I may rest my limbes, weake with the Chace
Of thee, an hower before thou cam'st at least.
PERIGOT: Beshrewe my Tardy stepps, here shalt thou rest
Uppon this holy banck no deadly snake,
Uppon this Turffe her selfe in foulds doth make,
Here is no poyson, for the Toade to feed,
Here boldly spread thy handes, no venomd weed,
Dares blister them, No slymy snaile dare creepe,
Over thy face when thou art fast a sleepe,
Here never durst the bablinge Cuckoe spitt.
No slough of falling Starr, did ever hitt.
Uppon this Bancke, let this thy Cabin bee.
This other set with violets for mee.
AMORET: Thou dost not love mee *Perigot*;
PERIGOT: Faire mayde
You onely love to heare it often sayd;
You do not doubt,
AMORET: Beleeve me, but I do.
PERIGOT: What shall we now begin againe to woe,
Tis the best way to make your lover last,
To play with him, when you have caught him fast.
AMORET: By *Pan* I sweare I loved *Perigot*,
And by yon Moone, I thinke thou lovest me not.
PERIGOT: By *Pan* I sweare and if I falsely sweare:

Let him not guard my flockes, let Foxes teare,
My Earelyest lambes, and wolves whilst I do sleepe
Fall on the rest, a Rot amonge my sheepe;
I love thee better, then the carefull Ewe,
The new yeand lambe that is of her owne hew,
I dote upon thee, more than that young lambe,
Doth on the Bagg, that feedes him from his dam.
Were there a sort of wolves got in my fould,
And one rann after thee, both young and ould,
Should be devour'd, and it should be my strife,
To save thee, whome I love above, my life,

AMORET: How shall I trust thee when I see thee chuse
Another bedd, and dost my side refuse,

PERIGOT: T'was onely that the chast thoughts, might be showen,
Twixt thee and me, although we were alone,

AMORET: Come *Perigot*, will show his power that hee
Can make his Amoret, though she weary bee,
Rise nimbly from her Couch, and come to his.
Here take my Amoret imbrace and kisse:

PERIGOT: What meanes my love;

AMORET: To do as lover shud.
That are to be injoyed not to be woed.
Ther's nere a Shepheardesse in all the plaine,
Can kisse thee with more Art, ther's none can faine.
More wanton trickes,

PERIGOT: Forbeare deare soule to trye,
Whether my heart be pure, Ile rather dye,
Then nourish one thought to dishonour thee,

AMORET: Still thinkst thou such a thing as Chastitie,
Is amongst woemen, Perigot thers none,
That with her love is in a wood alone,
And wood come home a Mayde, be not abus'd,
With thy fond first beleife, let time be usd,
Why dost thou rise,

PERIGOT: My true heart, thou hast slaine,
AMORET: Fayth *Perigot*, Ile plucke the downe againe,
PERIGOT: Let goe thou Serpent, that into me brest,
Hast with thy Cunning div'd art not in jest?
AMORET: Sweete love lye downe.
PERIGOT: Since this I live to see,
Some bitter North wind blast my flockes and mee.
AMORET: You swore you lov'd, yet will not do my will.
PERIGOT: O be as thou wert once, Ile love thee still.
AMORET: I am, as still I was, and all my kind,
Though others showes we have poore men to blynd.
PERIGOT: Then here I end all love, and rest my vaine,
Beleeife should ever draw me in againe,
Before thy face that hast my youth mislead,
I end my life, my blood be on thy head.
AMORET: O hold thy hands thy *Amoret* doth cry.
PERIGOT: Thou counsayl'st well, first *Amoret* shall dye,
That is the cause of my Eternall smart.
AMORET: O hold.
PERIGOT: This steele shall peirce thy lustfull hart:
[*He runs after her.*]
[*The Sullen Shepheard stepes out and uncharmes her.*]

SULLEN: Up and downe every where,
I strewe the hearbs to purge the Ayre,
Let your Odor drive hence,
All mistes that dazell sence,
Hearbes and springs whose hydden might:
Alters shapes, and mocks the fight.
Thus I charge ye to undo;
All before I brought yee to,
Let her flye, let her scape,
Give againe her owne shape.

[*c.* 1610]

BEN JONSON

The Sad Shepherd

from the *Prologue*

But here's an Heresie of late let fall;
That Mirth by no meanes fits a *Pastorall;*
Such say so, who can make none, he presumes:
Else, there's no Scene, more properly assumes
The Sock. For whence can sport in kind arise,
But from the Rurall Routs and Families?
Safe on this ground then, wee not feare to day,
To tempt your laughter by our rustick *Play.*
Wherin if we distaste, or be cry'd downe,
Wee thinke wee therefore shall not leave the Towne;
Nor that the Fore-wits, that would draw the rest
Unto their liking, alwayes like the best.
The wise, and knowing *Critick* will not say,
This worst, or better is, before he weigh,
Where every piece be perfect in the kind:
And then, though in themselves he difference find,
Yet if the place require it where they stood,
The equall fitting makes them equall good.
You shall have Love and Hate, and Jealousie,
As well as Mirth, and Rage, and Melancholy:
Or whatsoever else may either move,
Or stirre affections, and your likings prove.
But that no stile for *Pastorall* should goe
Current, but what is stamp'd with *Ah*, and *O;*
Who judgeth so, may singularly erre;
As if all *Poesie* had one Character:
In which what were not written, were not right,
Or that the man who made such one poore flight,
In his whole life, had with his winged skill
Advanc'd him upmost on the *Muses* hill.

When he like *Poet* yet remains, as those
Are *Painters* who can only make a *Rose*.
From such your wits redeeme you, or your chance,
Lest to a greater height you doe advance
Of Folly, to contemne those that are knowne
Artificers, and trust such as are none.

Act I, Scene 4

[ROBIN-HOOD, CLARION, MELLIFLEUR, LIONEL, AMIE, ALKEN, TUCK, SERVANTS, *with musick of all sorts.*]

ROBIN: Welcome bright *Clarion*, and sweet *Mellifleur*,
The courteous *Lionel*, faire *Amie*; all
My friends and neighbours, to the Jolly Bower
Of *Robin-hood*, and to the greene-wood Walkes:
Now that the shearing of your sheepe is done,
And the wash'd Flocks are lighted of their wooll,
The smoother Ewes are ready to receive
The mounting Rams againe; and both doe feed,
As either promist to increase your breed
At earning time; and bring you lusty twins.
Why should, or you, or wee so much forget
The season in our selves: as not to make
Use of our youth, and spirits, to awake
The nimble Horne-pipe, and the Timburine,
And mixe our Songs, and Dances in the Wood,
And each of us cut downe a Triumph-bough?
Such are the Rites, the youthfull *June* allow.
CLARION: They were, gay *Robin*, but the sowrer sort
Of Shepherds now disclaime in all such sport:
And say, our Flocks, the while, are poorely fed,
When with such vanities the Swaines are led.
TUCK: Would they, wise *Clarion*, were not hurried more

With Covetise and Rage, when to their store
They adde the poore mans Eaneling[1], and dare sell
Both Fleece, and Carkasse, not gi'ing him the Fell.
When to one Goat, they reach that prickly weed,
Which maketh all the rest forbeare to feed;
Or strew *Tods* haires, or with their tailes doe sweepe
The dewy grasse, to d'off the simpler sheepe;
Or digge deepe pits, their Neighbours Neat to vexe,
To drowne the Calves, and crack the Heifers necks.
Or with pretence of chasing thence the Brock,
Send in a curre to worrie the whole Flock.

[1] young lamb

LIONEL: O Friar, those are faults that are not seene,
Ours open, and of worst example beene.
They call ours, *Pagan* pastimes, that infect
Our blood with ease, our youth with all neglect,
Our tongues with wantonnesse, our thoughts with lust;
And what they censure ill, all others must.

ROBIN: I doe not know, what their sharpe sight may see
Of late, but I should thinke it still might be
(As 'twas) a happy age, when on the Plaines,
The Wood-men met the Damsells, and the Swaines
The Neat'ards, Plow-men, and the Pipers loud,
And each did dance, some to the Kit, or Crowd,
Some to the Bag-pipe, some the Tabret mov'd,
And all did either love, or were belov'd.

LIONEL: The dextrous Shepherd then would try his sling,
Then dart his Hooke at Daysies, then would sing,
Sometimes would wrastle.

CLARION: I, and with a Lasse:
And give her a new garment in the grasse;
After a course at Barley-breake, or Base[2].

LIONEL: And all these deeds were seene without offence,
Or the least hazard o' their innocence.

[2] old games rather like the modern 'prisoner's base'

ROBIN: Those charitable times had no mistrust.
Shepherds knew how to love, and not to lust.

[First performed *c.* 1612, published 1640]

JOSEPH RUTTER

From *The Shepheard's Holy-Day,*
Act I, Scene 4

MIRTILLUS: But shepherds, did you never hear that once
There was an age, the nearest to the gods:
An age we rather praise than imitate;
When no man's will nor woman's was enforc'd
To any bent but its own motion?
Each follow'd nature's laws, and by instinct
Did love the fairest, and enjoy their wishes:
Love then, not tied to any interest
Of blood or fortune, hasten'd to his end
Without control, nor did the shepherd number
Her sheep that was his choice, but every grace
That did adorn her beauteous mind or face.
Riches with love then were not valued –
Pure, uncompounded lov – ethat could despise
The whole world's riches for a mistress' eyes.

Act III, Scene I

DELIA, SYLVIA

SYLVIA: Alas, my Delia! thou dost mistake,
My liberty is of no worth to me,

Since that my love, I fear, will ne'er be free:
Nor do I care what idle ladies talk
Of my departure or my strange disguise,
To colour my intents; I am above
Their envy or their malice:
But for th' unlucky chance that sent to me
The over-curious eyes of him I hate –
Thou knows't the man.

DELIA: Yes, you mean Cleander,
Son to Eubulus, who is now your keeper:
What star directed him to find you out?

SYLVIA: His love, forsooth; for so he colour'd his
Unseason'd boldness: told me he was not able
To want my sight: and so, when every one
Had given o'er their strict inquiry of me,
He only, with too much officiousness,
Observ'd me in the woods, walking alone:
And when I would have shunn'd him, which perhaps
Had I not done, he had not so well known me:
He came and utter'd, as his manner was,
His tedious complaints; until at length
He brought me with him, making no resistance:
And to ingratiate himself the more,
He said he would convey me where my father
Should have no knowledge of me. I refused it;
Willing, however, to be rid of him.
And now, you know, it is a full month since
I did return to Court, but left my heart
Behind me in those fields wherein I joy'd.

DELIA: Madam, has not the Court more pleasure in it
Than the dull country, which can represent
Nothing but what does taste of solitude?
'Twas something else that carried you away.

SYLVIA: 'Tis true, my Delia; for though thou wert
Privy to my departure, yet the cause

Thou couldst not tell, which I will now unfold;
And think I trust my honour in thy hands,
And maiden modesty: 'twas love that did it.
DELIA: Love, madam! Sure, it is impossible
You should find anything there worth your love.
SYLVIA: Thou knowst the shepherds that do dwell about
This place which, for their entertainments only,
The king my father built, did use to come,
As now they do, being sent for unto Court:
I ever lik'd their sports, their harmless mirth,
And their contentions, which were void of malice,
And wish'd I had been born just such an one.
DELIA: Your state is better, madam, as you are.
SYLVIA: But I confess the rather, 'cause there was
One amongst them of a more comely grace
(Though none of them did seem uncomely to me)
Call'd Thyrsis; and with him methought I could
Draw out my life rather than any other,
Such things my fancy then suggested to me:
So well he sung, so passionate his love
Show'd in his verse, thereto so well express'd,
As any one would judge it natural:
Yet never felt he flame, till this of me:
Often he came, and oft'ner was desir'd
Of me; nor did I shame in public there
Before my father to commend his graces;
Which when I did, the whole Court, as they use,
Consented with me, and did strive to make them
Greater than I or any else could think them:
At last I was surpris'd, I could not help it;
My fate with love consenting, so would have it:
Then did I leave the Court – I've told thee all.
DELIA: 'Tis strange! but, madam, though in that disguise,
How could you hope (a stranger) to be lov'd
Of him you held so dear?

SYLVIA: I feign'd myself
Of Smyrna, and from thence some goats I had
And sheep, with them a rich commodity.
Near him I bought me land to feed them; he
Seem'd glad of it, and thinking me a stranger,
Us'd me with such civility and friendship,
As one would little look for of a shepherd;
And did defend me from the avarice
Of the old shepherds, which did think to make
A prey of what I had. At length I saw
He did address himself with fear to me,
Still gazing on me. Knowing my love to him,
I easily believ'd he lov'd me too –
For love, alas! is ever credulous –
And though I was resolv'd (having my end,
Which was no more than to discourse with him)
Never to let him know what flame I felt;
Yet when I saw his tears, and heard his vows –
Persuasive speakers for affection –
I could not choose but open to his view
My loving heart; yet with this caution,
That he should ever bear respect unto
My honour and my virgin chastity:
Which then he vow'd, and his ambition
Never was more than to attain a kiss,
Which yet he hardly got. Thou seest, sweet Delia,
How willingly I dwell upon this theme.
But can'st thou help me, now that I have open'd
My wound unto thee?

[1635]

THE SEVENTEENTH-CENTURY PASTORAL

'The *Golden-Age* was when the world was yong' for Fulke Greville and his fellow 'Spenserians', but for most poets after about 1610 the pastoral age had not only receded but had disappeared from view. Writers of Pastoral in the years between the accession of James I and the outbreak of the Civil War – where they are to be found – concur in Drayton's location of the Golden Age within the historical development of the English Pastoral. The second book of William Browne's *Britannia's Pastorals* opens with a nostalgic eulogy of Spenser, and the sense of an era having past is prevalent. The dominant model for such writers is the later Spenser, of *The Faerie Queene*. It has been argued that in Browne we have the first evidence of an actual observed English landscape – a move, that is, away from the classical towards the romantic – but, as in works like Phineas Fletcher's *The Purple Island*, it is the formal rehearsal of past artificiality that is most striking. The Golden Age has passed, and as the life of the Court becomes increasingly subjected to external political pressures the possibility of a celebration of a courtly idealism is ever more problematic.

The metaphysical poets were rarely interested in a pastoral tradition – Donne's 'The Baite' is little more than an exercise-piece, one in a long and ever more tedious series of replies to Marlowe's long-dead 'Passionate Sheepheard'. The imagery of the metaphysicals, where it is not concerned with personal salvation, is insistently contemporary, full of references to a new mercantile age, to commerce, exploration, political struggle and conquest. The poetry is critical of the values of such an age undoubtedly, but the poets no longer see a viable alternative in a world of pastoral innocence. In place of a vision of a simple, harmonized society, the metaphysicals looked for a resolution of contemporary problems in terms of the individual, be it in the area of the religious or the secular. A pastoral tradition which had arisen in reaction to an awakening of an individualist philosophy in the Renaissance had little to offer a writer intent on exploring the new world of scientific rationalism. The poetry of the metaphysical period is largely that of an urban culture which no longer feels sufficient connection with a rural alternative, an alternative which had anyway become ever more an artifice and a way of avoiding the contemporary and the threatening. The poet's problems were to be faced either in their urban context or by a turning inwards; a school of poetry which could call into question the whole manner of discussing human relationships taken over from Petrarch and an Italian tradition would clearly have little use for that other foreign importation, the Pastoral.

Where there is any expression of the pastoral vision it is either from poets looking back (those who looked through Drayton to Spenser) to an aristocratic culture that had all but passed, or (as in the example discussed from the *Duchess of Malfi*) as an implicit assumption in urban and court satire. At the same time, however, the seventeenth century sees the emergence of a different kind of pastoral voice, one that expresses no longer a merely idealized view of the countryside surrounding the town which housed the poet, and one which makes for the first time hesitant moves in the direction of 'realism'. The two sonnets of Drummond (another 'Spenserian') that we have included are very similar in theme, both praising an actual retreat from an urban world of politics and commerce. It is a theme that derives chiefly from Horace – Pope's 'Ode to Solitude' is included as a later example of juvenile borrowing from the Horatian – but its origins may also be sought in a non-pastoral area, the essay-form as developed by Montaigne. This turning away from the 'real' world of affairs is very much like the 'turning inwards' of the metaphysicals, and in a writer such as Cowley the two become merged. The country is seen as a place where the individual is free to find himself. What is different about this rural alternative is that it purports to have a specific geographical location – that is, the poet is not wandering around a classical landscape, but is supposedly living in the country with a roof over his head and a plot of land to work for his food. The seventeenth century produced many 'imitations' of Horace's 'Epode, In Praise of a Country Life', and, although space will not permit examples, the opening of that of Jonson will make the point:

> Happie is he, that from all Businese cleere,
> As the old race of Mankind were,
> With his owne Oxen tills his Sires left lands,
> And is not in the Usurers bands:
> Nor Souldier-like started with rough alarmes,
> Nor dreads the Seas inraged harmes:
> But flees the Barre and Courts, with the proud bords,
> And waiting Chambers of great Lords.

The group ritual of the older pastoral is replaced by an emphasis on the individual's relationship to his own land – the possession of 'paternal acres' is all-important. The poet never imagines himself living below his own social level, as a shepherd or traditional pastoral figure, so that the fantasy of country property – and fantasy it is, for Jonson like most celebrators of such a retreat possessed not a single field to till – does at least have a solid connection with the poet's life.

What is being celebrated here is more than an imaginative escape from the pressures of urban life; it is also the possibility of economic freedom for the writer. The fantasy is an adaptation of the situation of the pastoral poet to that of his patron, the landowner. What these poems represent is a 'bourgeois' version of the myth, with the poet, no longer cast as shepherd or clown, in the role of gentry-farmer supporting himself single-handedly – or probably with the aid of a buxom country wife – in such a way as to leave ample time for the main business of philosophical reflection. The patronage of the manor house is replaced by the freedom of the self-sufficient small farm.

But if the manor house had meant restriction, it had also meant security. As a microcosm of the larger society it symbolized both power and patronage, and stood in a relationship of mutual dependence with the rural community around it. The values of this world are invoked by Jonson in 'To Penshurst', when however this harmonious relationship is not the rule but the exception. The poet eats, as do the 'farmer and the clowne', the same food as the 'lord and lady', and he is happy to celebrate their munificence. The house which had given birth to the Pastoral – Sidney had lived there – still remains as a final embodiment of the pastoral myth of aristocratic organization; farmers and classical gods walk the same fields. As in Carew's 'To Saxham', the fish, flesh and fowl of the estate queue happily for their turn to be eaten; the humour is deliberate and indicates the ultimate impossibility of the vision. Jonson may express a nostalgia for what Penshurst represents but he is too much the realist not to realize that it is something that has passed.

Herrick's 'The Hock-Cart' is an attempt, from a Cavalier perspective, to deal honestly with the nature of the bond between the landowner and his workers. The union of the two groups is achieved in the ritual of the harvest-feast – a recurrent theme in the Pastoral – when the workers put down their tools to celebrate their master in feast and song. But the relationship is harsher than that; the harvest-feast slurs over the reality. The following morning will see the old order of ruler and ruled re-established, and the brief equality of the feast will cease. Like the oxen that pull their ploughs, the workers will resume their toil;

> And, you must know, your Lords word's true,
> Feed him ye must, whose food fils you.
> And that this pleasure is like raine,
> Not sent ye for to drowne your paine,
> But for to make it spring againe.

This strain, which becomes ever more evident throughout the century, makes it increasingly difficult for the serious perpetuation of this kind of pastoral celebration. Civil strife and the growth of a new landowning class would complete the process. When Pope refers to a vision of a restored 'manor house' community a century later, his appeal is one of political nostalgia. The account of rural organization had always been a mythical one, and the nearer it approaches to 'realism' the more its bones are revealed to all.

This sense of the passing of an age finds its greatest expression in Milton's 'Lycidas' (1637). The poem is a revitalization of an old form – the pastoral elegy – and also, in effect, an elegy for the Pastoral. The poet mourns the death of the young shepherd, Lycidas – Edward King, a young Cambridge scholar – and argues that with his death, the possibility of the traditional Pastoral has ended. Milton had already, in 'L'Allegro' (*c.* 1631), drawn heavily on the earlier Pastoral. Milton's shepherds are unable to play a pastoral role; the sheep are untended and hungry; the shearers have lost their skills; and the poet disturbs nature in his sorrow, preventing the coming of Spring and a new pastoral cycle. But 'Lycidas' is not just the culmination of the 'idealized' tradition. The world of the traditional Pastoral is opposed by that of the Christian myth, and the poem concludes with a resolution of the two in the resurrection of Lycidas into a heavenly paradise – not the now impossible earthly one – leaving the poet with renewed hope, to wander in 'fresh woods, and pastures new'. Although the poem is full of echoes of the past – the inclusion of anti-clerical satire, for instance, is sanctioned by Spenser's 'Fifth Eclogue' – the tone is not finally one of impossible nostalgia. The world of Lycidas has passed, and the poet, having assimilated the past, must find his own way in the new world. The conclusion is optimistic and indicative of an emergent Protestant consciousness on Milton's part, with the emphasis falling on the individual's break with the tradition.

There is a considerable amount of reference to the world of conventional Pastoral in *Paradise Lost* as well. In Book IX the reader's pastoral expectations are played upon for dramatic effect with the presentation of Satan 'as one who long in populous City pent'; but it is in Book IV that we find a full fusion of the classical and the christian Pastoral. No account of the Garden of Eden could conceivably ignore the pastoral tradition, and it is not too surprising to find 'Universal Pan' walking the same groves as Adam and Eve. In Book IV, Milton leaves the grand epic style for a quieter, pastoral voice.

His Paradise is very like Blake's state of 'Innocence' in which the beasts of the earth pose no threat to man, and God's creatures live the 'happiest life (of) simplicitie and spotless innocence'. But Milton does not see Paradise as a pre-Rousseauite home for 'natural-man'. He is concerned to present the Garden as a planted Garden, a creation of the universal architect, and in opposition to the chaos that is the world of Satan and unbridled passion. The pastoral represented an ordered nature for man before the Fall, an environment which offered no threat.

The opposition of created Garden and unspoilt Nature is obviously central to the Pastoral, but it is an opposition that may take many forms. Untamed Nature may be a place of repose from the vexations of the town, or a threat to man in organized society; the Garden may appear as a recognition of the essential harmony of the natural order, or a denial of it. The poet who is most concerned with the ambiguities of this opposition in the seventeenth century is Andrew Marvell. In his 'mower' poems, the cultivated Garden is not an indication – as it is in Milton – of an ordered Universe, but is an urban phenomenon, the product of 'Luxurious Man' after the Fall. It is only in the exotic 'Bermudas' that Marvell's puritan emigrés can find an unaltered paradise, far from the possibility of urban 'knowledge'. 'The Mower against Gardens' suggests the impossibility of harmony between man and his environment, and thus offers a serious threat to the entire pastoral tradition. But there is no simple praise of the natural life, for wild Nature is always threatening. The figure of the innocent but ineffective Shepherd is rejected in favour of the Mower with his destructive relationship to the land, 'depopulating all the ground'. The mower does not respond to the natural, as does the shepherd, but struggles against it, reducing it to order. So that although he is hostile towards the artificiality of cultivation, it is his job precisely to tame Nature, to tailor it more neatly for urban man. This ambiguity of attitude becomes even more complicated when we realize that there is no straightforward identification by Marvell with the mower. In 'Ametas and Thestylis making Hay-Ropes' – a poem whose apparent simplicity is deceptive – the world of urban metaphysical wit is thrown over for the natural rural activity of weaving, in imagery which combines the idea of work, dancing and copulation. Again the sterility of the city is opposed by the natural activities of the country, but activities which have a sense of pattern, of order.

The problems raised by Marvell's poetry are many and complex, and it is in 'The Garden' that he comes nearest to resolving them. The poem contrasts the efforts of ambitious urban man who labours incessantly to win the 'Palm ... Oke, or Bayes', with a vision of a natural paradise in which the individual, free from society, has the whole of Nature dancing attendance:

> What wond'rous Life in this I lead!
> Ripe Apples drop about my head;
> The Luscious Clusters of the Vine
> Upon my Mouth do crush their Wine.

But – although Marvell clearly conjures with imagery of a sensual Garden of Eden, the poem does not adopt a nostalgic Golden Age tone; nor is Marvell acceding wholly to the Horatian tradition of 'retreat'. He regards the original Eden as an idealized pastoral condition before the demands of human relationships enforced a separation of needs and desires, and considers how to achieve this paradise once more. Thus the Garden is both a place of natural retreat, where the trees 'weave the Garlands of repose' allowing the poet to think in serenity; and a created retreat, giving evidence of the hand of a gardener. The Garden is a paradise of the imagination, to be found by a turning inwards:

> Mean while the Mind, from pleasure less,
> Withdraws into its happiness:
> The Mind, that Ocean where each kind
> Does streight its own resemblance find;
> Yet it creates, transcending these,
> Far other Worlds, and other Seas;
> Annihilating all that's made
> To a green Thought in a green Shade.

The Garden is a world within the world and not a separation from it; it is a state of individual harmony that has no geographical placement, and is not to be achieved by the labour of men as conventionally understood. The traditional oppositions of the Pastoral are reconciled in Marvell's 'happy Garden-state', and the Golden Age is relocated in the world of puritan individualism.

The Baite

Come live with mee, and bee my love,
And we will some new pleasures prove
Of golden sands, and christall brookes,
With silken lines, and silver hookes.

There will the river whispering runne
Warm'd by thy eyes, more then the Sunne.
And there the'inamor'd fish will stay,
Begging themselves they may betray.

When thou wilt swimme in that live bath,
Each fish, which every channell hath,
Will amorously to thee swimme,
Gladder to catch thee, then thou him.

If thou, to be so seene, beest loath,
By Sunne, or Moone, thou darknest both,
And if my selfe have leave to see,
I need not their light, having thee.

Let others freeze with angling reeds,
And cut their legges, with shells and weeds,
Or treacherously poore fish beset,
With strangling snare, or windowie net:

Let coarse bold hands, from slimy nest
The bedded fish in banks out-wrest,
Or curious traitors, sleavesilke flies
Bewitch poore fishes wandring eyes.

For thee, thou needst no such deceit,
For thou thy selfe art thine owne bait;

That fish, that is not catch'd thereby,
Alas, is wiser farre then I.

[1633]

From *Ecclogue*

Unseasonable man, statue of ice,
  What could to countries solitude entice
Thee, in this yeares cold and decrepit time?
  Natures instinct drawes to the warmer clime
Even small birds, who by that courage dare,
  In numerous fleets, saile through their Sea, the aire.
What delicacie can in fields appeare,
  Whil'st Flora'herselfe doth a freeze jerkin weare?
Whil'st windes do all the trees and hedges strip
  Of leafes, to furnish roddes enough to whip
Thy madnesse from thee; and all springs by frost
  Have taken cold, and their sweet murmures lost;
If thou thy faults or fortunes would'st lament
  With just solemnity, do it in Lent.

[1633]

BEN JONSON

To Penshurst

Thou art not, Penshurst, built to envious show,
Of touch, or marble; nor canst boast a row
Of polish'd pillars, or a roofe of gold:
Thou hast no lantherne, whereof tales are told;
Or stayre, or courts; but stand'st an ancient pile,

And these grudg'd at, art reverenc'd the while.
Thou joy'st in better markes, of soyle, of ayre,
Of wood, of water: therein thou art faire.
Thou hast thy walkes for health, as well as sport:
Thy Mount, to which the Dryads doe resort,
Where Pan, and Bacchus their high feasts have made,
Beneath the broad beech, and the chest-nut shade;
That taller tree, which of a nut was set,
At his great birth, where all the Muses met.
There, in the writhed barke, are cut the names
Of many a Sylvane, taken with his flames.
And thence, the ruddy Satyres oft provoke
The lighter Faunes, to reach thy Ladies oke.
Thy copp's, too, nam'd of Gamage, thou hast there,
That never failes to serve thee season'd deere,
When thou would'st feast, or exercise thy friends.
The lower land, that to the river bends,
Thy sheepe, thy bullocks, kine, and calves doe feed:
The middle grounds thy mares, and horses breed.
Each banke doth yeeld thee coneyes; and the topps
Fertile of wood, Ashore, and Sydney's copp's,
To crowne thy open table, doth provide
The purpled pheasant, with the speckled side:
The painted partrich lyes in every field,
And, for thy messe, is willing to be kill'd.
And if the high swolne Medway faile thy dish,
Thou hast thy ponds, that pay thee tribute fish,
Fat, aged carps, that runne into thy net.
And pikes, now weary their owne kinde to eat,
As loth, the second draught, or cast to stay,
Officiously, at first, themselves betray.
Bright eeles, that emulate them, and leape on land,
Before the fisher, or into his hand.
Then hath thy orchard fruit, thy garden flowers,
Fresh as the ayre, and new as are the houres.

The earely cherry, with the later plum,
Fig, grape, and quince, each in his time doth come:
The blushing apricot, and woolly peach
Hang on thy walls, that every child may reach.
And though thy walls be of the countrey stone,
They'are rear'd with no mans ruine, no mans grone,
There's none, that dwell about them, wish them downe;
But all come in, the farmer, and the clowne:
And no one empty-handed, to salute
Thy lord, and lady, though they have no sute,
Some bring a capon, some a rurall cake,
Some nuts, some apples; some that thinke they make
The better cheeses, bring 'hem; or else send
By their ripe daughters, whom they would commend
This way to husbands; and whose baskets beare
An embleme of themselves, in plum, or peare.
But what can this (more then expresse their love)
Adde to thy free provisions, farre above
The neede of such? whose liberall boord doth flow,
With all, that hospitalitie doth know!
Where comes no guest, but is allow'd to eate,
Without his feare, and of the lords owne meate:
Where the same beere, and bread, and self-same wine,
That is his Lordships, shall be also mine.
And I not faine to sit (as some, this day,
At great mens tables) and yet dine away.
Here no man tells my cups; nor, standing by,
A waiter, doth my gluttony envy:
But gives me what I call, and lets me eate,
He knowes, below, he shall finde plentie of meate,
Thy tables hoord not up for the next day,
Nor, when I take my lodging, need I pray
For fire, or lights, or livorie: all is there;
As if thou, then, wert mine, or I reign'd here:
There's nothing I can wish, for which I stay.

That found King James, when hunting late, this way,
With his brave sonne, the Prince, they saw thy fires
Shine bright on every harth as the desires
Of thy Penates had beene set on flame,
To entertayne them; or the countrey came,
With all their zeale, to warme their welcome here.
What (great, I will not say, but) sodayne cheare
Did'st thou, then, make 'hem! and what praise was heap'd
On thy good lady, then! who, therein, reap'd
The just reward of her high huswifery:
To have her linnen, plate, and all things nigh,
When shee was farre: and not a roome, but drest,
As if it had expected such a guest!
These, Penshurst, are thy praise, and yet not all.
Thy lady's noble, fruitfull, chaste withall.
His children thy great lord may call his owne:
A fortune, in this age, but rarely knowne.
They are, and have beene taught religion: Thence
Their gentler spirits have suck'd innocence.
Each morne, and even, they are taught to pray,
With the whole household, and may, every day,
Reade, in their vertuous parents noble parts,
The mysteries of manners, armes, and arts.
Now, Penshurst, they that will proportion thee
With other edifices, when they see
Those proud, ambitious heaps, and nothing else,
May say, their lords have built, but thy lord dwells.

[1616]

To Sir Robert Wroth

How blest art thou, canst love the countrey, Wroth,
  Whether by choice, or fate, or both;
And, though so neere the citie, and the court.
  Art tane with neithers vice, nor sport:

That at great times, art no ambitious guest
  Of Sheriffes dinner, or Maiors feast.
Nor com'st to view the better cloth of state;
  The richer hangings, or crowne-plate;
Nor throng'st (when masquing is) to have a sight
  Of the short braverie of the night;
To view the jewells, stuffes, the paines, the wit
  There wasted, some not paid for yet!
But canst, at home, in thy securer rest,
  Live, with un-bought provision blest;
Free from proud porches, or their guilded roofes,
  'Mongst loughing heards, and solide hoofes:
Along'st the curled woods, and painted meades,
  Through which a serpent river leades
To some coole, courteous shade, which he calls his,
  And makes sleepe softer then it is!
Or, if thou list the night in watch to breake,
  A-bed canst heare the loud stag speake,
In spring, oft roused for thy masters sport,
  Who, for it, makes thy house his court;
Or with thy friends, the heart of all the yeere,
  Divid'st, upon the lesser Deere;
In autumne, at the Partrich makes a flight,
  And giv'st thy gladder guests the sight;
And, in the winter, hunt'st the flying hare,
  More for thy exercise, then fare;
While all, that follow, their glad eares apply
  To the full greatnesse of the cry:
Or hauking at the river, or the bush,
  Or shooting at the greedie thrush,
Thou dost with some delight the day out-weare,
  Although the coldest of the yeere!
The whil'st, the severall seasons thou hast seene
  Of flowrie fields, of cop'ces greene,

The mowed meddowes, with the fleeced sheepe,
  And feasts, that either shearers keepe;
The ripened eares, yet humble in their height,
  And furrowes laden with their weight;
The apple-harvest, that doth longer last;
  The hogs return'd home fat from mast;
The trees cut out in log; and those boughes made
  A fire now, that lent a shade!
Thus *Pan* and *Sylvane*, having had their rites,
  Comus puts in, for new delights;
And fills thy open hall with mirth, and cheere,
  As if in *Saturnes* raigne it were;
Apollo's harpe, and *Hermes* lyre resound,
  Nor are the *Muses* strangers found:
The rout of rurall folke come thronging in,
  (Their rudenesse then is thought no sinne)
Thy noblest spouse affords them welcome grace;
  And the great *Heroes*, of her race,
Sit mixt with losse of state, or reverence.
  Freedome doth with degree dispense.
The jolly wassall walkes the often round,
  And in their cups, their cares are drown'd:
They thinke not, then, which side the cause shall leese,
  Nor how to get the lawyer fees.
Such, and no other was that age, of old,
  Which boasts t'have had the head of gold.
And such since thou canst make thine owne content,
  Strive, *Wroth*, to live long innocent.
Let others watch in guiltie armes, and stand
  The furie of a rash command,
Goe enter breaches, meet the cannons rage,
  That they may sleepe with scarres in age.
And shew their feathers shot, and cullors torne,
  And brag, that they were therefore borne.

Let this man sweat, and wrangle at the barre,
  For every price, in every jarre,
And change possessions, oftner with his breath,
  Then either money, warre, or death:
Let him, then hardest sires, more disinherit,
  And each where boast it as his merit,
To blow up orphanes, widdowes, and their states;
  And thinke his power doth equall *Fates*.
Let that goe heape a masse of wretched wealth,
  Purchas'd by rapine, worse then stealth,
And brooding o're it sit, with broadest eyes,
  Not doing good, scarce when he dyes.
Let thousands more goe flatter vice, and winne,
  By being organes to great sinne,
Get place, and honor, and be glad to keepe
  The secrets, that shall breake their sleepe:
And, so they ride in purple, eate in plate,
  Though poyson, thinke it a great fate.
But thou, my *Wroth*, if I can truth apply,
  Shalt neither that, nor this envy:
Thy peace is made; and, when man's state is well,
  'Tis better, if he there can dwell.
God wisheth, none should wracke on a strange shelfe:
  To him, man's dearer, then to himselfe.
And, howsoever we may thinke things sweet,
  He alwayes gives what he knowes meet;
Which who can use is happy: Such be thou.
  Thy morning's, and thy evening's vow
Be thankes to him, and earnest prayer, to finde
  A body sound, with sounder minde;
To doe thy countrey service, thy selfe right;
  That neither want doe thee affright,
Nor death; but when thy latest sand is spent,
  Thou maist thinke life, a thing but lent.

[1616]

From *Cælica*

Sonnet XLIV

The *Golden-Age* was when the world was yong,
Nature so rich, as Earth did need no sowing,
Malice not knowne, the Serpents had not stung,
Wit was but sweet Affections overflowing.

Desire was free, and Beauties first-begotten;
Beauty then neither net, nor made by art,
Words out of thoughts brought forth, and not forgotten,
The Lawes were inward that did rule the heart.

The *Brasen Age* is now when Earth is worne,
Beauty growne sicke, Nature corrupt and nought,
Pleasure untimely dead as soone as borne,
Both words and kindnesse strangers to our thought:

If now this changing World doe change her head,
Cælica, what have her new Lords for to boast?
The old Lord knowes Desire is poorely fed,
And sorrowes not a wavering province lost,
  Since in the guilt-Age *Saturne* rul'd alone,
  And in this painted, *Planets* every one.

[1633]

PHINEAS FLETCHER

From *The Purple Island; or, The Isle of Man*, Canto I

Let others trust the seas, dare death and hell,
Search either *Inde*, vaunt of their scarres and wounds;
Let others their deare breath (nay silence) sell
To fools, and (swoln, not rich) stretch out their bounds
  By spoiling those that live, and wronging dead;
  That they may drink in pearl, and couch their head
In soft, but sleeplesse down; in rich, but restlesse bed.

Oh let them in their gold quaffe dropsies down;
Oh let them surfets feast in silver bright:
While sugar hires the taste the brain to drown,
And bribes of sauce corrupt false appetite,
  His masters rest, health, heart, life, soul to sell.
  Thus plentie, fulnesse, sicknesse, ring their knell:
Death weds and beds them; first in grave, and then in hell.

But (ah!) let me under some *Kentish* hill
Neare rowling *Medway* 'mong my shepherd peers,
With fearlesse merrie-make, and piping still,
Securely passe my few and slow-pac'd yeares:
  While yet the great *Augustus* of our nation
  Shuts up old *Janus* in this long cessation,
Strength'ning our pleasing ease, and gives us sure vacation.

There may I, master of a little flock,
Feed my poore lambes, and often change their fare:
My lovely mate shall tend my sparing stock,
And nurse my little ones with pleasing care;

Whose love and look shall speak their father plain.
Health be my feast, heav'n hope, content my gain:
So in my little house my lesser heart shall reigne.

The beech shall yeeld a cool safe canopie,
While down I sit, and chaunt to th'echoing wood:
Ah singing might I live, and singing die!
So by fair *Thames*, or silver *Medwayes* floud,
The dying swan, when yeares her temples pierce,
In musick strains breathes out her life and verse;
And chaunting her own dirge tides on her watry herse.

What shall I then need seek a patron out,
Or begge a favour from a mistris eyes,
To fence my song against the vulgar rout,
Or shine upon me with her Geminies?
What care I, if they praise my slender song?
Or reck I, if they do me right, or wrong?
A shepherds blisse nor stands nor falls to ev'ry tongue.

[1633]

WILLIAM DRUMMOND

'Deare Wood, and you sweet solitarie Place'

Deare Wood, and you sweet solitarie Place,
Where from the vulgare I estranged live,
Contented more with what your Shades mee give,
Than if I had what *Thetis* doth embrace:
What snakie Eye growne jealous of my Peace,

Now from your silent Horrours would mee drive?
When Sunne progressing in his glorious Race
Beyond the *Twinnes*, doth neare our Pole arrive.
What sweet Delight a quiet Life affords,
And what it is to bee of Bondage free,
Farre from the madding Worldlings hoarse Discords,
Sweet flowrie Place I first did learne of thee:
  Ah! if I were mine owne, your dear Resorts
  I would not change with *Princes stately Courts.*

[1614]

'Thrise happie hee, who by some shadie Grove'

Thrise happie hee, who by some shadie Grove
Farre from the clamorous World doth live his owne,
Though solitarie, yet who is not alone,
But doth converse with that *Eternall Love.*
O how more sweet is Birds harmonious Mone,
Or the soft Sobbings of the widow'd Dove?
Than those smoothe Whisp'rings neare a Princes Throne,
Which Good make doubtfull, doe the Evill approve.
O how more sweet is *Zephyres* wholesome Breath,
And Sighs perfum'd, which doe the Flowres unfold,
Than that Applause vaine *Honour* doth bequeath?
How sweete are Streames to Poyson drunke in Gold?
  The World is full of Horrours, Falshoods, Slights,
  Woods silent Shades have only true Delights.

[1630]

WILLIAM BROWNE

From *Britannia's Pastorals*, Book II, Song 2

The Muses friend (gray-eyde *Aurora*) yet
Held all the Meadowes in a cooling sweat,
The milke-white *Gossamores* not upwards snow'd,
Nor was the sharpe and usefull steering goad
Laid on the strong-neckt Oxe; no gentle bud
The *Sun* had dryde; the cattle chew'd the cud
Low level'd on the grasse; no Flyes quicke sting
Inforc'd the Stonehorse[1] in a furious ring
To teare the passive earth, nor lash his taile
About his buttockes broad; the slimy Snayle
Might on the wainscot, (by his many mazes
Winding *Meanders* and selfe-knitting traces)
Be follow'd, where he stucke, his glittering slime
Not yet wipt off. It was so earely time
The carefull *Smith* had in his sooty forge
Kindled no coale; nor did his hammers urge
His neighbours patience: *Owles* abroad did flye,
And day as then might plead his infancy.
Yet of faire *Albion* the westerne Swaines
Were long since up, attending on the plaines
When *Nereus* daughter with her mirthfull hoast
Should summon them, on their declining coast.
  But since her stay was long: for feare the Sunne
Should finde them idle, some of them begunne
To leape and wrastle, others threw the barre
Some from the company removed are
To meditate the songs they meant to play,
Or make a new *Round* for next *Holiday*:
Some tales of love their love-sicke fellowes told:

[1] stallion

Others were seeking stakes to pitch their fold.
This, all alone was mending of his Pipe;
That, for his lasse sought fruits most sweet most ripe.
Here, (from the rest) a lonely shepheards boy
Sits piping on a hill, as if his joy
Would still endure, or else that ages frost
Should never make him thinke what he had lost.
Yonder a shepheardesse knits by the springs,
Her hands still keeping time to what shee sings:
Or seeming, by her song, those fairest hands
Were comforted in working. Neere the sands
Of some sweet River sits a musing lad,
That moanes the losse of what he sometime had,
His Love by death bereft: when fast by him
An aged Swaine takes place, as neere the brim
Of's grave as of the River; shewing how
That as those floods, which passe along right now
Are follow'd still by others from their spring,
And in the Sea have all their burying:
Right so our times are knowne, our ages found,
(Nothing is permanent within this *Round*:)
One age is now, another *that* succeedes,
Extirping all things which the former breedes:
Another followes that, doth new times raise
New yeers, new months, new weeks, new hours, new days,
Mankinde thus goes like Rivers from their spring
And in the Earth have all their burying.
Thus sate the olde man counselling the yong;
Whilst, underneath a tree which over-hung
The silver streame, (as, some delight it tooke
To trim his thicke boughes in the Chrystall Brooke)
Were set a jocund crew of youthfull Swaines
Wooing their sweeting with dilicious straynes.
Sportive *Oreades* the hils descended,
The *Hamadryades* their hunting ended,

And in the high woods left the long-liv'd *Harts*
To feede in peace, free from their winged Darts;
Floods, Mountaines, Vallies, Woods, each vacant lyes
Of *Nimphs* that by them danc'd their *Haydigyes*[2]:
For all those *Powers* were ready to embrace
The present meanes, to give our Shepheards grace.
And underneath this tree (till *Thetis* came)
Many resorted; where a Swaine, of name
Lesse, then of worth: (and we doe never owne
Nor apprehend, him best, that most is knowne.)
Fame is uncertaine, who so swiftly flyes
By th'unregarded *shed* where *Vertue* lyes
Shee (ill inform'd of *Vertues* worth) pursu'th
(In hast) *Opinion* for the simple *Truth*.
True Fame is ever likened to our shade,
Hee soonest misseth her, that most hath made
To over-take her; who so takes his wing,
Regardlesse of her, shee'll be following:
Her true proprietie she thus discovers,
'Loves her contemners, and contemnes her lovers.'
Th'applause of common people never yet
Pursu'd this Swaine; hee knew't the counterfeit
Of setled praise, and therefore at his songs
Though all the Shepheards and the gracefull throngs
Of Semigods compar'd him with the best
That ever touch'd a Reede, or was addrest
In shepheards coate, he never would approve
Their Attributes, given in sincerest love;
Except he truely knew them, as his merit.
Fame gives a second life to such a spirit.

[2] a country dance; cf. also 'Ametas and Thestylis . . .', p. 216.

[1616]

ROBERT HERRICK

To his Muse

Whither, *Mad maiden* wilt thou roame?
Farre safer 'twere to stay at home:
Where thou mayst sit, and piping please
The poore and private *Cottages.*
Since *Coats,* and *Hamlets,* best agree
With this thy meaner Minstralsie.
There with the Reed, thou mayst expresse
The Shepherds Fleecie happinesse:
And with thy *Eclogues* intermixe
Some smooth, and harmlesse *Beucolicks.*
There on a Hillock thou mayst sing
Unto a handsome Shephardling;
Or to a Girle (that keeps the Neat)
With breath more sweet then Violet.
There, there, (perhaps) such Lines as These
May take the simple *Villages.*
But for the Court, the Country wit
Is despicable unto it.
Stay then at home, and doe not goe
Or flie abroad to seeke for woe.
Contempts in Courts and Cities dwell;
No *Critick* haunts the Poore mans Cell:
Where thou mayst hear thine own Lines read
By no one tongue, there, censured.
That man's unwise will search for Ill,
And may prevent it, sitting still.

[1648]

A Pastorall upon the birth of Prince Charles Presented to the King, and Set by Mr Nic: Laniere

[*The Speakers,* MIRTILLO, AMINTAS, *and* AMARILLIS]

AMINTAS: Good day, *Mirtillo.*
MIRTILLO: And to you no lesse:
And all faire Signs lead on our Shepardesse.
AMARILLIS: With all white luck to you.
MIRTILLO: But say, What news
Stirs in our Sheep-walk?
AMINTAS: None, save that my Ewes,
My Weathers, Lambes, and wanton Kids are well,
Smooth, faire, and fat, none better I can tell:
Or that this day *Menalchas* keeps a feast
For his Sheep-shearers.
MIRTILLO: True, these are the least.
But dear *Amintas,* and sweet *Amarillis,*
Rest but a while here, by this bank of Lillies,
And lend a gentle eare to one report
The Country has.
AMINTAS: From whence?
AMARILLIS: From whence?
MIRTILLO: The Court
Three dayes before the shutting in of *May,*
(With whitest Wool be ever crown'd that day!)
To all our joy, a sweet-fac't child was borne,
More tender then the childhood of the Morne.
CHORUS: *Pan* pipe to him, and bleats of lambs and sheep,
Let Lullaby the pretty Prince asleep!
MIRTILLO: And that his birth sho'd be more singular,
At Noone of Day, was seene a silver Star,
Bright as the Wise-men's Torch, which guided them
To Gods sweet Babe, when borne at *Bethlehem;*
While Golden Angels (some have told to me)
Sung out his Birth with Heav'nly Minstralsie.

AMINTAS: O rare! But is't a trespasse if we three
Sho'd wend along his Baby-ship to see?
MIRTILLO: Not so, not so.
CHORUS: But if it chance to prove
At most a fault, 'tis but a fault of love.
AMARILLIS: But deare *Mirtillo*, I have heard it told,
Those learned men brought *Incense, Myrrhe,* and *Gold*,
From Countries far, with Store of Spices, (sweet)
And laid them downe for Offrings at his feet.
MIRTILLO: 'Tis true indeed; and each of us will bring
Unto our smiling, and our blooming King,
A neat, though not so great an Offering.
AMARILLIS: A Garland for my Gift shall be
Of flowers, ne'r suckt by th' theeving Bee:
And all most sweet; yet all lesse sweet then he.
AMINTAS: And I will beare along with you
Leaves dropping downe the honyed dew,
With oaten pipes, as sweet, as new.
MIRTILLO: And I a Sheep-hook will bestow,
To have his little King-ship know,
As he is Prince, he's Shepherd too.
CHORUS: Come let's away, and quickly let's be drest,
And quickly give, *The swiftest Grace is best.*
And when before him we have laid our treasures,
We'll blesse the Babe, Then back to Countrie pleasures.

[1648]

The Hock-Cart, or *Harvest Home*

To the Right Honourable, Mildmay, *Earle of* Westmorland

Come Sons of Summer, by whose toile,
We are the Lords of Wine and Oile:
By whose tough labours, and rough hands,
We rip up first, then reap our lands.

Crown'd with the eares of corne, now come,
And, to the Pipe, sing Harvest home.
Come forth, my Lord, and see the Cart
Drest up with all the Country Art.
See, here a *Maukin*[1], there a sheet, [1] a working-woman
As spotlesse pure, as it is sweet:
The Horses, Mares, and frisking Fillies,
(Clad, all, in Linnen, white as Lillies.)
The Harvest Swaines, and Wenches bound
For joy, to see the *Hock-cart* crown'd.
About the Cart, heare, how the Rout
Of Rurall Younglings raise the shout;
Pressing before, some coming after,
Those with a shout, and these with laughter.
Some blesse the Cart; some kisse the sheaves;
Some prank them up with Oaken leaves:
Some crosse the Fill-horse[2]; some with great [2] shaft-horse
Devotion, stroak the home-borne wheat:
While other Rusticks, lesse attent
To Prayers, then to Merryment,
Run after with their breeches rent.
Well, on, brave boyes, to your Lords Hearth,
Glitt'ring with fire; where, for your mirth,
Ye shall see first the large and cheefe
Foundation of your Feast, Fat Beefe:
With Upper Stories, Mutton, Veale
And Bacon, (which makes full the meale)
With sev'rall dishes standing by,
As here a Custard, there a Pie,
And here all tempting Frumentie.
And for to make the merry cheere,
If smirking Wine be wanting here,
There's that, which drowns all care, stout Beere
Which freely drink to your Lords health,
Then to the Plough, (the Common-wealth)

Next to your Flailes, your Fanes, your Fatts;
Then to the Maids with Wheaten Hats:
To the rough Sickle, and crookt Sythe,
Drink frollick boyes, till all be blythe.
Feed, and grow fat; and as ye eat,
Be mindfull, that the lab'ring Neat
(As you) may have their fill of meat.
And know, besides, ye must revoke
The patient Oxe unto the Yoke,
And all goe back unto the Plough
And Harrow, (though they'r hang'd up now.)
And, you must know, your Lords word's true,
Feed him ye must, whose food fils you.
And that this pleasure is like raine,
Not sent ye for to drowne your paine,
But for to make it spring againe.

[1648]

To Phillis *to love, and live with him*

Live, live with me, and thou shalt see
The pleasures Ile prepare for thee:
What sweets the Country can afford
Shall blesse thy Bed, and blesse thy Board.
The soft sweet Mosse shall be thy bed,
With crawling Woodbine over-spread:
By which the silver-shedding streames
Shall gently melt thee into dreames.
Thy clothing next, shall be a Gowne
Made of the Fleeces purest Downe.
The tongues of Kids shall be thy meate;
Their Milke thy drinke; and thou shalt eate
The Pastes of Filberts for thy bread
With Cream of Cowslips buttered:

Thy Feasting-Tables shall be Hills
With *Daisies* spread, and *Daffadils*;
Where thou shalt sit, and *Red-brest* by,
For meat, shall give thee melody.
Ile give thee Chaines and Carkanets
Of *Primroses* and *Violets*.
A Bag and Bottle thou shalt have;
That richly wrought, and This as brave;
So that as either shall expresse
The Wearer's no meane Shepheardesse.
At Sheering-times, and yearely Wakes,
When *Themilis* his pastime makes,
There thou shalt be; and be the wit,
Nay more, the Feast, and grace of it.
On Holy-dayes, when Virgins meet
To dance the Heyes with nimble feet;
Thou shalt come forth, and then appeare
The *Queen of Roses* for that yeere.
And having danc't ('bove all the best)
Carry the Garland from the rest.
In Wicker-baskets Maids shal bring
To thee, (my dearest Shepharling)
The blushing Apple, bashfull Peare,
And shame-fac't Plum, (all simp'ring there).
Walk in the Groves, and thou shalt find
The name of *Phillis* in the Rind
Of every straight, and smooth-skin tree;
Where kissing that, Ile twice kisse thee.
To thee a Sheep-hook I will send,
Be-pranckt with Ribbands, to this end,
This, this alluring Hook might be
Lesse for to catch a sheep, then me.
Thou shalt have Possets, Wassails fine,
Not made of Ale, but spiced Wine;

To make thy Maids and selfe free mirth,
All sitting neer the glitt'ring Hearth.
Thou sha't have Ribbands, Roses, Rings,
Gloves, Garters, Stockings, Shooes, and Strings
Of winning Colours, that shall move
Others to Lust, but me to Love.
These (nay) and more, thine own shal be,
If thou wilt love, and live with me.

[1648]

His content in the Country

Here, here I live with what my Board,
Can with the smallest cost afford.
Though ne'r so mean the Viands be,
They well content my *Prew* and me.
Or Pea, or Bean, or Wort, or Beet,
What ever comes, content makes sweet:
Here we rejoyce, because no Rent
We pay for our poore Tenement:
Wherein we rest, and never feare
The Landlord, or the Usurer.
The Quarter-day do's ne'r affright
Our Peacefull slumbers in the night.
We eate our own, and batten more,
Because we feed on no mans score:
But pitie those, whose flanks grow great,
Swel'd with the Lard of others meat.
We blesse our Fortunes, when we see
Our own beloved privacie:
And like our living, where w'are known
To very few, or else to none.

[1648]

A Dialogue betwixt himselfe and Mistresse Eliza: Wheeler, *under the name of* Amarillis

My dearest Love, since thou will go,
And leave me here behind thee;
For love or pitie let me know
The place where I may find thee.

AMARILLIS: In country Meadowes pearl'd with Dew,
And set about with Lillies;
There filling Maunds with Cowslips, you
May find your *Amarillis*.

HERRICK: What have the Meades to do with thee,
Or with thy youthfull houres?
Live thou at Court, where thou mayst be
The *Queen* of men, not flowers.
Let Country wenches make 'em fine
With Poesies, since 'tis fitter
For thee with richest Jemmes to shine,
And like the Starres to glitter.

AMARILLIS: You set too high a rate upon
A Shepheardess so homely;

HERRICK: Believe it (dearest) ther's not one
I'th' Court that's halfe so comly.
I prithee stay. (AM:) I must away,
Lets kiss first, then we'l sever.

AMBO: And though we bid adieu to day,
Wee shall not part for ever.

[1648]

FRANCIS QUARLES

On the Plough-man

I heare the whistling *Plough-man*, all day long,
Sweetning his labour with a chearefull song:
His Bed's a Pad of *Straw*; His dyet course;
In both, he fares not better then his *Horse*:
He seldome slakes his thirst, but from the *Pumpe*,
And yet his heart is blithe; his visage, plumpe;
His thoughts are nere acquainted with such things,
As *Griefes* or *Feares*; He onely sweats, and sings:
Whenas the Landed *Lord*, that cannot dine
Without a Qualme, if not refresht with *Wine*;
That cannot judge that controverted case,
'Twixt meat and mouth, without the *Bribe* of Sauce;
That claimes the service of the purest linnen,
To pamper and to shroud his dainty skin in,
Groanes out his dayes, in lab'ring to appease
The rage of either *Buisnes*, or *Disease*:
Alas, his silken *Robes*, his costly *Diet*
Can lend a little pleasure, but no *Quiet*:
The untold summes of his descended wealth
Can give his Body plenty, but not *Health*:
The one, in Paynes, and want, possesses all;
T' other, in Plenty, finds no peace at all;
'Tis strange! And yet the cause is easly showne;
T' one's at *God's* finding; t' other, at his *owne*.

[1635]

THOMAS CAREW

To Saxham

Though frost, and snow, lockt from mine eyes
That beautie which without dore lyes;
Thy gardens, orchards, walkes, that so
I might not all thy pleasures know;
Yet (*Saxham*) thou within thy gate,
Art of thy selfe so delicate;
So full of native sweets, that blesse
Thy roofe with inward happinesse;
As neither from, nor to thy store
Winter takes ought, or Spring addes more.
The cold and frozen ayre had sterv'd
Much poore, if not by thee preserv'd;
Whose prayers have made thy Table blest
With plenty, far above the rest.
The season hardly did afford
Course cates unto thy neighbours board,
Yet thou hadst daintyes, as the skie
Had only been thy Volarie;
Or else the birds, fearing the snow
Might to another deluge grow:
The Pheasant, Partiridge, and the Larke,
Flew to thy house, as to the Arke.
The willing Oxe, of himselfe came
Home to the slaughter, with the Lambe,
And every beast did thither bring
Himselfe, to be an offering.
The scalie herd, more pleasure tooke,
Bath'd in thy dish, then in the brooke:
Water, Earth, Ayre, did all conspire,
To pay their tributes to thy fire,

Whose cherishing flames themselves divide
Through every roome, where they deride
The night, and cold abroad; whilst they
Like suns within, keepe endlesse day.
Those chearfull beames send forth their light,
To all that wander in the night,
And seeme to becken from aloofe,
The weary Pilgrim to thy roofe;
Where if refresh't, he will away,
Hee's fairly welcome, or if stay
Farre more, which he shall hearty find,
Both from the Master, and the Hinde.
The strangers welcome, each man there
Stamp'd on his chearfull brow, doth weare;
Nor doth this welcome, or his cheere
Grow lesse, 'cause he staies longer here.
There's none observes (much lesse repines)
How often this man sups or dines.
Thou hast no Porter at the doore
T'examine, or keep back the poore;
Nor locks, nor bolts; thy gates have bin
Made onely to let strangers in;
Untaught to shut, they doe not feare
To stand wide open all the yeare;
Carelesse who enters, for they know,
Thou never didst deserve a foe;
And as for theeves, thy bountie's such,
They cannot steale, thou giv'st so much.

[1640]

THOMAS RANDOLPH

An Ode to Mr Anthony Stafford *to hasten him into the country*

Come spurre away,
I have no patience for a longer stay;
But must goe downe,
And leave the chargeable noise of this great Towne.
I will the country see,
Where old simplicity,
Though hid in gray
Doth looke more gay
Then foppery in plush and scarlat clad.
Farewell you City-wits that are
Almost at Civill warre;
'Tis time that I grow wise, when all the world grows mad.

More of my dayes
I will not spend to gaine an Idiots praise;
Or to make sport
For some slight Punie of the Innes of Court.
Then worthy *Stafford* say
How shall we spend the day,
With what delights
Shorten the nights?
When from this tumult we are got secure;
Where mirth with all her freedome goes
Yet shall no finger loose;
Where every worde is thought, and every thought is pure.

There from the tree
Wee'l cherries plucke, and pick the strawbery.
And every day

Go see the wholesome Country Girles make hay.
Whose browne hath lovlier grace,
Then any painted face,
That I doe know
Hide-Parke can show.
Where I had rather gaine a kisse then meet
(Though some of them in greater state
Might court my love with plate)
The beauties of the *Cheape*, and wives of *Lumbardstreet*.

But thinke upon
Some other pleasures, these to me are none,
Why doe I prate
Of woemen, that are things against my fate?
I never meane to wed,
That torture to my bed.
My Muse is shee
My Love shall bee.
Let Clownes get wealth, and heires; when I am gone,
And the great Bugbeare grisly death
Shall take this idle breath
If I a Poem leave, that Poem is my Sonne.

Of this, no more;
Wee'l rather tast the bright *Pomona's* store.
No fruit shall scape
Our pallats, from the damsen, to the grape.
Then full we'l seek a shade,
And heare what musique's made;
How Philomell
Her tale doth tell:
And how the other Birds doe fill the quire;
The Thrush and Blackbird lend their throats
Warbling melodious notes;
Wee will all sports enjoy, which others but desire.

Ours is the skie,
Where at what fowle we please our Hauke shall flye;
Nor will we spare
To hunt the crafty foxe or timorous hare;
But let our hounds runne loose
In any ground they'l choose,
The Bucke shall fall,
The stagge and all:
Our pleasures must from their owne warrants bee,
For to my *Muse*, if not to mee,
I'me sure all game is free;
Heaven, Earth, are all but parts of her great Royalty.

And when we meane
To tast of *Bacchus* blessings now and then,
And drinke by stealth
A cup or two to noble *Barkleys* health.
I'le take my pipe and try
The *Phrygian* melody;
Which he that heares
Lets through his eares
A madnesse to distemper all the braine.
Then I another pipe will take
And *Dorique* musique make,
To Civilize with graver notes our wits againe.

[1638]

L'Allegro

Hence loathed Melancholy
  Of *Cerberus*, and blackest midnight born,
In *Stygian* Cave forlorn
  'Mongst horrid shapes, and shreiks, and sights unholy,
Find out som uncouth cell,
  Wher brooding darknes spreads his jealous wings,
And the night-Raven sings;
  There under *Ebon* shades, and low-brow'd Rocks,
As ragged as thy Locks,
  In dark *Cimmerian* desert ever dwell.
But com thou Goddes fair and free,
In Heav'n ycleap'd *Euphrosyne*,
And by men, heart-easing Mirth,
Whom lovely *Venus* at a birth
With two sister Graces more
To Ivy-crowned *Bacchus* bore;
Or whether (as som Sager sing)
The frolick Wind that breathes the Spring,
Zephir with *Aurora* playing,
As he met her once a Maying,
There on Beds of Violets blew,
And fresh-blown Roses washt in dew,
Fill'd her with thee a daughter fair,
So bucksom, blith, and debonair.
Haste thee nymph, and bring with thee
Jest and youthful Jollity,
Quips and Cranks, and wanton Wiles,
Nods, and Becks, and Wreathed Smiles,
Such as hang on *Hebe's* cheek,
And love to live in dimple sleek;

Sport that wrincled Care derides,
And Laughter holding both his sides.
Com, and trip it as ye go
On the light fantastick toe,
And in thy right hand lead with thee,
The Mountain Nymph, sweet Liberty;
And if I give thee honour due,
Mirth, admit me of thy crue
To live with her, and live with thee,
In unreproved pleasures free;
To hear the Lark begin his flight,
And singing startle the dull night,
From his watch-towre in the skies,
Till the dappled dawn doth rise;
Then to com in spight of sorrow,
And at my window bid good morrow,
Through the Sweet-Briar, or the Vine,
Or the twisted Eglantine.
While the Cock with lively din,
Scatters the rear of darknes thin,
And to the stack, or the Barn dore,
Stoutly struts his Dames before,
Oft list'ning how the Hounds and horn,
Clearly rouse the slumbring morn,
From the side of som Hoar Hill,
Through the high wood echoing shrill.
Som time walking not unseen
By Hedge-row Elms, on Hillocks green,
Right against the Eastern gate,
Where the great Sun begins his state,
Rob'd in flames, and Amber light,
The clouds in thousand Liveries dight,
While the Plowman neer at hand,
Whistles ore the Furrow'd Land,
And the Milkmaid singeth blithe,

And the Mower whets his sithe,
And every Shepherd tells his tale
Under the Hawthorn in the dale.
Streit mine eye hath caught new pleasures
Whilst the Lantskip round it measures,
Russet Lawns, and Fallows Gray,
Where the nibling flocks do stray,
Mountains on whose barren brest
The labouring clouds do often rest:
Meadows trim with Daisies pide,
Shallow Brooks, and Rivers wide.
Towers, and Battlements it sees
Boosom'd high in tufted Trees,
Where perhaps som beauty lies,
The Cynosure of neighbouring eyes.
Hard by, a Cottage chimney smokes,
From betwixt two aged Okes,
Where *Corydon* and *Thyrsis* met,
Are at their savory dinner set
Of Hearbs, and other Country Messes,
Which the neat-handed *Phillis* dresses;
And then in haste her Bowre she leaves,
With *Thestylis* to bind the Sheaves;
Or if the earlier season lead
To the tann'd Haycock in the Mead,
Som times with secure delight
The up-land Hamlets will invite,
When the merry Bells ring round,
And the jocond rebecks sound
To many a youth, and many a maid,
Dancing in the Chequer'd shade;
And young and old com forth to play
On a Sunshine Holyday,
Till the live-long day-light fail,
Then to the Spicy Nut-brown Ale,

With stories told of many a feat,
How *Faery Mab* the junkets eat,
She was pincht, and pull'd she sed,
And he by Friars Lanthorn led
Tells how the drudging *Goblin* swet,
To ern his Creame-bowle duly set,
When in one night, ere glimps of morn,
His shadowy Flale hath thresh'd the Corn
That ten day-labourers could not end,
Then lies him down the Lubbar Fend[1],
And stretch'd out all the Chimney's length,
Basks at the fire his hairy strength;
And Crop-full out of dores he flings,
Ere the first Cock his Mattin rings.
Thus don the Tales, to bed they creep,
By whispering Windes soon lull'd asleep.
Towred Cities please us then,
And the busie humm of men,
Where throngs of Knights and Barons bold,
In weeds of Peace high triumphs hold,
With store of Ladies, whose bright eies
Rain influence, and judge the prise
Of Wit, or Arms, while both contend
To win her Grace, whom all commend.
There let *Hymen* oft appear
In Saffron robe, with Taper clear,
And pomp, and feast, and revelry,
With mask, and antique Pageantry,
Such sights as youthfull Poets dream
On Summer eeves by haunted stream.
Then to the well-trod stage anon,
If *Jonsons* learned Sock be on,
Or sweetest *Shakespear* fancies childe,
Warble his native Wood-notes wilde;
And ever against eating Cares,

[1] a beneficent goblin (fiend) who works at night

Lap me in soft *Lydian* Aires,
Married to immortal verse
Such as the meeting soul may pierce
In notes, with many a winding bout
Of lincked sweetnes long drawn out,
With wanton heed, and giddy cunning,
The melting voice through mazes running;
Untwisting all the chains that ty
The hidden soul of harmony.
That *Orpheus* self may heave his head
From golden slumber on a bed
Of heapt *Elysian* flowres, and hear
Such streins as would have won the ear
Of *Pluto*, to have quite set free
His half regain'd *Eurydice*.
These delights, if thou canst give,
Mirth with thee, I mean to live.

[Written 1632]

From *A Mask presented at Ludlow-Castle*

COMUS: Can any mortal mixture of Earths mould
Breath such Divine inchanting ravishment?
Sure somthing holy lodges in that brest,
And with these raptures moves the vocal air
To testifie his hidd'n residence;
How sweetly did they float upon the wings
Of silence, through the empty-vaulted night
At every fall smoothing the Raven doune
Of darknes till it smil'd: I have oft heard
My Mother *Circe* with the Sirens three,
Amidst the flowry-kirtl'd *Naiades*
Culling their potent hearbs, and balefull drugs,
Who as they sung, would take the prison'd soul,

And lap it in *Elysium*, *Scylla* wept,
And chid her barking waves into attention,
And fell *Charybdis* murmur'd soft applause:
Yet they in pleasing slumber lull'd the sense,
And in sweet madnes rob'd it of it self,
But such a sacred, and home-felt delight,
Such sober certainty of waking bliss
I never heard till now. Ile speak to her
And she shall be my Queen. Hail forren wonder
Whom certain these rough shades did never breed
Unlesse the Goddes that in rurall shrine
Dwell'st here with *Pan*, or *Silvan*, by blest Song
Forbidding every bleak unkindly Fog
To touch the prosperous growth of this tall Wood.
LADY: Nay gentle Shepherd ill is lost that praise
That is addrest to unattending Ears,
Not any boast of skill, but extreme shift
How to regain my sever'd company
Compell'd me to awake the courteous Echo
To give me answer from her mossie Couch.
COMUS: What chance good Lady hath bereft you thus?
LADY: Dim darknes, and this leavy Labyrinth.
COMUS: Could that divide you from neer-ushering guides?
LADY: They left me weary on a grassie terf.
COMUS: By falsehood, or discourtesie, or why?
LADY: To seek i'th vally som cool friendly Spring.
COMUS: And left your fair side all unguarded Lady?
LADY: They were but twain, and purpos'd quick return.
COMUS: Perhaps fore-stalling night prevented them.
LADY: How easie my misfortune is to hit!
COMUS: Imports their loss, beside the present need?
LADY: No less then if I should my brothers loose.
COMUS: Were they of manly prime, or youthful bloom?
LADY: As smooth as *Hebe's* their unrazor'd lips.
COMUS: Two such I saw, what time the labour'd Oxe

In his loose traces from the furrow came,
And the swink't hedger at his Supper sate;
I saw them under a green mantling vine
That crawls along the side of yon small hill,
Plucking ripe clusters from the tender shoots,
Their port was more then human, as they stood;
I took it for a faery vision
Of som gay creatures of the element
That in the colours of the Rainbow live
And play i'th plighted clouds. I was aw-strook,
And as I past, I worshipt; if those you seek
It were a journey like the path to Heav'n,
To help you find them. [LA:] Gentle villager
What readiest way would bring me to that place?
COMUS: Due west it rises from this shrubby point.
LADY: To find out that, good Shepherd, I suppose,
In such a scant allowance of Star-light,
Would overtask the best Land-Pilots art,
Without the sure guess of well-practiz'd feet.
COMUS: I know each lane, and every alley green
Dingle or bushy dell of this wilde Wood,
And every bosky bourn from side to side
My daily walks and ancient neighbourhood,
And if your stray attendance be yet lodg'd,
Or shroud within these limits, I shall know
Ere morrow wake, or the low roosted lark
From her thatch't pallat rowse, if otherwise
I can conduct you Lady to a low
But loyal cottage, where you may be safe
Till further quest'. [LA:] Shepherd I take thy word,
And trust thy honest offer'd courtesie,
Which oft is sooner found in lowly sheds
With smoaky rafters, then in tapstry Halls
And Courts of Princes, where it first was nam'd,
And yet is most pretended: In a place

Less warranted then this, or less secure
I cannot be, that I should fear to change it.
Eie me blest Providence, and square my triall
To my proportion'd strength. Shepherd lead on . . .

[1634]

Lycidas

In this Monody the Author bewails a learned Friend, unfortunatly drown'd in his Passage from Chester *on the* Irish *Seas, 1637. And by occasion foretels the ruine of our corrupted Clergy then in their height.*

Yet once more, O ye Laurels, and once more
Ye Myrtles brown, with Ivy never-sear,
I com to pluck your Berries harsh and crude,
And with forc'd fingers rude,
Shatter your leaves before the mellowing year.
Bitter constraint, and sad occasion dear,
Compels me to disturb your season due:
For *Lycidas* is dead, dead ere his prime
Young *Lycidas*, and hath not left his peer:
Who would not sing for *Lycidas*? he well knew
Himself to sing, and build the lofty rhyme.
He must not flote upon his watry bear
Unwept, and welter to the parching wind,
Without the meed of som melodious tear.
Begin then, Sisters of the sacred well,
That from beneath the seat of *Jove* doth spring,
Begin, and somwhat loudly sweep the string.
Hence with denial vain, and coy excuse,
So may som gentle Muse
With lucky words favour my destin'd Urn,
And as he passes turn,

And bid fair peace be to my sable shrowd.
For we were nurst upon the self-same hill,
Fed the same flock, by fountain, shade, and rill.
  Together both, ere the high Lawns appear'd
Under the opening eye-lids of the morn,
We drove a field, and both together heard
What time the Gray-fly winds her sultry horn,
Batt'ning our flocks with the fresh dews of night,
Oft till the Star that rose, at Ev'ning, bright
Toward Heav'ns descent had slop'd his westering wheel.
Mean while the Rural ditties were not mute,
Temper'd to th'Oaten Flute,
Rough *Satyrs* danc'd, and *Fauns* with clov'n heel,
From the glad sound would not be absent long,
And old *Damœtas* lov'd to hear our song.
  But O the heavy change, now thou art gon,
Now thou art gon, and never must return!
Thee Shepherd, thee the Woods, and desert Caves,
With wilde Thyme and the gadding Vine o'regrown,
And all their echoes mourn.
The Willows, and the Hazle Copses green,
Shall now no more be seen,
Fanning their joyous Leaves to thy soft layes.
As killing as the Canker to the Rose,
Or Taint-worm to the weanling Herds that graze,
Or Frost to Flowers, that their gay wardrop wear,
When first the White-thorn blows;
Such, *Lycidas*, thy loss to Shepherds ear.
  Where were ye Nymphs when the remorseless deep
Clos'd o're the head of your lov'd *Lycidas*?
For neither were ye playing on the steep,
Where your old *Bards*, the famous *Druids* ly,
Nor on the shaggy top of *Mona* high,
Nor yet where *Deva* spreads her wisard stream:
Ay me, I fondly dream!

Had ye bin there . . . for what could that have don?
What could the Muse her self that *Orpheus* bore,
The Muse her self, for her inchanting son
Whom Universal nature did lament,
When by the rout that made the hideous roar,
His goary visage down the stream was sent,
Down the swift *Hebrus* to the *Lesbian* shore.
  Alas! What boots it with uncessant care
To tend the homely slighted Shepherds trade,
And strictly meditate the thankles Muse,
Were it not better don as others use,
To sport with *Amaryllis* in the shade,
Or with the tangles of *Neæra's* hair?
Fame is the spur that the clear spirit doth raise
(That last infirmity of Noble mind)
To scorn delights, and live laborious dayes;
But the fair Guerdon when we hope to find,
And think to burst out into sudden blaze,
Comes the blind *Fury* with th'abhorred shears,
And slits the thin-spun life. But not the praise,
Phœbus repli'd, and touch'd my trembling ears;
Fame is no plant that grows on mortal soil,
Nor in the glistering foil
Set off to th'world, nor in broad rumour lies,
But lives and spreds aloft by those pure eyes,
And perfet witnes of all-judging *Jove*;
As he pronounces lastly on each deed,
Of so much fame in Heav'n expect thy meed.
  O Fountain *Arethuse*, and thou honour'd floud,
Smooth-sliding *Mincius*, crown'd with vocall reeds,
That strain I heard was of a higher mood:
But now my Oate proceeds,
And listens to the Herald of the Sea
That came in *Neptune's* plea,
He ask'd the Waves, and ask'd the Fellon winds,

What hard mishap hath doom'd this gentle swain?
And question'd every gust of rugged wings
That blows from off each beaked Promontory;
They knew not of his story,
And sage *Hippotades* their answer brings,
That not a blast was from his dungeon stray'd,
The Ayr was calm, and on the level brine,
Sleek *Panope* with all her sisters play'd.
It was that fatall and perfidious Bark
Built in th'eclipse, and rigg'd with curses dark,
That sunk so low that sacred head of thine.
  Next *Camus*, reverend Sire, went footing slow,
His Mantle hairy, and his Bonnet sedge,
Inwrought with figures dim, and on the edge
Like to that sanguine flower inscrib'd with woe.
Ah! Who hath reft (quoth he) my dearest pledge?
Last came, and last did go,
The Pilot of the *Galilean* lake,
Two massy Keyes he bore of metals twain,
(The Golden opes, the Iron shuts amain)
He shook his Miter'd locks, and stern bespake,
How well could I have spar'd for thee young swain,
Anow of such as for their bellies sake,
Creep and intrude, and climb into the fold?
Of other care they little reck'ning make,
Then how to scramble at the shearers feast,
And shove away the worthy bidden guest;
Blind mouthes! that scarce themselves know how to hold
A Sheep-hook, or have learn'd ought els the least
That to the faithfull Herdmans art belongs!
What recks it them? What need they? They are sped;
And when they list, their lean and flashy songs
Grate on their scrannel Pipes of wretched straw,
The hungry Sheep look up, and are not fed,
But swoln with wind, and the rank mist they draw,

Rot inwardly, and foul contagion spread:
Besides what the grim Woolf with privy paw
Daily devours apace, and nothing sed,
But that two-handed engine at the door,
Stands ready to smite once, and smite no more.
  Return *Alpheus*, the dread voice is past,
That shrunk thy streams; Return *Sicilian* Muse,
And call the Vales, and bid them hither cast
Their Bels, and Flourets of a thousand hues.
Ye valleys low where the milde whispers use,
Of shades and wanton winds, and gushing brooks,
On whose fresh lap the swart Star sparely looks,
Throw hither all your quaint enameld eyes,
That on the green terf suck the honied showres,
And purple all the ground with vernal flowres.
Bring the rathe Primrose that forsaken dies,
The tufted Crow-toe, and pale Gessamine,
The white Pink, and the Pansie freakt with jeat,
The glowing Violet,
The Musk-rose, and the well-attir'd Woodbine,
With Cowslips wan that hang the pensive hed,
And every flower that sad embroidery wears:
Bid *Amaranthus* all his beauty shed,
And Daffadillies fill their cups with tears,
To strew the Laureat Herse where *Lycid* lies.
For so to interpose a little ease,
Let our frail thoughts dally with false surmise.
Ay me! Whilst thee the shores, and sounding Seas
Wash far away, where ere thy bones are hurld,
Whether beyond the stormy *Hebrides*,
Where thou perhaps under the whelming tide
Visit'st the bottom of the monstrous world;
Or whether thou to our moist vows deny'd,
Sleep'st by the fable of *Bellerus* old,
Where the great vision of the guarded Mount

Looks toward *Namancos* and *Bayona's* hold;
Look homeward Angel now, and melt with ruth,
And, O ye *Dolphins*, waft the haples youth.
  Weep no more, woful Shepherds weep no more,
For *Lycidas* your sorrow is not dead,
Sunk though he be beneath the watry floar,
So sinks the day-star in the Ocean bed,
And yet anon repairs his drooping head,
And tricks his beams, and with new spangled Ore,
Flames in the forehead of the morning sky:
So *Lycidas* sunk low, but mounted high,
Through the dear might of him that walk'd the waves;
Where other groves, and other streams along,
With *Nectar* pure his oozy Locks he laves,
And hears the unexpressive nuptiall Song,
In the blest Kingdoms meek of joy and love.
There entertain him all the Saints above,
In solemn troops, and sweet Societies
That sing, and singing in their glory move,
And wipe the tears for ever from his eyes.
Now *Lycidas* the Shepherds weep no more;
Henceforth thou art the Genius of the shore,
In thy large recompense, and shalt be good
To all that wander in that perilous flood.
  Thus sang the uncouth Swain to th'Okes and rills,
While the still morn went out with Sandals gray,
He touch'd the tender stops of various Quills,
With eager thought warbling his *Dorick* lay:
And now the Sun had stretch'd out all the hills,
And now was dropt into the Western bay;
At last he rose, and twitch'd his Mantle blew:
To morrow to fresh Woods, and Pastures new.

[1637]

JOHN MILTON

Paradise Lost

From Book IV

So on he fares, and to the border comes
Of *Eden*, where delicious Paradise,
Now nearer, Crowns with her enclosure green,
As with a rural mound the champain head
Of a steep wilderness, whose hairie sides
With thicket overgrown, grottesque and wilde,
Access deni'd; and over head up grew
Insuperable highth of loftiest shade,
Cedar, and Pine, and Firr, and branching Palm,
A Silvan Scene, and as the ranks ascend
Shade above shade, a woodie Theatre
Of stateliest view. Yet higher then thir tops
The verdurous Wall of Paradise up sprung:
Which to our general Sire gave prospect large
Into his nether Empire neighbouring round.
And higher then that Wall a circling row
Of goodliest Trees load'n with fairest Fruit,
Blossoms and Fruits at once of gold'n hue
Appeerd, with gay enameld colours mixt:
On which the Sun more glad impressd his beams
Then in fair Eevning Cloud, or humid Bow,
When God hath showrd the earth: so lovely seemd
That Lantskip: And of pure now purer aire
Meets his approach, and to the heart inspires
Vernal delight and joy, able to drive
All sadness but despair: now gentle gales
Fanning thir odoriferous wings dispense
Native perfumes, and whisper whence they stole
Those balmie spoiles. As when to them who saile
Beyond the *Cape of Hope*, and now are past
Mozambic, off at Sea North-East windes blow
Sabean Odours from the spicie shoare

Of *Arabie* the blest, with such delay
Well pleas'd they slack thir course, and many a League
Cheard with the grateful smell old Ocean smiles.
So entertaind those odorous sweets the Fiend
Who came thir bane, though with them better pleas'd
Then *Asmodeus* with the fishie fume,
That drove him, though enamourd, from the Spouse
Of *Tobits* Son, and with a vengeance sent
From *Media* post to *Ægypt*, there fast bound.
Now to th' ascent of that steep savage Hill
Satan had journied on, pensive and slow;
But furder way found none, so thick entwin'd,
As one continu'd brake, the undergrowth
Of shrubs and tangling bushes had perplext
All path of Man or Beast that passd that way:
One Gate there onely was, and that lookd East
On th' other side: which when th' Arch-fellon saw
Due entrance he disdaind, and in contempt,
At one slight bound high overleap'd all bound
Of Hill or highest Wall, and sheer within
Lights on his feet. As when a prowling Wolfe,
Whom hunger drives to seek new haunt for prey,
Watching where Shepherds pen thir Flocks at eeve
In hurdl'd Cotes amid the field secure,
Leaps ore the fence with ease into the Fould:
Or as a Thief bent to unhoord the cash
Of some rich Burgher, whose substantial dores,
Cross-barrd and bolted fast, fear no assault,
In at the window climbes, or ore the tiles;
So clomb this first grand Thief into Gods Fould:
So since into his Church lewd Hirelings climbe.
Thence up he flew, and on the Tree of Life,
The middle Tree and highest there that grew,
Sat like a Cormorant; yet not true Life
Thereby regaind, but sat devising Death

To them who liv'd; nor on the vertue thought
Of that life-giving Plant, but onely us'd
For prospect, what well us'd had bin the pledge
Of immortalitie. So little knows
Any, but God alone, to value right
The good before him, but perverts best things
To worst abuse, or to thir meanest use.
Beneath him with new wonder now he views
To all delight of human sense expos'd
In narrow room Natures whole wealth, yea more,
A Heav'n on Earth: for blissful Paradise
Of God the Garden was, by him in the East
Of *Eden* planted; *Eden* stretchd her Line
From *Auran* Eastward to the Royal Towrs
Of great *Seleucia*, built by *Grecian* Kings,
Or where the Sons of *Eden* long before
Dwelt in *Telassar*: in this pleasant soile
His farr more pleasant Garden God ordaind;
Out of the fertil ground he caus'd to grow
All Trees of noblest kind for sight, smell, taste;
And all amid them stood the Tree of Life,
High eminent, blooming Ambrosial Fruit
Of vegetable Gold; and next to Life
Our Death the Tree of Knowledge grew fast by,
Knowledge of Good bought dear by knowing ill.
Southward through *Eden* went a River large,
Nor chang'd his course, but through the shaggie hill
Passd underneath ingulft, for God had thrown
That Mountain as his Garden mould high rais'd
Upon the rapid current, which through veins
Of porous Earth with kindly thirst up drawn,
Rose a fresh Fountain, and with many a rill
Waterd the Garden; thence united fell
Down the steep glade, and met the nether Flood,
Which from his darksom passage now appeers,

And now divided into four main Streams,
Runs divers, wandring many a famous Realme
And Country whereof here needs no account,
But rather to tell how, if Art could tell,
How from that Saphire Fount the crisped Brooks,
Rowling on Orient Pearl and sands of Gold,
With mazie error under pendant shades
Ran Nectar, visiting each plant, and fed
Flours worthy of Paradise, which not nice Art
In Beds and curious Knots, but Nature boon
Powrd forth profuse on Hill and Dale and Plaine,
Both where the morning Sun first warmly smote
The op'n field, and where the unpierc't shade
Imbround the noontide Bowrs: Thus was this place,
A happy rural seat of various view;
Groves whose rich Trees wept odorous Gumms and Balme,
Others whose fruit burnisht with Gold'n Rinde
Hung amiable, *Hesperian* Fables true,
If true, here onely, and of delicious taste:
Betwixt them Lawns, or level Downs, and Flocks
Grasing the tender herb, were interpos'd,
Or palmie hilloc, or the flourie lap
Of som irriguous Valley spred her store,
Flours of all hue, and without Thorn the Rose:
Another side, umbrageous Grots and Caves
Of coole recess, ore which the mantling Vine
Layes forth her purple Grape, and gently creeps
Luxuriant; mean while murmuring waters fall
Down the slope hills, disperst, or in a Lake,
That to the fringed Bank with Myrtle crownd,
Her crystal mirror holds, unite thir streams.
The Birds thir quire apply; aires, vernal aires,
Breathing the smell of field and grove, attune
The trembling leaves, while Universal *Pan*
Knit with the *Graces* and the *Hours* in dance

Led on th'Eternal Spring. Not that faire field
Of *Enna*, where *Proserpin* gathring flours
Her self a fairer Floure by gloomie *Dis*
Was gatherd, which cost *Ceres* all that pain
To seek her through the World; nor that sweet Grove
Of *Daphne* by *Orontes*, and th' inspir'd
Castalian Spring, might with this Paradise
Of *Eden* strive; nor that *Nyseian* Ile
Girt with the River *Triton*, where old *Cham*,
Whom Gentiles *Ammon* call and *Libyan Jove*,
Hid *Amalthea* and her Florid Son
Young *Bacchus* from his Stepdame *Rhea's* eye;
Nor where *Abassin* Kings thir issue Guard,
Mount *Amara*, though this by som suppos'd
True Paradise under the *Ethiop* Line
By *Nilus* head, enclos'd with shining Rock,
A whole dayes journey high, but wide remote
From this *Assyrian* Garden, where the Fiend
Saw undelighted all delight, all kind
Of living Creatures new to sight and strange:
Two of farr nobler shape erect and tall,
Godlike erect, with native Honour clad
In naked Majestie seemd Lords of all,
And worthie seemd, for in thir looks Divine
The image of thir glorious Maker shon,
Truth, Wisdom, Sanctitude severe and pure,
Severe, but in true filial freedom plac't;
Whence true autoritie in men; though both
Not equal, as thir sex not equal seemd;
For contemplation hee and valour formd,
For softness shee and sweet attractive grace,
Hee for God onely, shee for God in him:
His fair large Front and Eye sublime declar'd
Absolute rule; and Hyacinthin Locks
Round from his parted forelock manly hung

Clustring, but not beneath his shoulders broad:
Shee as a vail down to the slender waste
Her unadorned gold'n tresses wore
Dissheveld, but in wanton ringlets wav'd
As the Vine curles her tendrils, which impli'd
Subjection, but requir'd with gentle sway,
And by her yielded, by him best receivd,
Yielded with coy submission, modest pride,
And sweet reluctant amorous delay.
Nor those mysterious parts were then conceald,
Then was not guiltie shame, dishonest shame
Of Natures works, honor dishonorable,
Sin-bred, how have ye troubl'd all mankind
With shews instead, meer shews of seeming pure,
And banisht from Mans life his happiest life,
Simplicitie and spotless innocence.
So passd they naked on, nor shunned the sight
Of God or Angel, for they thought no ill:
So hand in hand they passd, the lovliest pair
That ever since in loves imbraces met,
Adam the goodliest man of men since borne
His Sons, the fairest of her Daughters *Eve*.
Under a tuft of shade that on a green
Stood whispering soft, by a fresh Fountain side
They sat them down, and after no more toil
Of thir sweet Gardning labour then suffic'd
To recommend coole *Zephyr*, and made ease
More easie, wholsom thirst and appetite
More grateful, to thir Supper Fruits they fell,
Nectarin Fruits which the compliant boughes
Yielded them, side-long as they sat recline
On the soft downie Bank damaskt with flours:
The savourie pulp they chew, and in the rinde
Still as they thirsted scoop the brimming stream;
Nor gentle purpose, nor endearing smiles

Wanted, nor youthful dalliance as beseems
Fair couple, linkt in happie nuptial League,
Alone as they. About them frisking playd
All Beasts of th' Earth, since wilde, and of all chase
In Wood or Wilderness, Forrest or Den;
Sporting the Lion rampd, and in his paw
Dandl'd the Kid; Bears, Tygers, Ounces[1], Pards[2] — [1] lynxes
Gambold before them; th' unwieldy Elephant — [2] leopards
To make them mirth us'd all his might, and wreath'd
His Lithe Proboscis; close the Serpent sly
Insinuating, wove with Gordian twine
His breaded[3] train, and of his fatal guile — [3] plaited
Gave proof unheeded; others on the grass
Coucht, and now filld with pasture gazing sat,
Or Bedward ruminating: for the Sun
Declin'd was hasting now with prone carreer
To th' Ocean Iles, and in th' ascending Scale
Of Heav'n the Starrs that usher Eevning rose:
When *Satan* still in gaze, as first he stood,
Scarce thus at length faild speech recoverd sad.
O Hell! what doe mine eyes with grief behold,
Into our room of bliss thus high advanc't
Creatures of other mould, earth-born perhaps,
Not Spirits, yet to heav'nly Spirits bright
Little inferior; whom my thoughts persue
With wonder, and could love, so lively shines
In them Divine resemblance, and such grace
The hand that formd them on thir shape hath pourd.
Ah gentle pair, ye little think how nigh
Your change approaches, when all these delights
Will vanish and deliver ye to woe,
More woe, the more your taste is now of joy;
Happie; but for so happie ill secur'd
Long to continue, and this high seat your Heav'n
Ill fenc't for Heav'n to keep out such a foe

As now is enterd; yet no purpos'd foe
To you, whom I could pittie thus forlorne
Though I unpittied: League with you I seek,
And mutual amitie so streight, so close,
That I with you must dwell, or you with mee
Henceforth; my dwelling haply may not please
Like this fair Paradise, your sense, yet such
Accept your Makers work; he gave it me,
Which I as freely give; Hell shall unfould,
To entertain you two, her widest Gates,
And send forth all her Kings; there will be room,
Not like these narrow limits, to receive
Your numerous ofspring; if no better place,
Thank him who puts me loath to this revenge
On you who wrong me not for him who wrongd.
And should I at your harmless innocence
Melt, as I doe, yet public reason just,
Honour and Empire with revenge enlarg'd,
By conquering this new World, compells me now
To do what else though damnd I should abhorre.

From Book IX

Thus saying, from her Husbands hand her hand
Soft she withdrew, and like a Wood-Nymph light
Oread or *Dryad*, or of *Delia's* Traine,
Betook her to the Groves, but *Delia's* self
In gate surpassd and Goddess-like deport,
Though not as shee with Bow and Quiver armd,
But with such Gardning Tools as Art yet rude,
Guiltless of fire had formd, or Angels brought.
To *Pales*, or *Pomona*, thus adornd,
Likest she seemed, *Pomona* when she fled
Vertumnus, or to *Ceres* in her Prime,

Yet Virgin of *Proserpina* from *Jove*.
Her long with ardent look his Eye persu'd
Delighted, but desiring more her stay.
Oft he to her his charge of quick returne
Repeated, shee to him as oft engag'd
To be returnd by Noon amid the Bowre,
And all things in best order to invite
Noontide repast, or Afternoons repose.
O much deceav'd, much failing, hapless *Eve*,
Of thy presum'd return! event perverse!
Thou never from that houre in Paradise
Foundst either sweet repast, or sound repose;
Such ambush hid among sweet Flours and Shades
Waited with hellish rancor imminent
To intercept thy way, or send thee back
Despoild of Innocence, of Faith, of Bliss.
For now, and since first break of dawne the Fiend,
Meer Serpent in appearance, forth was come,
And on his Quest, where likeliest he might finde
The onely two of Mankinde, but in them
The whole included Race, his purposd prey.
In Bowre and Field he sought, where any tuft
Of Grove or Garden-Plot more pleasant lay,
Thir tendance or Plantation for delight,
By Fountain or by shadie Rivulet
He sought them both, but wishd his hap might find
Eve separate, he wishd, but not with hope
Of what so seldom chanc'd, when to his wish,
Beyond his hope, *Eve* separate he spies,
Veild in a Cloud of Fragrance, where she stood,
Half spi'd, so thick the Roses bushing round
About her glowd, oft stooping to support
Each Flour of slender stalk, whose head though gay
Carnation, Purple, Azure, or spect with Gold,

Hung drooping unsustaind, them she upstaies
Gently with Mirtle band, mindless the while,
Her self, though fairest unsupported Flour,
From her best prop so farr, and storm so nigh.
Neerer he drew, and many a walk travers'd
Of stateliest Covert, Cedar, Pine, or Palme,
Then voluble and bold, now hid, now seen
Among thick-woven Arborets and Flours
Imborderd on each Bank, the hand of *Eve*:
Spot more delicious then those Gardens feignd
Or of reviv'd *Adonis*, or renownd
Alcinous, host of old *Laertes* Son,
Or that, not Mystic, where the Sapient King
Held dalliance with his faire *Egyptian* Spouse.
Much he the Place admir'd, the Person more.
As one who long in populous City pent,
Where Houses thick and Sewers annoy the Aire,
Forth issuing on a Summers Morn to breathe
Among the pleasant Villages and Farmes
Adjoind, from each thing met conceaves delight,
The smell of Grain, or tedded Grass, or Kine,
Or Dairie, each rural sight, each rural sound;
If chance with Nymphlike step fair Virgin pass,
What pleasing seemd, for her now pleases more,
Shee most, and in her look summs all Delight.

[1667]

SIR JOHN DENHAM

From *Cooper's Hill*

My eye descending from the Hill, surveys
Where *Thames* amongst the wanton vallies strays.
Thames, the most lov'd of all the Oceans sons,
By his old Sire to his embraces runs,
Hasting to pay his tribute to the sea,
Like mortal life to meet Eternity.
Though with those streams he no resemblance hold,
Whose foam is Amber, and their Gravel Gold;
His genuine, and less guilty wealth t' explore,
Search not his bottom, but survey his shore;
Ore which he kindly spreads his spacious wing,
And hatches plenty for th' ensuing Spring.
Nor then destroys it with too fond a stay,
Like Mothers which their Infants overlay.
Nor with a sudden and impetuous wave,
Like profuse Kings, resumes the wealth he gave.
No unexpected inundations spoyl
The mowers hopes, nor mock the plowmans toyl.
But God-like his unwearied Bounty flows;
First loves to do, then loves the Good he does.
Nor are his Blessings to his banks confin'd,
But free, and common, as the Sea or Wind;
When he to boast, or to disperse his stores
Full of the tributes of his grateful shores,
Visits the world, and in his flying towers
Brings home to us, and makes both *Indies* ours;
Finds wealth where 'tis, bestows it where it wants
Cities in deserts, woods in Cities plants.

[1642]

RICHARD LOVELACE

From *Aramantha*
A Pastorall

Up with the jolly Bird of Light
Who sounds his third Retreat to Night;
Faire *Aramantha* from her bed
Ashamed starts, and rises Red
As the Carnation-mantled Morne,
Who now the blushing Robe doth spurne,
And puts on angry Gray, whilst she
The *Envy of a Deity*
Arayes her limbes, too rich indeed
To be inshrin'd in such a Weed;
Yet lovely 'twas and strait, but fit;
Not made for her, but she to it:
By Nature it sate close and free,
As the just bark unto the Tree:
Unlike Loves Martyrs of the Towne,
All day imprison'd in a Gown,
Who Rackt in Silke 'stead of a Dresse,
Are cloathed in a Frame or Presse,
And with that liberty and room,
The dead expatiate in a Tombe.
No Cabinets with curious Washes,
Bladders, and perfumed Plashes;
No venome-temper'd water's here,
Mercury is banished this Sphere:
Her Payle's all this, in which wet Glasse,
She both doth cleanse and view her Face.
Far hence all *Iberian* smells,
Hot Amulets, Pomander spells;
Fragrant Gales, cool Ay'r, the fresh,

And naturall Odour of her Flesh,
Proclaim her sweet from th' Wombe as Morne.
Those colour'd things were made not borne,
Which fixt within their narrow straits,
Do looke like their own counterfeyts.
So like the Provance Rose she walkt,
Flowerd with Blush, with Verdure stalkt;
Th' Officious Wind her loose Hayre Curles,
The Dewe her happy linnen purles,
But wets a Tresse, which instantly
Sol with a Crisping Beame doth dry.
  Into the Garden is she come,
Love and Delights *Elisium*;
If ever Earth show'd all her store,
View her discolourd budding Floore;
Here her glad Eye she largely feedes,
And stands 'mongst them, as they 'mong weeds;
The flowers in their best aray,
As to their Queen their Tribute pay,
And freely to her Lap proscribe
A Daughter out of ev'ry Tribe:
Thus as she moves, they all bequeath
At once the Incense of their Breath.
  The noble *Heliotropian*
Now turnes to her, and knowes no Sun;
  And as her glorious face doth vary,
So opens loyall golden *Mary*;
Who if but glanced from her fight,
Straight shuts again as it were Night.
  The *Violet* (else lost ith' heap)
Doth spread fresh purple for each step;
With whose Humility possest,
Sh' inthrones the *poore Girle* in her breast:
The *July-flow'r* that hereto thriv'd,
Knowing her self no longer liv'd,

But for one look of her, upheaves,
Then 'stead of tears straight sheds her leaves.
  Now the rich robed *Tulip*, who
Clad all in Tissue close doth woe,
Her (sweet to th' eye but smelling sower)
She gathers to adorn her Bower.
  But the proud *Hony-suckle* spreads
Like a Pavilion her Heads,
Contemnes the wanting Commonalty,
That but to two ends usefull be,
And to her lips thus aptly plac't,
With *smell* and *Hue* presents her *Tast*.
  So all their due Obedience pay,
Each thronging to be in her Way:
Faire *Aramantha* with her Eye
Thanks those that live, which else would dye:
The rest in silken fetters bound,
By *Crowning* her are *Crown* and *Crown'd*.
  And now the Sun doth higher rise,
Our *Flora* to the meadow hies:
The poore distressed Heifers low,
And as sh' approacheth gently bow,
Begging her charitable leasure
To strip them of their milkie Treasure.
  Out of the Yeomanry oth' Heard,
With grave aspect, and feet prepar'd,
A rev'rend Lady Cow drawes neare,
Bids *Aramantha* welcome here;
And from her privy purse lets fall
A Pearle or two, which seeme to call
This adorn'd adored Fayry
To the banquet of her Dayry.
  Soft *Aramantha* weeps to see
'Mongst men such inhumanitie,

That those who do receive in Hay,
And pay in silver twice a Day,
Should by their cruell barb'rous theft,
Be both of that, and life bereft.
  But 'tis decreed when ere this dies,
That she shall fall a Sacrifice
Unto the Gods, since those that trace
Her stemme, show 'tis a God-like race;
Descending in an even line
From Heifers, and from Steeres divine,
Making the honour'd extract full
In *Ió* and *Europa's* Bull.
She was the largest goodliest Beast,
That ever Mead or Altar blest;
Round as her Udder, and more white
Then is the *milkie way* in Night:
Her full broad Eye did sparkle fire,
Her breath was sweet as kind desire,
And in her beauteous crescent shone,
Bright as the Argent-horned Moone.
  But see! this whitenesse is obscure,
Cynthia spotted, she impure;
Her body writheld, and her eyes
Departing lights at obsequies:
Her lowing hot, to the fresh Gale,
Her breath perfumes the field withall;
To those two Suns that ever shine,
To those plump parts she doth inshrine,
To th' hovering Snow of either hand,
That *Love* and *Cruelty* command.
  After the breakfast on her Teat,
She takes her leave oth' mournfull Neat,
Who by her toucht now prize their life,
Worthy alone the *hallowed knife*.

[1648]

What I have further to say of the Country Life, shall be borrowed from the Poets, who were alwayes the most faithful and affectionate friends to it. Poetry was Born among the Shepherds . . . The truth is, no other place is proper for their work; one might as well undertake to Dance in a Crowd, as to make good Verses in the midst of Noise and Tumult.

As well might Corn as Verse, in Cities grow;
In vain the thankless Glebe we Plow and Sow,
Against th' unnatural Soil in vain we strive;
'Tis not a Ground, in which these Plants will thrive.

It will bear nothing but the Nettles or Thornes of Satyre, which grow most naturally in the worst Earth; and therefore almost all Poets, except those who were not able to eat Bread without the bounty of Great men, that is, without what they could get by Flattering of them, have not only withdrawn themselves from the Vices and Vanities of the Grand World, into the innocent happiness of a retired Life; but have commended and adorned nothing so much by their Ever-living Poems.

[*Of Agriculture*, 1668]

Of Solitude

I

Hail, old *Patrician* Trees, so great and good!
Hail, ye *Plebeian* underwood!
Where the Poetique Birds rejoyce,
And for their quiet Nests and plenteous Food
Pay with their grateful voice.

II

Hail, the poor Muses' richest Mannor Seat!
    Ye Countrey Houses and Retreat,
    Which all the happy Gods so Love,
That for you oft they quit their Bright and Great
    Metropolis above.

III

Here Nature does a House for me erect,
    Nature, the wisest Architect,
    Who those fond Artists does despise
That can the fair and living Trees neglect;
    Yet the Dead Timber prize.

IV

Here let me, careless and unthoughtful lying,
    Hear the soft winds, above me flying,
    With all their wanton Boughs dispute,
And the more tuneful Birds to both replying,
    Nor be myself, too Mute.

V

A Silver stream shall roll his waters neer,
    Gilt with the Sun-beams here and there
    On whose enamel'd Bank I'll walk,
And see how prettily they Smile, and hear
    How prettily they Talk.

VI

Ah wretched, and too Solitary Hee
    Who loves not his own company!
    He'l feel the weight of't many a day,
Unless he call in Sin or Vanity
    To help to bear't away.

VII

Oh Solitude, first state of Humain-kind!
    Which blest remain'd till man did find
    Even his own helpers Company.
As soon as two (alas!) together joyn'd,
    The Serpent made up Three.

VIII

Though God himself, through countless Ages Thee
    His sole Companion chose to be,
    Thee, Sacred Solitude, alone,
Before the Branchy head of Numbers Tree
    Sprang from the Trunk of One.

IX

Thou (though men think thine an unactive part)
    Dost break and tame th' unruly heart,
    Which else would know no setled pace,
Making it move, well mannag'd by thy Art,
    With Swiftness and with Grace.

X

Thou the faint beams of Reasons scatter'd Light
    Dost, like a Burning glass, unite,
    Dost multiply the feeble Heat,
And fortifie the strength, till thou dost bright
    And noble Fires beget.

XI

Whilst this hard Truth I teach, methinks, I see
    The monster *London* laugh at me;
    I should at thee too, foolish City,
If it were fit to laugh at Misery;
    But thy Estate I pity.

XII

Let but thy wicked men from out thee go,
    And the Fools that crowd thee so,
    Even thou, who dost thy Millions boast,
A Village less than *Islington* wilt grow,
    A Solitude almost.

[1656]

From *The Garden*

For God, the universal Architect,
    'T had been as easie to erect
A Louvre or Escurial or a Tower,
That might with Heav'n communication hold,
As *Babel* vainly thought to do of old:
    He wanted not the skill or power,
    In the Worlds Fabrick those were shown,
And, the Materials were all his own.
But well he knew what place would best agree
With Innocence, and with Felicity:
And we else where still seek for them in vain
If any part of either yet remain;
If any part of either we expect,
This may our judgment in the search direct;
God the first Garden made, and the first City, *Kain*.

[1667]

Bermudas

Where the remote *Bermudas* ride
In th' Oceans bosome unespy'd,
From a small Boat, that row'd along,
The listning Winds receiv'd this Song.
  What should we do but sing his Praise
That led us through the watry Maze,
Unto an Isle so long unknown,
And yet far kinder than our own?
Where he the huge Sea-Monsters wracks,
That lift the Deep upon their Backs.
He lands us on a grassy Stage;
Safe from the Storms, and Prelat's rage.
He gave us this eternal Spring,
Which here enamells every thing;
And sends the Fowl's to us in care,
On daily Visits through the Air.
He hangs in shades the Orange bright,
Like golden Lamps in a green Night.
And does in the Pomgranates close,
Jewels more rich than *Ormus* show's.
He makes the Figs our mouths to meet;
And throws the Melons at our feet.
But Apples plants of such a price,
No Tree could ever bear them twice.
With Cedars, chosen by his hand,
From *Lebanon*, he stores the Land.
And makes the hollow Seas, that roar,
Proclaime the Ambergris on shoar.
He cast (of which we rather boast)
The Gospels Pearl upon our Coast.

And in these Rocks for us did frame
A Temple, where to sound his Name.
Oh let our Voice his Praise exalt,
Till it arrive at Heavens Vault:
Which thence (perhaps) rebounding, may
Eccho beyond the *Mexique Bay*.
Thus sung they, in the *English* boat,
An holy and a chearful Note,
And all the way, to guide their Chime,
With falling Oars they kept the time.

[1681]

The Mower against Gardens

Luxurious Man, to bring his Vice in use,
  Did after him the World seduce:
And from the fields the Flow'rs and Plants allure,
  Where Nature was most plain and pure.
He first enclos'd within the Gardens square
  A dead and standing pool of Air:
And a more luscious Earth for them did knead,
  Which stupifi'd them while it fed.
The Pink grew then as double as his Mind;
  The nutriment did change the kind.
With strange perfumes he did the Roses taint.
  And Flow'rs themselves were taught to paint.
The Tulip, white, did for complexion seek;
  And learn'd to interline its cheek:
Its Onion root they then so high did hold,
  That one was for a Meadow sold.
Another World was search'd, through Oceans new,
  To find the *Marvel of Peru*.
And yet these Rarities might be allow'd,
  To Man, that sov'raign thing and proud;

Had he not dealt between the Bark and Tree,
  Forbidden mixtures there to see.
No Plant now knew the Stock from which it came;
  He grafts upon the Wild the Tame:
That the uncertain and adult'rate fruit
  Might put the Palate in dispute.
His green *Seraglio* has its Eunuchs too;
  Lest any Tyrant him out-doe.
And in the Cherry he does Nature vex,
  To procreate without a Sex.
'Tis all enforc'd; the Fountain and the Grot;
  While the sweet Fields do lye forgot:
Where willing Nature does to all dispence
  A wild and fragrant Innocence:
And *Fauns* and *Fairyes* do the Meadows till,
  More by their presence then their skill.
Their Statues polish'd by some ancient hand,
  May to adorn the Gardens stand:
But howso'ere the Figures do excel,
  The *Gods* themselves with us do dwell.

[1681]

Damon the Mower

I

Heark how the Mower *Damon* Sung,
With love of *Juliana* stung!
While ev'ry thing did seem to paint
The Scene more fit for his complaint.
Like her fair Eyes the day was fair;
But scorching like his am'rous Care.
Sharp like his Sythe his Sorrow was,
And wither'd like his Hopes the Grass.

II

Oh what unusual Heats are here,
Which thus our Sun-burn'd Meadows sear!
The Grass-hopper its pipe gives ore;
And hamstring'd Frogs can dance no more.
But in the brook the green Frog wades;
And Grass-hoppers seek out the shades.
Only the Snake, that kept within,
Now glitters in its second skin.

III

This heat the Sun could never raise,
Nor Dog-star so inflame's the dayes.
It from an higher Beauty grow'th,
Which burns the Fields and Mower both:
Which made the Dog, and makes the Sun
Hotter then his own *Phaeton*.
Not *July* causeth these Extremes,
But *Juliana's* scorching beams.

IV

Tell me where I may pass the Fires
Of the hot day, or hot desires.
To what cool Cave shall I descend,
Or to what gelid Fountain bend?
Alas! I look for Ease in vain,
When Remedies themselves complain.
No moisture but my Tears do rest,
Nor Cold but in her Icy Breast.

V

How long wilt Thou, fair Shepheardess,
Esteem me, and my Presents less?
To Thee the harmless Snake I bring,
Disarmed of its teeth and sting.

To Thee *Chameleons* changing-hue,
And Oak leaves tipt with hony due.
Yet Thou ungrateful hast not sought
Nor what they are, nor who them brought.

VI

I am the Mower *Damon*, known
Through all the Meadows I have mown.
On me the Morn her dew distills
Before her darling Daffadils.
And, if at Noon my toil me heat,
The Sun himself licks off my Sweat.
While, going home, the Ev'ning sweet
In cowslip-water bathes my feet.

VII

What, though the piping Shepherd stock
The plains with an unnum'red Flock,
This Sithe of mine discovers wide
More ground then all his Sheep do hide.
With this the golden fleece I shear
Of all these Closes ev'ry Year.
And though in Wooll more poor then they,
Yet am I richer far in Hay.

VIII

Nor am I so deform'd to sight,
If in my Sithe I looked right;
In which I see my Picture done,
As in a crescent Moon the Sun.
The deathless Fairyes take me oft
To lead them in their Danses soft:
And, when I tune my self to sing,
About me they contract their Ring

IX

How happy might I still have mow'd,
Had not Love here his Thistles sow'd!
But now I all the day complain,
Joyning my Labour to my Pain;
And with my Sythe cut down the Grass,
Yet still my Grief is where it was:
But, when the Iron blunter grows,
Sighing I whet my Sythe and Woes.

X

While thus he threw his Elbow round,
Depopulating all the Ground,
And, with his whistling Sythe, does cut
Each stroke between the Earth and Root,
The edged Stele by careless chance
Did into his own Ankle glance;
And there among the Grass fell down,
By his own Sythe, the Mower mown.

XI

Alas! said He, these hurts are slight
To those that dye by Loves despight.
With Shepherds-purse, and Clowns-all-heal,
The Blood I stanch, and Wound I seal.
Only for him no Cure is found,
Whom *Julianas* Eyes do wound.
'Tis death alone that this must do:
For Death thou art a Mower too.

[1681]

Ametas and Thestylis making Hay-Ropes

I

AMETAS:

Think'st Thou that this Love can stand,
Whilst Thou still dost say me nay?
Love unpaid does soon disband:
Love binds Love as Hay binds Hay.

II

THESTYLIS:

Think'st Thou that this Rope would twine
If we both should turn one way?
Where both parties so combine,
Neither Love will twist nor Hay.

III

AMETAS:

Thus you vain Excuses find,
Which your selve and us delay:
And Love tyes a Womans Mind
Looser then with Ropes of Hay.

IV

THESTYLIS:

What you cannot constant hope
Must be taken as you may.

V

AMETAS:

Then let's both lay by our Rope,
And go kiss within the Hay*.

[1681]

* Among other things, this is the name of a country dance.

The Garden

I

How vainly men themselves amaze
To win the Palm, the Oke, or Bayes;
And their uncessant Labours see
Crown'd from some single Herb or Tree,
Whose short and narrow verged Shade
Does prudently their Toyles upbraid;
While all Flow'rs and all Trees do close
To weave the Garlands of repose.

II

Fair quiet, have I found thee here,
And Innocence thy Sister dear!
Mistaken long, I sought you then
In busie Companies of Men.
Your sacred Plants, if here below,
Only among the Plants will grow.
Society is all but rude,
To this delicious Solitude.

III

No white nor red was ever seen
So am'rous as this lovely green.
Fond Lovers, cruel as their Flame,
Cut in these Trees their Mistress name.
Little, Alas, they know, or heed,
How far these Beauties Hers exceed!
Fair Trees! where s'eer your barkes I wound,
No Name shall but your own be found.

IV

When we have run our Passions heat,
Love hither makes his best retreat.

The *Gods*, that mortal Beauty chase,
Still in a Tree did end their race.
Apollo hunted *Daphne* so,
Only that She might Laurel grow.
And *Pan* did after *Syrinx* speed,
Not as a Nymph, but for a Reed.

V

What wond'rous Life in this I lead!
Ripe Apples drop about my head;
The Luscious Clusters of the Vine
Upon my Mouth do crush their Wine;
The Nectaren, and curious Peach,
Into my hands themselves do reach;
Stumbling on Melons, as I pass,
Insnar'd with Flow'rs, I fall on Grass.

VI

Mean while the Mind, from pleasure less,
Withdraws into its happiness:
The Mind, that Ocean where each kind
Does streight its own resemblance find;
Yet it creates, transcending these,
Far other Worlds, and other Seas;
Annihilating all that's made
To a green Thought in a green Shade.

VII

Here at the Fountains sliding foot,
Or at some Fruit-trees mossy root,
Casting the Bodies Vest aside,
My Soul into the boughs does glide:
There like a Bird it sits, and sings,
Then whets, and combs its silver Wings

And, till prepar'd for longer flight,
Waves in its Plumes the various Light.

VIII

Such was that happy Garden-state,
While Man there walk'd without a Mate:
After a Place so pure, and sweet,
What other Help could yet be meet!
But 'twas beyond a Mortal's share
To wander solitary there:
Two Paradises 'twere in one
To live in Paradise alone.

IX

How well the skilful Gardner drew
Of flow'rs and herbes this Dial new;
Where from above the milder Sun
Does through a fragrant Zodiack run;
And, as it works, th' industrious Bee
Computes its time as well as we.
How could such sweet and wholsome Hours
Be reckon'd but with herbs and flow'rs!

[1681]

AUGUSTAN PASTORAL

The court culture which briefly reasserts itself at the Restoration in 1660 runs counter to the broader social development of the century. The pastoral voice never finds expression as a celebration of an aristocratic world-view. Rather it becomes a joke, a last amused gesture at the middle-class puritan culture whose advancement it had temporarily halted. It is a pastoral reflecting decadence not nostalgia, a product of a culture that has outlived its dominance. The elegant love lyrics of the later Cavalier poets frequently hint, beneath their surface cynicism, at a world of pastoral values. But it is the distance between the insistently basic imagery of sexual relationships and the niceties of pastoral innocence – as in Rochester's 'Chloris' poems – that is important. When Flatman writes of the rakish Rochester as having lived the life of a pastoral swain, he does not expect the identification to be taken seriously for one moment; it is to the defiant non-innocence of Rochester that he wishes to direct our attention. Restoration Comedy denied the possibility of social mobility that the earlier drama had increasingly allowed, and reflects the values of a besieged culture. The countryside – even as an idealized setting – is no longer an alternative. There is only the world of the court and of fashionable London. When Dorimant offers protestations of romantic love to Harriet at the end of Etherege's *Man of Mode* (1676), she correctly takes him to task: 'This is more dismal than the Country. Emilia, pity me who am going to that sad place – Kaw, kaw, kaw – There's music in the worst cry in London; my Dill and Cucumbers to pickle.' To the Restoration audience, the country was a void, a place of unlife.

But even Restoration Comedy does gradually acknowledge the presence of an audience less courtly and more representative of the realities of political power; the conflict between town and country becomes more ambiguous, and the marriage of different class interests a possibility. Aristocratic attitudes are assimilated into the larger cultural tradition, so that a poet such as Pope, who is not of the court, has, in his early poetry, a version of the Pastoral that appears to cling to a past that the poet can evidently no longer believe in.

Pope, in his *Discourse on Pastoral Poetry* (1717), regards an actual historical location of a pastoral age as an irrelevance: 'Pastoral is an image of what they call the golden age. So that we are not to describe our shepherds as shepherds at this day really are, but as they may be conceived then to have been; when the best of men followed the employment.' Pope makes an easy separation between what '*they* call' and what '*we* are ... to describe'. The idealization of the shepherd's life must predominate over any urge to naturalism, and any pretence of a believable contemporary setting – or indeed of any setting other than an imagined one – should be abandoned. For Pope as for Spenser – both taking Virgil as their model – the Pastoral was the first stage in the development of the poet; but for Spenser, the Pastoral had been a natural voice to adopt. Pope's Pastorals are defiantly artificial in their adherence to the neo-classical, in a way that does not reflect his social role – as it had for Spenser. Pope is well aware of the possibility of humour:

> Where'er you walk, cool gales shall fan the glade,
> Trees, where you sit, shall crowd into a shade:
> Where'er you tread, the blushing flow'rs shall rise,
> And all things flourish where you turn your eyes.

This is an adaptation of an aristocratic view of the natural order, smoothened and polished for the amusement of the coffee-house. This is not to say that the Pastoral did not have a more serious aspect for Pope. He is too much the urban poet to offer a credible rural Idyll, but what the Pastoral did provide was a convenient mythology for his essentially nostalgic political philosophy, and what above is an amusing conceit will elsewhere reflect quite seriously Pope's idea of the harmony of man and his environment.

> Here earth and water seem to strive again,
> Not Chaos-like together crush'd and bruis'd,
> But, as the world, harmoniously confus'd:
> Where order in variety we see . . .

Nature presents no threat to man, and the apparent social confusion surrounding the poet does in fact have an underlying sense of order. Such a vision of society is at odds with the actual society in which Pope was writing and represents an attempt to hang on to what he sees as an earlier harmonious society. This invocation of the Pastoral at the beginning of 'Windsor Forest', despite its claim to be a contemporary depiction of England under Queen Anne – 'peace and plenty tell, a STUART reigns' – makes use of all that machinery of a nostalgic Golden Age that Pope had perhaps unwittingly discredited in his *Discourse*. The passage is a magnificent piece of propaganda for an already lost cause, for a world of settled, conservative values, in the face of a threatening, aggressive individualism. It is an attempt to stop social and historical development in a moment of pastoral stasis – like the figures on Keats's Urn. Earth and water, like the social elements in the nation, 'strive', but the result is harmony, 'order in variety', and not the Chaos of Milton's Satan – a Chaos of 'democracy' or even Civil War.

This simplistic view of social organization does not survive long, and there is little evidence of the Pastoral in Pope's later poetry. For Pope, the Pastoral was always associated with the old culture, and he was never able to transform it from his experience of the new. Where it does occur, as at the end of the attack on Timon's Villa in the 'Epistle to Burlington', it is presented as a mythical counter to man's over-sophistication. Nature, while it is not a Chaos – although Pope came increasingly to have doubts about this – should not be too organized either. Timon's Garden usurps the natural order of society, imposing rigid patterns and ignoring the natural contours of the country. The image of the Garden as a symbol of both the society and its culture is clearly important, and has links in Pope with the Miltonic Paradise and contemporary theories of landscaping. The Garden is the ultimate pastoral creation, the organization by man of nature into art. Timon's creation is an unnatural one, not only lacking in taste, but threatening the view of social organization that Pope was finding it ever more difficult to believe in. Ironically, by this absurd expenditure on house and garden, Timon does fulfil his traditional role in the scheme, as provider of work for the local community. The pastoral expression remains only as an uncertain possibility:

> Another age shall see the golden Ear
> Imbrown the Slope, and nod on the Parterre,
> Deep Harvests bury all his pride has plann'd,
> And laughing Ceres re-assume the land.

In comparison with the lengthily elaborate imagery of the Villa, this rehearsal of arcadian prophecy cannot – despite its breezy tone – have convinced even Pope. It is doubtful whether the modern, self-made Timon would have known 'laughing Ceres' from the manager of his estate.

Pope's neo-classical position derives largely from the necessity of confronting the emergent middle-class culture with a positive alternative to its emphasis on the contemporary, on the uniqueness of the individual's experience, and, above all, on the *material*. When Ambrose Philips, in his *Pastorals* (1708), insisted on the Englishness of the myth and of the landscapes he describes, Pope, in an article in the *Guardian*, the irony of which escaped many readers, damned his own *Pastorals* in favour of those of Philips. Pope quoted enthusiastically a 'Pastoral Ballad' in the West Country dialect, which he has supposedly stumbled on:

> CICILY: Rager, go vetch that kee, or else the zun
> Will quite be go, bevore c'have haf a don.

The fact that so many readers were unable to detect Pope's easy gibe indicates the nature of the division perfectly. The 'Pastoral Ballad' has an apparent rural authenticity which anticipates nineteenth-century attempts at dialect poetry. The neo-classic meets the 'naturalistic' head-on. Of course, Philips's efforts do contain much of the dead lumber of the past, but there is a certain freshness, a feeling of something very near direct observation. The conclusion of the 'Second Pastoral', after some less-than-successful dialogue – although at least the cause of Colinet's lament does have some possible basis in a countryside of fixed communities – with the onset of evening and the resolution of the shepherd's problems, introduces a poetic voice that is not to be found again in English poetry until Gray draws upon the passage for the opening of his 'Elegy':

> And now behold the sun's departing ray,
> O'er yonder hill, the sign of ebbing day:
> With songs the jovial hinds return from plough;
> And unyoked heifers, loitering homeward, low.

The 'jovial hinds' are a stock image, but the overall mood of these lines is something that begins to liberate the Pastoral from the confines of classicism.

The idea of talking about – or nearly talking about – ordinary people, and the resultant lowness of subject-matter, comes under frequent attack. Late in the eighteenth century, a translator of Virgil found it necessary to apologize for the inclusion of such vulgar words as 'cow' and 'dung', fearing its effect on the reader's sensibilities; and, although this is an extreme reaction, the suspicion of a too earthy verisimilitude is deep-rooted. Swift's 'Pastoral Dialogue' and Jago's 'The Scavengers' burlesque the 'naturalistic' Pastoral with their emphasis on the vulgarity and the nastiness of the swains' activities. Jago's characters bemoan the lack of dung on modern streets, and reminisce lovingly on the abundance of it in days gone by, and Swift's indulge in an insistent banter of rough sexual innuendo. Swift gradually 'weeds' his 'Dialogue' of its classical reference as the bawdy low-life content increases. This Pastoral–burlesque, which becomes almost a genre in its own right, is completely urban in its orientation, and very often, as with 'The Scavengers', transfers the pastoral action to the town.

In Gay's *The Shepherd's Week*, the situation is more complex. Gay's Pastorals are usually taken to be straight ridicule of the 'naturalistic' school, written at the instigation of Pope. Whether this explanation of their genesis is correct or not, it does not solve the problem of interpretation. In 'Tuesday', Marian laments her lover's defection to her rival, Cicily. Marian represents the worthy attributes of the cottage, tending and caring faithfully for her man,

What I have done for thee will Cic'ly do?

Her life is one of hard agricultural toil, and has little room in it for the elaborate love debate of the traditional Pastoral. Gay appears to be mocking the 'naturalistic' by allowing the earth-bound girl to express her love so resolutely and in such low language, but the poem concludes firmly on the side of unromantic 'reality', and the values of the external world. Goody Dobbins brings her cow to be served – just as Marian's rival is being served by Colin – causing her to forgo her tears in the cause of material gain and the routine of work:

With apron blue to dry her tears she sought,
Then saw the cow well serv'd, and took a groat.

It is not Ambrose Philips's naturalism that is under attack, but the falsity of his urban sentimentalism. Gay, although writing in an urban environment and for an urban audience, had at least a youth spent in the country to draw from. The uncertainty which the poem displays is a result of Gay's own uncertainty about his position in the struggle between the old and the new that was taking place in pastoral fields. The naturalistic school had rejected the artificiality of the neo-classic pastoral but had retained the convenient expression of rural innocence – convenient, because allowing of a sentimental, entirely urban response. Gay, in 'The Birth of the Squire', is firm in his dismissal of such sentiments. His model is that *Eclogue* of Virgil which, because of its theme of the restoration of the Golden Age by Pollio, had been most frequently invoked in religious and political prophecy. The Squire whose birth is celebrated, might be expected to return his community to the ideals of the 'manor house' society, but Gay does not allow such an innocent view of the country. The poem ends in a magnificent vision of sordid death:

The mighty bumper trembles in his hands;
Boldly he drinks, and like his glorious Sires,
In copious gulps of potent ale expires.

Whatever expectation we still might have of a future Golden Age is frustrated.

Let Pastoral never venture upon a lofty subject, let it not recede one jot from its proper matter, but be employ'd about Rustick affairs; such as are mean and humble in themselves; and such are the affairs of shepherds, especially their Loves, but those must be pure and innocent; not disturb'd by vain suspitious jealousy, nor polluted by Rapes; The Rivals must not fight, and their emulations must be without quarellings.

. . . Nature is chiefly to be lookt upon (for nothing that is disagreeable to Nature can please) yet that will hardly prevail naked, by it self, and without the polishing of Art.

[René Rapin, *A Treatise De Carmine Pastorale,* first English translation 1684]

We meet with certain wild Animals, male and female, spread over the Country. They are black and tann'd, united to the Earth, which they are always digging and turning up and down with an unweary'd resolution. They have something like an articulate voice, when they stand on their feet they discover a manlike face, and indeed are men, at night they retire into their Burries, where they live on black Bread, Water and Raysons. They spare other men the trouble of sowing, labouring, and reaping for their maintenance, and deserve, one would think, that they should not want the Bread they themselves sow.

[La Bruyère, *Caractères,* first English translation 1699]

Society in time was brought to perfection, or rather declin'd and was perverted; and Man took up Employments that seem'd to them of greater consequence . . . Towns and Cities were built everywhere, and mighty States at last were founded and establisht. Then those who lived in the Country became Slaves to those who dwelt in Cities, and the Pastoral Life being grown the lot of the most wretched sort of People, no longer inspir'd any delightful Thought.

[Bernard Bovier de Fontenelle, 'Of Pastorals', first English translation 1695]

CHARLES COTTON

The Retirement

Stanzes Irreguliers to Mr. Izaak Walton

I

Farewell thou busie World, and may
We never meet again:
Here I can eat, and sleep, and pray,
And do more good in one short day,
Than he who his whole Age out wears
Upon the most conspicuous Theaters,
Where nought but Vice and Vanity do reign.

II

Good God! how sweet are all things here!
How beautifull the Fields appear!
How cleanly do we feed and lie!
Lord! what good hours do we keep!
How quietly we sleep!
What Peace, what Unanimity!
How innocent from the leud Fashion,
Is all our bus'ness, all our Conversation!

III

Oh how happy here's our leisure!
Oh how innocent our pleasure!
Oh ye Vallies, oh ye Mountains!
Oh ye Groves and Chrystall Fountains,
How I love at liberty,
By turns to come and visit ye!

IV

O Solitude, the Soul's best Friend,
That man acquainted with himself dost make,

And all his Maker's Wonders to intend;
With thee I here converse at will,
And would be glad to do so still;
For it is thou alone, that keep'st the Soul awake.

V

How calm and quiet a delight
It is, alone
To read, and meditate, and write,
By none offended, nor offending none;
To walk, ride, sit, or sleep at one's own ease,
And pleasing a man's self, none other to displease!

VI

Oh my beloved Nymph! fair Dove,
Princess of rivers, how I love
Upon thy flow'ry Banks to lie,
And view thy Silver stream,
When gilded by a Summer's Beam!
And in it, all thy wanton Fry
Playing at liberty,
And with my Angle upon them
The All of Treachery
I ever learn'd to practise and to try!

VII

Such streams *Rome's* yellow *Tiber* cannot show,
Th'Iberian *Tagus*, nor Ligurian *Po*;
The *Meuse*, the *Danube*, and the *Rhine*,
Are puddle-water all compar'd with thine;
And *Loyres* pure streams yet too polluted are
With thine much purer to compare:
The rapid *Garonne*, and the winding *Seine*
Are both too mean,

Beloved *Dove*, with thee
To vie priority;
Nay, *Tame* and *Isis*, when conjoyn'd, submit,
And lay their Trophies at thy Silver Feet.

VIII

Oh my beloved Rocks! that rise
To awe the Earth, and brave the Skies,
From some aspiring Mountain's crown
How dearly do I love,
Giddy with pleasure, to look down,
And from the Vales to view the noble heights above!

IX

Oh my beloved Caves! from Dog-star heats,
And hotter Persecution safe retreats,
What safety, privacy, what true delight,
In the artificial Night
Your gloomy entrails make,
Have I taken, do I take!
How oft, when grief has made me fly
To hide me from Society,
Even of my dearest Friends, have I
In your recesses friendly shade
All my sorrows open laid,
And my most secret woes entrusted to your privacy!

X

Lord! would men let me alone,
What an over-happy one
Should I think my self to be,
Might I in this desart place,
Which most men by their voice disgrace,
Live but undisturb'd and free!
Here in this despis'd recess

Would I maugre Winter's cold,
And the Summer's worst excess,
Try to live out to sixty full years old,
And all the while
Without an envious eye
On any thriving under Fortune's smile,
Contented live, and then contented die.

[1689]

THOMAS SHADWELL

From *The Libertine*
Act V

[*Enter two Shepherds, and two Nymphs*]

FIRST SHEPHERD:
Come Nymphs and Shepherds, haste away
To the happy sports within these shady Groves;
In pleasant lives time slides away apace,
But with the wretched seems to creep too slow.

FIRST NYMPH:
Our happy leisure we imploy in Joys,
As innocent as they are pleasant. We,
Strangers to strife, and to tumultuous noise,
To baneful envy, and to wretched cares,
In rural pleasures spend our happy days,
And our soft nights in calm and quiet sleeps.

SECOND SHEPHERD:
No rude Ambition interrupts our rest,
Nor base and guilty thoughts how to be great.

SECOND NYMPH:

In humble Cottages we have such contents,
As uncorrupted Nature does afford,
Which the Great, that surfeit under gilded Roofs,
And wanton in Down Beds, can never know.

FIRST SHEPHERD:

Nature is here, not yet debauch'd by Art,
'Tis as it was in *Saturn's* happy days:
Minds are not here by Luxury invaded.
A homely Plenty, with sharp Appetite,
Does lightsome health, and vigorous strength impart.

FIRST NYMPH:

A chast cold Spring does here refresh our Thirst,
Which by no feverish surfeit is increas'd;
Our food is such as Nature meant for Men,
Ere with the Vicious, Eating was an Art.

SECOND NYMPH:

In noisy Cities riot is pursued,
And leud Luxurious Living softens Men,
Effeminates Fools in Body and in Mind,
Weakens their Appetites, and decays their Nerves.

SECOND SHEPHERD:

With filthy steams from their excess of Meat,
And cloudy vapours rais'd from dangerous Wine,
Their heads are never clear or free to think.
They waste their Lives in a continual mist.

FIRST SHEPHERD:

Some subtil and ill Men chuse Temperance,
Not as a Vertue, but a Bawd to Vice,
And vigilantly wait to ruine those,
Whom Luxury and Ease have lull'd asleep.

SECOND SHEPHERD:

Yes, in the clamorous Courts of tedious Law,
Where what is meant for a relief's a grievance;
Or in King's Palaces, where Cunning strives

Not to advance King's Interests, but its own.

FIRST NYMPH:

There they in a continual hurry live,
And seldom can, for all their subtile Arts,
Lay their Foundations sure; but some
Are undermin'd, others blown down by storms.

SECOND NYMPH:

Their subtilty is but a Common Road
Of flattering great Men, and opposing little;
Smiling on all they meet, and loving none.

FIRST SHEPHERD:

In populous Cities, Life is all a storm;
But we enjoy a sweet perpetual calm:
Here our own Flocks we keep, and here
I and my *Phillis* can embrace unenvy'd.

SECOND SHEPHERD:

And I and *Celia* without Jealousie:
But hark, the Pipes begin; now for our sports.

A Symphony of Rustick Musick

Nymphs and Shepherds come away,
In these Groves let's sport and play;
Where each day is a Holy day,
Sacred to Ease and happy Love,
To Dancing, Musick, Poetry:
Your Flocks may now securely rove,
Whilst you express your jollity.

[1676]

JOHN WILMOT, EARL OF ROCHESTER

Song

As Chloris full of harmless thought
  Beneath the willows lay,
Kind love a comely shepherd brought
  To pass the time away.

She blushed to be encountered so
  And chid the amorous swain,
But as she strove to rise and go,
  He pulled her back again.

A sudden passion seized her heart
  In spite of her disdain;
She found a pulse in every part,
  And love in every vein.

'Ah, youth!' quoth she, 'What charms are these
  That conquer and surprise?
Ah, let me – for unless you please,
  I have no power to rise.'

She faintly spoke, and trembling lay,
  For fear he should comply,
But virgins' eyes their hearts betray
  And give their tongues the lie.

Thus she, who princes had denied
  With all their pompous train,
Was in the lucky minute tried
  And yielded to the swain.

[1676]

Song

Fair Chloris in a pigsty lay;
   Her tender herd lay by her.
She slept; in murmuring gruntlings they,
Complaining of the scorching day,
   Her slumbers thus inspire.

She dreamt whilst she with careful pains
   Her snowy arms employed
In ivory pails to fill out grains,
One of her love-convicted swains
   Thus hasting to her cried:

'Fly, nymph! Oh, fly ere 'tis too late
   A dear, loved life to save;
Rescue your bosom pig from fate
Who now expires, hung in the gate
   That leads to Flora's cave.

'Myself had tried to set him free
   Rather than brought the news,
But I am so abhorred by thee
That ev'n thy darling's life from me
   I know thou wouldst refuse.'

Struck with the news, as quick she flies
   As blushes to her face;
Not the bright lightning from the skies,
Nor love, shot from her brighter eyes,
   Move half so swift a pace.

This plot, it seems, the lustful slave
   Had laid against her honor,

Which not one god took care to save,
For he pursues her to the cave
   And throws himself upon her.

Now pierced is her virgin zone;
   She feels the foe within it.
She hears a broken amorous groan,
The panting lover's fainting moan,
   Just in the happy minute.

Frighted she wakes, and waking frigs.
   Nature thus kindly eased
In dreams raised by her murmuring pigs
And her own thumb between her legs,
   She's innocent and pleased.

[1680]

THOMAS FLATMAN

On the Death of the Earl of Rochester
Pastoral

I

As on his death-bed gasping Strephon lay,
      Strephon the wonder of the plains,
      The noblest of th' Arcadian swains;
Strephon the bold, the witty, and the gay:
With many a sigh and many a tear he said,
Remember me, ye Shepherds, when I'm dead.

II

Ye trifling glories of this world, adieu,
And vain applauses of the age;
For when we quit this earthly stage,
Believe me, shepherds, for I tell you true;
Those pleasures which from virtuous deeds we have,
Procure the sweetest slumbers in the grave.

III

Then since your fatal hour must surely come,
Surely your heads lie low as mine,
Your bright meridian sun decline;
Beseech the mighty Pan to guard you home,
If to Elysium you would happy fly,
Live not like Strephon, but like Strephon die.

[1682]

CHARLES SACKVILLE, EARL OF DORSET

Knotting

At Noon, in a Sunshiny Day,
The brighter Lady of the *May*,
Young Chloris innocent and gay,
Sat Knotting in a Shade:

Each slender Finger play'd its Part,
With such Activity and Art,
As would inflame a youthful Heart,
And warm the most decay'd.

Her fav'rite Swain, by Chance, came by,
He saw no Anger in her Eye;
Yet when the bashful Boy drew nigh,
  She would have seem'd afraid.

She let her ivory Needle fall,
And hurl'd away the twisted Ball;
But strait gave Strephon such a Call,
  As would have rais'd the Dead.

Dear gentle Youth, is't none but Thee?
With Innocence I dare be free;
By so much Truth and Modesty
  No Nymph was e'er betray'd.

Come lean thy Head upon my Lap;
While thy smooth Cheeks I stroke and clap,
Thou may'st securely take a Nap.
  Which he, poor Fool, obey'd.

She saw him yawn, and heard him snore,
And found him fast asleep all o'er.
She sigh'd, and could endure no more,
  But starting up, she said,

Such Virtue shall rewarded be:
For this thy dull Fidelity,
I'll trust you with my Flocks, not Me,
  Pursue thy grazing Trade;

Go milk thy Goats, and shear thy Sheep,
And watch all Night thy Flocks to keep;
Thou shalt no more be lull'd asleep
  By Me mistaken Maid.

[1701]

JOHN DRYDEN

From *To My Honour'd Kinsman* John Driden

How Blessed is He, who leads a Country Life,
Unvex'd with anxious Cares, and void of Strife!
Who studying Peace, and shunning Civil Rage,
Enjoy'd his Youth, and now enjoys his Age:
All who deserve his Love, he makes his own;
And, to be lov'd himself, needs only to be known.
  Just, Good, and Wise, contending Neighbours come
From your Award to wait their final Doom;
And, Foes before, return in Friendship home.
Without their Cost, you terminate the Cause;
And save th' Expence of long Litigious Laws:
Where Suits are travers'd; and so little won,
That he who conquers, is but last undone:
  Such are not your Decrees; but so design'd,
The Sanction leaves a lasting Peace behind;
Like your own Soul, Serene; a Pattern of your Mind.
  Promoting Concord, and composing Strife,
Lord of your self, uncumber'd with a Wife;
Where, for a Year, a Month, perhaps a Night,
Long Penitence succeeds a short Delight:
Minds are so hardly match'd, that ev'n the first,
Though pair'd by Heav'n, in Paradise, were curs'd.
For Man and Woman, though in one they grow,
Yet, first or last, return again to Two.
He to God's Image, She to His was made;
So, farther from the Fount, the Stream at random stray'd.
  How cou'd He stand, when, put to double Pain,
He must a Weaker than himself sustain!
Each might have stood perhaps; but each alone;
Two Wrestlers help to pull each other down.

Not that my Verse wou'd blemish all the Fair;
But yet, if *some* be Bad, 'tis Wisdom to beware;
And better shun the Bait, than struggle in the Snare.
Thus have you shunn'd, and shun the married State,
Trusting as little as you can to Fate.
No porter guards the Passage of your Door;*
T' admit the Wealthy, and exclude the Poor:
For God, who gave the Riches, gave the Heart
To sanctifie the Whole, by giving Part:
Heav'n, who foresaw the Will, the Means has wrought,
And to the Second Son, a Blessing brought:
The First-begotten had his Father's Share,
But you, like *Jacob*, are *Rebecca's* Heir.
So may your Stores, and fruitful Fields increase;
And ever be you bless'd, who live to bless.
As *Ceres* sow'd where e'er her Chariot flew;
As Heav'n in Desarts rain'd the Bread of Dew,
So free to Many, to Relations most,
You feed with Manna your own *Israel*-Host.
With Crowds attended of your ancient Race,
You seek the Champian-Sports, or Sylvan-Chace:
With well-breath'd Beagles, you surround the Wood,
Ev'n then, industrious of the Common Good:
And often have you brought the wily Fox
To suffer for the Firstlings of the Flocks;
Chas'd ev'n amid the Folds; and made to bleed,
Like Felons, where they did the murd'rous Deed.
This fiery Game, your active Youth maintain'd:
Not yet, by years extinguish'd, though restrain'd:
You season still with Sports your serious Hours;
For Age but tastes of Pleasures, Youth devours.
The Hare, in Pastures or in Plains is found,
Emblem of Humane Life, who runs the Round;

* Cf. 'To Saxham', p. 174.

And, after all his wand'ring Ways are done,
His Circle fills, and ends where he begun,
Just as the Setting meets the Rising Sun.
  Thus Princes ease their Cares: But happier he,
Who seeks not Pleasure thro' Necessity,
Than such as once on slipp'ry Thrones were plac'd;
And chasing, sigh to think themselves are chas'd.
  So liv'd our Sires, e'er Doctors learn'd to kill,
And multiply'd with theirs, the Weekly Bill:
The first Physicians by Debauch were made:
Excess began, and Sloth sustains the Trade.
Pity the gen'rous Kind their Cares bestow
To search forbidden Truths; (a Sin to know:)
To which, if Humane Science cou'd attain,
The Doom of Death, pronounc'd by God, were vain.
In vain the Leech wou'd interpose Delay;
Fate fastens first, and vindicates the Prey.

*

By Chace our long-liv'd Fathers earned their Food;
Toil strung the Nerves, and purifi'd the Blood:
But we, their Sons, a pamper'd Race of Men,
Are dwindl'd down to threescore Years and ten.
Better to hunt in Fields, for Health unbought,
Than see the Doctor for a nauseous Draught.
The Wise, for Cure, on Exercise depend;
God never made his Work, for Man to mend.
  The Tree of Knowledge, once in *Eden* plac'd,
Was easie found, but was forbid the Taste:
O, had our Grandsire walk'd without his Wife,
He first had sought the better Plant of Life!
Now, both are lost: Yet, wandring in the dark,
Physicians for the Tree have found the Bark.

They, lab'ring for Relief of Humane Kind,
With sharpen'd sight some Remedies may find:
Th' Apothecary-Train is wholly blind.
From Files, a Random-*Recipe* they take,
And Many Deaths of One Prescription make.
Garth, gen'rous as his Muse, prescribes and gives;*
The Shop-Man sells; and by Destruction lives:
Ungrateful Tribe! who, like the Viper's Brood,
From Med'cine issuing, suck their Mother's Blood!
Let These obey; and let the Learn'd prescribe,
That Man may die, without a double Bribe:
Let Them, but under their Superiours, kill,
When Doctors first have sign'd the bloody Bill:
He scapes the best, who Nature to repair,
Draws Phisick from the Fields, in Draughts of Vital Air.
You hoard not Health, for your own private use,
But on the Publick spend the rich Produce.
When, often urg'd, unwilling to be Great,
Your Country calls you from your lov'd Retreat,
And sends to Senates, charg'd with Common Care,
Which none more shuns; and none can better bear.
Where cou'd they find another form'd so fit,
To poise, with solid Sense, a spritely Wit!
Were these both wanting, (as they both abound)
Where cou'd so firm Integrity be found?
Well-born and Wealthy; wanting no Support,
You steer betwixt the Country and the Court:
Nor gratifie whate'er the Great desire,
Nor grudging give, what Publick Needs require.

[1700]

* A reference to Garth's poem, *The Dispensary*.

A Ballad of Andrew *and* Maudlin

Andrew and *Maudlin*, *Rebecca* and *Will*,
  Margaret and *Thomas*, and *Jockey* and *Mary*;
Kate o'th' Kitchin, and *Kit* of the Mill,
  Dick the Plow-man, and *Joan* of the Dairy,
To solace their Lives, and to sweeten their Labour,
All met on a time with a Pipe and Tabor.

Andrew was Cloathed in Shepherd's Grey;
  And *Will* had put on his Holiday Jacket;
Beck had a Coat of *Popin-jay*,
  And *Madge* had a Ribbon hung down to her Placket;
Meg and *Mell* in Frize, *Tom* and *Jockey* in Leather,
And so they began all to Foot it together.

Their Heads and their Arms about them they flung,
  With all the Might and Force they had;
Their Legs went like Flays, and as loosely hung,
  They Cudgel'd their Arses as if they were Mad;
Their Faces did shine, and their Fires did kindle,
While the Maids they did trip and turn like a Spindle.

Andrew chuck'd *Maudlin* under the Chin,
  Simper she did like a Furmity Kettle;
The twang of whose blubber lips made such a din,
  As if her Chaps had been made of Bell-metal:
Kate Laughed heartily at the same smack,
And loud she did answer it with a Bum-crack.

At no *Whitsun-Ale* there e'er yet had been,
  Such Fraysters and Friskers[1] as these Lads and Lasses;
From their Faces the Sweat ran down to be seen,

[1] noisy frolickers

But sure I am, much more from their Arses;
For had you but seen't, you then would have sworn,
You never beheld the like since you were Born.

Here they did fling, and there they did hoist,
Here a hot Breath, and there went a Savour;
Here they did glance, and there they did gloist,
Here they did Simper, and there they did Slaver;
Here was a Hand, and their was a Placket,
Whilst, hey! their Sleeves went Flicket-a-flacket.

The Dance being ended, they Sweat and they Stunk,
The Maidens did smirk it, the Youngsters did Kiss 'em;
Cakes and Ale flew about, they clapp'd hands and drunk,
They laugh'd and they gigl'd until they bepist 'em;
They laid the Girls down, and gave each a green Mantle,
While their Breasts and their Bellies went Pintle a Pantle.

[1700]

THOMAS PARNELL

Health, An Eclogue

Now early Shepherds o'er the Meadow pass,
And print long Foot-steps in the glittering Grass;
The Cows neglectful of their Pasture stand,
By turns obsequious to the Milker's Hand.

When *Damon* softly trod the shaven Lawn,
Damon, a Youth from City Cares withdrawn·

Long was the pleasing Walk he wander'd thro',
A cover'd Arbour clos'd the distant view;
There rests the *Youth*, and, while the feather'd Throng
Raise their wild Musick, thus contrives a Song.

Here, wafted o'er by mild *Etesian* Air,
Thou Country *Goddess*, beauteous *Health*, repair!
Here let my Breast thro' quivering Trees inhale
Thy rosy Blessings with the Morning Gale.
What are the Fields, or Flow'rs, or all I see?
Ah! tasteless all, if not enjoy'd with thee.

Joy to my soul! I feel the *Goddess* nigh,
The Face of Nature cheers as well as I;
O'er the flat Green refreshing Breezes run,
The smiling Dazies blow beneath the Sun,
The Brooks run purling down with silver Waves,
The planted Lanes rejoice with dancing Leaves,
The chirping Birds from all the Compass rove
To tempt the tuneful Echoes of the Grove:
High sunny Summits, deeply shaded Dales,
Thick Mossy Banks, and flow'ry winding Vales,
With various Prospect gratify the Sight,
And scatter fix'd Attention in Delight.

Come, Country *Goddess*, come; nor thou suffice,
But bring thy Mountain-sister, *Exercise*.
Call'd by thy lively Voice, she turns her Pace,
Her winding Horn proclaims the finish'd Chace;
She mounts the Rocks, she skims the level Plain,
Dogs, Hawks, and Horses, crowd her early Train;
Her hardy Face repels the tanning Wind,
And Lines and Meshes loosely float behind.
All these as Means of Toil the Feeble see,
But these are helps to Pleasure join'd with thee.

Let *Sloth* lye softning till high Noon in Down,
Or lolling fan her in the sult'ry Town,
Unnerv'd with Rest; and turn her own Disease,
Or foster others in luxurious Ease:
I mount the Courser, call the deep-mouth'd Hounds
The Fox unkennell'd flies to covert Grounds;
I lead where Stags through tangled Thickets tread,
And shake the Saplings with their branching Head;
I make the Faulcons wing their airy Way,
And soar to seize, or stooping strike their Prey;
To snare the Fish I fix the luring Bait;
To wound the Fowl I load the Gun with Fate.
'Tis thus through change of Exercise I range,
And Strength and Pleasure rise from every Change.
  Here, beauteous *Health*, for all the Year remain;
  When the next comes, I'll charm thee thus again.

O come, thou *Goddess* of my rural Song,
And bring thy Daughter, calm *Content*, along,
Dame of the ruddy Cheek and laughing Eye,
From whose bright Presence Clouds of Sorrow fly:
For her I mow my Walks, I platt my Bow'rs,
Clip my low Hedges, and support my Flow'rs;
To welcome her, this Summer Seat I drest,
And here I court her when she comes to Rest;
When she from Exercise to learned Ease
Shall change again, and teach the Change to please.

Now Friends conversing my soft Hours refine,
And *Tully's Tusculum* revives in mine:
Now to grave Books I bid the Mind retreat,
And such as make me rather Good than Great;
Or o'er the Works of easy *Fancy* rove,
Where Flutes and Innocence amuse the Grove;
The native *Bard* that on *Sicilian* Plains

First sung the lowly Manners of the Swains,
Or *Maro's* Muse, that in the fairest Light
Paints rural Prospects and the Charms of Sight:
These soft *Amusements* bring *Content* along,
And *Fancy*, void of Sorrow, turns to *Song*.
  Here, beauteous *Health*, for all the Year remain;
  When the next comes, I'll charm thee thus again.

[1722]

JOHN PHILIPS

From *Cyder*,

Book II

  A thousand Accidents the Farmer's Hopes
Subvert, or checque, uncertain all his Toil,
'Till lusty Autumn's luke-warm Days, allay'd
With gentle Colds, insensibly confirm
His ripening Labours: Autumn to the Fruits
Earth's various Lap produces, Vigour gives
Equal, intenerating milky Grain,
Berries, and Sky-dy'd Plums, and what in Coat
Rough, or soft Rind, or bearded Husk, or Shell;
Fat *Olives*, and *Pistacio*'s fragrant Nut,
And the *Pine*'s tastful Apple: Autumn paints
Ausonian Hills with Grapes, whilst *English* Plains
Blush with pomaceous Harvests, breathing Sweets.
O let me now, when the kind early Dew
Unlocks th' embosom'd Odors, walk among
The well rang'd Files of Trees, whose full-ag'd Store

Diffuse *Ambrosial* Steams, than *Myrrh*, or *Nard*
More grateful, or perfuming flow'ry *Beane*!
Soft whisp'ring Airs, and the Larks mattin Song
Then woo to musing, and becalm the Mind
Perplex'd with irksome Thoughts. Thrice happy time,
Best Portion of the various Year, in which
Nature rejoyceth, smiling on her Works
Lovely, to full Perfection wrought! but ah,
Short are our Joys, and neighb'ring Griefs disturb
Our pleasant Hours. Inclement Winter dwells
Contiguous; forthwith frosty Blasts deface
The blithsome Year: Trees of their shrivel'd Fruits
Are widow'd, dreery Storms o'er all prevail.
Now, now's the time; e'er hasty Suns forbid
To work, disburthen thou thy sapless *Wood*
Of its rich Progeny; the turgid Fruit
Abounds with mellow Liquor; now exhort
Thy Hinds to exercise the pointed Steel
On the hard Rock, and give a wheely Form
To the expected Grinder: Now prepare
Materials for thy Mill, a sturdy Post
Cylindric, to support the Grinder's Weight
Excessive, and a flexile Sallow' entrench'd,
Rounding, capacious of the juicy Hord.
Nor must thou not be mindful of thy Press
Long e'er the Vintage; but with timely Care
Shave the Goat's shaggy Beard, least thou too late,
In vain should'st seek a Strainer, to dispart
The husky, terrene Dregs, from purer Must.
Be cautious next a proper Steed to find,
Whose Prime is past; the vigorous Horse disdains
Such servile Labours, or, if forc'd, forgets
His past Atchievements, and victorious Palms.
Blind *Bayard* rather, worn with Work, and Years,
Shall roll th' unweildy Stone; with sober Pace

He'll tread the circling Path 'till dewy Eve,
From early Day-spring, pleas'd to find his Age
Declining, not unuseful to his Lord.

Some, when the Press, by utmost Vigour screw'd,
Has drain'd the pulpous Mass, regale their Swine
With the dry Refuse; thou, more wise shalt steep
Thy Husks in Water, and again employ
The pondrous Engine. Water will imbibe
The small Remains of Spirit, and acquire
A vinous Flavour; this the Peasants blith
Will quaff, and whistle, as thy tinkling Team
They drive, and sing of *Fusca's* radiant Eyes,
Pleas'd with the medly Draught. Nor shalt thou now
Reject the *Apple-Cheese*, tho' quite exhaust;
Ev'n now 'twill cherish, and improve the Roots
Of sickly Plants; new Vigor hence convey'd
Will yield an Harvest of unusual Growth.
Such Profit springs from Husks discreetly us'd!

[1708]

ALEXANDER POPE

If we would copy Nature, it may be useful to take this Idea along with us, that Pastoral is an image of what they call the golden age. So that we are not to describe our shepherds as shepherds at this day really are, but as they may be conceived then to have been; when the best of men followed the employment. To carry this resemblance yet farther, it would not be amiss to give these shepherds some skill in astronomy, as far as it may be useful to that sort of life. And an air of piety to the Gods should shine through the Poem, which so visibly appears in all the works of antiquity: and it ought to preserve some relish of the old way of writing; the connections should be loose, the narrations and descriptions short, and the periods concise. Yet it is not sufficient that the sentences only be brief, the whole Eclogue should be so too. For we cannot suppose Poetry in those days to have been the business of men, but their recreation at vacant hours.

[A Discourse on Pastoral Poetry, 1717]

Summer, the Second Pastoral

Or, Alexis

To Dr Garth

A Shepherd's Boy (he seeks no better name)
Led forth his flocks along the silver Thame,
Where dancing sun-beams on the waters play'd,
And verdant alders form'd a quiv'ring shade.
Soft as he mourn'd, the streams forgot to flow,
The flocks around a dumb compassion show,
The Naiads wept in ev'ry wat'ry bow'r,
And Jove consented in a silent show'r.
Accept, O Garth, the Muse's early lays,
That adds this wreath of Ivy to thy Bays;
Hear what from Love unpractis'd hearts endure,
From Love, the sole disease thou canst not cure.
Ye shady beeches, and ye cooling streams,
Defence from Phœbus', not from Cupid's beams,
To you I mourn, nor to the deaf I sing,
The woods shall answer, and their echo ring.
The hills and rocks attend my doleful lay,
Why art thou prouder and more hard than they?
The bleating sheep with my complaints agree,

They parch'd with heat, and I inflam'd by thee.
The sultry Sirius burns the thirsty plains,
While in thy heart eternal winter reigns.
  Where stray ye Muses, in what lawn or grove,
While your Alexis pines in hopeless love?
In those fair fields where sacred Isis glides,
Or else where Cam his winding vales divides?
As in the crystal spring I view my face,
Fresh rising blushes paint the wat'ry glass;
But since those graces please thy eyes no more,
I shun the fountains which I sought before.
Once I was skill'd in ev'ry herb that grew,
And ev'ry plant that drinks the morning dew;
Ah wretched shepherd, what avails thy art,
To cure thy lambs, but not to heal thy heart!
  Let other swains attend the rural care,
Feed fairer flocks, or richer fleeces share:
But nigh yon' mountain let me tune my lays,
Embrace my Love, and bind my brows with bays.
That flute is mine which Colin's tuneful breath
Inspir'd when living, and bequeath'd in death;
He said; Alexis, take this pipe, the same
That taught the groves my Rosalinda's name:
But now the reeds shall hang on yonder tree,
For ever silent, since despis'd by thee.
Oh! were I made by some transforming pow'r
The captive bird that sings within thy bow'r!
Then might my voice thy list'ning ears employ,
And I those kisses he receives, enjoy.
  And yet my numbers please the rural throng,
Rough Satyrs dance, and Pan applauds the song:
The Nymphs, forsaking ev'ry cave and spring,
Their early fruit, and milk-white turtles bring;
Each am'rous nymph prefers her gifts in vain,
On you their gifts are all bestow'd again.

For you the swains the fairest flow'rs design,
And in one garland all their beauties join;
Accept the wreath which you deserve alone,
In whom all beauties are compriz'd in one.
  See what delights in sylvan scenes appear!
Descending Gods have found Elysium here.
In woods bright Venus with Adonis strayed,
And chaste Diana haunts the forest-shade.
Come, lovely nymph, and bless the silent hours,
When swains from sheering seek their nightly bow'rs;
When weary reapers quit the sultry field,
And crown'd with corn, their thanks to Ceres yield,
This harmless grove no lurking viper hides,
But in my breast the serpent Love abides.
Here bees from blossoms sip the rosy dew,
But your Alexis knows no sweets but you.
Oh deign to visit our forsaken seats,
The mossy fountains, and the green retreats!
Where'er you walk, cool gales shall fan the glade,
Trees, where you sit, shall crowd into a shade:
Where'er you tread, the blushing flow'rs shall rise,
And all things flourish where you turn your eyes.
Oh! how I long with you to pass my days,
Invoke the Muses, and resound your praise!
Your praise the birds shall chant in ev'ry grove,
And winds shall waft it to the pow'rs above.
But would you sing, and rival Orpheus' strain,
The wond'ring forests soon should dance again,
The moving mountains hear the pow'rful call,
And headlong streams hang list'ning in their fall!
  But see, the shepherds shun the noon-day heat,
The lowing herds to murm'ring brooks retreat,
To closer shades the panting flocks remove;
Ye Gods! and is there no relief for Love?
But soon the sun with milder rays descends

To the cool ocean, where his journey ends:
On me love's fiercer flames for ever prey,
By night he scorches, as he burns by day.

[1709]

If any are of opinion, that there is a necessity of admitting these classical legends into our serious compositions, in order to give them a more poetical turn; I would recommend to their consideration the pastorals of Mr [*Ambrose*] *Philips. One would have thought it impossible for this kind of poetry to have subsisted without fawns and satyrs, wood-nymphs and water-nymphs, with all the tribe of rural deities. But we see he has given a new life, and a more natural beauty to this way of writing by substituting in the place of these antiquated fables, the superstitious mythology which prevails among the shepherds of our own country.*

[Joseph Addison, *Spectator*, 1712]

AMBROSE PHILIPS

The Second Pastoral

THENOT, COLINET

THENOT:

Is it not Colinet I lonesome see,
Leaning with folded arms against the tree?
Or is it age, of late, bedims my sight? –
'Tis Colinet, indeed, in woful plight.
Thy cloudy look, why melting into tears,
Unseemly, now the sky so bright appears?

Why in this mournful manner art thou found,
Unthankful lad, when all things smile around?
Or hear'st not lark and linnet jointly sing,
Their notes blithe-warbling to salute the spring?

COLINET:

Though blithe their notes, not so my wayward fate;
Nor lark would sing, nor linnet, in my state.
Each creature, Thenot, to his task is born,
As they to mirth and music, I to mourn.
Waking, at midnight, I my woes renew,
My tears oft mingling with the falling dew.

THENOT:

Small cause, I ween, has lusty youth to plain:
Or, who may then, the weight of eld sustain,
When every slackening nerve begins to fail,
And the load presseth as our days prevail?
Yet, though with years my body downward tend,
As trees beneath their fruit, in autumn bend;
Spite of my snowy head, and icy veins,
My mind a cheerful temper still retains:
And why should man, mishap what will, repine,
Sour every sweet, and mix with tears his wine?
But tell me, then: it may relieve thy woe,
To let a friend thine inward ailment know.

COLINET:

Idly 'twill waste thee, Thenot, the whole day,
Shouldst thou give ear to all my grief can say.
Thine ewes will wander; and the heedless lambs,
In loud complaints, require their absent dams.

THENOT:

See Lightfoot, he shall tend them close: and I,
'Tween whiles, across the plain will glance mine eye.

COLINET:

Where to begin I know not, where to end:
Doth there one smiling hour my youth attend?
Though few my days, as well my follies show,
Yet are those days all clouded o'er with woe:
No happy gleam of sunshine doth appear,
My lowering sky, and wintry months, to cheer.
My piteous plight in yonder naked tree,
Which bears the thunder-scar, too plain I see:
Quite destitute it stands of shelter kind,
The mark of storms, and sport of every wind:
The riven trunk feels not the' approach of spring,
Nor birds among the leafless branches sing:
No more, beneath thy shade, shall shepherds throng,
With jocund tale, or pipe, or pleasing song.
Ill-fated tree! and more ill-fated I!
From thee, from me, alike the shepherds fly.

THENOT:

Sure thou in hapless hour of time wast born,
When blighting mildews spoil the rising corn,
Or blasting winds o'er blossom'd hedge-rows pass,
To kill the promised fruits, and scorch the grass,
Or when the moon, by wizard charm'd, foreshows,
Blood-stain'd in foul eclipse, impending woes.
Untimely born, ill-luck betides thee still.

COLINET:

And can there, Thenot, be a greater ill!

THENOT:

Nor fox, nor wolf, nor rot among our sheep,
From this good shepherd's care his flock may keep:
Against ill-luck, alas! all forecast fails;
Nor toil by day, nor watch by night, avails.

COLINET:

Ah me, the while! ah me, the luckless day!
Ah, luckless lad! befits me more to say.
Unhappy hour! when, fresh in youthful bud,
I left, Sabrina fair, thy silvery flood.
Ah, silly I! more silly than my sheep,
Which on thy flowery banks I wont to keep.
Sweet are thy banks! Oh, when shall I, once more,
With ravish'd eyes review thine amell'd shore!
When in the crystal of thy water, scan
Each feature faded, and my colour wan?
When shall I see my hut, the small abode
Myself did raise, and cover o'er with sod?
Small though it be, a mean and humble cell,
Yet is there room for peace and me to dwell.

THENOT:

And what enticement charm'd thee, far away
From thy loved home, and led thy heart astray?

COLINET:

A lewd desire, strange lads and swains to know:
Ah, God! that ever I should covet woe!
With wandering feet unbless'd, and fond of fame,
I sought I know not what besides a name.

THENOT:

Or sooth to say, didst thou not hither roam
In search of grains more plenty than at home?
A rolling-stone is, ever, bare of moss;
And to their cost, green years old proverbs cross.

COLINET:

Small need there was, in random search of gain,
To drive my pining flock athwart the plain,
To distant Cam. Fine gain at length, I trow,
To hoard up to myself such deal of woe!

My sheep quite spent, through travel and ill-fare,
And, like their keeper, ragged grown and bare;
The damp, cold greensward, for my nightly bed,
And some slant willow's trunk to rest my head.
Hard is to bear of pinching cold the pain;
And hard is want to the unpractised swain:
But neither want, nor pinching cold, is hard,
To blasting storms of calumny compared!
Unkind as hail it falls: the pelting shower
Destroys the tender herb, and budding flower.

THENOT:

Slander, we shepherds count the vilest wrong:
And what wounds sorer than an evil tongue?

COLINET:

Untoward lads, the wanton imps of spite,
Make mock of all the ditties I indite.
In vain, O Colinet, thy pipe, so shrill,
Charms every vale, and gladdens every hill;
In vain thou seek'st the coverings of the grove,
In the cool shade to sing the pains of love:
Sing what thou wilt, ill-nature will prevail;
And every elf hath skill enough to rail.
But yet, though poor and artless be my vein,
Menalcas seems to like my simple strain:
And while that he delighteth in my song,
Which to the good Menalcas doth belong,
Nor night, nor day, shall my rude music cease;
I ask no more, so I Menalcas please.

THENOT:

Menalcas, lord of these fair fertile plains,
Preserves the sheep, and o'er the shepherds reigns:
For him our yearly wakes and feasts we hold,
And choose the fairest firstling from the fold:

He, good to all who good deserve, shall give
Thy flock to feed, and thee at ease to live;
Shall curb the malice of unbridled tongues,
And bounteously reward thy rural songs.

COLINET:

First, then, shall lightsome birds forget to fly,
The briny ocean turn to pastures dry,
And every rapid river cease to flow,
Ere I unmindful of Menalcas grow.

THENOT:

This night thy care with me forget; and fold
Thy flock with mine, to ward the' injurious cold.
New milk, and clouted cream, mild cheese and curd,
With some remaining fruit of last year's hoard,
Shall be our evening fare; and for the night,
Sweet herbs and moss, which gentle sleep invite:
And now behold the sun's departing ray,
O'er yonder hill, the sign of ebbing day:
With songs the jovial hinds return from plough;
And unyoked heifers, loitering homeward, low.

[1708]

The Fifth Pastoral

CUDDY:

In rural strains we first our music try,
And, bashful, into woods and thickets fly,
Mistrusting then our skill; yet if through time
Our voice, improving, gain a pitch sublime,
Thy growing virtues, Sackville, shall engage
My riper verse, and more aspiring age.
  The sun, now mounted to the noon of day,
Began to shoot direct his burning ray;

When, with the flocks, their feeders sought the shade
A venerable oak wide-spreading made:
What should they do to pass the loitering time?
As fancy led, each form'd his tale in rhyme:
And some the joys, and some the pains of love,
And some to set out strange adventures, strove;
The trade of wizards some, and Merlin's skill,
And whence, to charms, such empire o'er the will.
Then, Cuddy last (who Cuddy can excel
In neat device?) his tale began to tell.
'When shepherds flourish'd in Eliza's reign,
There lived in high repute a jolly swain,
Young Colin Clout*; who well could pipe and sing,
And by his notes invite the lagging spring.
He, as his custom was, at leisure laid
In woodland bower, without a rival play'd,
Soliciting his pipe to warble clear,
Enchantment sweet as ever wont to hear
Belated wayfarers, from wake or fair
Detain'd by music, hovering on in air:
Drawn by the magic of the' enticing sound,
What troops of mute admirers flock'd around!
The steerlings left their food; and creatures, wild
By nature form'd, insensibly grew mild.
He makes the gathering birds about him throng,
And loads the neighbouring branches with his song.
There, with the crowd, a nightingale of fame,
Jealous, and fond of praise, to listen came:
She turn'd her ear, and pause by pause, with pride,
Like echo to the shepherd's pipe replied.
The shepherd heard with wonder, and again,
To try her more, renew'd his various strain:
To all the various strain she plies her throat,
And adds peculiar grace to every note.

* The reference is to Spenser's Colin.

If Colin, in complaining accent grieve,
Or brisker motion to his measure give,
If gentle sounds he modulate, or strong,
She, not a little vain, repeats the song:
But so repeats, that Colin half-despised
His pipe and skill, around the country prized;
"And sweetest songster of the winged kind,
What thanks, (said he) what praises, shall I find
To equal thy melodious voice? In thee
The rudeness of my rural fife I see;
From thee I learn no more to vaunt my skill."
Aloft in air she sat, provoking still
The vanquish'd swain. Provoked, at last, he strove
To show the little minstrel of the grove
His utmost powers, determined once to try
How art, exerting, might with nature vie;
For vie could none with either in their part,
With her in nature, nor with him in art.
He draws in breath, his rising breath to fill:
Throughout the wood his pipe is heard to shrill.
From note to note, in haste, his fingers fly;
Still more and more the numbers multiply:
And now they trill, and now they fall and rise,
And swift and slow they change with sweet surprise.
Attentive she doth scarce the sounds retain:
But to herself first cons the puzzling strain,
And tracing, heedful, note by note repays
The shepherd in his own harmonious lays,
Through every changing cadence runs at length,
And adds in sweetness what she wants in strength.
Then Colin threw his fife disgraced aside,
While she loud triumph sings, proclaiming wide
Her mighty conquest, and within her throat
Twirls many a wild unimitable note,
To foil her rival. What could Colin more?

A little harp of maple ware he bore:
The little harp was old, but newly strung,
Which, usual, he across his shoulders hung.
"Now take, delightful bird, my last farewell,
(He said) and learn from hence thou dost excel
No trivial artist!" and anon he wound
The murmuring strings, and order'd every sound;
Then earnest to his instrument he bends,
And both hands pliant on the strings extends;
His touch the strings obey, and various move,
The lower answering still to those above:
His fingers, restless, traverse to and fro,
As in pursuit of harmony they go:
Now, lightly skimming, o'er the strings they pass,
Like winds which gently brush the plying grass,
While melting airs arise at their command:
And now, laborious, with a weighty hand
He sinks into the cords with solemn pace,
To give the swelling tones a bolder grace;
And now the left, and now by turns the right,
Each other chase, harmonious both in flight:
Then his whole fingers blend a swarm of sounds,
Till the sweet tumult through the harp rebounds.
Cease, Colin, cease, thy rival cease to vex;
The mingling notes, alas! her ear perplex:
She warbles, diffident, in hope and fear,
And hits imperfect accents here and there,
And fain would utter forth some double tone,
When soon she falters, and can utter none:
Again she tries, and yet again she fails;
For still the harp's united power prevails:
Then Colin play'd again, and playing sung:
She, with the fatal love of glory stung,
Hears all in pain: her heart begins to swell:
In piteous notes she sighs, in notes which tell

Her bitter anguish: he still singing plies
His limber joints: her sorrows higher rise.
How shall she bear a conqueror, who, before,
No equal through the grove in music bore?
She droops, she hangs her flagging wings, she moans,
And fetcheth from her breast melodious groans.
Oppress'd with grief at last too great to quell,
Down, breathless, on the guilty harp she fell.
Then Colin loud lamented o'er the dead,
And unavailing tears profusely shed,
And broke his wicked strings, and cursed his skill;
And best to make atonement for the ill,
If, for such ill, atonement might be made,
He builds her tomb beneath a laurel shade
Then adds a verse, and sets with flowers the ground,
And makes a fence of winding osiers round.
"A verse and tomb is all I now can give;
And here thy name, at least, (he said) shall live".'
  Thus ended Cuddy with the setting sun,
And, by his tale, unenvied praises won.

[1708]

Pastoral Poetry . . . transports us into a kind of Fairy-Land . . . It is a Dream. 'Tis a Vision, which we wish may be real, and we believe that it is true.

[Thomas Tickell, *Guardian*, 22, 1713]

The Italians *and* French *being dispatched, I come now to the* English, *whom I shall treat with such Meekness as becomes a good Patriot; and shall so far recommend this our Island as a proper Scene for Pastoral under certain Regulations, as will satisfie the courteous Reader that I am in the Landed Interest.*

I must in the first place observe, that our Countrymen have so good an Opinion of the Ancients, and think so modestly of themselves, that the generality of Pastoral Writers have either stolen all from the Greeks *and* Romans, *or so servilely imitated their Manners and Customs, as makes them very ridiculous. In looking over some* English *Pastorals a few Days ago, I perused at least fifty lean Flocks, and reckoned up an hundred left-handed Ravens, besides blasted Oaks, withering Meadows, and weeping Deities. Indeed most of the occasional Pastorals we have, are built upon one and the same Plan. A Shepherd asks his Fellow, why he is so pale, if his favourite Sheep hath strayed, if his Pipe be broken, or* Phyllis *unkind? He answers, None of these Misfortunes have befallen him, but one much greater, for* Damon *(or sometimes the God* Pan*) is dead. This immediately causes the other to make Complaints, and call upon the lofty Pines and Silver Streams to join in the Lamentation. While he goes on, his Friend interrupts him, and tells him that* Damon *lives, and shows him a Track of Light in the Skies to confirm it; then invites him to Chestnuts and Cheese. Upon this Scheme most of the noble Families in* Great Britain *have been comforted; nor can I meet with any Right Honourable Shepherd that doth not die and live again, after the manner of the aforesaid* Damon.

[Thomas Tickell, *Guardian*, 30, 1713]

JOHN GAY

Great marvell hath it been (and that not unworthily) to diverse worthy wits, that in this our Island of Britain, *in all rare sciences so greatly abounding, more especially in all kinds of Poesie highly flourishing, no* Poet *(though otherways of notable cunning in roundelays) hath hit on the right simple Eclogue after the true ancient guise of* Theocritus, *before this mine attempt.*

Other Poet travailing in this plain high-way of Pastoral know I none. Yet, certes, such it behoveth a Pastoral to be, as nature in the country affordeth; and the manners also meetly copied from the rustical folk therein. In this also my love to my native country Britain *much pricketh me forward, to describe aright the manners of our own honest and laborious plough-men, in no wise sure more unworthy a* British *Poet's imitation, than those of* Sicily *or* Arcadie; *albeit, not ignorant I am, what a rout and rabblement of critical gallimawfy hath been made of late days by certain young men of insipid delicacy, concerning, I wist not what,* Golden Age, *and other outragious conceits, to which they would confine Pastoral. Whereof, I avow, I account nought at all, knowing no age so justly to be instiled* Golden, *as this of our* Soveraign Lady Queen ANNE.

[*The Shepherd's Week,* from 'The Proeme to the Courteous Reader', 1714]

Tuesday; or, *The Ditty*
From *The Shepherd's Week*

MARIAN

Young *Colin Clout*, a lad of peerless meed,
Full well could dance, and deftly tune the reed;
In ev'ry wood his carrols sweet were known,
At ev'ry wake his nimble feats were shown.
When in the ring the rustick routs he threw,
The damsels pleasures with his conquests grew;
Or when aslant the cudgel threats his head,
His danger smites the breast of ev'ry maid,
But chief of *Marian. Marian* lov'd the swain,
The Parson's maid, and neatest of the plain.
Marian, that soft could stroke the udder'd cow,
Or lessen with her sieve the barley mow;
Marbled with sage the hardn'ing cheese she press'd,
And yellow butter *Marian*'s skill confess'd;

But *Marian* now devoid of country cares,
Nor yellow butter nor sage cheese prepares.
For yearning love the witless maid employs,
And *Love*, say swains, *all busie heed destroys.*
Colin makes mock at all her piteous smart,
A lass, who *Cic'ly* hight, had won his heart,
Cic'ly the western lass who tends the kee,
The rival of the Parson's maid was she.
In dreary shade now *Marian* lyes along,
And mixt with sighs thus wails in plaining song.
  Ah woful day! ah woful noon and morn!
When first by thee my younglings white were shorn,
Then first, I ween, I cast a lover's eye,
My sheep were silly, but more silly I.
Beneath the shears they felt no lasting smart,
They lost but fleeces while I lost a heart.
  Ah *Colin*! canst thou leave thy Sweetheart true!
What I have done for thee will *Cic'ly* do?
Will she thy linnen wash or hosen darn,
And knit thee gloves made of her own-spun yarn?
Will she with huswife's hand provide thy meat,
And ev'ry *Sunday* morn thy neckcloth plait?
Which o'er thy kersey doublet spreading wide,
In service-time drew *Cic'ly*'s eyes aside.
  Where-e'er I gad I cannot hide my care,
My new disasters in my look appear.
White as the curd my ruddy cheek is grown,
So thin my features that I'm hardly known;
Our neighbours tell me oft in joking talk
Of ashes, leather, oatmeal, bran and chalk;
Unwittingly of *Marian* they devine,
And wist not that with thoughtful love I pine.
Yet *Colin Clout*, untoward shepherd swain,
Walks whistling blithe, while pitiful I plain.
  Whilom with thee 'twas *Marian*'s dear delight

To moil all day, and merry-make at night.
If in the soil you guide the crooked share,
Your early breakfast is my constant care.
And when with even hand you strow the grain,
I fright the thievish rooks from off the plain,
In misling days when I my thresher heard,
With nappy beer I to the barn repair'd;
Lost in the musick of the whirling flail,
To gaze on thee I left the smoaking pail;
In harvest when the Sun was mounted high,
My leathern bottle did thy drought supply;
When-e'er you mow'd I follow'd with the rake,
And have full oft been sun-burnt for thy sake;
When in the welkin gath'ring show'rs were seen,
I lagg'd the last with *Colin* on the green;
And when at eve returning with thy carr,
Awaiting heard the gingling bells from far;
Strait on the fire the sooty pot I plac't,
To warm thy broth I burnt my hands for haste.
When hungry thou stood'st *staring, like an Oaf*,
I slic'd the luncheon from the barly loaf,
With crumbled bread I thicken'd well thy mess.
Ah, love me more, or love thy pottage less!
  Last *Friday*'s eve, when as the sun was set,
I, near yon stile, three sallow gypsies met.
Upon my hand they cast a poring look,
Bid me beware, and thrice their heads they shook,
They said that many crosses I must prove,
Some in my worldly gain, but most in love.
Next morn I miss'd three hens and our old cock,
And off the hedge two pinners and a smock.
I bore these losses with a christian mind,
And no mishaps could feel, while thou wert kind.
But since, alas! I grew my *Colin*'s scorn,
I've known no pleasure, night, or noon, or morn.

Help me, ye gypsies, bring him home again,
And to a constant lass give back her swain.
Have I not sate with thee full many a night,
When dying embers were our only light,
When ev'ry creature did in slumbers lye,
Besides our cat, my *Colin Clout*, and I?
No troublous thoughts the cat or *Colin* move,
While I alone am kept awake by love.
Remember, *Colin*, when at last year's wake,
I bought the costly present for thy sake,
Couldst thou spell o'er the posie on thy knife,
And with another change thy state of life?
If thou forget'st, I wot, I can repeat,
My memory can tell the verse so sweet.
As this is grav'd upon this knife of thine,
So is thy image on this heart of mine.
But woe is me! Such presents luckless prove,
For *Knives*, they tell me, *always sever Love.*
Thus *Marian* wail'd, her eyes with tears brimfull,
When Goody *Dobbins* brought her cow to bull.
With apron blue to dry her tears she sought,
Then saw the cow well serv'd, and took a groat.

[1714]

To the most Honourable the Earl of OXFORD, The Lord High Treasurer

The Epigrammatical Petition of your Lordship's most humble servant, John Gay

I'm no more to converse with the swains,
But go where fine people resort;
One can live without money on plains,
But never without it at court.

Yet if when with swains I did gambol,
  I array'd me in silver and blue,
When abroad and in courts I shall ramble,
  Pray, my Lord, how much money will do?

[1720]

The Birth of the Squire

An Eclogue in Imitation of the Pollio *of* Virgil

  Ye sylvan Muses, loftier strains recite,
Not all in shades, and humble cotts delight.
Hark! the bells ring; along the distant grounds
The driving gales convey the swelling sounds;
Th' attentive swain, forgetful of his work,
With gaping wonder, leans upon his fork.
What sudden news alarms the waking morn?
To the glad Squire a hopeful heir is born.
Mourn, mourn, ye stags; and all ye beasts of chase,
This hour destruction brings on all your race:
See the pleas'd tenants duteous off'rings bear,
Turkeys and geese and grocer's sweetest ware;
With the new health the pond'rous tankard flows,
And old *October* reddens ev'ry nose.
Beagles and spaniels round his cradle stand,
Kiss his moist lip and gently lick his hand;
He joys to hear the shrill horn's ecchoing sounds,
And learns to lisp the names of all the hounds.
With frothy ale to make his cup o'er-flow,
Barley shall in paternal acres grow;
The bee shall sip the fragrant dew from flow'rs,
To give metheglin[1] for his morning hours;
For him the clustring hop shall climb the poles,
And his own orchard sparkle in his bowles.

[1] mead

His Sire's exploits he now with wonder hears,
The monstrous tales indulge his greedy ears;
How when youth strung his nerves and warm'd his veins,
He rode the mighty *Nimrod* of the plains:
He leads the staring infant through the hall,
Points out the horny spoils that grace the wall;
Tells, how this stag thro' three whole Countys fled,
What rivers swam, where bay'd, and where he bled.
Now he the wonders of the fox repeats,
Describes the desp'rate chase, and all his cheats;
How in one day beneath his furious speed,
He tir'd seven coursers of the fleetest breed;
How high the pale he leapt, how wide the ditch,
When the hound tore the haunches of the witch!
These stories which descend from son to son,
The forward boy shall one day make his own.
Ah, too fond mother, think the time draws nigh,
That calls the darling from thy tender eye;
How shall his spirit brook the rigid rules,
And the long tyranny of grammar schools?
Let younger brothers o'er dull authors plod,
Lash'd into *Latin* by the tingling rod;
No, let him never feel that smart disgrace:
Why should he wiser prove than all his race?
When rip'ning youth with down o'ershades his chin,
And ev'ry female eye incites to sin;
The milk-maid (thoughtless of her future shame)
With smacking lip shall raise his guilty flame;
The dairy, barn, the hay-loft and the grove
Shall oft' be conscious of their stolen love.
But think, *Priscilla*, on that dreadful time,
When pangs and watry qualms shall own thy crime;
How wilt thou tremble when thy nipple's prest,
To see the white drops bathe thy swelling breast!
Nine moons shall publickly divulge thy shame,

And the young Squire forestall a father's name.
When twice twelve times the reaper's sweeping hand
With levell'd harvests has bestrown the land,
On fam'd *St. Hubert*'s feast, his winding horn
Shall cheer the joyful hound and wake the morn:
This memorable day his eager speed
Shall urge with bloody heel the rising steed.
O check the foamy bit, nor tempt thy fate,
Think on the murders of a five-bar gate!
Yet prodigal of life, the leap he tries,
Low in the dust his groveling honour lies,
Headlong he falls, and on the rugged stone
Distorts his neck, and cracks the collar bone;
O ventr'ous youth, thy thirst of game allay,
Mayst thou survive the perils of this day!
He shall survive; and in late years be sent
To snore away Debates in *Parliament*.
The time shall come, when his more solid sense
With nod important shall the laws dispense;
A Justice with grave Justices shall sit,
He praise their wisdom, they admire his wit.
No greyhound shall attend the tenant's pace,
No rusty gun the farmer's chimney grace;
Salmons shall leave their covers void of fear,
Nor dread the thievish net or triple spear;
Poachers shall tremble at his awful name,
Whom vengeance now o'ertakes for murder'd game.
Assist me, *Bacchus*, and ye drunken Pow'rs,
To sing his friendships and his midnight hours!
Why dost thou glory in thy strength of beer,
Firm-cork'd, and mellow'd till the twentieth year;
Brew'd or when *Phœbus* warms the fleecy sign,
Or when his languid rays in *Scorpio* shine.
Think on the mischiefs which from hence have sprung!
It arms with curses dire the wrathful tongue;

Foul scandal to the lying lip affords,
And prompts the mem'ry with injurious words.
O where is wisdom, when by this o'erpower'd?
The State is censur'd, and the maid deflowr'd!
And wilt thou still, O Squire, brew ale so strong?
Hear then the dictates of prophetic song.
  Methinks I see him in his hall appear,
Where the long table floats in clammy beer,
'Midst mugs and glasses shatter'd o'er the floor,
Dead-drunk his servile crew supinely snore;
Triumphant, o'er the prostrate brutes he stands,
The mighty bumper trembles in his hands;
Boldly he drinks, and like his glorious Sires,
In copious gulps of potent ale expires.

[1720]

ALEXANDER POPE

Ode on Solitude

Happy the man, whose wish and care
  A few paternal acres bound,
Content to breathe his native air,
    In his own ground.

Whose herds with milk, whose fields with bread,
  Whose flocks supply him with attire,
Whose trees in summer yield him shade,
    In winter fire.

Blest, who can unconcern'dly find
Hours, days, and years slide soft away,
In health of body, peace of mind,
Quiet by day,

Sound sleep by night; study and ease,
Together mixt; sweet recreation,
And innocence, which most does please
With meditation.

Thus let me live, unseen, unknown;
Thus unlamented let me die;
Steal from the world, and not a stone
Tell where I lie.

[1717]

From *Windsor Forest*

The Groves of Eden, vanish'd now so long,
Live in description, and look green in song:
These, were my breast inspir'd with equal flame,
Like them in beauty, should be like in fame.
Here hills and vales, the woodland and the plain,
Here earth and water seem to strive again,
Not Chaos-like together crush'd and bruis'd,
But, as the world, harmoniously confus'd:
Where order in variety we see,
And where, tho' all things differ, all agree.
Here waving groves a chequer'd scene display,
And part admit, and part exclude the day;
As some coy nymph her lover's warm address
Nor quite indulges, nor can quite repress.
There, interspers'd in lawns and op'ning glades,
Thin trees arise that shun each other's shades.
Here in full light the russet plains extend:

There wrapt in clouds the blueish hills ascend.
Ev'n the wild heath displays her purple dyes,
And 'midst the desert fruitful fields arise,
That crown'd with tufted trees and springing corn,
Like verdant isles the sable waste adorn.
Let India boast her plants, nor envy we
The weeping amber or the balmy tree,
While by our oaks the precious loads are born,
And realms commanded which those trees adorn.
Not proud Olympus yields a nobler sight,
Tho' Gods assembled grace his tow'ring height,
Than what more humble mountains offer here,
Where, in their blessings, all those Gods appear.
See Pan with flocks, with fruits Pomona crown'd,
Here blushing Flora paints th'enamel'd ground,
Here Ceres' gifts in waving prospect stand,
And nodding tempt the joyful reaper's hand;
Rich Industry sits smiling on the plains,
And peace and plenty tell, a STUART reigns.

[1713]

From *An Essay on Man*, Epistle I

Ask for what end the heav'nly bodies shine,
Earth for whose use? Pride answers, ''Tis for mine:
For me kind Nature wakes her genial pow'r,
Suckles each herb, and spreads out ev'ry flow'r;
Annual for me, the grape, the rose renew
The juice nectareous, and the balmy dew;
For me, the mine a thousand treasures brings;
For me, health gushes from a thousand springs;
Seas roll to waft me, suns to light me rise;
My foot-stool earth, my canopy the skies.'

[1733]

AARON HILL

From *A Dialogue between Damon and Philemon Concerning the Preference of a Town Life to a Country Life*

PHILEMON:

If truth, dear swain! with freedom might advise,
Thou may'st be happy, for I know thee wise;
Quit for a trial once, this meagre air,
And all impartial to thy friend repair.
Then wilt thou ever fix'd with me remain,
And envious rustics tempt thee back in vain.
Thus some raw youth, on a domestic shore,
With terror hears th' encircling surges roar;
Trembling, he sees the threat'ning tempest roll,
And ev'ry rising billow lifts his soul:
But when a riper age has call'd him o'er,
To try the pleasures of some foreign shore,
Sad he returns, nor will at home remain,
But pants to taste abandon'd joys again.
Your muse, in vain, of boasted prospect sings;
Your flow'ry meadows, and your murm'ring springs:
Poor short-liv'd scenes of shadow-skimming joy,
Whose pride a change of season can destroy!
The rising floods your valleys over-flow,
And winter spreads your hills, with sheets of snow:
Autumnal winds strip bare your gawdy trees,
And cold December nights your purling currents freeze.
But we, more happy, constant blessings share,
Nor hang our comforts in the changeful air:
Our diff'ring seasons have their different sport,
The park, the play, the tavern, and the court!
Our rolling hours can sweetly wear away,

The utmost moments of the longest day:
When tir'd with business, we would care decline,
We drown the weight of thought in gen'rous wine:
By that made sprightly, to the park repair,
And eloquently silent, court the fair:
Thence, to the theatre, inspir'd we move,
And feast at once, on mingled wit and love!
These and a thousand nameless new delights,
Make our days fruitful, and enrich our nights;
While you, 'midst few repeated pastimes live,
Nor ever taste the joy which changing pleasures give.

DAMON:

'Tis true, Philemon, our autumnal storms
Disrobe our trees, and strip their quiv'ring forms:
'Tis true, our liveliest beauties are but short,
Short as the joys which recommend your court:
But these new charms, in following springs obtain,
While those, once set, shall never rise again.
In vain your plays allure; all there, that's fine,
Does faintly to our artless beauties shine.
Their scenes as grossly imitate our groves,
As their lewd actors our soft past'ral loves.
Frequent their comedies to please the town,
Descend to borrow, hence, some wit-grac'd clown.
The park, their folly's larger stage charms less;
An ill-mix'd scene of noise, grimace, and dress!
The court, 'tis true, shines out with tempting state;
For ruin, angling there, to catch the great,
Hides the hook, wisely, with attractive bait!
The joy which wine can give, like smoky fires,
Obscure their sight whose fancy it inspires.
Thus, like old Sodom's fruit, that seat of sin,
Your pleasures, fair without, are worms and dust within.

PHILEMON:

Assist me, sacred sisters! aid my voice,
And guide lost Damon to a nobler choice!
The crowds of rustics, who to town repair,
And quit, for vulgar hopes, their native air,
Are gross-form'd vapours heavily exhal'd,
Where profit's sunny influence has prevail'd;
But those alone, my friend, are beams for me
Which draw such limpid innocence as thee!
What pleasures reap you from the unprun'd field,
Which cities cannot more completely yield?
If, to some peace-blest cot we would retire,
An hour's short journey crowns the soft desire:
There, strait we taste the sweets so prais'd by you,
And then return to those you never knew!
Ev'n heav'n approves not solitude, else why
Did his great will direct society?
Why did the ancients else to towns repair,
And quit, for houses, tents and open air?
Would the great Hebrew favourite of Heav'n,
To whom both pow'r and wisdom's charms were giv'n,
Would he on Sion's hills have fix'd his seat,
Had rural pleasures been, in truth, most sweet?

[1753]

A Receipt for a Pastoral Elegy

Take Damon and Thyrsis, both of which Virgil will lend you with all his Heart; put them in a Cave together; be sure it is garnish'd well with Cypress, and don't forget a murmuring Stream, which may help you to a Rhyme or Smile upon Occasion. Let them lament Daphnis or Pastorella; or take any other Name, which you think will run off smoothly in your Verse . . . Blast an old Oak or two, wither your Flowers secundum Artem, season it with Prodigies quantum sufficit and 'twill make an excellent Elegy.

[*London Magazine*, 1738]

JONATHAN SWIFT

A Pastoral Dialogue

DERMOT, SHEELAH

A nymph and Swain, *Sheelah* and *Dermot* hight,
Who wont to weed the Court of *Gosford Knight*,
While each with stubbed Knife remov'd the Roots
That rais'd between the Stones their daily Shoots;
As at their Work they sate in counterview,
With mutual Beauty smit, their Passion grew.
Sing heavenly Muse in sweetly flowing Strain,
The soft Endearments of the Nymph and Swain.

DERMOT:

My Love to *Sheelah* is more firmly fixt
Than strongest Weeds that grow these Stones betwixt:
My Spud these Nettles from the Stones can part,
No Knife so keen to weed thee from my Heart.

SHEELAH:

My Love for gentle *Dermot* faster grows
Than yon tall Dock that rises to thy Nose.
Cut down the Dock, 'twill sprout again: but O!
Love rooted out, again will never grow.

DERMOT:

No more that Bry'r thy tender Leg shall rake:
(I spare the Thistle for Sir *Arthur*'s sake.)

Sharp are the Stones, take thou this rushy Matt;
The hardest Bum will bruise with sitting squat.

SHEELAH:

Thy Breeches torn behind, stand gaping wide;
This Petticoat shall save thy dear Back-side;
Nor need I blush, although you feel it wet;
Dermot, I vow, 'tis nothing else but Sweat.

DERMOT:

At an old stubborn Root I chanc'd to tug,
When the Dean threw me this Tobacco-plug:
A longer half-p'orth never did I see;
This, dearest *Sheelah*, thou shalt share with me.

SHEELAH:

In at the Pantry-door this Morn I slipt,
And from the Shelf a charming Crust I whipt:
Dennis was out, and I got hither safe;
And thou, my dear, shalt have the bigger half.

DERMOT:

When you saw *Tady* at long-bullets play,
You sat and lows'd him all the Sun-shine Day.
How could you, *Sheelah*, listen to his Tales,
Or crack such Lice as his betwixt your Nails?

SHEELAH:

When you with *Oonah* stood behind a Ditch,
I peept, and saw you kiss the dirty Bitch.
Dermot, how could you touch those nasty Sluts!
I almost wisht this Spud were in your Guts.

DERMOT:

If *Oonah* once I kiss'd, forbear to chide:
Her Aunt's my Gossip by my Father's Side:
But, if I ever touch her Lips again,
May I be doom'd for Life to weed in Rain.

SHEELAH:

Dermot, I swear, tho' *Tady's* Locks could hold
Ten thousand Lice, and ev'ry Louse was gold,
Him on my Lap you never more should see;
Or may I loose my Weeding-knife – and Thee.

DERMOT:

O, could I earn for thee, my lovely Lass,
A pair of Brogues to bear thee dry to Mass!
But see, where *Norah* with the Sowins[1] comes –
Then let us rise, and rest our weary Bums.

[1] a bran mash

[1732]

ALEXANDER POPE

From *An Epistle to Bathurst*

Old Cotta sham'd his fortune and his birth,
Yet was not Cotta void of wit or worth:
What tho' (the use of barb'rous spits forgot)
His kitchen vy'd in coolness with his grot?
His court with nettles, moats with cresses stor'd,
With soups unbought and sallads blest his board.
If Cotta liv'd on pulse, it was no more
Than Bramins, Saints, and Sages did before;
To cram the Rich was prodigal expence,
And who would take the Poor from Providence?
Like some lone Chartreux stands the good old Hall,
Silence without, and Fasts within the wall,
No rafter'd roofs with dance and tabor sound,
No noontide-bell invites the country round;
Tenants with sighs the smoakless tow'rs survey,
And turn th' unwilling steeds another way:

Benighted wanderers, the forest o'er,
Curse the sav'd candle, and unop'ning door;
While the gaunt mastiff growling at the gate,
Affrights the beggar whom he longs to eat.
Not so his Son, he mark'd this oversight,
And then mistook reverse of wrong for right.
(For what to shun will no great knowledge need,
But what to follow, is a task indeed.)
What slaughter'd hecatombs, what floods of wine,
Fill the capacious Squire, and deep Divine!
Yet no mean motive this profusion draws,
His oxen perish in his country's cause;
'Tis *George* and *Liberty* that crowns the cup,
And Zeal for that great House which eats him up.
The woods recede around the naked seat,
The Sylvans groan – no matter – for the Fleet:
Next goes his Wool – to clothe our valiant bands,
Last, for his Country's love, he sells his Lands.
To town he comes, completes the nation's hope,
And heads the bold Train-bands, and burns a Pope.
And shall not Britain now reward his toils,
Britain, that pays her Patriots with her Spoils?
In vain at Court the Bankrupt pleads his cause,
His thankless Country leaves him to her Laws.
The Sense to value Riches with the Art
T'enjoy them, and the Virtue to impart,
Not meanly, nor ambitiously pursu'd,
Not sunk by sloth, nor rais'd by servitude;
To balance Fortune by a just expense,
Join with Oeconomy, Magnificence;
With Splendour, Charity; with Plenty, Health;
Oh teach us, *Bathurst*! yet unspoil'd by wealth!
That secret rare, between th' extremes to move
Of mad Good-nature, and of mean self-love.

[1733]

From *An Epistle to Burlington*

At Timon's Villa let us pass a day,
Where all cry out, 'What sums are thrown away!'
So proud, so grand, of that stupendous air,
Soft and Agreeable come never there.
Greatness, with Timon, dwells in such a draught
As brings all Brobdignag before your thought.
To compass this, his building is a Town,
His pond an Ocean, his parterre a Down:
Who but must laugh, the Master when he sees?
A puny insect, shiv'ring at a breeze.
Lo! what huge heaps of littleness around!
The whole, a labour'd Quarry above ground.
Two Cupids squirt before: a Lake behind
Improves the keenness of the Northern wind.
His Gardens next your admiration call,
On ev'ry side you look, behold the Wall!
No pleasing Intricacies intervene,
No artful wildness to perplex the scene;
Grove nods at grove, each Alley has a brother,
And half the platform just reflects the other.
The suff'ring eye inverted Nature sees,
Trees cut to Statues, Statues thick as trees,
With here a Fountain, never to be play'd,
And there a Summer-house, that knows no shade.
Here Amphitrite sails thro' myrtle bow'rs;
There Gladiators fight, or die, in flow'rs;
Un-water'd see the drooping sea-horse mourn,
And swallows roost in Nilus' dusty Urn.
My Lord advances with majestic mien,
Smit with the mighty pleasure, to be seen:
But soft – by regular approach – not yet –
First thro' the length of yon hot Terrace sweat,
And when up ten steep slopes you've dragg'd your thighs,

Just at his Study-door he'll bless your eyes.
  His Study! with what Authors is it stor'd?
In Books, not Authors, curious is my Lord;
To all their dated Backs he turns you round:
These Aldus printed, those Du Suëil has bound.
Lo some are Vellom, and the rest as good
For all his Lordship knows, but they are Wood.
For Locke or Milton 'tis in vain to look,
These shelves admit not any modern book.
  And now the Chapel's silver bell you hear,
That summons you to all the Pride of Pray'r:
Light quirks of Music, broken and uneven,
Make the soul dance upon a Jig to Heav'n.
On painted Cielings you devoutly stare,
Where sprawl the Saints of Verrio or Laguerre,
On gilded clouds in fair expansion lie,
And bring all Paradise before your eye.
To rest, the Cushion and soft Dean invite,
Who never mentions Hell to ears polite.
  But hark! the chiming Clocks to dinner call;
A hundred footsteps scrape the marble Hall:
The rich Buffet well-colour'd Serpents grace,
And gaping Tritons spew to wash your face.
Is this a dinner? this a Genial room?
No, 'tis a Temple, and a Hecatomb,
A solemn Sacrifice, perform'd in state,
You drink by measure, and to minutes eat.
So quick retires each flying course, you'd swear
Sancho's dread Doctor and his Wand were there.
Between each Act the trembling salvers ring,
From soup to sweet-wine, and God bless the King.
In plenty starving, tantaliz'd in state,
And complaisantly help'd to all I hate,
Treated, caress'd, and tir'd, I take my leave,
Sick of his civil Pride from Morn to Eve;

I curse such lavish cost, and little skill,
And swear no Day was ever past so ill.*
  Yet hence the Poor are cloath'd, the Hungry fed;
Health to himself, and to his Infants bread
The Lab'rer bears: What his hard Heart denies,
His charitable Vanity supplies.
  Another age shall see the golden Ear
Imbrown the Slope, and nod on the Parterre,
Deep Harvests bury all his pride has plann'd,
And laughing Ceres re-assume the land.
  Who then shall grace, or who improve the Soil?
Who plants like Bathurst, or who builds like Boyle.
'Tis Use alone that sanctifies Expence,
And Splendor borrows all her rays from Sense.
  His Father's Acres who enjoys in peace,
Or makes his Neighbours glad, if he encrease;
Whose chearful Tenants bless their yearly toil,
Yet to their Lord owe more than to the soil;
Whose ample Lawns are not asham'd to feed
The milky heifer and deserving steed;
Whose rising Forests, not for pride or show,
But future Buildings, future Navies grow:
Let his plantations stretch from down to down,
First shade a Country, and then raise a Town.

[1731]

* Cf. 'To Penshurst', p. 150.

MATTHEW GREEN

From *The Spleen*

Forced by soft violence of prayer,
The blithsome goddess sooths my care;
I feel the deity inspire,
And thus she models my desire.
Two hundred pounds, half-yearly paid,
Annuity securely made,
A farm some twenty miles from town,
Small, tight, salubrious, and my own:
Two maids, that never saw the town,
A serving man not quite a clown;
A boy to help to tread the mow,
And drive, while t'other holds the plough;
A chief, of temper form'd to please,
Fit to converse, and keep the keys;
And better to preserve the peace,
Commission'd by the name of niece;
With understandings of a size
To think their master very wise.
May Heaven ('tis all I wish for) send
One genial room to treat a friend,
Where decent cupboard, little plate,
Display benevolence, not state.
And may my humble dwelling stand
Upon some chosen spot of land:
A pond before full to the brim,
Where cows may cool, and geese may swim;
Behind a green, like velvet neat,
Soft to the eye and to the feet;
Where odorous plants, in evening fair,
Breathe all around ambrosial air;

From Eurus, foe to kitchen ground,
Fenced by a slope with bushes crown'd,
Fit dwelling for the feather'd throng,
Who pay their quitrents with a song;
With opening views of hill and dale,
Which sense and fancy too regale,
Where the half-cirque, which vision bounds,
Like amphitheatre surrounds;
And woods, impervious to the breeze,
Thick phalanx of embodied trees,
From hills through plains in dusk array
Extended far, repel the day.

[1737]

WILLIAM SOMERVILLE

From *The Chase*, Book I

First let the kennel be the huntsman's care,
Upon some little eminence erect,
And fronting to the ruddy dawn; its courts
On either hand wide-opening to receive
The sun's all-cheering beams, when mild he shines,
And gilds the mountain tops. For much the pack
(Roused from their dark alcoves) delight to stretch,
And bask, in his invigorating ray:
Warn'd by the streaming light, and merry lark,
Forth rush the jolly clan; with tuneful throats
They carol loud, and in grand chorus join'd

Salute the new-born day. For not alone
The vegetable world, but men and brutes
Own his reviving influence, and joy
At his approach. Fountain of light! if chance
Some envious cloud veil thy refulgent brow,
In vain the Muse's aid; untouch'd, unstrung,
Lies my mute harp, and thy desponding bard
Sits darkly musing o'er the' unfinish'd lay.
   Let no Corinthian pillars prop the dome,
A vain expense, on charitable deeds
Better disposed, to clothe the tatter'd wretch
Who shrinks beneath the blast, to feed the poor
Pinch'd with afflictive want: for use, not state,
Gracefully plain, let each apartment rise.
O'er all let cleanliness preside, no scraps
Bestrew the pavement, and no half-pick'd bones,
To kindle fierce debate, or to disgust
That nicer sense, on which the sportsman's hope,
And all his future triumphs must depend.
Soon as the growling pack with eager joy
Have lapped their smoking viands, morn or eve,
From the full cistern lead the ductile streams,
To wash thy court, well-paved, nor spare thy pains,
For much to health will cleanliness avail.
Seek'st thou for hounds to climb the rocky steep,
And brush the' entangled covert, whose nice scent
O'er greasy fallows, and frequented roads
Can pick the dubious way? Banish far off
Each noisome stench, let no offensive smell
Invade thy wide enclosure, but admit
The nitrous air and purifying breeze.
   Water and shade no less demand thy care:
In a large square the' adjacent field enclose,
There plant in equal ranks the spreading elm,
Or fragrant lime; most happy thy design,

If at the bottom of thy spacious court,
A large canal, fed by the crystal brook,
From its transparent bosom shall reflect
Downward thy structure and inverted grove.
Here when the sun's too potent gleams annoy
The crowded kennel, and the drooping pack,
Restless and faint, loll their unmoisten'd tongues,
And drop their feeble tails; to cooler shades
Lead forth the panting tribe; soon shalt thou find
The cordial breeze their fainting hearts revive:
Tumultuous soon they plunge into the stream,
There lave their reeking sides, with greedy joy
Gulp down the flying wave, this way and that
From shore to shore they swim, while clamour loud
And wild uproar torments the troubled flood:
Then on the sunny bank they roll and stretch
Their dripping limbs, or else in wanton rings
Coursing around, pursuing and pursued,
The merry multitude disporting play.

[1735]

WILLIAM PATTISON

A Harvest Scene

Behold –
The *Green* Fields *Yellowing* into Corny Gold!
White o'er their Ranks, an Old Man half appears,
How hale he Looks, tho' hoar'd with seventy Years;
His Prospect mounts, slow-pac'd, he strives to climb,
And seems some antient Monument of Time;

Propt o'er his Staff the reverend Father stands,
And views Heaven's Blessings with up-lifted Hands;
Gleeful in Heart computes the Year's Increase,
And portions out, in Thought, his homely Race,
His homely Race before, his Hopes improve,
And labour in Obedience for his Love;
Sweepy they Cut, then Bind the Sheafy-Grain,
And bend beneath the Burthen of the Plain;
His chearful Eyes, with silent Praises crown
Their Toils, and Smile at Vigour once his own;
Till the Mid-Sun to second Nature's Call,
Noon-marks the distant Steeple's Ivy'd Wall,
Thence warn'd, he waves his Arms, with giddy Haste,
The circling Summons to a cool Repaste.

[1728]

WHIGS AND POST-AUGUSTANS

With the publication of James Thomson's *Seasons* in 1730, the nature of the Pastoral suddenly becomes a good deal less problematic, anyway at first sight; for now and then Thomson cheerfully and quite unambiguously presents the mid-eighteenth century in England as the Golden Age. There is no nostalgia in Thomson's Pastoral; his ideal is directly before his eyes, the successful, commercial, polished England of the Whig ministries and the advancing agricultural revolution. But this lack of nostalgia does not involve a lack of classical reference: the English Golden Age has more affinities to the age of Augustus than to the first, primitive Golden Age of Saturn, and the valley of the Thames becomes for Thomson a new Roman *campagna*, which flourishes in the certainty that history is progressive, and has no fear of a decay like that of post-Augustan Rome. The landscape is a perfect balance of cultivated field and ornamented park, the one paying for the other, the second dignifying the first. And Thomson never lets us forget that the prosperity of this British *campagna* is the gift of Industry and Commerce – is the result, that is, of the very labour the absence of which had seemed to all earlier writers the chief attraction of the Golden Age. The owners of the lands that Thomson describes are proud to live by the sweat of someone's brow, if not their own.

We might expect that this self-consciously modernized version of Pastoral would have led to something like a new naturalism – and in particular to a hard look at the labourers who produced the wealth of England, now that their labour is no longer a thing to be regretted. But when agricultural labourers do appear in this poem – and they do frequently, in long and excellent set-piece descriptions of rural tasks – it is either as personified Industry, the eighteenth-century poet's equivalent of a modern economist's Labour, as though their work was being done for them by an unseen Goddess; or else as workers whose 'happy labour' is congenial to them, the natural complement of their physique and character. All this involves Thomson in a pair of contradictory attitudes to nature; so that when his emphasis is upon the achievement of British Agriculture, nature appears to him as potentially hostile, something which must be subjugated by an invisible labour-force; but when the laborious process of subjugation is being described, it suddenly ceases to be laborious at all, and the earth gives up her bounty to the eager rustic with no unpleasant effort on his part; for to fulfil their part in Thomson's Augustan England, the workers must work, but still be as happy as if they were not working.

But in fact Thomson's version of Pastoral is more subtle than what has been said so far would suggest. He is aware of an opposition in values between his commercial England and the Golden Age; he is intrigued by the opposing views of nature, as at once the enemy of man and his bountiful provider. These oppositions are not resolved in any way that might endanger the apparent harmony of rural life in England which is based upon them; but they are very fully explored in Thomson's extraordinary descriptions of nature in the tropics. In the vast savannahs, Thomson discovers the synthesis of nature's hostility and her productivity – in these regions, it is the astonishing fertility of the landscape that makes it so terrifying:

> Along these lonely regions, where, retired
> From little scenes of art, great Nature dwells
> In awful solitude, and naught is seen
> But the wild herds that own no master's stall,
> Prodigious rivers roll their fattening seas . . .

This synthesis encourages Thomson to express a contempt for the 'little scenes' of England that the arts of agriculture or gardening have tamed; but it is worth noticing that the synthesis is achieved in a context where labour is unnecessary (nature is herself the luxuriant provider) and also absent (the savannahs are deserted). And no sooner has Thomson discovered a Golden Age on the old terms of the Pastoral –

a 'Ceres void of pain' – than he insists against this discovery that there is no true civilization without labour, no humanity without art, and can thus almost justify the contradictions arising from his attempt to reconcile the commercial and the pastoral.

These two contradictory attitudes to nature in Thomson's poem may be regarded as parts of two separate strains of pastoral, or more properly rural, literature in the eighteenth century. On the one hand Thomson's poem leads to what is really a version of Anti-Pastoral, the poetry of the Sublime and the Picturesque, which is suspicious of improvement in agriculture and which concentrates on images of nature which resist the attempts of man to cultivate and control her; on the other, it is related to that variety of optimistic Pastoral that most often finds expression in the Georgic. Thomson did not originate the Georgic tradition in England, nor is his work strictly considered a part of it; but it does share the progressive, bourgeois, mercantile values of a number of formal Georgic poems produced in the early and middle eighteenth century. That there had already been by 1730 an increasing middle-class interest in the practical aspects of rural life for several decades is evident from the new interest taken by writers of Pastoral in Virgil's *Georgics*, which first became popular at the end of the seventeenth century, and appear in a flood of translations – aimed at a literate audience but one not versed in a classical tradition – in the following century. The *Georgics* differ from the *Eclogues* in their interest in the 'how' of country life; they are ostensibly didactic, and are concerned at a fairly detailed level with the most effective methods of husbandry; and they display a considerable knowledge of agricultural practice. Addison's *Essay on the Georgics* (1693) is the first work specifically on this area of Virgil's poetry to appear in English, in contrast with the great amount of earlier material on – and translations of – the *Eclogues*. John Philips's *Cyder* is one of the earliest attempts to render the spirit of the *Georgics* into English; Philips chooses to write on the production of the lowly English drink, in preference to the nobler wine of the Continent. His language is, however, self-consciously elevated, owing much more to the Miltonic epic style than to the quieter voice of the naturalistic Pastoral, and in this way Philips tries, though not very successfully, to give the humble activities of apple-growing and cider-production a seriousness which he clearly thinks his reader might otherwise consider they lacked.

The eighteenth century abounds with other attempts at the Georgic – Dyer's *Fleece*, Grainger's *Sugar-Cane*, and Smart's *Hop Garden* are three of the most distinguished – and the interest in the practicalities of rural affairs comes to need less and less defending, until about the 1770s at least, from the charge of triviality. As a result, the English Georgic comes to present a view of the peasant as industrious, hardworking; a view which – often in the same poem – is in awkward conflict with the idea of the peasant as languid, with time on his hands, the character he brings with him from conventional Pastoral. The only poet who pays much attention to this conflict is Dyer, whose poem confidently reconciles the pastoral and mercantile in a way no-one else could manage, and offers a view of England in which the merchant is humanized by the simple virtues of the shepherd, the shepherd is animated by the energy of the merchant, and the interests of both are united by the progress of 'the homely fleece', from the valleys of Shropshire, through the fast-growing wool-towns of the north, and thence to all the trading-posts of America and Asia.

The Georgic always stood – from the time of Virgil arguably, but always in England – in a problematic relationship with the values of the town. To begin with, the conventional self-consciousness of the Georgic poet about the proper language of the kind suggests an appeal for the approval of the town, which contrasts with the official purpose of the Georgic, to instruct those in the country. And yet, while the Georgic is not apparently hostile to the town, as are the poets of (for example) the Horatian 'Happy the man' tradition, the poet who asserts the dignity of rural pursuits usually does so in a way which suggests an implicit appeal away from the over-abundant and misdirected energy of urban life. Then again, the mid-eighteenth-century writer of Georgics was usually anxious to see the particular rural industry of which he was singing as part of a national economic structure, and he praised it by the same mercantile, and essentially urban, value-system as he would have praised the expansion of trade or the invention of the steam-pump. These disjunctions became slowly more apparent as the century progressed, and (among other things) the position of the writer was seen to have changed; and poets like Goldsmith, doing without a patron and trying to live by what he could sell in a competitive urban literary market, or like Cowper, self-consciously amateur and withdrawn from urban and commercial pressures, were increasingly less likely to find inspiration in the improvement of agriculture, or in the assertion of John Langhorne, standing Pope on his head, that 'Peace and Plenty own a Brunswick reigns.' Soon after the mid-century, enthusiasm for the more energetic values of the Georgic falters; its epitaph will be found in Cowper's instructions on the cultivation of cucumbers, in *The Task*. There is a proper emphasis on the profitability of the enterprise; a minute and almost (if such a thing were possible for Cowper) indelicate attention to detail; a diction as lofty as can be imagined; and it is no hard task at all for Cowper to exploit the absurd hiatus between cucumbers and the grand style.

The key poem in this rediscovery of the pessimistic roots of Pastoral is certainly Gray's 'Elegy Written in a Country Churchyard', a poem whose overwhelming and immediate popularity surprised its author more than anyone. Gray's 'Elegy' draws together many strings of the pastoral tradition in tune with a new emphasis on sentiment, and on the refinements of feeling. Gray takes up from the Horatian tradition, or what we have called the 'Happy the man' school, the theme of rural retreat – the desire of the poet to remove himself from the life of the town and the possibility of wealth and fame, in favour of the obscure life of the cottager. The poem concludes with an epitaph on one thus retired:

Here rests his head upon the lap of Earth
A Youth to Fortune and to Fame unknown.
Fair Science frown'd not on his humble birth,
And Melancholy mark'd him for her own.

The tone of melancholy characterizes the entire elegy; it is a mood that is found in embryo in the more successful passages of Ambrose Philips's *Pastorals*, and in those poems as in this it is produced by the tension between the expression of an admiration for rural contentment, and the desire for recognition by the 'madding crowd'. The landscape in the opening lines of the elegy is depicted at dusk, in the final moments of the day, and it is a setting which is in keeping with the philosophic tone of the rest of the poem. Gray cannot see himself as a part of those who worship at 'the shrine of Luxury and Pride'; he feels cut off from the urban world of Augustan poetry, and seeks refuge in the solitude of the country; and yet the moral conclusions he advances against the mercantile values of the urban middle-class culture he seeks to escape from are simply the quiet virtues – generosity, modesty – of that same culture. The pastoral tradition is here deployed to stress Gray's sense of isolation, his inability to share the ideals of his literary contemporaries. The 'ivy-mantled tow'r', the 'mopeing owl', the 'dark unfathom'd caves' all are parts of what is to become a familiar Gothic landscape, a decay which will come to all civilizations, however confident they are in their conviction that the movement of history is a progression towards perfection. The 'Elegy' is both the final synthesis of the Augustan culture – the poet as spokesman for his audience – and the first expression of a hesitant romanticism – the poet separated from his audience. It is a signpost on the road out of Arcadia, pointing back where we have come from, and forward along the path that the main body of pastoral literature was afterwards to follow.

That the design of pastoral poetry is, to represent the undisturbed felicity of the golden age is an empty notion which . . . I think, all rational critics have agreed to extirpate and explode.

[Joseph Warton, 'An Essay on the Genius and Writings of Alexander Pope', 1756]

In this age, pastoral poetry is enriched in a manner unknown to the Antients. Philosophy has . . . aggrandized and adorned the universe; it is now a much more striking object than in the ages of ignorance: the progress of science . . . has made the palace of the world, and its inhabitants, better known . . . Poems may be written which require a very considerable knowledge of nature, and their authors may, not withstanding, hope to find readers.

[Jean-François Saint-Lambert, *Monthly Review*, 1769]

If we search the writings of Virgil for the true definition of a pastoral it will be found a poem in which any action or passion is represented by its effects upon a country life . . . In this definition . . . there is no mention of the golden age. I cannot indeed easily discover why it is thought necessary to refer descriptions of a rural state to remote times.

[Samuel Johnson, *The Rambler*, 1750]

JAMES THOMSON

The Seasons

From *Summer*

Now swarms the village o'er the jovial mead –
The rustic youth, brown with meridian toil,
Healthful and strong; full as the summer rose
Blown by prevailing suns, the ruddy maid,
Half naked, swelling on the sight, and all
Her kindled graces burning o'er her cheek.
Even stooping age is here; and infant hands
Trail the long rake, or, with the fragrant load
O'ercharged, amid the kind oppression roll.
Wide flies the tedded grain; all in a row
Advancing broad, or wheeling round the field,
They spread their breathing harvest to the sun,
That throws refreshful round a rural smell;
Or, as they rake the green-appearing ground,
And drive the dusky wave along the mead,
The russet hay-cock rises thick behind
In order gay: while heard from dale to dale,
Waking the breeze, resounds the blended voice
Of happy labour, love, and social glee.
Or, rushing thence, in one diffusive band
They drive the troubled flocks, by many a dog
Compelled, to where the mazy-running brook
Forms a deep pool, this bank abrupt and high,
And that fair-spreading in a pebbled shore.
Urged to the giddy brink, much is the toil,
The clamour much of men and boys and dogs
Ere the soft, fearful people to the flood
Commit their woolly sides. And oft the swain,
On some impatient seizing, hurls them in:

Emboldened then, nor hesitating more,
Fast, fast they plunge amid the flashing wave,
And, panting, labour to the farther shore.
Repeated this, till deep the well-washed fleece
Has drunk the flood, and from his lively haunt
The trout is banished by the sordid stream.
Heavy and dripping, to the breezy brow
Slow move the harmless race; where, as they spread
Their swelling treasures to the sunny ray,
Inly disturbed, and wondering what this wild
Outrageous tumult means, their loud complaints
The country fill; and, tossed from rock to rock,
Incessant bleatings run around the hills.
At last, of snowy white the gathered flocks
Are in the wattled pen innumerous pressed,
Head above head; and, ranged in lusty rows,
The shepherds sit, and whet the sounding shears.
The housewife waits to roll her fleecy stores,
With all her gay-drest maids attending round.
One, chief, in gracious dignity enthroned,
Shines o'er the rest, the pastoral queen, and rays
Her smiles sweet-beaming on her shepherd-king;
While the glad circle round them yield their souls
To festive mirth, and wit that knows no gall.
Meantime, their joyous task goes on apace;
Some mingling stir the melted tar, and some
Deep on the new-shorn vagrant's heaving side
To stamp his master's cipher ready stand;
Others the unwilling wether drag along;
And, glorying in his might, the sturdy boy
Holds by the twisted horns the indignant ram.
Behold where bound, and of its robe bereft
By needy man, that all-depending lord,
How meek, how patient, the mild creature lies!
What softness in its melancholy face,

What dumb complaining innocence appears!
Fear not, yet gentle tribes! 'tis not the knife
Of horrid slaughter that is o'er you waved;
No, 'tis the tender swain's well-guided shears,
Who having now, to pay his annual care,
Borrowed your fleece, to you a cumbrous load
Will send you bounding to your hills again.
A simple scene! yet hence Britannia sees
Her solid grandeur rise: hence she commands
The exalted stores of every brighter clime,
The treasures of the sun without his rage:
Hence, fervent all with culture, toil, and arts,
Wide glows her land: her dreadful thunder hence
Rides o'er the waves sublime, and now, even now,
Impending hangs o'er Gallia's humbled coast;
Hence rules the circling deep, and awes the world.

*

Bear me, Pomona! to thy citron groves;
To where the lemon and the piercing lime,
With the deep orange glowing through the green,
Their lighter glories blend. Lay me reclined
Beneath the spreading tamarind, that shakes,
Fanned by the breeze, its fever-cooling fruit.
Deep in the night the massy locust sheds
Quench my hot limbs; or lead me through the maze,
Embowering endless, of the Indian fig;
Or, thrown at gayer ease on some fair brow,
Let me behold, by breezy murmurs cooled,
Broad o'er my head the verdant cedar wave,
And high palmettos lift their graceful shade.
Oh, stretched amid these orchards of the sun,
Give me to drain the cocoa's milky bowl,
And from the palm to draw its freshening wine!

More bounteous far than all the frantic juice
Which Bacchus pours. Nor, on its slender twigs
Low-bending, be the full pomegranate scorned;
Nor, creeping through the woods, the gelid race
Of berries. Oft in humble station dwells
Unboastful worth, above fastidious pomp.
Witness, thou best Anana, thou the pride
Of vegetable life, beyond whate'er
The poet's imaged in the golden age:
Quick let me strip thee of thy tufty coat,
Spread thy ambrosial stores, and feast with Jove!
  From these the prospect varies. Plains immense
Lie stretched below, interminable meads
And vast savannas, where the wandering eye,
Unfixt, is in a verdant ocean lost.
Another Flora there, of bolder hues
And richer sweets beyond our garden's pride,
Plays o'er the fields, and showers with sudden hand
Exuberant spring – for oft these valleys shift
Their green-embroidered robe to fiery brown,
And swift to green again, as scorching suns
Or streaming dews and torrent rains prevail.
Along these lonely regions, where, retired
From little scenes of art, great Nature dwells
In awful solitude, and naught is seen
But the wild herds that own no master's stall,
Prodigious rivers roll their fattening seas;
On whose luxuriant herbage, half-concealed,
Like a fallen cedar, far diffused his train,
Cased in green scales, the crocodile extends.
The flood disparts: behold! in plaited mail
Behemoth rears his head. Glanced from his side,
The darted steel in idle shivers flies:
He fearless walks the plain, or seeks the hills,

Where, as he crops his varied fare, the herds,
In widening circle round, forget their food
And at the harmless stranger wondering gaze.

★

Nor less thy world, Columbus, drinks refreshed
The lavish moisture of the melting year.
Wide o'er his isles the branching Oronoque
Rolls a brown deluge, and the native drives
To dwell aloft on life-sufficing trees –
At once his dome, his robe, his food, and arms.
Swelled by a thousand streams, impetuous hurled
From all the roaring Andes, huge descends
The mighty Orellana. Scarce the muse
Dares stretch her wing o'er this enormous mass
Of rushing water; scarce she dares attempt
The sea-like Plata, to whose dread expanse,
Continuous depth, and wondrous length of course
Our floods are rills. With unabated force
In silent dignity they sweep along,
And traverse realms unknown, and blooming wilds,
And fruitful deserts – worlds of solitude
Where the sun smiles and seasons teem in vain,
Unseen and unenjoyed. Forsaking these,
O'er peopled plains they fair-diffusive flow
And many a nation feed, and circle safe
In their soft bosom many a happy isle,
The seat of blameless Pan, yet undisturbed
By Christian crimes and Europe's cruel sons.
Thus pouring on they proudly seek the deep,
Whose vanquish'd tide, recoiling from the shock,
Yields to this liquid weight of half the globe;
And Ocean trembles for his green domain.
But what avails this wondrous waste of wealth,

This gay profusion of luxurious bliss,
This pomp of Nature? what their balmy meads,
Their powerful herbs, and Ceres void of pain?
By vagrant birds dispersed and wafting winds,
What their unplanted fruits? what the cool draughts,
The ambrosial food, rich gums, and spicy health
Their forests yield? their toiling insects what,
Their silky pride and vegetable robes?
Ah! what avail their fatal treasures, hid
Deep in the bowels of the pitying earth,
Golconda's gems, and sad Potosi's mines
Where dwelt the gentlest children of the Sun?
What all that Afric's golden rivers roll,
Her odorous woods, and shining ivory stores?
Ill-fated race! the softening arts of peace,
Whate'er the humanizing muses teach,
The godlike wisdom of the tempered breast,
Progressive truth, the patient force of thought,
Investigation calm whose silent powers
Command the world, the light that leads to Heaven,
Kind equal rule, the government of laws,
And all-protecting freedom which alone
Sustains the name and dignity of man –
These are not theirs. The parent sun himself
Seems o'er this world of slaves to tyrannize,
And, with oppressive ray the roseate bloom
Of beauty blasting, gives the gloomy hue
And feature gross – or, worse, to ruthless deeds,
Mad jealousy, blind rage, and fell revenge
Their fervid spirit fires. Love dwells not there,
The soft regards, the tenderness of life,
The heart-shed tear, the ineffable delight
Of sweet humanity: these court the beam
Of milder climes – in selfish fierce desire

And the wild fury of voluptuous sense
There lost. The very brute creation there
This rage partakes, and burns with horrid fire.

*

Which way, Amanda, shall we bend our course?
The choice perplexes. Wherefore should we choose?
All is the same with thee. Say, shall we wind
Along the streams? or walk the smiling mead?
Or court the forest glades? or wander wild
Among the waving harvests? or ascend,
While radiant Summer opens all its pride,
Thy hill, delightful Shene? Here let us sweep
The boundless landscape; now the raptured eye,
Exulting swift, to huge Augusta send,
Now to the sister hills that skirt her plain,
To lofty Harrow now, and now to where
Majestic Windsor lifts his princely brow.
In lovely contrast to this glorious view,
Calmly magnificent, then will we turn
To where the silver Thames first rural grows.
There let the feasted eye unwearied stray;
Luxurious, there, rove through the pendent woods
That nodding hang o'er Harrington's retreat;
And, stooping thence to Ham's embowering walks,
Beneath whose shades, in spotless peace retired,
With her the pleasing partner of his heart,
The worthy Queensberry yet laments his Gay,
And polished Cornbury woos the willing muse,
Slow let us trace the matchless vale of Thames;
Fair-winding up to where the muses haunt
In Twit'nam's bowers, and for their Pope implore
The healing god; to royal Hampton's pile,
To Clermont's terraced height, and Esher's groves,

Where in the sweetest solitude, embraced
By the soft windings of the silent Mole,
From courts and senates Pelham finds repose.
Enchanting vale! beyond whate'er the muse
Has of Achaia or Hesperia sung!
O vale of bliss! O softly-swelling hills!
On which the power of cultivation lies,
And joys to see the wonders of his toil.
  Heavens! what a goodly prospect spreads around,
Of hills, and dales, and woods, and lawns, and spires,
And glittering towns, and gilded streams, till all
The stretching landskip into smoke decays!
Happy Britannia! where the Queen of Arts,
Inspiring vigour, Liberty, abroad
Walks unconfined even to thy farthest cots,
And scatters plenty with unsparing hand.
  Rich is thy soil, and merciful thy clime;
Thy streams unfailing in the Summer's drought;
Unmatched thy guardian-oaks; thy valleys float
With golden waves; and on thy mountains flocks
Bleat numberless; while, roving round their sides,
Bellow the blackening herds in lusty droves.
Beneath, thy meadows glow, and rise unquelled
Against the mower's scythe. On every hand
Thy villas shine. Thy country teems with wealth;
And Property assures it to the swain,
Pleased and unwearied in his guarded toil.
  Full are thy cities with the sons of art;
And trade and joy, in every busy street,
Mingling are heard: even Drudgery himself,
As at the car he sweats, or, dusty, hews
The palace stone, looks gay. Thy crowded ports,
Where rising masts an endless prospect yield,
With labour burn, and echo to the shouts
Of hurried sailor, as he hearty waves

His last adieu, and, loosening every sheet,
Resigns the spreading vessel to the wind.

[1727]

From *Autumn*

These are thy blessings, Industry, rough power!
Whom labour still attends, and sweat, and pain;
Yet the kind source of every gentle art
And all the soft civility of life:
Raiser of human kind! by nature cast
Naked and helpless out amid the woods
And wilds to rude inclement elements;
With various seeds of art deep in the mind
Implanted, and profusely poured around
Materials infinite; but idle all,
Still unexerted, in the unconscious breast
Slept the lethargic powers; Corruption still
Voracious swallowed what the liberal hand
Of Bounty scattered o'er the savage year.
And still the sad barbarian roving mixed
With beasts of prey; or for his acorn meal
Fought the fierce tusky boar – a shivering wretch!
Aghast and comfortless when the bleak north,
With winter charged, let the mixed tempest fly,
Hail, rain, and snow, and bitter-breathing frost.
Then to the shelter of the hut he fled,
And the wild season, sordid, pined away;
For home he had not: home is the resort
Of love, of joy, of peace and plenty, where,
Supporting and supported, polished friends
And dear relations mingle into bliss.
But this the rugged savage never felt,
Even desolate in crowds; and thus his days

Rolled heavy, dark, and unenjoyed along –
A waste of time! till Industry approached,
And roused him from his miserable sloth;
His faculties unfolded; pointed out
Where lavish Nature the directing hand
Of Art demanded; showed him how to raise
His feeble force by the mechanic powers,
To dig the mineral from the vaulted earth,
On what to turn the piercing rage of fire,
On what the torrent, and the gathered blast;
Gave the tall ancient forest to his axe;
Taught him to chip the wood, and hew the stone,
Till by degrees the finished fabric rose;
Tore from his limbs the blood-polluted fur,
And wrapt them in the woolly vestment warm,
Or bright in glossy silk, and flowing lawn;
With wholesome viands filled his table, poured
The generous glass around, inspired to wake
The life-refining soul of decent wit;
Nor stopped at barren bare necessity;
But, still advancing bolder, led him on
To pomp, to pleasure, elegance, and grace;
And, breathing high ambition through his soul,
Set science, wisdom, glory in his view,
And bade him be the lord of all below.
  Then gathering men their natural powers combined,
And formed a public; to the general good
Submitting, aiming, and conducting all.
For this the patriot-council met, the full,
The free, and fairly represented whole;
For this they planned the holy guardian laws,
Distinguished orders, animated arts,
And, with joint force Oppression chaining, set
Imperial Justice at the helm, yet still
To them accountable: nor slavish dreamed

That toiling millions must resign their weal
And all the honey of their search to such
As for themselves alone themselves have raised.
  Hence every form of cultivated life
In order set, protected, and inspired
Into perfection wrought. Uniting all,
Society grew numerous, high, polite,
And happy. Nurse of art, the city reared
In beauteous pride her tower-encircled head;
And, stretching street on street, by thousands drew,
From twining woody haunts, or the tough yew
To bows strong-straining, her aspiring sons.

[1730]

JOHN ARMSTRONG

From *The Art of Preserving Health,* Book III

  Behold the labourer of the glebe, who toils
In dust, in rain, in cold and sultry skies;
Save but the grain from mildews and the flood,
Nought anxious he what sickly stars ascend.
He knows no laws by Æsculapius given;
He studies none. Yet him nor midnight fogs
Infest, nor those envenom'd shafts that fly
When rabid Sirius fires the' autumnal noon.
His habit pure with plain and temperate meals,
Robust with labour, and by custom steel'd
To every casualty of varied life;

Serene he bears the peevish eastern blast,
And uninfected breathes the mortal south.
  Such the reward of rude and sober life;
Of labour such. By health the peasant's toil
Is well repaid; if exercise were pain
Indeed, and temperance pain. By arts like these
Laconia nursed of old her hardy sons;
And Rome's unconquer'd legions urged their way,
Unhurt, through every toil in every clime.
  Toil, and be strong. By toil the flaccid nerves
Grow firm, and gain a more compacted tone;
The greener juices are by toil subdued.
Mellow'd, and subtilized; the vapid old
Expell'd, and all the rancour of the blood.

[1744]

RICHARD JAGO

The Scavengers
A Town Eclogue

Awake, my Muse, prepare a loftier theme;
The winding valley, and the dimpled stream
Delight not all: quit, quit the verdant field,
And try what dusty streets and alleys yield.
  Where Avon wider flows and gathers fame,
Stands a fair town, and Warwick is its name;
For useful arts entitled once to share
The gentle Ethelfleda's guardian care:
Nor less for deeds of chivalry renown'd,

When her own Guy was with her laurels crown'd.
Now siren Sloth holds here her tranquil reign,
And binds in silken bonds the feeble train.
No frowning knights, in uncouth armour laced,
Seek now for monsters on the dreary waste:
In these soft scenes they chase a gentler prey,
No monsters! but as dangerous as they.
In different forms as sure destruction lies;
They have no claws 'tis true – but they have eyes.
  Last of the toiling race there lived a pair,
Bred up in labour, and inured to care;
To sweep the streets their task from sun to sun,
And seek the nastiness which others shun.
More plodding wight or dame you ne'er shall see,
He Gaffer Pestel hight, and Gammer she.
  As at their door they sat one summer's day,
Old Pestel first essay'd the plaintive lay:
His gentle mate the plaintive lay return'd,
And thus alternately their cares they mourn'd –

OLD PESTEL:

Alas! was ever such fine weather seen,
How dusty are the roads, the streets how clean!
How long, ye Almanacs, will it be dry?
Empty my cart how long, and idle I?
E'en at the best the times are not so good
But 'tis hard work to scrape a livelihood.
The cattle in the stalls resign their life,
And balk the shambles, and the' unbloody knife.
While farmers sit at home in pensive gloom,
And turnpikes threaten to complete my doom.

WIFE:

Well! for the turnpike, that will do no hurt;
Some say the managers are friends to dirt.
But much I fear this murrain where 'twill end,

For sure the cattle did our door befriend.
Oft have I hail'd them, as they stalk'd along,
Their fat the butchers pleased, but me their dung.

OLD PESTEL:

See what a little dab of dirt is here!
But yields all Warwick more, O tell me where?
Yet, on this spot, though now so naked seen,
Heaps upon heaps, and loads on loads, have been:
Bigger, and bigger, the proud dunghill grew,
Till my diminished house was hid from view.

WIFE:

Ah! Gaffer Pestel, what brave days were those,
When higher than our house our muckhill rose!
The growing mount I view'd with joyful eyes,
And mark'd what each load added to its size.
Wrapp'd in its fragrant steam we often sat,
And to its praises held delightful chat.
Nor did I e'er neglect my mite to pay,
To swell the goodly heap from day to day.
A cabbage once I bought; but small the cost –
Nor do I think the farthing all was lost.
Again you sold its well digested store,
To dung the garden where it grew before.

OLD PESTEL:

What though the beaux and powder'd coxcombs jeer'd,
And at the scavenger's employment sneer'd,
Yet then at night content I told my gains,
And thought well paid their malice and my pains.
Why toils the tradesman, but to swell his store?
Why craves the wealthy landlord still for more?
Why will our gentry flatter, fawn, and lie?
Why pack the cards, and what d'ye call't – the die?
All, all, the pleasing paths of gain pursue,

And wade through thick and thin, as we folks do.
Sweet is the scent that from advantage springs,
And nothing dirty which good interest brings.

WIFE:

When goody Dobbins call'd me nasty bear,
And talk'd of kennels, and the ducking chair,
With patience I could hear the scolding quean,
For sure 'twas dirtiness that kept me clean:
Clean was my gown on Sundays, if not fine,
Nor Mrs ***'s cap so white as mine.
A slut in silk or kersey is the same,
Nor sweetest always is the finest dame.

Thus wail'd they pleasure past, and present cares,
While the starved hog join'd his complaint with theirs:
To still his grunting different ways they tend,
To West Street he, and she to Cotton End.

[1784]

WILLIAM COLLINS

Ode

On the Death of Mr Thomson

I

In yonder Grave a *Druid* lies
  Where slowly winds the stealing Wave!
The *Year's* best Sweets shall duteous rise
  To deck *it's Poet's* sylvan Grave!

II

In yon deep Bed of whisp'ring Reeds
  His airy Harp shall now be laid,
That He, whose Heart in Sorrow bleeds
  May love thro' Life the soothing Shade.

III

Then Maids and Youths shall linger here,
  And while it's Sounds at distance swell,
Shall sadly seem in Pity's Ear
  To hear the *Woodland Pilgrim's* Knell.

IV

Remembrance oft shall haunt the Shore
  When *Thames* in Summer-wreaths is drest,
And oft suspend the dashing Oar
  To bid his gentle Spirit rest!

V

And oft as *Ease* and *Health* retire
  To breezy Lawn, or Forest deep,
The Friend shall view yon whit'ning Spire,
  And 'mid the varied Landschape weep.

VI

But Thou, who own'st that Earthy Bed,
  Ah! what will ev'ry Dirge avail?
Or Tears, which *Love* and *Pity* shed
  That mourn beneath the gliding Sail!

VII

Yet lives there one, whose heedless Eye
  Shall scorn thy pale Shrine glimm'ring near?
With Him, Sweet Bard, may *Fancy* die,
  And Joy desert the blooming Year.

VIII

But thou, lorn *Stream*, whose sullen Tide
No sedge-crown'd *Sisters* now attend,
Now waft me from the green Hill's Side
Whose cold Turf hides the buried *Friend*!

IX

And see, the Fairy Valleys fade,
Dun *Night* has veil'd the solemn View!
– Yet once again, Dear parted *Shade*
Meek *Nature's Child* again adieu!

X

The genial Meads assign'd to bless
Thy Life, shall mourn thy early Doom,
Their Hinds, and Shepherd-Girls shall dress
With simple Hands thy rural Tomb.

XI

Long, long, thy Stone and pointed Clay
Shall melt the musing *Briton's* Eyes,
O! *Vales*, and *Wild Woods*, shall He say
In yonder Grave *Your Druid* lies!

[1749]

A Song from Shakespear's *Cymbelyne*

Sung by Guiderus *and* Arviragus *over* Fidele, *suppos'd to be dead*

I

To fair *Fidele's* grassy Tomb
Soft Maids, and Village Hinds shall bring
Each op'ning Sweet, of earliest Bloom,
And rifle all the breathing Spring.

II

No wailing Ghost shall dare appear
  To vex with Shrieks this quiet Grove:
But Shepherd Lads assemble here,
  And melting Virgins own their Love.

III

No wither'd Witch shall here be seen,
  No Goblins lead their nightly Crew:
The Female Fays shall haunt the Green,
  And dress thy Grave with pearly Dew!

IV

The Redbreast oft at Ev'ning Hours
  Shall kindly lend his little Aid:
With hoary Moss, and gather'd Flow'rs,
  To deck the Ground where thou art laid.

V

When howling Winds, and beating Rain,
  In Tempests shake the sylvan Cell:
Or midst the Chace on ev'ry Plain,
  The tender Thought on thee shall dwell.

VI

Each lonely Scene shall thee restore,
  For thee the Tear be duly shed:
Belov'd, till Life could charm no more;
  And mourn'd, till Pity's self be dead.

[1744]

Ode to Evening

If ought of oaten stop, or pastoral song,
May hope, chaste *Eve*, to soothe thy modest ear,
Like thy own solemn springs,
Thy springs, and dying gales,
O Nymph reserv'd, while now the bright-hair'd sun
Sits in yon western tent, whose cloudy skirts,
With brede ethereal wove,
O'erhang his wavy bed:
Now air is hush'd, save where the weak-ey'd bat,
With short shrill shriek flits by on leathern wing,
Or where the Beetle winds
His small but sullen horn,
As oft he rises 'midst the twilight path,
Against the pilgrim born in heedless hum:
Now teach me, Maid compos'd,
To breathe some softn'd strain,
Whose numbers stealing thro' thy darkning vale,
May not unseemly with its stillness suit,
As musing slow, I hail
Thy genial lov'd return!
For when thy folding star arising shews
His paly circlet, at his warning lamp
The fragrant Hours[1], and Elves
Who slept in flow'rs the day,
And many a Nymph who wreaths her brows with sedge,
And sheds the fresh'ning dew, and lovelier still,
The *Pensive Pleasures* sweet
Prepare thy shadowy car.
Then lead, calm Vot'ress, where some sheety lake
Cheers the lone heath, or some time-hallow'd pile,
Or up-land fallows grey
Reflect its last cool gleam.
But when chill blust'ring winds, or driving rain,

[1] female divinities who preside over the seasons

Forbid my willing feet, be mine the hut,
    That from the mountain's side,
    Views wilds, and swelling floods,
And hamlets brown, and dim-discover'd spires,
And hears their simple bell, and marks o'er all
    Thy dewy fingers draw
    The gradual dusky veil.
While Spring shall pour his show'rs, as oft he wont,
And bathe thy breathing tresses, meekest Eve!
    While Summer loves to sport,
    Beneath thy ling'ring light;
While sallow Autumn fills thy lap with leaves;
Or Winter yelling thro' the troublous air,
    Affrights thy shrinking train,
    And rudely rends thy robes;
So long, sure-found beneath the Sylvan shed,
Shall *Fancy*, *Friendship*, *Science*, rose-lip'd *Health*,
    Thy gentlest influence own,
    And hymn thy fav'rite name!

[1746]

JOSEPH WARTON

To Solitude

Thou, that at deep dead of night
Walk'st forth beneath the pale moon's light
In robe of flowing black array'd,
While cypress leaves thy brows o'ershade;
Listening to the crowing cock,

And the distant sounding clock;
Or, sitting in thy cavern low,
Dost hear the bleak winds loudly blow,
Or the hoarse death-boding owl,
Or village mastiff's wakeful howl,
While through thy melancholy room
A dim lamp casts an awful gloom;
Thou, that on the meadow green,
Or daisied upland art not seen,
But wandering by the dusky nooks,
And the pensive falling brooks,
Or near some rugged, herbless rock,
Where no shepherd keeps his flock!
Musing maid, to thee I come,
Hating the tradeful city's hum;
Oh, let me calmly dwell with thee;
From noisy mirth and business free,
With meditation seek the skies,
This folly-fetter'd world despise!

[1746]

To Evening

Hail, meek-eyed maiden, clad in sober gray,
  Whose soft approach the weary woodman loves;
As homeward bent to kiss his prattling babes,
  Jocund he whistles through the twilight groves.

When Phœbus sinks behind the gilded hills,
  You lightly o'er the misty meadows walk;
The drooping daisies bathe in honey dews,
  And nurse the nodding violet's slender stalk.

The panting dryads, that in day's fierce heat
  To inmost bowers, and cooling caverns ran;
Return to trip in wanton evening dance;
  Old Sylvan too returns, and laughing Pan.

To the deep wood the clamorous rooks repair,
  Light skims the swallow o'er the watery scene;
And, from the sheepcote and fresh furrow'd field,
  Stout ploughmen meet, to wrestle on the green.

The swain, that artless sings on yonder rock,
  His supping sheep and lengthening shadow spies;
Pleased with the cool, the calm, refreshful hour,
  And with hoarse humming of unnumber'd flies.

Now every passion sleeps: desponding Love,
  And pining Envy, ever restless Pride;
A holy calm creeps o'er my peaceful soul,
  Anger, and mad Ambition's storms subside.

O modest Evening! oft let me appear
  A wandering votary in thy pensive train;
Listening to every wildly warbling throat
  That fills with farewell sweet thy darkening plain.

[1746]

From *The Enthusiast*

  Happy the first of men ere yet confined
To smoky cities; who in sheltering groves,
Warm caves, and deep-sunk valleys lived and loved,
By cares unwounded: what the sun and showers,
And genial earth untillaged could produce,
They gather'd grateful, or the acorn brown,
Or blushing berry; by the liquid lapse

Of murmuring waters call'd to slake their thirst,
Or with fair nymphs their sunbrown limbs to bathe;
With nymphs who fondly clasp'd their favourite youths,
Unawed by shame, beneath the beechen shade,
Nor wiles nor artificial coyness knew.
  Then doors and walls were not; the melting maid
Nor frowns of parents fear'd, nor husband's threats;
Nor had cursed gold their tender hearts allured:
Then beauty was not venal. Injured Love,
O, whither, god of raptures, art thou fled?
While Avarice waves his golden wand around,
Abhorr'd magician! and his costly cup
Prepares with baneful drugs, to' enchant the souls
Of each low thoughted fair to wed for gain.
  In earth's first infancy (as sung the bard,
Who strongly painted what he boldly thought)
Though the fierce north oft smote with iron whip
Their shivering limbs, though oft the bristly boar
Or hungry lion woke them with their howls,
And scared them from their mossgrown caves to rove
Houseless and cold in dark tempestuous nights;
Yet were not myriads in embattled fields
Swept off at once, nor had the raging seas
O'erwhelm'd the foundering bark and shrieking crew;
In vain the glassy ocean smiled to tempt
The jolly sailor unsuspecting harm,
For commerce ne'er had spread her swelling sails,
Nor had the wondering nereids ever heard
The dashing oar: then Famine, Want, and Pain
Sunk to the grave their fainting limbs; but us
Diseaseful dainties, riot and excess,
And feverish luxury destroy. In brakes
Or marshes wild, unknowingly they cropp'd
Herbs of malignant juice; to realms remote
While we for powerful poisons madly roam,

From every noxious herb collecting death.
What though unknown to those primeval sires
The well arch'd dome, peopled with breathing forms
By fair Italia's skilful hand, unknown
The shapely column, and the crumbling busts
Of awful ancestors in long descent?
Yet why should man, mistaken, deem it nobler
To dwell in palaces, and high roof'd halls,
Than in God's forests, architect supreme!
Say, is the Persian carpet, than the field's
Or meadow's mantle gay, more richly woven;
Or softer to the votaries of ease
Than bladed grass perfumed with dewdropp'd flowers?
O taste corrupt! that luxury and pomp,
In specious names of polish'd manners veil'd,
Should proudly banish Nature's simple charms!
All beauteous Nature! by thy boundless charms
Oppress'd, O, where shall I begin thy praise.
Where turn the' ecstatic eye, how ease my breast
That pants with wild astonishment and love!
Dark forests, and the opening lawn, refresh'd
With ever gushing brooks, hill, meadow, dale.
The balmy bean-field, the gay clover'd close,
So sweetly interchanged, the lowing ox,
The playful lamb, the distant waterfall
Now faintly heard, now swelling with the breeze;
The sound of pastoral reed from hazel bower,
The choral birds, the neighing steed that snuffs
His dappled mate, stung with intense desire;
The ripen'd orchard when the ruddy orbs
Betwixt the green leaves blush, the azure skies,
The cheerful sun that through earth's vitals pours
Delight and health and heat; all, all conspire
To raise, to sooth, to harmonize the mind,
To lift on wings of praise, to the great Sire

Of being and of beauty, at whose nod
Creation started from the gloomy vault
Of dreary Chaos, while the grisly king
Murmur'd to feel his boisterous power confined.

[1744]

THOMAS GRAY

Elegy Written in a Country Churchyard

The Curfew tolls the knell of parting day,
The lowing herd wind slowly o'er the lea,
The plowman homeward plods his weary way,
And leaves the world to darkness and to me.

Now fades the glimmering landscape on the sight,
And all the air a solemn stillness holds,
Save where the beetle wheels his droning flight,
And drowsy tinklings lull the distant folds;

Save that from yonder ivy-mantled tow'r
The mopeing owl does to the moon complain
Of such, as wand'ring near her secret bow'r,
Molest her ancient solitary reign.

Beneath those rugged elms, that yew-tree's shade,
Where heaves the turf in many a mould'ring heap,
Each in his narrow cell for ever laid,
The rude Forefathers of the hamlet sleep.

The breezy call of incense-breathing Morn,
The swallow twitt'ring from the straw-built shed,
The cock's shrill clarion, or the echoing horn,
No more shall rouse them from their lowly bed.

For them no more the blazing hearth shall burn,
Or busy housewife ply her evening care:
No children run to lisp their sire's return,
Or climb his knees the envied kiss to share.

Oft did the harvest to their sickle yield,
Their furrow oft the stubborn glebe has broke;
How jocund did they drive their team afield!
How bow'd the woods beneath their sturdy stroke!

Let not Ambition mock their useful toil,
Their homely joys, and destiny obscure;
Nor Grandeur hear with a disdainful smile,
The short and simple annals of the poor.

The boast of heraldry, the pomp of pow'r,
And all that beauty, all that wealth e'er gave,
Awaits alike th' inevitable hour.
The paths of glory lead but to the grave.

Nor you, ye Proud, impute to These the fault,
If Mem'ry o'er their Tomb no Trophies raise,
Where thro' the long-drawn isle and fretted vault
The pealing anthem swells the note of praise.

Can storied urn or animated bust
Back to its mansion call the fleeting breath?
Can Honour's voice provoke the silent dust,
Or Flatt'ry sooth the dull cold ear of Death?

Perhaps in this neglected spot is laid
Some heart once pregnant with celestial fire;
Hands, that the rod of empire might have sway'd,
Or wak'd to extasy the living lyre.

But Knowledge to their eyes her ample page
Rich with the spoils of time did ne'er unroll;
Chill Penury repress'd their noble rage,
And froze the genial current of the soul.

Full many a gem of purest ray serene,
The dark unfathom'd caves of ocean bear:
Full many a flower is born to blush unseen,
And waste its sweetness on the desert air.

Some village-Hampden, that with dauntless breast
The little Tyrant of his fields withstood;
Some mute inglorious Milton here may rest,
Some Cromwell guiltless of his country's blood.

Th' applause of list'ning senates to command,
The threats of pain and ruin to despise,
To scatter plenty o'er a smiling land,
And read their hist'ry in a nation's eyes,

Their lot forbad: nor circumscrib'd alone
Their growing virtues, but their crimes confin'd;
Forbad to wade through slaughter to a throne,
And shut the gates of mercy on mankind,

The struggling pangs of conscious truth to hide,
To quench the blushes of ingenuous shame,
Or heap the shrine of Luxury and Pride
With incense kindled at the Muse's flame.

Far from the madding crowd's ignoble strife,
Their sober wishes never learn'd to stray;
Along the cool sequester'd vale of life
They kept the noiseless tenor of their way.

Yet ev'n these bones from insult to protect
Some frail memorial still erected nigh,
With uncouth rhimes and shapeless sculpture deck'd,
Implores the passing tribute of a sigh.

Their name, their years, spelt by th' unletter'd muse,
The place of fame and elegy supply:
And many a holy text around she strews,
That teach the rustic moralist to die.

For who to dumb Forgetfulness a prey,
This pleasing anxious being e'er resign'd,
Left the warm precincts of the chearful day,
Nor cast one longing ling'ring look behind?

On some fond breast the parting soul relies,
Some pious drops the closing eye requires;
Ev'n from the tomb the voice of Nature cries,
Ev'n in our Ashes live their wonted Fires.

For thee, who mindful of th' unhonour'd Dead
Dost in these lines their artless tale relate;
If chance, by lonely contemplation led,
Some kindred Spirit shall inquire thy fate,

Haply some hoary-headed Swain may say,
'Oft have we seen him at the peep of dawn
'Brushing with hasty steps the dews away
'To meet the sun upon the upland lawn.

'There at the foot of yonder nodding beech
'That wreathes its old fantastic roots so high,
'His listless length at noontide would he stretch,
'And pore upon the brook that babbles by.

'Hard by yon wood, now smiling as in scorn,
'Mutt'ring his wayward fancies he would rove,
'Now drooping, woeful wan, like one forlorn,
'Or craz'd with care, or cross'd in hopeless love.

'One morn I miss'd him on the custom'd hill,
'Along the heath and near his fav'rite tree;
'Another came; nor yet beside the rill,
'Nor up the lawn, nor at the wood was he;

'The next with dirges due in sad array
'Slow thro' the church-way path we saw him born.
'Approach and read (for thou can'st read) the lay,
'Grav'd on the stone beneath yon aged thorn.'

The Epitaph

Here rests his head upon the lap of Earth
A Youth to Fortune and to Fame unknown.
Fair Science frown'd not on his humble birth,
And Melancholy mark'd him for her own.

Large was his bounty, and his soul sincere,
Heav'n did a recompence as largely send:
He gave to Mis'ry all he had, a tear,
He gain'd from Heav'n ('twas all he wish'd) a friend.

No farther seek his merits to disclose,
Or draw his frailties from their dread abode,
(There they alike in trembling hope repose,)
The bosom of his Father and his God.

[1750]

CHRISTOPHER SMART

A Morning Piece

Or an hymn for the hay-maker

Quin etiam Gallum noctem explaudentibus alis
Auroram clara consuetum voce vocare.
Lucretius

Brisk Chanticleer his matins had begun,
And broke the silence of the night.
And thrice he call'd aloud the tardy sun,
And thrice he hail'd the dawn's ambiguous light;
Back to their graves the fear-begotten phantoms run.

Strong Labour got up. – With his pipe in his mouth,
He stoutly strode over the dale,
He lent new perfumes to the breath of the south,
On his back hung his wallet and flail.
Behind him came Health from her cottage of thatch,
Where never physician had lifted the latch.

First of the village *Colin* was awake,
And thus he sung reclining on his rake.
Now the rural graces three
Dance beneath yon maple tree;
First the vestal Virtue, known
By her adamantine zone;
Next to her in rosy pride,
Sweet Society the bride;
Last Honesty, full seemly drest
In her cleanly home-spun vest.
The abbey bells in wak'ning rounds
The warning peal have giv'n;

And pious Gratitude resounds
        Her morning hymn to heav'n.

All nature wakes – the birds unlock their throats,
And mock the shepherd's rustic notes.
        All alive o'er the lawn,
        Full glad of the dawn,
        The little lambkins play,
Sylvia and Sol arise, – and all is day –
        Come, my mates, let us work,
        And all hands to the fork,
While the Sun shines, our hay-cocks to make,
        So fine is the day,
        And so fragrant the hay,
That the meadow's as blith as the wake.

        Our voices let's raise
        In Phœbus's praise,
Inspir'd by so glorious a theme,
        Our musical words
        Shall be join'd by the birds,
And we'll dance to the tune of the stream.

[1750]

The Hop Garden

From Book I

The land that answers best the farmer's care,
And silvers to maturity the Hop:
When to inhume the plants; to turn the glebe;
And wed the tendrils to th' aspiring poles:
Under what sign to pluck the crop, and how
To cure, and in capacious sacks infold,
I teach in verse Miltonian. Smile the muse,
And meditate an honour to that land
Where first I breath'd, and struggled into life,
Impatient, Cantium, to be call'd thy son.
Oh! cou'd I emulate Dan Sydney's Muse,
Thy Sydney, Cantium – He, from court retir'd,
In Penshurst's sweet Elysium sung delight,
Sung transport to the soft-responding streams
Of Medway, and enliven'd all her groves:
While ever near him, goddess of the green,
Fair Pembroke sat and smil'd immense applause.
With vocal fascination charm'd the Hours,
Unguarded left Heav'n's adamantine gate,
And to his lyre, swift as the winged sounds
That skim the air, danc'd unperceiv'd away.
Had I such pow'r, no peasants toil, no hops
Shou'd e'er debase my lay: far nobler themes,
The high achievements of thy warrior kings
Shou'd raise my thoughts, and dignify my song.
But I, young rustic, dare not leave my cot,
For so enlarg'd a sphere – ah! muse beware,
Lest the loud larums of the braying trump,
Lest the deep drum shou'd drown thy tender reed,
And mar its puny joints: me, lowly swain,
Every unshaven arboret, me the lawns,
Me the voluminous Medway's silver wave,

Content inglorious, and the hopland shades!
Yeomen and countrymen, attend my song:
Whether you shiver in the marshy Weald,
Egregious shepherds of unnumber'd flocks,
Whose fleeces, poison'd into purple, deck
All Europe's kings: or in fair Madum's vale
Imparadis'd, blest denizons, ye dwell;
Or Dorovernia's awful tow'rs ye love:
Or plough Tunbridgia's salutiferous hills
Industrious, and with draughts chalybiate heal'd,
Confess divine Hygeia's blissful seat;
The muse demands your presence, ere she tune
Her monitory voice; observe her well,
And catch the wholesome dictates as they fall.

From Book II

Ye smiling nymphs, th' inseparable train
Of saffron Ceres; ye, that gamesome dance,
And sing to jolly Autumn, while he stands
With his right hand poizing the scales of heav'n,
And while his left grasps Amalthea's horn:
Young chorus of fair Bacchanals, descend,
And leave awhile the sickle; yonder hill,
Where stand the loaded hop-poles, claims your care.
There mighty Bacchus stradling cross the bin,
Waits your attendance – There he glad reviews
His paunch, approaching to immensity
Still nearer, and with pride of heart surveys
Obedient mortals, and the world his own.
See! from the great metropolis they rush,
Th'industrious vulgar. They, like prudent bees,
In Kent's wide garden roam, expert to crop

The flow'ry hop, and provident to work,
Ere winter numb their sunburnt hands, and winds
Engaol them, murmuring in their gloomy cells.
From these, such as appear the rest t' excel
In strength and young agility, select.
These shall support with vigour and address
The bin-man's weighty office; now extract
From the sequacious earth the pole, and now
Unmarry from the closely clinging vine.
O'er twice three pickers, and no more, extend
The bin-man's sway; unless thy ears can bear
The crack of poles continual, and thine eyes
Behold unmoved the hurrying peasant tear
Thy wealth, and throw it on the thankless ground.
But first the careful planter will consult
His quantity of acres and his crop,
How many and how large his kilns; and then
Proportion'd to his wants the hands provide.
But yet of greater consequence and cost,
One thing remains unsung, a man of faith
And long experience, in whose thund'ring voice
Lives hoarse authority, potent to quell
The frequent frays of the tumultuous crew.
He shall preside o'er all thy hop-land store,
Severe dictator! His unerring hand,
And eye inquisitive, in heedful guise,
Shall to the brink the measure fill, and fair
On the twin registers the work record.

[1752]

JOHN DYER

The Fleece

From Book I

At shearing-time, along the lively vales,
Rural festivities are often heard:
Beneath each blooming arbor all is joy
And lusty merriment: while on the grass
The mingled youth in gaudy circles sport,
We think the golden age again return'd,
And all the fabled Dryades in dance.
Leering they bound along, with laughing air,
To the shrill pipe, and deep remurm'ring cords
Of th' ancient harp, or tabor's hollow sound.
While th' old apart, upon a bank reclin'd,
Attend the tuneful carol, softly mixt
With ev'ry murmur of the sliding wave,
And ev'ry warble of the feather'd choir;
Music of paradise! which still is heard,
When the heart listens; still the views appear
Of the first happy garden, when content
To nature's flow'ry scenes directs the sight.
Yet we abandon those Elysian walks,
Then idly for the lost delight repine:
As greedy mariners, whose desp'rate sails
Skim o'er the billows of the foamy flood,
Fancy they see the less'ning shores retire,
And sigh a farewell to the sinking hills.
Could I recall those notes, which once the muse
Heard at a shearing, near the woody sides
Of blue-topp'd Wreakin. Yet the carols sweet,
Through the deep maze of the memorial cell,
Faintly remurmur. First arose in song

Hoar-headed *Damon*, venerable swain,
The soothest shepherd of the flow'ry vale.
'This is no vulgar scene: no palace roof
'Was e'er so lofty, nor so nobly rise
'Their polish'd pillars, as these aged oaks,
'Which o'er our fleecy wealth and harmless sports
'Thus have expanded wide their shelt'ring arms,
'Thrice told an hundred summers. Sweet content,
'Ye gentle shepherds, pillow us at night.'
  'Yes, tuneful *Damon*, for our cares are short,
'Rising and falling with the chearful day,'
Colin reply'd, 'and pleasing weariness
'Soon our unaching heads to sleep inclines.
'Is it in cities so? where, poets tell,
'The cries of sorrow sadden all the streets,
'And the diseases of intemp'rate wealth.
'Alas, that any ills from wealth should rise!
  'May the sweet nightingale on yonder spray,
'May this clear stream, these lawns, those snow-white lambs,
'Which, with a pretty innocence of look,
'Skip on the green, and race in little troops;
'May that great lamp, which sinks behind the hills,
'And streams around variety of lights,
'Recall them erring: This is *Damon's* wish.
  'Huge Breaden's stony summit once I climb'd
'After a kiddling: *Damon*, what a scene!
'What various views unnumber'd spread beneath!
'Woods, tow'rs, vales, caves, dells, cliffs, and torrent floods;
'And here & there, between the spiry rocks,
'The broad flat sea. Far nobler prospect these,
'Than gardens black with smoke in dusty towns,
'Where stenchy vapours often blot the sun:
'Yet flying from his quiet, thither crowds

'Each greedy wretch for tardy-rising wealth,
'Which comes too late; that courts the taste in vain,
'Or nauseates with distempers. Yes, ye rich,
'Still, still be rich, if thus ye fashion life;
'And piping, careless silly shepherds we,
'We silly shepherds, all intent to feed
'Our snowy flocks, and wind the sleeky fleece.'
'Deem not, howe'er, our occupation mean,'
Damon reply'd, 'while the *Supreme* accounts
'Well of the faithful shepherd, rank'd alike
'With king and priest: they also shepherds are;
'For so th' All-seeing stiles them, to remind
'Elated man, forgetful of his charge.'
'But haste, begin the rites: see purple Eve
'Stretches her shadows: all ye nymphs and swains
'Hither assemble. Pleas'd with honours due,
'*Sabrina*, guardian of the crystal flood,
'Shall bless our cares, when she by moonlight clear
'Skims o'er the dales, and eyes our sleeping folds:
'Or in hoar caves, around Plynlymmon's brow,
'Where precious min'rals dart their purple gleams,
'Among her sisters she reclines; the lov'd
'Vaga, profuse of graces, Ryddol rough,
'Blithe Ystwith, and Clevedoc swift of foot;
'And mingles various seeds of flow'rs, and herbs
'In the divided torrents, ere they burst
'Thro' the dark clouds, & down the mountain roll.
'Nor taint-worm shall infect the yeaning herds,
'Nor penny-grass, nor spearwort's pois'nous leaf.'
He said: with light fantastic toe, the nymphs
Thither assembled, thither ev'ry swain;
And o'er the dimpled stream a thousand flow'rs,
Pale lilies, roses, violets, and pinks,
Mix'd with the greens of burnet, mint, and thyme,
And trefoil, sprinkled with their sportive arms.

Such custom holds along th' irriguous vales,
From Wreakin's brow to rocky Dolvoryn,
Sabrina's early haunt, ere yet she fled
The search of Guendolen, her stepdame proud,
With envious hate enrag'd. The jolly chear,
Spread on a mossy bank, untouch'd abides,
Till cease the rites: and now the mossy bank
Is gayly circled, and the jolly chear
Dispers'd in copious measure; early fruits,
And those of frugal store, in husk or rind;
Steep'd grain, and curdled milk with dulcet cream
Soft temper'd, in full merriment they quaff,
And cast about their gibes; and some apace
Whistle to roundelays: their little ones
Look on delighted: while the mountain-woods,
And winding vallies, with the various notes
Of pipe, sheep, kine, and birds, and liquid brooks,
Unite their echoes: near at hand the wide
Majestic wave of Severn slowly rolls
Along the deep-divided glebe: the flood,
And trading bark with low contracted sail,
Linger among the reeds and copsy banks
To listen; and to view the joyous scene.

From Book II

When many-colour'd ev'ning sinks behind
The purple woods and hills, and opposite
Rises, full-orb'd, the silver harvest-moon,
To light th' unwearied farmer, late afield
His scatter'd sheaves collecting; then expect
The artists, bent on speed, from pop'lous Leeds,
Norwich, or Froome; they traverse every plain,
And ev'ry dale, where farm or cottage smokes:

Reject them not; and let the season's price
Win thy soft treasures: let the bulky wain
Through dusty roads roll nodding; or the bark,
That silently adown the the cerule stream
Glides with white sails, dispense the downy freight
To copsy villages on either side,
And spiry towns, where ready diligence,
The grateful burden to receive, awaits,
Like strong *Briareus*, with his hundred hands.

From Book IV

Rejoice, ye nations! vindicate the sway
Ordain'd for common happiness. Wide, o'er
The globe terraqueous, let Britannia pour
The fruits of plenty from her copious horn.
What can avail to her, whose fertile earth
By ocean's briny waves are circumscrib'd,
The armed host, and murd'ring sword of war,
And conquest o'er her neighbours? She ne'er breaks
Her solemn compacts in the lust of rule:
Studious of arts and trade, she ne'er disturbs
The holy peace of states. 'Tis her delight
To fold the world with harmony, and spread,
Among the habitations of mankind,
The various wealth of toil, and what her fleece,
To clothe the naked, and her skilful looms,
Peculiar give. Ye too, rejoice, ye swains;
Increasing commerce shall reward your cares.
A day will come, if not too deep we drink
The cup, which luxury on careless wealth,
Pernicious gift, bestows; a day will come,
When, thro' new channels sailing, we shall clothe
The Californian coast, and all the realms

That stretch from Anian's streights to proud Japan;
And the green isles, which on the left arise
Upon the glassy brine, whose various capes
Not yet are figured on the sailor's chart:
Then ev'ry variation shall be told
Of the magnetic steel; and currents mark'd,
Which drive the heedless vessel from her course.
  That portion too, of land, a tract immense,
Beneath th' Antarctic spread, shall then be known,
And new plantations on its coast arise.
Then rigid winter's ice no more shall wound
The only naked animal; but man
With the soft fleece shall every-where be clothed.
The exulting muse shall then, in vigour fresh,
Her flight renew; mean-while, with weary wing,
O'er ocean's wave returning, she explores
Siluria's flowery vales, her old delight,
The shepherds' haunts, where the first springs arise
Of Britain's happy trade, now spreading wide,
Wide as th' Atlantic and Pacific seas,
Or as air's vital fluid o'er the globe.

[1757]

WILLIAM SHENSTONE

He repeats the song of Colin

A discerning Shepherd lamenting the state of the woollen manufactory

Ergo omni studio glaciem ventosque nivales,
Quo minus est illis curæ mortalis egestas,
Avertes: victumque feres. *Virgil*

Thou, therefore, in proportion to their lack
Of human aid, with all thy care defend
From frozen seasons and inclement blasts,
And give them timely food.

Near Avon's bank, on Arden's flowery plain,
A tuneful shepherd charm'd the listening wave,
And sunny Cotsol' fondly loved the strain,
Yet not a garland crowns the shepherd's grave!

Oh! lost Ophelia! smoothly flow'd the day,
To feel his music with my flames agree,
To taste the beauties of his melting lay,
To taste, and fancy it was dear to thee.

When for his tomb, with each revolving year,
I steal the musk-rose from the scented brake,
I strew my cowslips, and I pay my tear,
I'll add the myrtle for Ophelia's sake.

Shivering beneath a leafless thorn he lay,
When Death's chill rigour seized his flowing tongue:
The more I found his faltering notes decay,
The more prophetic truth sublimed the song.

'Adieu, my flocks! (he said) my wonted care,
By sunny mountain or by verdant shore;
May some more happy hand your fold prepare,
And may you need your Colin's crook no more!

'And you, ye shepherds! lead my gentle sheep;
To breezy hills or leafy shelters lead;
But if the sky with showers incessant weep,
Avoid the putrid moisture of the mead.

Where the wild thyme perfumes the purpled heath,
  Long loitering, there your fleecy tribes extend –
But what avails the maxims I bequeath?
  The fruitless gift of an officious friend!

'Ah! what avails the timorous lambs to guard,
  Though nightly cares with daily labours join,
If foreign sloth obtain the rich reward,
  If Gallia's craft the ponderous fleece purloin?

'Was it for this, by constant vigils worn,
  I met the terrors of an early grave?
For this I led them from the pointed thorn?
  For this I bathed them in the lucid wave?

'Ah heedless Albion! too benignly prone
  Thy blood to lavish and thy wealth resign!
Shall every other virtue grace thy throne,
  But quick-eyed Prudence never yet be thine?

'From the fair natives of this peerless hill
  Thou gavest the sheep that browse Iberian plains;
Their plaintive cries the faithless region fill,
  Their fleece adorns an haughty foe's domains.

'Ill-fated flocks; from cliff to cliff they stray;
  Far from their dams, their native guardians, far!
Where the soft shepherd, all the livelong day,
  Chants his proud mistress to his hoarse guitar.

'But Albion's youth her native fleece despise;
  Unmoved they hear the pining shepherd's moan:
In silky folds each nervous limb disguise,
  Allured by every treasure but their own.

'Oft have I hurried down the rocky steep,
  Anxious to see the wintry tempest drive:
"Preserve, (said I,) preserve your fleece, my sheep!
  Ere long will Phillis, will my love, arrive."

'Ere long she came: ah, woe is me! she came,
  Robed in the Gallic loom's extraneous twine;
For gifts like these they give their spotless fame,
  Resign their bloom, their innocence resign.

'Will no bright maid, by worth, by titles known,
  Give the rich growth of British hills to fame?
And let her charms, and her example, own
  That Virtue's dress and Beauty's are the same?

'Will no famed chief support this generous maid?
  Once more the patriot's arduous path resume?
And, comely from his native plains array'd,
  Speak future glory to the British loom?

'What power unseen my ravish'd fancy fires?
  I pierce the dreary shade of future days?
Sure 'tis the Genius of the land inspires,
  To breathe my latest breath in ***'s praise.

'O might my breath for ***'s praise suffice,
  How gently should my dying limbs repose!
O might his future glory bless mine eyes,
  My ravish'd eyes! how calmly would they close!

'*** was born to spread the general joy;
  By virtue rapt, by party uncontroll'd;
Britons for Britain shall the crook employ;
  Britons for Britain's glory shear the fold.'

[1764]

From *Hope,*
A Pastoral Ballad

My banks they are furnish'd with bees,
  Whose murmur invites one to sleep;
My grottos are shaded with trees,
  And my hills are white-over with sheep.
I seldom have met with a loss,
  Such health do my fountains bestow;
My fountains, all border'd with moss,
  Where the hare-bells and violets grow.

Not a pine in my grove is there seen,
  But with tendrils of woodbine is bound;
Not a beech's more beautiful green
  But a sweetbriar entwines it around:
Not my fields, in the prime of the year,
  More charms than my cattle unfold;
Not a brook that is limpid and clear,
  But it glitters with fishes of gold.

One would think she might like to retire
  To the bower I have labour'd to rear;
Not a shrub that I heard her admire,
  But I hasted and planted it there.
O how sudden the jessamine strove
  With the lilac to render it gay!
Already it calls for my love
  To prune the wild branches away.

From the plains, from the woodlands and groves,
  What strains of wild melody flow!
How the nightingales warble their loves
  From thickets of roses that blow!

And when her bright form shall appear,
  Each bird shall harmoniously join
In a concert so soft and so clear,
  As – she may not be fond to resign.

I have found out a gift for my fair;
  I have found where the wood-pigeons breed;
But let me that plunder forbear,
  She will say 'twas a barbarous deed:
For he ne'er could be true, she averr'd,
  Who could rob a poor bird of its young;
And I loved her the more when I heard
  Such tenderness fall from her tongue.

I have heard her with sweetness unfold,
  How that pity was due to – a dove;
That it ever attended the bold,
  And she call'd it the sister of Love.
But her words such a pleasure convey,
  So much I her accents adore,
Let her speak, and whatever she say,
  Methinks I should love her the more.

Can a bosom so gentle remain
  Unmov'd when her Corydon sighs?
Will a nymph that is fond of the plain,
  These plains and this valley despise?
Dear regions of silence and shade!
  Soft scenes of contentment and ease!
Where I could have pleasingly stray'd,
  If aught, in her absence, could please.

But where does my Phyllida stray?
  And where are her grots and her bow'rs?

Are the groves and the valleys as gay,
  And the shepherds as gentle as ours?
The groves may perhaps be as fair,
  And the face of the valleys as fine;
The swains may in manners compare,
  But their love is not equal to mine.

[1755]

On Certain Pastorals

So rude and tuneless are thy lays,
  The weary audience vow –
'Tis not the' Arcadian swain that sings,
  But 'tis his herds that low.

[1764]

JOHN CUNNINGHAM

Corydon

To the Memory of William Shenstone, Esq.

Come, shepherds, we'll follow the hearse,
  We'll see our loved Corydon laid:
Though sorrow may blemish the verse,
  Yet let a sad tribute be paid.
They call'd him the pride of the plain;
  In sooth he was gentle and kind!
He mark'd on his elegant strain
  The graces that glow'd in his mind.

On purpose he planted yon trees,
  That birds in the covert might dwell;
He cultured his thyme for the bees,
  But never would rifle their cell:
Ye lambkins that play'd at his feet,
  Go bleat – and your master bemoan;
His music was artless and sweet,
  His manners as mild as your own.

No verdure shall cover the vale;
  No bloom on the blossoms appear;
The sweets of the forest shall fail,
  And winter discolour the year.
No birds in our hedges shall sing
  (Our hedges so vocal before),
Since he that should welcome the Spring,
  Salutes the gay season no more.

His Phillis was fond of his praise.
  And poets came round in a throng;
They listn'd – they envied his lays,
  But which of them equal'd his song?
Ye shepherds, henceforward be mute,
  For lost is the pastoral strain;
So give me my Corydon's flute,
  And thus – let me break it in twain.

[1766]

Content

O'er moorlands and mountains, rude, barren, and bare,
  As wilder'd and wearied I roam,
A gentle young shepherdess sees my despair,
  And leads me – o'er lawns – to her home:

Yellow sheaves from rich Ceres her cottage had crown'd,
   Green rushes were strew'd on her floor,
Her casement sweet woodbines crept wantonly round,
   And deck'd the sod seats at her door.

We sat ourselves down to a cooling repast;
   Fresh fruits! and she cull'd me the best:
While thrown from my guard by some glances she cast,
   Love slily stole into my breast!
I told my soft wishes; she sweetly replied
   (Ye virgins, her voice was divine!)
'I've rich ones rejected, and great ones denied,
   But take me, fond shepherd – I'm thine.'

Her air was so modest, her aspect so meek!
   So simple, yet sweet, were her charms!
I kiss'd the ripe roses that glow'd on her cheek,
   And lock'd the dear maid in my arms.
Now jocund together we tend a few sheep,
   And if, by yon prattler, the stream,
Reclined on her bosom, I sink into sleep,
   Her image still softens my dream.

Together we range o'er the slow rising hills,
   Delighted with pastoral views,
Or rest on the rock whence the streamlet distils,
   And point out new themes for my muse.
To pomp or proud titles she ne'er did aspire,
   The damsel's of humble descent;
The cottager Peace is well known for her sire,
   And shepherds have named her Content.

[1766]

ROBERT LLOYD

From *The Cit's Country Box*

Vos sapere et solos aio bene vivere, quorum,
Conspicitur nitidis fundata pecunia villis.

Horace

The wealthy Cit, grown old in trade,
Now wishes for the rural shade,
And buckles to his one-horse chair,
Old *Dobbin*, or the founder'd mare;
While wedg'd in closely by his side,
Sits Madam, his unwieldy bride,
With *Jacky* on a stool before 'em,
And out they jog in due decorum.
Scarce past the turnpike half a mile,
How all the country seems to smile!
And as they slowly jog together,
The Cit commends the road and weather;
While madam doats upon the trees,
And longs for ev'ry house she sees,
Admires its views, its situation,
And thus she opens her oration.
  What signify the loads of wealth,
Without that richest jewel, health?
Excuse the fondness of a wife,
Who doats upon your precious life!
Such ceaseless toil, such constant care,
Is more than human strength can bear.
One may observe it in your face –
Indeed, my dear, you break apace:
And nothing can your health repair,
But exercise and country air,
Sir Traffic has a house, you know,

About a mile from *Cheney-Row*;
He's a *good* man, indeed 'tis true,
But not so *warm*, my dear, as you:
And folks are always apt to sneer –
One would not be out-done my dear!
  Sir Traffic's name so well apply'd
Awak'd his brother merchant's pride;
And Thrifty, who had all his life
Paid utmost deference to his wife.
Confess'd her arguments had reason,
And by th' approaching summer season,
Draws a few hundreds from the stocks,
And purchases his country box.
  Some three or four mile out of town,
(An hour's ride will bring you down,)
He fixes on his choice abode,
Not half a furlong from the road:
And so convenient does it lay,
The stages pass it ev'ry day:
And then so snug, so mighty pretty,
To have an house so near the city!
Take but your places at the Boar
You're set down at the very door.
  Well then, suppose them fix'd at last,
White-washing, painting, scrubbing past,
Hugging themselves in ease and clover,
With all the fuss of moving over;
Lo, a new heap of whims are bred!
And wanton in my lady's head.
  Well to be sure, it must be own'd,
It is a charming spot of ground;
So sweet a distance for a ride,
And all about so *countrified!*
'Twould come but to a trifling price
To make it quite a paradise;

I cannot bear those nasty rails,
Those ugly broken mouldy pales:
Suppose, my dear, instead of these,
We build a railing, all Chinese.
Although one hates to be expos'd;
'Tis dismal to be thus enclos'd;
One hardly any object sees –
I wish you'd fell those odious trees.
Objects continual passing by
Were something to amuse the eye,
But to be pent within the walls –
One might as well be at St Paul's.
Our house, beholders would adore,
Was there a level lawn before,
Nothing its views to incommode,
But quite laid open to the road;
While ev'ry trav'ler in amaze,
Should on our little mansion gaze,
And pointing to the choice retreat,
Cry, that's Sir Thrifty's country seat.

[1757]

JAMES GRAINGER

From *The Sugar-Cane*

Of composts shall the muse descend to sing,
Nor soil her heavenly plumes? The sacred muse
Nought sordid deems, but what is base; nought fair
Unless true virtue stamp it with her seal.
Then, planter, wouldst thou double thine estate,

Never, ah! never be asham'd to tread
Thy dung-heaps, where the refuse of thy mills,
With all the ashes all thy coppers yield,
With weeds, mould, dung, and stale, a compost form,
Of force to fertilize the poorest soil.
  But, planter, if thy lands lie far remote,
And of access are difficult; on these
Leave the cane's sapless foliage; and with pens
Wattled (like those the muse hath oft times seen,
When frolic fancy led her youthful steps
In green Dorchestria's plains), the whole enclose:
There well thy stock with provender supply;
The well-fed stock will soon that food repay.
  Some of the skilful teach, and some deny,
That yams improve the soil. In meagre lands,
'Tis known the yam will ne'er to bigness swell;
And from each mould the vegetable tribes,
However frugal, nutriment derive:
Yet may their sheltering vines, their drooping leaves,
Their roots dividing the tenacious glebe,
More than refund the sustenance they draw.
  Whether the fattening compost in each hole
'Tis best to throw, or on the surface spread,
Is undetermin'd: trials must decide.
Unless kind rains and fostering dews descend,
To melt the compost's fertilizing salts,
A stinted plant, deceitful of thy hopes,
Will from those beds slow spring where hot dung lies:
But, if 'tis scatter'd generously o'er all,
The cane will better bear the solar blaze;
Less rain demand; and, by repeated crops
Thy land improv'd, its gratitude will show.

[1764]

MARK AKENSIDE

From *The Pleasures of Imagination*, Book IV

O ye dales
Of Tyne, and ye most ancient woodlands; where,
Oft as the giant flood obliquely strides,
And his banks open, and his lawns extend,
Stops short the pleased traveller to view,
Presiding o'er the scene, some rustic tower
Founded by Norman or by Saxon hands:
O ye Northumbrian shades, which overlook
The rocky pavement and the mossy falls
Of solitary Wensbeck's limpid stream;
How gladly I recall your well-known seats,
Beloved of old, and that delightful time
When, all alone, for many a summer's day,
I wandered through your calm recesses, led
In silence by some powerful hand unseen.
Nor will I e'er forget you; nor shall e'er
The graver tasks of manhood, or the advice
Of vulgar wisdom, move me to disclaim
Those studies which possessed me in the dawn
Of life, and fixed the colour of my mind
For every future year: whence even now
From sleep I rescue the clear hours of morn,
And, while the world around lies overwhelmed
In idle darkness, am alive to thoughts
Of honourable fame, of truth divine
Or moral, and of minds to virtue won
By the sweet magic of harmonious verse.

[1744]

Inscription for a Grotto

To me, whom, in their lays, the shepherds call
Actæa, daughter of the neighbouring stream,
This cave belongs. The fig-tree and the vine,
Which o'er the rocky entrance downward shoot,
Were placed by Glycon. He, with cowslips pale,
Primrose, and purple lychnis, decked the green
Before my threshold, and my shelving walls
With honeysuckle covered. Here, at noon,
Lulled by the murmur of my rising fount,
I slumber: here my clustering fruits I tend;
Or from the humid flowers at break of day,
Fresh garlands weave, and chase from all my bounds
Each thing impure or noxious. Enter in,
O stranger, undismayed. Nor bat, nor toad
Here lurks: and, if thy breast of blameless thoughts
Approve thee, not unwelcome shalt thou tread
My quiet mansion: chiefly, if thy name
Wise Pallas and the immortal Muses own.

[1772]

To the Honourable Charles Townshend; *from the Country*

I

Say, Townshend, what can London boast
To pay thee for the pleasures lost,
  The health to-day resigned;
When Spring from this her favourite seat
Bade Winter hasten his retreat,
  And met the western wind.

II

Oh! knew'st thou how the balmy air,
The sun, the azure heavens prepare
To heal thy languid frame,
No more would noisy courts engage;
In vain would lying faction's rage
Thy sacred leisure claim.

III

Oft I looked forth, and oft admired;
Till with the studious volume tired
I sought the open day;
And sure, I cried, the rural gods
Expect me in their green abodes,
And chide my tardy lay.

IV

But ah! in vain my restless feet
Traced every silent shady seat
Which knew their forms of old:
Nor Naiad by her fountain laid,
Nor Wood-nymph tripping through her glade,
Did now their rites unfold:

V

Whether to nurse some infant oak
They turn the slowly-tinkling brook,
And catch the pearly showers;
Or brush the mildew from the woods,
Or paint with noontide beams the buds,
Or breathe on opening flowers.

VI

Such rites, which they with Spring renew,
The eyes of care can never view;
And care hath long been mine:

And hence, offended with their guest,
Since grief of love my soul oppressed,
    They hide their toils divine.

VII

But soon shall thy enlivening tongue
This heart, by dear affliction wrung,
    With noble hope inspire:
Then will the sylvan powers again
Receive me in their genial train,
    And listen to my lyre.

VIII

Beneath yon Dryad's lonely shade
A rustic altar shall be paid,
    Of turf with laurel framed:
And thou the inscription wilt approve;
'This for the peace which, lost by love,
    By friendship was reclaimed.'

[1772]

WILLIAM MASON

From *The English Garden*, Book II

Nor is that cot, of which fond fancy draws
This casual picture, alien from our theme.
Revisit it at morn; its opening latch,
Though penury and toil within reside,

Shall pour thee forth a youthful progeny
Glowing with health and beauty (such the dower
Of equal heaven): See how the ruddy tribe
Throng round the threshold, and, with vacant gaze,
Salute thee; call the loiterers into use,
And form of these thy fence, the living fence
That graces what it guards. Thou think'st, perchance,
That, skill'd in Nature's heraldry, thy art
Has, in the limits of yon fragrant tuft,
Marshal'd each rose, that to the eye of June
Spreads its peculiar crimson; do not err,
The loveliest still is wanting; the fresh rose
Of Innocence, it blossoms on their cheek,
And, lo, to thee they bear it! striving all,
In panting race, who first shall reach the lawn,
Proud to be call'd thy shepherds. Want, alas!
Has o'er their little limbs her livery hung,
In many a tatter'd fold, yet still those limbs
Are shapely; their rude locks start from their brow,
Yet, on that open brow, its dearest throne,
Sits sweet Simplicity. Ah, clothe the troop
In such a russet garb as best befits
Their pastoral office; let the leathern scrip
Swing at their side, tip thou their crook with steel,
And braid their hat with rushes, then to each
Assign his station; at the close of eve,
Be it their care to pen in hurdled cote
The flock, and when the matin prime returns,
Their care to set them free; yet watching still
The liberty they lend, oft shalt thou hear
Their whistle shrill, and oft their faithful dog
Shall with obedient barkings fright the flock
From wrong or robbery. The livelong day
Meantime rolls lightly o'er their happy heads;
They bask on sunny hillocks, or disport

In rustic pastime, while that loveliest grace,
Which only lives in action unrestrain'd,
To every simple gesture lends a charm.

[1775]

JOHN SCOTT

Theron; or, *The Praise of Rural Life* From *Moral Eclogues*

Scene – *A Heath.*
Season – *Spring;* Time – *Morning.*

Fair Spring o'er Nature held her gentlest sway;
Fair Morn diffused around her brightest ray;
Thin mists hung hovering on the distant trees,
Or roll'd from off the fields before the breeze.
The shepherd Theron watch'd his fleecy train,
Beneath a broad oak, on the grassy plain.
A heath's green wild lay pleasant to his view,
With shrubs and field-flowers deck'd of varied hue:
There hawthorns tall their silver bloom disclosed,
Here flexile broom's bright yellow interposed;
There purple orchis, here pale daisies spread,
And sweet May lilies richest odour shed.
From many a copse and blossom'd orchard near,
The voice of birds melodious charm'd the ear;
There shrill the lark and soft the linnet sung,
And loud through air the throstle's music rung.
The gentle swain the cheerful scene admired;
The cheerful scene the song of joy inspired: –

'Chant on (he cried), ye warblers on the spray!
Bleat on, ye flocks that in the pastures play!
Low on, ye herds, that range the dewy vales!
Murmur, ye rills! and whisper soft, ye gales!
How bless'd my lot, in these sweet fields assign'd
Where peace and leisure sooth the tuneful mind;
Where yet some pleasing vestiges remain
Of unperverted Nature's golden reign,
When Love and Virtue ranged Arcadian shades,
With undesigning youths and artless maids!
For us, though destined to a later time,
A less luxuriant soil, less genial clime,
For us the country boasts enough to charm,
In the wild woodland or the cultured farm.
Come, Cynthio, come! in town no longer stay;
From crowds, and noise, and folly haste away!
The fields, the meads, the trees are all in bloom,
The vernal showers awake a rich perfume.
Where Damon's mansion, by the glassy stream,
Rears its white walls that through green willows gleam,
Annual the neighbours hold their shearing day;
And blithe youths come, and nymphs in neat array:
Those shear their sheep, upon the smooth turf laid,
In the broad plane's or trembling poplar's shade;
These for their friends the' expected feast provide,
Beneath cool bowers along the' enclosure's side.
To view the toil, the glad repast to share,
Thy Delia, my Melania shall be there;
Each kind and faithful to her faithful swain,
Loves the calm pleasures of the pastoral plain.
Come, Cynthio, come! If towns and crowds invite,
And noise and folly promise high delight;
Soon the tired soul disgusted turns from these –
The rural prospect only long can please!'

[1778]

From *Rural Business*

FIRST:

The care of farms we sing – attend the strain –
What skill, what toil shall best procure you gain;
How different culture different ground requires;
While Wealth rewards whom Industry inspires.

SECOND:

When thy light land on scorching gravel lies,
And to the springing blade support denies;
Fix on the wintry tilth the frequent fold,
And mend with cooling marl or untried mould.

THIRD:

If thy strong loam superfluous wet retain,
Lead through thy fields the subterraneous drain,
And o'er the surface mellowing stores expand
Of fiery lime or incoherent sand.

FIRST:

In vacant corners, on the hamlet waste,
The ample dunghill's steaming heap be placed;
There many a month fermenting to remain,
Ere thy slow team disperse it o'er the plain.

SECOND:

The prudent farmer all manure provides,
The mire of roads, the mould of hedge-row sides;
For him their mud the stagnant ponds supply;
For him their soil, the stable and the sty.

THIRD:

For this the swain, on Kennet's winding shore,
Digs sulphurous peat along the sable moor:
For this, where Ocean bounds the stormy strand,
They fetch dank seaweed to the neighbouring land.

FIRST:

Who barren heaths to tillage means to turn,
Must, ere he plough, the greensward pare and burn;
Where rise the smoking hillocks o'er the field,
The saline ashes useful compost yield.

SECOND:

Where sedge or rushes rise on spongy soils,
Or rampant moss the impoverish'd herbage spoils,
Corrosive soot with liberal hand bestow;
The improving pasture soon its use will show.

THIRD:

Hertfordian swains on airy hills explore
The chalk's white vein, a fertilizing store:
This, from deep pits in copious baskets drawn,
Amends alike the arable and lawn.

FIRST:

Who spends too oft in indolence the day
Soon sees his farm his base neglect betray;
His useless hedge-greens docks and nettles bear,
And the tough cammock clogs his shining share.

SECOND:

Thy weedy fallows let the plough pervade,
Till on the top the' inverted roots are laid:
There left to wither in the noontide ray,
Or by the spiky harrow clear'd away.

THIRD:

When wheat's green stem the ridge begins to hide,
Let the sharp weedhook's frequent aid be tried,
Lest thy spoil'd crop at harvest thou bemoan,
With twitch and twining bindweed overgrown.

FIRST:

Much will rank melilot thy grain disgrace,
And darnel, fellest of the weedy race:
To' extirpate these, might care or cost avail,
To' extirpate these nor care nor cost should fail.

SECOND:

When the foul furrow fetid mayweed fills,
The weary reaper oft complains of ills;
As his keen sickle grides along the lands,
The acrid herbage oft corrodes his hands.

THIRD:

Wield oft thy scythe along the grassy layes,
Ere the rude thistle its light down displays;
Else that light down upon the breeze will fly,
And a new store of noxious plants supply.

FIRST:

Would ye from tillage ample gains receive,
With change of crops the' exhausted soil relieve;
Next purple clover let brown wheat be seen,
And bearded barley after turnips green.

SECOND:

Bid here dark peas or tangled vetches spread,
There buckwheat's white flower faintly tinged with red;
Bid here potatoes' deep green stems be born,
And yellow cole the enclosure there adorn.

THIRD:

Here let tall rye or fragrant beans ascend,
Or oats their ample panicles extend;
There rest thy glebe, left fallow not in vain,
To feel the summer's sun and winter's rain.

FIRST:

The skill'd in culture oft repay their toil
By choice of plants adapted to their soil;

The spiky saintfoin best on chalk succeeds,
The lucern hates cold clays and moory meads.

SECOND:

Best on loose sands, where brakes and briars once rose,
Its deep-fringed leaves the yellow carrot shows;
Best on stiff loam rough teasels rear their heads,
And brown coriander's odorous umbel spreads.

THIRD:

On barren mountains, bleak with chilly air,
Forbidding pasturage or the ploughman's care,
Laburnum's boughs a beauteous bloom disclose,
Or spiry pines a gloomy grove compose.

FIRST:

On rushy marshes, rank with watery weeds,
Clothe the clear'd soil with groves of waving reeds;
Of them the gardener annual fences forms,
To shield his tender plants from vernal storms.

[1782]

JOHN LANGHORNE

From *Studley Park*

What pleasing scenes the landscape wide displays!
The' enchanting prospect bids for ever gaze.
Hail, charming fields, of happy swains the care!
Hail, happy swains, possess'd of fields so fair!
In peace your plenteous labours long enjoy;
No murdering wars shall waste, nor foes destroy;

While western gales Earth's teeming womb unbind,
The seasons change, and bounteous suns are kind.
To social towns, see! wealthy Commerce brings
Rejoicing Affluence on his silver wings.
On verdant hills, see! flocks innumerous feed,
Or thoughtful listen to the lively reed.
See! golden harvests sweep the bending plains;
'And Peace and Plenty own a Brunswick reigns.'*

[1766]

WILLIAM COWPER

From *Retirement*

Ye groves (the statesman at his desk exclaims,
Sick of a thousand disappointed aims),
My patrimonial treasure and my pride,
Beneath your shades your grey possessor hide,
Receive me languishing for that repose
The servant of the public never knows.
Ye saw me once (ah, those regretted days
When boyish innocence was all my praise!)
Hour after hour delightfully allot
To studies then familiar, since forgot,
And cultivate a taste for ancient song,
Catching its ardour as I mus'd along;
Nor seldom, as propitious heav'n might send,
What once I valued and could boast, a friend,
Were witnesses how cordially I press'd
His undissembling virtue to my breast;

* A reference to Pope's *Windsor Forest*; see p. 276.

Receive me now, not uncorrupt as then,
Nor guiltless of corrupting other men,
But vers'd in arts that, while they seem to stay
A falling empire, hasten its decay.
To the fair haven of my native home,
The wreck of what I was, fatigu'd, I come;
For once I can approve the patriot's voice,
And make the course he recommends my choice;
We meet at last in one sincere desire,
His wish and mine both prompt me to retire.
'Tis done – he steps into the welcome chaise,
Lolls at his ease behind four handsome bays,
That whirl away from business and debate
The disincumber'd Atlas of the state.
Ask not the boy, who when the breeze of morn
First shakes the glittering drops from every thorn
Unfolds his flock, then under bank or bush
Sits linking cherry stones, or platting rush,
How fair is freedom? – he was always free:
To carve his rustic name upon a tree,
To snare the mole, or with ill-fashion'd hook,
To draw th' incautious minnow from the brook,
Are life's prime pleasures in his simple view,
His flock the chief concern he ever knew –
She shines but little in his heedless eyes,
The good we never miss we rarely prize:
But ask the noble drudge in state affairs,
Escap'd from office and its constant cares,
What charms he sees in freedom's smile express'd,
In freedom lost so long, now repossess'd;
The tongue whose strains were cogent as commands,
Rever'd at home, and felt in foreign lands,
Shall own itself a stamm'rer in that cause,
Or plead its silence as its best applause.
He knows indeed that, whether dress'd or rude,

Wild without art, or artfully subdu'd,
Nature in ev'ry form inspires delight,
But never mark'd her with so just a sight.
Her hedge-row shrubs, a variegated store,
With woodbine and wild roses mantled o'er,
Green balks and furrow'd lands, the stream that spreads
Its cooling vapour o'er the dewy meads,
Downs that almost escape th' inquiring eye,
That melt and fade into the distant sky,
Beauties he lately slighted as he pass'd,
Seem all created since he travell'd last.
Master of all th' enjoyments he design'd,
No rough annoyance rankling in his mind,
What early philosophic hours he keeps,
How regular his meals, how sound he sleeps!
Not sounder he that on the mainmast head,
While morning kindles with a windy red,
Begins a long look-out for distant land,
Nor quits, till ev'ning watch, his giddy stand,
Then swift descending with a seaman's haste,
Slips to his hammock, and forgets the blast.
He chooses company, but not the squire's,
Whose wit is rudeness, whose good breeding tires;
Nor yet the parson's, who would gladly come,
Obsequious when abroad, though proud at home;
Nor can he much affect the neighb'ring peer,
Whose toe of emulation treads too near;
But wisely seeks a more convenient friend,
With whom, dismissing forms, he may unbend!
A man whom marks of condescending grace
Teach, while they flatter him, his proper place:
Who comes when call'd, and at a word withdraws,
Speaks with reserve, and listens with applause;
Some plain mechanic, who, without pretence
To birth or wit, nor gives nor takes offence;

On whom he rests well-pleas'd his weary pow'rs,
And talks and laughs away his vacant hours.
The tide of life, swift always in its course,
May run in cities with a brisker force,
But no where with a current so serene,
Or half so clear, as in the rural scene.
Yet how fallacious is all earthly bliss,
What obvious truths the wisest heads may miss;
Some pleasures live a month, and some a year,
But short the date of all we gather here;
No happiness is felt, except the true,
That does not charm the more for being new.
This observation, as it chanc'd, not made,
Or if the thought occurr'd, not duly weigh'd,
He sighs – for, after all, by slow degrees,
The spot he lov'd has lost the pow'r to please;
To cross his ambling pony day by day,
Seems at the best but dreaming life away;
The prospect, such as might enchant despair,
He views it not, or sees no beauty there;
With aching heart, and discontented looks,
Returns at noon to billiards or to books,
But feels, while grasping at his faded joys,
A secret thirst of his renounc'd employs.
He chides the tardiness of ev'ry post,
Pants to be told of battles won or lost,
Blames his own indolence, observes, though late,
'Tis criminal to leave a sinking state,
Flies to the levee, and, receiv'd with grace,
Kneels, kisses hands, and shines again in place.

[1782]

THOMAS BATCHELOR

From *The Progress of Agriculture*

Great queen of arts! when shall thy blissful sway,
From every heart, command the grateful lay?
For, hark! – methinks far other notes I hear,
Which, sad and solemn, strike my wounded ear;
Beneath yon willow sits a minstrel swain,
Nor Wealth nor Grandeur hearken to his strain;
While lonely there, his plaintive notes arise,
The drops of anguish glisten in his eyes.
– 'Sweet-smiling vale! that nurs'd my infant years,
Whose scenes enchanted, and whose name endears!
Still glow thy fields in summer's fruitful ray,
Thy harvests flourish, all thy meads are gay;
But not for me fair Nature spreads her store,
Life's smiling prospects must be mine no more!
'Ye blissful hours! which once this breast has known,
When half the village sow'd and reap'd their own;
When social feelings glow'd in ev'ry breast,
Each master gen'rous, and each servant blest;
When competence, and peace, and rural joy,
Smil'd in each cottage, cheer'd each days employ;
Alas! your beams are vanish'd from the plain,
As with'ring flow'rets fade in winter's iron reign.
'Friends of my youth, who bade my fortunes rise,
Death's ruthless hand for ever seals your eyes,
Where yonder high tow'r lifts its ivy'd head,
Ye rest, reposing on your clay-cold bed:
Envied retreat! – while your surviving heirs
Inherit life with its ten thousand cares!
'Fled is your long-accumulating store,
Your houses, meadows, fields, are theirs no more;

Where long your race manur'd and till'd the soil,
With easy competence and healthful toil,
Monopoly has rear'd her gorgon head,
To strike the source of rural comforts dead!
  'I ask not Science to withdraw her hand,
Nor hoary Custom still to rule the land;
Prais'd be the scene when ev'ry hill and plain
Exulting owns fair Cultivation's reign;
When verdant fences o'er each field extend,
Limits define, and property defend:
Ye noble few, whose patriot-bosoms glow
In this fair cause, may glory gild your brow!
– But say, ye great! who bid, o'er all the isle,
Green pastures spread where harvests wont to smile,
Who change, for herds, the life-supporting grain,
With *woolly tribes* displace the reaper train,
Who build a *palace* for the wealthier few,
But drive to squallid huts the *ruin'd* crew;
Shall not those wretched sons of Want repine?
Yes – helpless myriads mix their sighs with mine!'

[1804]

GILBERT WHITE

The Naturalist's Summer-Evening Walk

. . . equidem credo, quia sit divinitus illis
Ingenium. *Virgil*

When day declining sheds a milder gleam,
What time the may-fly haunts the pool or stream;
When the still owl skims round the grassy mead,

What time the timorous hare limps forth to feed;
Then be the time to steal adown the vale,
And listen to the vagrant cuckoo's tale;
To hear the clamorous curlew call his mate,
Or the soft quail his tender pain relate;
To see the swallow sweep the dark'ning plain
Belated, to support her infant train;
To mark the swift in rapid giddy ring
Dash round the steeple, unsubdu'd of wing:
Amusive birds! – say where your hid retreat
When the frost rages and the tempests beat;
Whence your return, by such nice instinct led,
When spring, soft season, lifts her bloomy head?
Such baffled searches mock man's prying pride,
The *God* of *Nature* is your secret guide!
  While deep'ning shades obscure the face of day,
To yonder bench leaf-shelter'd let us stray,
Till blended objects fail the swimming sight,
And all the facing landscape sinks in night;
To hear the drowsy dor[1] come brushing by
With buzzing wing, or the shrill cricket cry;
To see the feeding bat glance through the wood;
To catch the distant falling of the flood;
While o'er the cliff th' awaken'd churn-owl hung
Through the still gloom protracts his chattering song;
While high in air, and pois'd upon his wings,
Unseen, the soft enamour'd woodlark sings:
These, *Nature*'s works, the curious mind employ,
Inspire a soothing melancholy joy:
As fancy warms, a pleasing kind of pain
Steals o'er the cheek, and thrills the creeping vein!
  Each rural sight, each sound, each smell, combine;
The tinkling sheep-bell, or the breath of kine;
The new-mown hay that scents the swelling breeze,
Or cottage-chimney smoking through the trees.

[1] the dung-beetle (which flies by night)

The chilling night-dews fall: – away, retire;
For see, the glow-worm lights her amorous fire!
Thus, e'er night's veil had half obscur'd the sky,
Th' impatient damsel hung her lamp on high:
True to the signal, by love's meteor led,
Leander hasten'd to his Hero's bed.

[1789]

SOME VERSIONS OF ANTI-PASTORAL

Whatever the opposition between Gray's version of Pastoral and Thomson's, the condition of the agricultural labourer was seen by both men as one of comfortable jollity. The labourers in *The Seasons* are delighted, as we have seen, at the bounty of nature towards their employers; and for Gray the happiness of the ploughman, jocund as he drives his team afield, is at once a lesson of patience, and the expression of a social glee from which the poet is excluded. It is against both these versions, then, that the realism of George Crabbe, and the extreme pessimism of Goldsmith, are directed; in the first part of *The Village* (1783), Crabbe insists that the pastoral vision distorts, and that the agricultural labourer is brutalized and impoverished; in Goldsmith's *The Deserted Village* (1770), the labourer is presented as having been in recent times contented and dignified, in something like a Golden Age, but one which has been destroyed rather than created by the advance of the mercantile spirit in agriculture. The attitudes of both men had been anticipated in some respects, however, by earlier writers, and Crabbe in particular owes a good deal to the early work of Stephen Duck, whose *The Thresher's Labour* describes the life of the labourer in agriculture from his own experience, and without the detachment of earlier attempts at naturalism:

> But when the scorching Sun is mounted high,
> And no kind Barns with friendly Shade are nigh;
> Our weary Scythes entangle in the Grass,
> While Streams of Sweat run trickling down apace.

Duck rejects the vision of the literary Pastoral as later Crabbe was to do:

> Can we, like Shepherds, tell a merry Tale;
> The Voice is lost, drown'd by the louder Flail.

There is no smiling, paternalistic employer to welcome them from their work – 'Rogues, d'ye think that this will do?' – and the harvest-feast is seen for what arguably it was, a 'cheat' to oil the routine of industry. What is most remarkable about the poem is its formulation of the essential boringness of farm-work:

> Think what a painful Life we daily lead;
> Each Morning early rise, go late to Bed.

Nor is the labourer free from toil while he sleeps, for his nights are full of disturbed dreams of his Herculean labours. The seasonal cycle so dear to the writers of Pastoral, of birth, maturity, death and rebirth, becomes for Duck simply the hopeless inevitability of continual work; after the labour of the harvest comes the labour of sowing, of weeding. The only, temporary consolation is in alcoholic stupor.

To stress these aspects of *The Thresher's Labour* is, however, to read the poem too much through twentieth-century eyes. Duck is intent on describing life in the country as it really is; but of course the only poetic language available to him is that of the courtly, of the neo-classical literary tradition. *The Thresher's Labour* vacillates between intense naturalism and an extreme neo-classical formalism:

> Ye Reapers, cast your Eyes around the Field;
> And view, the various Scenes its Beauties yield:
> Then look again, with a more tender Eye,
> To think how soon it must in Ruin lie!

It is hard to equate these philosophic swains with the sweating labourers in other parts of the poem, but the poetic models from which Duck learned to write made it almost inevitable that the individuality of his own experience would be subsumed by the wider tradition. Nor was Duck ever given a chance to develop an original poetic voice within the tradition – he was taken up by the court, and his poetry rapidly lost whatever individuality it had possessed in his anxiety to conform with the expectations of his patrons.

The complaints that 'honest Duck' was for a while able to make, and which are taken up and developed by Crabbe, amount to a refusal to pastoralize, to idealize, the agricultural labourer on any terms; for both men it is in the nature of farm-work to be unrewarding, and for Crabbe the question of whether there can ever have been a Golden Age was an academic one. What mattered was that in the eighteenth century the condition of the labourer was unendurable.

> No shepherds now, in smooth alternate verse,
> Their country's beauty or their nymphs' rehearse;
> Yet still for these we frame the tender strain,
> Still in our lays fond Corydons complain,
> And shepherds' boys their amorous pains reveal,
> The only pains, alas! they never feel.

The Village is not simply, of course, an argument against a literary tradition, but against the deliberate idealization of the English labourer in almost all eighteenth-century discussion of him, which allowed the Pastoral to flourish and the poor to starve:

> Or will you praise that homely, healthy fare,
> Plenteous and plain, that happy peasants share!
> Oh! trifle not with wants you cannot feel,
> Nor mock the misery of a stinted meal;
> Homely, not wholesome, plain, not plenteous, such
> As you who praise would never deign to touch.

It is important to distinguish the nature of these complaints from the sort of complaint made by Goldsmith, and, following him, by Ebenezer Elliott in *The Splendid Village*, and by John Clare in *The Parish*, that there was until recently a time when there was dignity in agricultural labour; when according to Goldsmith, 'every rood of ground maintained its man':

> For him light labour spread her wholesome store,
> Just gave what life required, but gave no more:
> His best companions, innocence and health;
> And his best riches, ignorance of wealth.

In the Golden Age these poets remember – the memory is perhaps dimmer for Elliott than for Goldsmith and Clare – the society of the village was still a unified one, which admitted social differences but not social divisions. But that time had been destroyed, for Goldsmith by the entry into rural society of a new class of landowners, the ex-merchants of 'trade's unfeeling train'; for Clare and Elliott by the inflationary agriculture of the Napoleonic Wars and the consequent agricultural depression; and for Clare also by the enclosure of his native parish, Helpston.

In pointing to the distinction between these two traditions one critic, Raymond Williams, has argued that Crabbe's description of the condition of the rural poor, as it must always have been during the long development of agricultural capitalism, is 'real history'; while Goldsmith, Clare, and a number of later writers remained to some extent deceived by the pastoral vision and the memories of feudalism, and put forward a mythological history of the degradation of labour which, whether it occurred in 1770, 1800, or 1830, is always for them a happening in the recent past. But this case against Goldsmith and Clare is perhaps a mistaken one, which rests on a confusion between the form of their protest and its content, and on an over-abstract idea of the nature of historical change. It is true enough that the protests of these poets and others like them find expression in the conventional nostalgia of the pastoral tradition, and in complaints whose substance appears and reappears throughout the seventeenth, eighteenth and nineteenth centuries. The important question, however, is why these complaints appear where they do and when they do. And the changes described by Goldsmith and Clare, although sometimes expressed in a generalized and conventional pessimism, are particular, local changes; considered in the lump they were certainly only parts of a long and painful agricultural revolution, with no beginning and no end, but they must have been quite convulsive in the local communities in which they occurred – in Goldsmith's Auburn ('a little village, distant about fifty miles from town') and Clare's Helpston. If this is so, a view of history in terms of a Golden Age and after is perfectly justified, in the local terms in which Goldsmith and Clare want their poems in the first instance to be understood; so that in the late eighteenth century, and especially in the early nineteenth, the period of inflation and depression, of Corn Laws and Game Laws, the conventional nostalgia of the Pastoral became the entirely appropriate expression of agricultural discontent.

Pastoral poetry is a native of happier climates, where the face of nature, and the manners of the people are widely different from those of our northern regions. What is reality on the soft Arcadian and Sicilian plains, is all fiction here.

[John Aikin, 'Essay on Ballads and Pastoral Songs', 1772]

If rural life no longer present us with shepherds singing and piping for a bowl or a crook, why persist, in violation of all probability, to introduce such characters? If pastoral cannot exist without them, let us cease to compose it.

[Nathan Drake, *Literary Hours*, 1798]

STEPHEN DUCK

From *The Thresher's Labour*

Soon as the golden Harvest quits the Plain,
And *Ceres'* Gift's reward the Farmer's Pain;
What Corn each Sheaf will yield, intent to hear,
And guess from thence the Profits of the Year,
He calls his Reapers forth: Around we stand,
With deep Attention, waiting his Command.
To each our Task he readily divides,
And pointing, to our diff'rent Stations guides.
As he directs, to distant Barns we go;
Here two for Wheat, and there for Barley two.
But first, to shew what he expects to find,
These Words, or Words like these, disclose his Mind.

'So dry the Corn was carry'd from the Field,
'So easily 'twill thresh, so well 'twill yield;
'Sure large Day's Works I well may hope for now:
'Come, strip, and try; let's see what you can do.'

Divested of our Cloaths, with Flail in Hand,
At proper Distance, Front to Front we stand:
And first the Threshal's gently swung, to prove,
Whether with just Exactness it will move:
That once secure, we swiftly whirl them round,
From the strong Planks our Crab-tree Staves rebound,
And echoing Barns return the rattling Sound.
Now in the Air our knotty Weapons fly,
And now with equal Force descend from high;
Down one, one up, so well they keep the Time,
The *Cyclops'* Hammers could not truer chime;
Nor with more heavy Strokes could *Ætna* groan,

When *Vulcan* forg'd the Arms for *Thetis'* Son.
In briny Streams our Sweat descends apace,
Drops from our Locks, or trickles down our Face.
No Intermission in our Work we know;
The noisy Threshal must for ever go.
Their Master absent, others safely play;
The sleeping Threshal does itself betray.
Nor yet, the tedious Labour to beguile,
And make the passing Minutes sweetly smile,
Can we, like Shepherds, tell a merry Tale;
The Voice is lost, drown'd by the louder Flail.
But we may think – Alas! what pleasing Thing,
Here, to the Mind, can the dull Fancy bring?
Our Eye beholds no pleasing Object here,
No chearful Sound diverts our list'ning Ear.
The Shepherd well may tune his Voice to sing,
Inspir'd with all the Beauties of the Spring.
No Fountains murmur here, no Lambkins play,
No Linnets warble, and no Fields look gay;
'Tis all a gloomy, melancholy Scene,
Fit only to provoke the Muse's Spleen.
When sooty Pease we thresh, you scarce can know
Our native Colour, as from Work we go:
The Sweat, the Dust, and suffocating Smoke,
Make us so much like *Ethiopians* look,
We scare our Wives, when Ev'ning brings us home;
And frighted Infants think the Bugbear come.
Week after Week, we this dull Task pursue,
Unless when winn'wing Days produce a new;
A new, indeed, but frequently a worse!
The Threshal yields but to the Master's Curse.
He counts the Bushels, counts how much a Day;
He swears we've idled half our Time away:
'Why, look ye, Rogues, d'ye think that this will do?
'Your Neighbours thrash as much again as you.'

Now in our Hands we wish our noisy Tools,
To drown the hated Names of Rogues and Fools.
But wanting these, we just like School-boys look,
When angry Masters view the blotted Book:
They cry, 'their Ink was faulty, and their Pen;'
We, 'the Corn threshes bad, 'twas cut too green.'

But soon as *Winter* hides his hoary Head,
And Nature's Face is with new Beauty spread;
The lovely *Spring* appears, refreshing Show'rs
New cloath the Field with Grass, and blooming Flow'rs.
Next to her the rip'ning *Summer* presses on,
And SOL begins his longest Race to run.
Before the Door our welcome Master stands;
Tells us the ripen'd Grass requires our Hands.
The grateful Tiding presently imparts
Life to our Looks, and Spirits to our Hearts.
We with the happy Season may be fair;
And, joyful, long to breathe in op'ner Air.
This Change of Labour seems to give such Ease,
With Thoughts of Happiness ourselves we please.
But, ah! how rarely's Happiness complete!
There's always Bitter mingled with the Sweet.
When first the Lark sings Prologue to the Day,
We rise, admonish'd by his early Lay;
This new Employ with eager Haste to prove,
This new Employ, becomes so much our Love.
Alas! that human Joys shou'd change so soon!
Our Morning Pleasure turns to Pain at Noon.
The Birds salute us, as to Work we go,
And with new Life our Bosoms seem to glow.
On our right Shoulder hangs the crooked Blade,
The Weapon destin'd to uncloath the Mead:
Our left supports the Whetstone, Scrip, and Beer;
This for our Scythes, and these ourselves to chear.

And now the Field, design'd to try our Might,
At length appears, and meets our longing Sight.
The Grass and Ground we view with careful Eyes,
To see which Way the best Advantage lies;
And, Hero-like, each claims the foremost Place.
At first our Labour seems a sportive Race:
With rapid Force our sharpen'd Blades we drive,
Strain ev'ry Nerve, and Blow for Blow we give.
All strive to vanquish, tho' the Victor gains,
No other Glory, but the greatest Pains.

But when the scorching Sun is mounted high,
And no kind Barns with friendly Shade are nigh;
Our weary Scythes entangle in the Grass,
While Streams of Sweat run trickling down apace.
Our sportive Labour we too late lament;
And wish that Strength again we vainly spent.

Thus, in the Morn, a Courser have I seen
With headlong Fury scour the level Green;
Or mount the hills, if Hills are in his Way,
As if no Labour could his Fire allay;
Till *Phoebus*, shining with meridian Heat,
Has bath'd his panting Sides in briny Sweat:
The lengthen'd Chace scarce able to sustain,
He measures back the Hills and Dales with Pain.

With Heat and Labour tir'd, our Scythes we quit,
Search out a shady Tree and down we sit:
From Scrip and Bottle hope new Strength to gain;
But Scrip and Bottle too are try'd in vain.
Down our parch'd Throats we scarce the Bread can get;
And, quite o'erspent with Toil, but faintly eat,
Nor can the Bottle only answer all;
The Bottle and the Beer are both too small.

Time flows: Again we rise from off the Grass;
Again each Mower takes his proper Place;
Not eager now, as late, our Strength to prove;
But all contented regular to move.
We often whet, and often view the Sun;
As often wish, his tedious Race was run.
At length he veils his purple Face from Sight,
And bids the weary Labourer, Good Night.
Homewards we move, but spent so much with Toil,
We slowly walk, and rest at ev'ry Stile.
Our good expecting Wives, who think we stay,
Got to the Door, soon eye us in the Way.
Then from the Pot the Dumplin's catch'd in Haste,
And homely by its Side the Bacon plac'd.
Supper and Sleep by Morn new Strength supply;
And out we set again, our Work to try;
But not so early quite, nor quite so fast,
As, to our Cost, we did the Morning past.

★

Let those who feast at Ease on dainty Fare
Pity the Reapers, who their Feasts prepare:
For Toils scarce ever ceasing press us now;
Rest never does, but on the Sabbath, show;
And barely that our Masters will allow.
Think what a painful Life we daily lead;
Each Morning early rise, go late to Bed;
Nor, when asleep, are we secure from Pain;
We then perform our Labours o'er again:
Our mimic Fancy ever restless seems;
And what we act awake, she acts in Dreams.
Hard Fate! our Labours ev'n in Sleep don't cease;
Scarce *Hercules* e'er felt such Toils as these!

But soon we rise the bearded Crop again,
Soon *Phoebus'* Rays well dry the golden Grain.
Pleas'd with the Scene, our Master glows with Joy;
Bids us for carrying all our Force employ;
When straight Confusion o'er the Field appears,
And stunning Clamour fill the Workmen's Ears;
The Bells and clashing Whips alternate sound,
And rattling Waggons thunder o'er the Ground.
The Wheat, when carry'd, Pease, and other Grain,
We soon secure, and leave a fruitless Plain;
In noisy Triumph the last Load moves on,
And loud Huzza's proclaim the Harvest done.

Our Master, joyful at the pleasing Sight,
Invites us all to feast with him at Night.
A Table plentifully spread we find,
And jugs of huming Ale to chear the Mind;
Which he, too gen'rous, pushes round so fast,
We think no Toils to come, nor mind the past.
But the next Morning soon reveals the Cheat,
When the same Toils we must again repeat;
To the same Barns must back again return,
To labour there for Room for next Year's Corn.

Thus, as the Year's revolving Course goes round,
No Respite from our Labour can be found:
Like *Sisyphus*, our Work is never done;
Continually rolls back the restless Stone.
New-growing Labours still succeed the past;
And growing always new, must always last.

[1736]

OLIVER GOLDSMITH

From *The Deserted Village*

Sweet Auburn! loveliest village of the plain,
Where health and plenty cheer'd the labouring swain,
Where smiling spring its earliest visit paid,
And parting summer's lingering blooms delay'd:
Dear lovely bowers of innocence and ease,
Seats of my youth, when every sport could please:
How often have I loiter'd o'er thy green,
Where humble happiness endear'd each scene!
How often have I paused on every charm,
The shelter'd cot, the cultivated farm,
The never failing brook, the busy mill,
The decent church that topp'd the neighbouring hill,
The hawthorn bush, with seats beneath the shade,
For talking age and whispering lovers made!
How often have I bless'd the coming day,
When toil remitting lent its turn to play,
And all the village train, from labour free,
Led up their sports beneath the spreading tree:
While many a pastime circled in the shade,
The young contending as the old survey'd;
And many a gambol frolick'd o'er the ground,
And slights of art and feats of strength went round.
And still, as each repeated pleasure tired,
Succeeding sports the mirthful band inspired;
The dancing pair that simply sought renown,
By holding out to tire each other down;
The swain mistrustless of his smutted face,
While secret laughter titter'd round the place;
The bashful virgin's sidelong looks of love,
The matron's glance that would those looks reprove.

These were thy charms, sweet village! sports like these,
With sweet succession, taught e'en toil to please;
These round thy bowers their cheerful influence shed,
These were thy charms – but all these charms are fled.
  Sweet smiling village, loveliest of the lawn,
Thy sports are fled, and all thy charms withdrawn;
Amidst thy bowers the tyrant's hand is seen,
And desolation saddens all thy green:
One only master grasps the whole domain,
And half a tillage stints thy smiling plain;
No more thy glassy brook reflects the day,
But choked with sedges works its weedy way;
Along thy glades, a solitary guest,
The hollow-sounding bittern guards its nest;
Amidst thy desert walks the lapwing flies,
And tires their echoes with unvaried cries.
Sunk are thy bowers in shapeless ruin all,
And the long grass o'ertops the mouldering wall;
And, trembling, shrinking from the spoiler's hand,
Far, far away thy children leave the land.
  Ill fares the land, to hastening ills a prey,
Where wealth accumulates, and men decay;
Princes and lords may flourish or may fade;
A breath can make them, as a breath has made:
But a bold peasantry, their country's pride,
When once destroy'd, can never be supplied.
  A time there was, ere England's griefs began,
When every rood of ground maintained its man;
For him light labour spread her wholesome store,
Just gave what life required, but gave no more:
His best companions, innocence and health;
And his best riches, ignorance of wealth.
  But times are altered; trade's unfeeling train
Usurp the land and dispossess the swain;
Along the lawn, where scattered hamlets rose,

Unwieldy wealth, and cumbrous pomp repose;
And every want to oppulence allied,
And every pang that folly pays to pride.
These gentle hours that plenty bade to bloom,
Those calm desires that asked but little room,
Those healthful sports that graced the peaceful scene,
Lived in each look, and brightened all the green;
These far departing seek a kinder shore,
And rural mirth and manners are no more.

*

Beside yon straggling fence that skirts the way
With blossom'd furze, unprofitably gay,
There, in his noisy mansion, skill'd to rule,
The village master taught his little school:
A man severe he was, and stern to view,
I knew him well, and every truant knew;
Well had the boding tremblers learn'd to trace
The day's disasters in his morning face;
Full well they laugh'd with counterfeited glee
At all his jokes, for many a joke had he;
Full well the busy whisper, circling round,
Convey'd the dismal tidings when he frown'd;
Yet he was kind, or if severe in aught,
The love he bore to learning was in fault;
The village all declared how much he knew;
'Twas certain he could write and cipher too;
Lands he could measure, terms and tides presage,
And e'en the story ran that he could gauge:
In arguing, too, the parson own'd his skill,
For e'en though vanquish'd he could argue still;
While words of learned length and thundering sound
Amazed the gazing rustics ranged around;
And still they gazed, and still the wonder grew

That one small head should carry all he knew.
But pass'd is all his fame. The very spot,
Where many a time he triumph'd, is forgot.
  Near yonder thorn that lifts its head on high,
Where once the signpost caught the passing eye,
Low lies that house where nut-brown draughts inspired,
Where gray-beard mirth and smiling toil retired,
Where village statesmen talk'd with looks profound,
And news much older than their ale went round.
Imagination fondly stoops to trace
The parlour splendours of that festive place;
The white-wash'd wall, the nicely sanded floor,
The varnish'd clock that click'd behind the door:
The chest contrived a double debt to pay,
A bed by night, a chest of drawers by day;
The pictures placed for ornament and use,
The twelve good rules, the royal game of goose;
The hearth, except when winter chill'd the day,
With aspen boughs and flowers and fennel gay;
While broken teacups, wisely kept for show,
Ranged o'er the chimney, glisten'd in a row.
  Vain transitory splendours! could not all
Reprieve the tottering mansion from its fall!
Obscure it sinks, nor shall it more impart
An hour's importance to the poor man's heart;
Thither no more the peasant shall repair
To sweet oblivion of his daily care;
No more the farmer's news, the barber's tale,
No more the woodman's ballad shall prevail;
No more the smith his dusky brow shall clear,
Relax his ponderous strength, and lean to hear;
The host himself no longer shall be found
Careful to see the mantling bliss go round;
Nor the coy maid, half willing to be press'd,
Shall kiss the cup to pass it to the rest.

Yes! let the rich deride, the proud disdain
These simple blessings of the lowly train;
To me more dear, congenial to my heart,
One native charm than all the gloss of art;
Spontaneous joys, where Nature has its play,
The soul adopts, and owns their firstborn sway;
Lightly they frolic o'er the vacant mind,
Unenvied, unmolested, unconfined.
But the long pomp, the midnight masquerade,
With all the freaks of wanton wealth array'd,
In these, ere triflers half their wish obtain,
The toiling pleasure sickens into pain;
And, e'en while fashion's brightest arts decoy,
The heart distrusting asks, if this be joy?
Ye friends to truth, ye statesmen, who survey
The rich man's joys increase, the poor's decay,
'Tis yours to judge how wide the limits stand
Between a splendid and a happy land.
Proud swells the tide with loads of freighted ore,
And shouting Folly hails them from her shore;
Hoards e'en beyond the miser's wish abound,
And rich men flock from all the world around.
Yet count our gains. This wealth is but a name
That leaves our useful products still the same.
Not so the loss. The man of wealth and pride
Takes up a space that many poor supplied;
Space for his lake, his park's extended bounds,
Space for his horses, equipage, and hounds;
The robe that wraps his limbs in silken sloth
Has robb'd the neighbouring fields of half their growth;
His seat, where solitary sports are seen,
Indignant spurns the cottage from the green;
Around the world each needful product flies,
For all the luxuries the world supplies:
While thus the land, adorn'd for pleasure all,

In barren splendour feebly waits the fall.
 As some fair female, unadorn'd and plain,
Secure to please while youth confirms her reign,
Slights every borrow'd charm that dress supplies,
Nor shares with art the triumph of her eyes;
But when those charms are pass'd, for charms are frail,
When time advances, and when lovers fail,
She then shines forth, solicitous to bless,
In all the glaring impotence of dress:
Thus fares the land, by luxury betray'd,
In Nature's simplest charms at first array'd;
But verging to decline, its splendours rise,
Its vistas strike, its palaces surprise;
While, scourged by famine, from the smiling land
The mournful peasant leads his humble band;
And while he sinks, without one arm to save,
The country blooms – a garden and a grave.

[1770]

CHARLES CHURCHILL

From *The Prophecy of Famine*

 Two boys, whose birth, beyond all question, springs
From great and glorious, though forgotten, kings,
Shepherds, of Scottish lineage, born and bred
On the same bleak and barren mountain's head,
By niggard nature doom'd on the same rocks
To spin out life, and starve themselves and flocks,
Fresh as the morning, which, enrobed in mist,

The mountain's top with usual dulness kiss'd,
Jockey and Sawney to their labours rose;
Soon clad I ween, where nature needs no clothes;
Where, from their youth enured to winter-skies,
Dress and her vain refinements they despise.
  Jockey, whose manly, high-boned cheeks to crown,
With freckles spotted, flamed the golden down,
With meikle art could on the bag-pipes play,
E'en from the rising to the setting day;
Sawney as long without remorse could bawl
Home's madrigals, and ditties from Fingal:
Oft' at his strains, all natural though rude,
The Highland lass forgot her want of food,
And, whilst she scratch'd her lover into rest,
Sunk pleased, though hungry, on her Sawney's breast.
  Far as the eye could reach, no tree was seen,
Earth, clad in russet, scorn'd the lively green:
The plague of locusts they secure defy,
For in three hours a grasshopper must die:
No living thing, whate'er its food, feasts there,
But the cameleon, who can feast on air.
No birds, except as birds of passage, flew;
No bee was known to hum, no dove to coo:
No streams, as amber smooth, as amber clear,
Were seen to glide, or heard to warble here:
Rebellion's spring, which through the country ran,
Furnish'd with bitter draughts, the steady clan:
No flowers embalm'd the air, but one white rose,
Which, on the tenth of June, by instinct blows;
By instinct blows at morn, and when the shades
Of drizzly eve prevail, by instinct fades.
  One and but one poor solitary cave,
Too sparing of her favours, nature gave;
That one alone (hard tax on Scottish pride!)
Shelter at once for man and beast supplied.

There snares without entangling briars spread,
And thistles, arm'd against the invader's head,
Stood in close ranks, all entrance to oppose;
Thistles now held more precious than the rose.
All creatures which, on nature's earliest plan,
Were form'd to loath, and to be loath'd by man;
Which owed their birth to nastiness and spite,
Deadly to touch, and hateful to the sight;
Creatures, which when admitted in the ark
Their saviour shunn'd, and rankled in the dark,
Found place within: marking her noisome road
With poison's trail, here crawl'd the bloated toad:
There webs were spread of more than common size,
And half-starved spiders prey'd on half-starved flies:
In quest of food, efts strove in vain to crawl;
Slugs, pinch'd with hunger, smear'd the slimy wall:
The cave around with hissing serpents rung;
On the damp roof unhealthy vapour hung;
And Famine, by her children always known,
As proud as poor, here fix'd her native throne.
  Here, for the sullen sky was overcast,
And summer shrunk beneath a wintry blast;
A native blast, which, arm'd with hail and rain,
Beat unrelenting on the naked swain,
The boys for shelter made; behind, the sheep,
Of which those shepherds every day *take keep*,
Sickly crept on, and with complainings rude,
On nature seem'd to call, and bleat for food.

JOCKEY:

  Sith to this cave, by tempest, we're confined,
And within *ken* our flocks, under the wind,
Safe from the pelting of this perilous storm,
Are laid *emong* yon' thistles, dry and warm,
What, Sawney, if by Shepherds' art we try

To mock the rigour of this cruel sky?
What if we tune some merry roundelay?
Well dost thou sing, nor ill doth Jockey play.

SAWNEY:

Ah! Jockey, ill advisest thou, I wis,
To think of songs at such a time as this:
Sooner shall herbage crown these barren rocks,
Sooner shall fleeces clothe these ragged flocks,
Sooner shall want seize shepherds of the south,
And we forget to live from hand to mouth,
Then Sawney, out of season, shall impart
The songs of gladness with an aching heart.

[1763]

GEORGE CRABBE

The Village

Book 1

The Village Life, and every care that reigns
O'er youthful peasants and declining swains;
What labour yields, and what, that labour past,
Age, in its hour of languor, finds at last;
What form the real Picture of the Poor,
Demand a song – the Muse can give no more.
Fled are those times, when, in harmonious strains,
The rustic poet praised his native plains:
No shepherds now, in smooth alternate verse,
Their country's beauty or their nymphs' rehearse;
Yet still for these we frame the tender strain,

Still in our lays fond Corydons complain,
And shepherds' boys their amorous pains reveal,
The only pains, alas! they never feel.
  On Mincio's banks, in Caesar's bounteous reign,
If Tityrus found the Golden Age again,
Must sleepy bards the flattering dream prolong,
Mechanic echoes of the Mantuan song?
From Truth and Nature shall we widely stray,
Where Virgil, not where Fancy, leads the way?
  Yes, thus the Muses sing of happy swains,
Because the Muses never knew their pains:
They boast their peasants' pipes; but peasants now
Resign their pipes and plod behind the plough;
And few, amid the rural-tribe, have time
To number syllables, and play with rhyme;
Save honest *Duck*, what son of verse could share
The poet's rapture and the peasant's care?
Or the great labours of the field degrade,
With the new peril of a poorer trade?
  From this chief cause these idle praises spring,
That themes so easy few forbear to sing;
For no deep thought the trifling subjects ask;
To sing of shepherds is an easy task:
The happy youth assumes the common strain,
A nymph his mistress, and himself a swain;
With no sad scenes he clouds his tuneful prayer,
But all, to look like her, is painted fair.
  I grant indeed that fields and flocks have charms
For him that grazes or for him that farms;
But when amid such pleasing scenes I trace
The poor laborious natives of the place,
And see the mid-day sun, with fervid ray,
On their bare heads and dewy temples play;
While some, with feebler heads and fainter hearts,
Deplore their fortune, yet sustain their parts –

Then shall I dare these real ills to hide
In tinsel trappings of poetic pride?
  No; cast by Fortune on a frowning coast,
Which neither groves nor happy valleys boast;
Where other cares than those the Muse relates,
And other shepherds dwell with other mates;
By such examples taught I paint the Cot,
As Truth will paint it, and as Bards will not:
Nor you, ye Poor, of letter'd scorn complain,
To you the smoothest song is smooth in vain;
O'ercome by labour, and bow'd down by time,
Feel you the barren flattery of a rhyme?
Can poets soothe you, when you pine for bread,
By winding myrtles round your ruin'd shed?
Can their light tales your weighty griefs o'erpower,
Or glad with airy mirth the toilsome hour?
  Lo! where the heath, with withering brake grown o'er,
Lends the light turf that warms the neighbouring poor,
From thence a length of burning sand appears,
Where the thin harvest waves its wither'd ears;
Rank weeds, that every art and care defy,
Reign o'er the land, and rob the blighted rye:
There thistles stretch their prickly arms afar,
And to the ragged infant threaten war;
There poppies nodding, mock the hope of toil;
There the blue bugloss paints the sterile soil;
Hardy and high, above the slender sheaf,
The slimy mallow waves her silky leaf;
O'er the young shoot the charlock throws a shade,
And clasping tares cling round the sickly blade;
With mingled tints the rocky coasts abound,
And a sad splendour vainly shines around.
So looks the nymph whom wretched arts adorn,
Betray'd by man, then left for man to scorn;
Whose cheek in vain assumes the mimic rose,

While her sad eyes the troubled breast disclose;
Whose outward splendour is but folly's dress,
Exposing most, when most it gilds distress.
  Here joyless roam a wild amphibious race,
With sullen woe display'd in every face;
Who, far from civil arts and social fly,
And scowl at strangers with suspicious eye.
  Here too the lawless merchant of the main
Draws from his plough th' intoxicated swain;
Want only claim'd the labour of the day,
But vice now steals his nightly rest away.
  Where are the swains, who, daily labour done,
With rural games play'd down the setting sun;
Who struck with matchless force the bounding ball,
Or made the pond'rous quoit obliquely fall;
While some huge Ajax, terrible and strong,
Engaged some artful stripling of the throng,
And fell beneath him, foil'd, while far around
Hoarse triumph rose, and rocks return'd the sound?
Where now are these? – Beneath yon cliff they stand,
To show the freighted pinnace where to land;
To load the ready steed with guilty haste,
To fly in terror o'er the pathless waste,
Or, when detected, in their straggling course,
To foil their foes by cunning or by force;
Or, yielding part (which equal knaves demand),
To gain a lawless passport through the land.
  Here, wand'ring long, amid these frowning fields,
I sought the simple life that Nature yields;
Rapine and Wrong and Fear usurp'd her place,
And a bold, artful, surly, savage race;
Who, only skill'd to take the finny tribe,
The yearly dinner, or septennial bribe,
Wait on the shore, and, as the waves run high,
On the tost vessel bend their eager eye,

Which to their coast directs its vent'rous way;
Theirs, or the ocean's, miserable prey.
   As on their neighbouring beach yon swallows stand,
And wait for favouring winds to leave the land;
While still for flight the ready wing is spread
So waited I the favouring hour, and fled;
Fled from these shores where guilt and famine reign,
And cried, Ah! hapless they who still remain;
Who still remain to hear the ocean roar,
Whose greedy waves devour the lessening shore;
Till some fierce tide, with more imperious sway,
Sweeps the low hut and all it holds away;
When the sad tenant weeps from door to door;
And begs a poor protection from the poor!
   But these are scenes where Nature's niggard hand
Gave a spare portion to the famish'd land;
Her's is the fault, if here mankind complain
Of fruitless toil and labour spent in vain;
But yet in other scenes more fair in view,
When Plenty smiles – alas! she smiles for few –
And those who taste not, yet behold her store,
Are as the slaves that dig the golden ore –
The wealth around them makes them doubly poor.
   Or will you deem them amply paid in health,
Labour's fair child, that languishes with wealth?
Go then! and see them rising with the sun,
Through a long course of daily toil to run;
See them beneath the dog-star's raging heat,
When the knees tremble and the temples beat;
Behold them, leaning on their scythes, look o'er
The labour past, and toils to come explore;
See them alternate suns and showers engage,
And hoard up aches and anguish for their age;
Through fens and marshy moors their steps pursue,
When their warm pores imbibe the evening dew;

Then own that labour may as fatal be
To these thy slaves, as thine excess to thee.
  Amid this tribe too oft a manly pride
Strives in strong toil the fainting heart to hide;
There may you see the youth of slender frame
Contend with weakness, weariness, and shame;
Yet, urged along, and proudly loth to yield,
He strives to join his fellows of the field:
Till long-contending nature droops at last,
Declining health rejects his poor repast,
His cheerless spouse the coming danger sees,
And mutual murmurs urge the slow disease.
  Yet grant them health, 'tis not for us to tell,
Though the head droops not, that the heart is well
Or will you praise that homely, healthy fare,
Plenteous and plain, that happy peasants share!
Oh! trifle not with wants you cannot feel,
Nor mock the misery of a stinted meal;
Homely, not wholesome, plain, not plenteous, such
As you who praise would never deign to touch.
  Ye gentle souls, who dream of rural ease,
Whom the smooth stream and smoother sonnet please;
Go! if the peaceful cot your praises share,
Go look within, and ask if peace be there;
If peace be his – that drooping weary sire,
Or theirs, that offspring round their feeble fire;
Or hers, that matron pale, whose trembling hand
Turns on the wretched hearth th' expiring brand!
  Not yet can Time itself obtain for these
Life's latest comforts, due respect and ease;
For yonder see that hoary swain, whose age
Can with no cares except its own engage;
Who, propt on that rude staff, looks up to see
The bare arms broken from the withering tree,*

* Cf. Ambrose Philips's 'Second Pastoral'.

On which, a boy, he climb'd the loftiest bough,
Then his first joy, but his sad emblem now.
He once was chief in all the rustic trade;
His steady hand the straightest furrow made;
Full many a prize he won, and still is proud
To find the triumphs of his youth allow'd:
A transient pleasure sparkles in his eyes,
He hears and smiles, then thinks again and sighs:
For now he journeys to his grave in pain;
The rich disdain him; nay, the poor disdain:
Alternate masters now their slave command,
Urge the weak efforts of his feeble hand,
And, when his age attempts its task in vain,
With ruthless taunts, of lazy poor complain.
Oft may you see him, when he tends the sheep,
His winter charge, beneath the hillock weep;
Oft hear him murmur to the winds that blow
O'er his white locks and bury them in snow,
When, roused by rage and muttering in the morn,
He mends the broken hedge with icy thorn: –
'Why do I live, when I desire to be
'At once from life and life's long labour free?
'Like leaves in spring, the young are blown away,
'Without the sorrows of a slow decay;
'I, like yon wither'd leaf, remain behind,
'Nipt by the frost, and shivering in the wind;
'There it abides till younger buds come on,
'As I, now all my fellow-swains are gone;
'Then, from the rising generation thrust,
'It falls, like me, unnoticed to the dust.
'These fruitful fields, these numerous flocks I see
'Are others' gain, but killing cares to me:
'To me the children of my youth are lords,
'Cool in their looks, but hasty in their words;
'Wants of their own demand their care; and who

'Feels his own want and succours others too?
'A lonely, wretched man, in pain I go,
'None need my help, and none relieve my woe;
'Then let my bones beneath the turf be laid,
'And men forget the wretch they would not aid.'
   Thus, groan the old, till, by disease oppress'd,
They taste a final woe, and then they rest.
   Theirs is yon House that holds the parish poor,
Whose walls of mud scarce bear the broken door;
There, where the putrid vapours, flagging, play,
And the dull wheel hums doleful through the day; –
There children dwell who know no parents' care;
Parents, who know no children's love, dwell there!
Heart-broken matrons on their joyless bed,
Forsaken wives, and mothers never wed;
Dejected widows with unheeded tears,
And crippled age with more than childhood fears;
The lame, the blind, and, far the happiest they!
The moping idiot, and the madman gay.
   Here too the sick their final doom receive,
Here brought, amid the scenes of grief, to grieve,
Where the loud groans from some sad chamber flow,
Mixt with the clamours of the crowd below;
Here, sorrowing, they each kindred sorrow scan,
And the cold charities of man to man:
Whose laws indeed for ruin'd age provide,
And strong compulsion plucks the scrap from pride;
But still that scrap is bought with many a sigh,
And pride embitters what it can't deny.
   Say, ye, opprest by some fantastic woes,
Some jarring nerve that baffles your repose;
Who press the downy couch, while slaves advance
With timid eye to read the distant glance;
Who with sad prayers the weary doctor tease,
To name the nameless ever-new disease;

Who with mock patience dire complaints endure,
Which real pain and that alone can cure;
How would ye bear in real pain to lie,
Despised, neglected, left alone to die?
How would ye bear to draw your latest breath,
Where all that's wretched paves the way for death?
  Such is that room which one rude beam divides,
And naked rafters form the sloping sides;
Where the vile bands that bind the thatch are seen,
And lath and mud are all that lie between;
Save one dull pane, that, coarsely patch'd, gives way
To the rude tempest, yet excludes the day:
Here, on a matted flock, with dust o'erspread,
The drooping wretch reclines his languid head;
For him no hand the cordial cup applies,
Or wipes the tear that stagnates in his eyes;
No friends with soft discourse his pain beguile,
Or promise hope, till sickness wears a smile.
  But soon a loud and hasty summons calls,
Shakes the thin roof, and echoes round the walls;
Anon, a figure enters, quaintly neat,
All pride and business, bustle and conceit;
With looks unalter'd by these scenes of woe,
With speed that, entering, speaks his haste to go,
He bids the gazing throng around him fly,
And carries fate and physic in his eye:
A potent quack, long versed in human ills,
Who first insults the victim whom he kills;
Whose murd'rous hand a drowsy Bench protect,
And whose most tender mercy is neglect.
  Paid by the parish for attendance here,
He wears contempt upon his sapient sneer;
In haste he seeks the bed where Misery lies,
Impatience mark'd in his averted eyes;
And, some habitual queries hurried o'er,

Without reply, he rushes on the door:
His drooping patient, long inured to pain,
And long unheeded, knows remonstrance vain;
He ceases now the feeble help to crave
Of man; and silent sinks into the grave.
  But ere his death some pious doubts arise,
Some simple fears, which 'bold bad' men despise;
Fain would he ask the parish priest to prove
His title certain to the joys above:
For this he sends the murmuring nurse, who calls
The holy stranger to these dismal walls:
And doth not he, the pious man, appear,
He, 'passing rich with forty pounds a year?'
Ah! no; a shepherd of a different stock,
And far unlike him, feeds this little flock:
A jovial youth, who thinks his Sunday's task
As much as God or man can fairly ask;
The rest he gives to loves and labours light,
To fields the morning, and to feasts the night;
None better skill'd the noisy pack to guide,
To urge their chase, to cheer them or to chide;
A sportsman keen, he shoots through half the day,
And, skill'd at whist, devotes the night to play:
Then, while such honours bloom around his head,
Shall he sit sadly by the sick man's bed,
To raise the hope he feels not, or with zeal
To combat fears that e'en the pious feel?
  Now once again the gloomy scene explore,
Less gloomy now; the bitter hour is o'er,
The man of many sorrows sighs no more. –
Up yonder hill, behold how sadly slow
The bier moves winding from the vale below:
There lie the happy dead, from trouble free,
And the glad parish pays the frugal fee:
No more, O Death! thy victim starts to hear

Churchwarden stern, or kingly overseer;
No more the farmer claims his humble bow,
Thou art his lord, the best of tyrants thou!
  Now to the church behold the mourners come,
Sedately torpid and devoutly dumb;
The village children now their games suspend,
To see the bier that bears their ancient friend:
For he was one in all their idle sport,
And like a monarch ruled their little court;
The pliant bow he form'd, the flying ball,
The bat, the wicket, were his labours all;
Him now they follow to his grave, and stand,
Silent and sad, and gazing, hand in hand;
While bending low, their eager eyes explore
The mingled relics of the parish poor.
The bell tolls late, the moping owl flies round,
Fear marks the flight and magnifies the sound;
The busy priest, detain'd by weightier care,
Defers his duty till the day of prayer;
And, waiting long, the crowd retire distrest,
To think a poor man's bones should lie unblest.

[1783]

WILLIAM HOLLOWAY

From *The Peasant's Fate*

  Few years are past, since, on the paddock green,
Beneath the hill, that old farm-house was seen,
Round which the barley-mows and wheat-ricks rose,

And cattle sought refreshment and repose.
The cock, proud marching with his cackling train,
Sought the barn-door, to pick the scatter'd grain;
The trotting sow her spotted offspring led,
And gobbling turkeys rear'd the crimson head.
The mistress there, and blooming daughters, drest
In russet stuffs, their new-made cheeses prest,
Summon'd the swine the full repast to share,
And rais'd their poultry with assiduous care, . . .
From whose increase their private fortune grew, . . .
Their ancient right, and still acknowledg'd due; . . .
While in the fields *young Master* held the plough,
Form'd the square load, or trod the fragrant mow:
Familiar still, he crack'd the ready joke,
And sure applause attended all he spoke.
For change, sometimes, with unremitting care,
He led his healthful flock to pastures fair,
Along the green-wood's verge would guard the fold
From crafty foxes and marauders bold;
The helpless lambs, with tender toil, would guide
To shelt'ring bush, or hay-stack's sunny side:
In herbs and simples he was skill'd full well,
He taught their virtues crude disease to quell;
And, on the festive eve of shearing, heard
His praise proclaim'd, his noblest, best reward!
By rains confin'd, the sounding flail he plied,
Nor scorn'd the meanest lab'rer by his side.
All day the rustic clamour fill'd the air,
And Health, Content, and Cheerfulness, were there.
  Ye, who have seen your country's better days,
When many an envying nation spoke her praise, . . .
Think ye her sons were then more brave, more wise,
More firmly bound by patriotic ties? . . .
Or is it our refinement to maintain,
That now the rich oppress, . . . the poor complain? . . .

If so, . . . O, perish the detested cause! . . .
Bend only we to *God*, and Nature's laws!
  Four miles from hence, across an odorous down,
Snug in the valley, lies the market-town,
From whence the humble hamlets, far and nigh,
Once in the week, their casual wants supply.
Thither our *Farmer* oft dispatch'd his team,
Ere the red east shot forth its golden gleam,
To bear his groaning gran'ry's choicest store, . . .
Its price adapted for the neighb'ring poor,
Whom, in all dealings, he remember'd still,
Nor deign'd, by sordid arts, his purse to fill. . . .
O, fair example! now no longer known,
Since grasping Av'rice serves *herself* alone!
The distant music of the waggon bells
Resounds in mellow echoes down the dells,
The hoarse horn warning from th' approaching wain,
To shun th' encounter in the narrow lane.
And, lo! the dairy mare is taught to wait,
With docile patience, at the barton gate,
Where she receives, in creaking panniers stow'd,
Eggs, poultry, butter, cream, . . . a precious load! . . .
And, mounting from an elm's fall'n trunk, the dame
Takes her proud seat, nor sighs for loftier fame.
One fav'rite ploughboy trudges by her side,
With wicker-basket, plenteously supplied;
His songs, his tales, excite the mistress' smiles,
And, o'er the dusty road, the hour beguiles.
  But, O, what rapture in each bosom wrought,
Whene'er the due-revolving seasons brought
The morn of wake, or fair! From sleepless night
They rose, impatient, ere the grey morn's light,
Collecting all the pleasure-loving train,
To share the joys and pastimes of the plain.
In milk-white frock, and buckskin breeches, clean,

The lusty ploughman rous'd his bosom's queen:
Wak'd from sweet dreams, she hears the rattling glass,
And at her lattice peeps, . . . a bonny lass!
The wakeful dairy-maid, on anxious watch,
Starts, as her shepherd lifts the clattering latch;
And, while in his her trembling hand is prest,
The half-form'd passion heaves her lab'ring breast.
Their's the pure bliss the virtuous only prove,
Unfelt, untasted by *licentious love*,
Which, like the baleful ivy, 'midst its joys,
Its object clasps, and, while it clasps, destroys.
From ev'ry village, trooping damsels come,
In native charms, and blushing beauty's bloom,
Unknown to *gossip Fame*, or seldom seen
Beyond the precincts of the cottage green.
So, in the mossy dell, coy violets rise,
Beneath the influence soft of April skies,
Sweet breathing only for the pensive swains,
Who trace, at early dawn, the lonely plains;
While foxgloves tall ascend, in storied pride,
And flaunt, unheeded, by the pathway side.

[1802]

JOHN CLARE

The Mores

Far spread the moorey ground a level scene
Bespread with rush and one eternal green
That never felt the rage of blundering plough

Though centurys wreathed springs blossoms on its brow
Still meeting plains that stretched them far away
In uncheckt shadows of green brown and grey
Unbounded freedom ruled the wandering scene
Nor fence of ownership crept in between
To hide the prospect of the following eye
Its only bondage was the circling sky
One mighty flat undwarfed by bush and tree
Spread its faint shadow of immensity
And lost itself which seemed to eke its bounds
In the blue mist the orisons[1] edge surrounds

[1] horizon's

Now this sweet vision of my boyish hours
Free as spring clouds and wild as summer flowers
Is faded all – a hope that blossomed free
And hath been once no more shall ever be
Inclosure came and trampled on the grave
Of labours rights and left the poor a slave
And memorys pride ere want to wealth did bow
Is both the shadow and the substance now
The sheep and cows were free to range as then
Where change might prompt nor felt the bonds of men
Cows went and came with evening morn and night
To the wild pasture as their common right
And sheep unfolded with the rising sun
Heard the swains shout and felt their freedom won
Tracked the red fallow field and heath and plain
Then met the brook and drank and roamed again
The brook that dribbled on as clear as glass
Beneath the roots they hid among the grass
While the glad shepherd traced their tracks along
Free as the lark and happy as her song
But now alls fled and flats of many a dye
That seemed to lengthen with the following eye
Moors loosing from the sight far smooth and blea[2]

[2] bleak

Where swopt the plover in its pleasure free
Are vanished now with commons wild and gay
As poets visions of lifes early day
Mulberry bushes where the boy would run
To fill his hands with fruit are grubbed[3] and done
And hedgrow briars – flower lovers overjoyed
Came and got flower pots – these are all destroyed
And sky bound mores in mangled garbs are left
Like mighty giants of their limbs bereft
Fence now meets fence in owners little bounds
Of field and meadow large as garden grounds
In little parcels little minds to please
With men and flocks imprisoned ill at ease
Each little path that led its pleasant way
As sweet as morning leading night astray
Where little flowers bloomed round a varied host
That travel felt delighted to be lost
Nor grudged the steps that he had taen as vain
When right roads traced his journeys and again
Nay on a broken tree hed[4] sit awhile
To see the mores and fields and meadows smile
Sometimes with cowslaps smothered – then all white
With daiseys – then the summers splendid sight
Of corn fields crimson oer the 'headach' bloomd
Like splendid armys for the battle plumed
He gazed upon them with wild fancys eye
As fallen landscapes from an evening sky
These paths are stopt – the rude philistines thrall
Is laid upon them and destroyed them all
Each little tyrant with his little sign
Shows where man claims earth glows no more divine
But paths to freedom and to childhood dear
A board sticks up to notice 'no road here'
And on the tree with ivy overhung

[3] i.e. grubbed up

[4] he'd

The hated sign by vulgar taste is hung
As tho the very birds should learn to know
When they go there they must no further go
This with the poor scared freedom bade good bye
And much they feel it in the smothered sigh
And birds and trees and flowers without a name
All sighed when lawless laws enclosure came
And dreams of plunder in such rebel schemes
Have found too truly that they were but dreams

[*c.* 1822]

The Lament of Swordy Well

Im swordy well a piece of land
Thats fell upon the town
Who worked me till I couldnt stand
& crush me now Im down

There was a time my bit of ground
Made freeman of the slave
The ass no pindard[1] dare to pound
When I his supper gave

[1] i.e. no pindar (a man who pounded stray animals) would

The gipseys camp was not affraid
I made his dwelling free
Till vile enclosure came & made
A parish slave of me

Alas dependance thou'rt a brute
Want only understands
His feelings wither branch & root
That falls in parish hands

The muck that clouts the ploughmans shoe
The moss that hides the stone
Now Im become the parish due
Is more than I can own

The silver springs grow naked dykes
Scarce own a bunch of rushes
When grain got high the tasteless tykes
Grubbed up trees banks & bushes

Though Im no man yet any wrong
Some sort of right may seek
& I am glad if een a song
Gives me the room to speak

Ive got among such grubbling geer[2]
& such a hungry pack
If I brought harvests twice a year
They'd bring me nothing back

[2] digging or scrabbling gear

& should the price of grain get high
Lord help to keep it low
I shant possess a butterflye
Nor get a weed to grow

I shant possess a yard of ground
To bid a mouse to thrive
For gain has put me in a pound
I scarce can keep alive

& me they turned me inside out
For sand & grit & stones
& turned my old green hills about
& picked my very bones

The bees flye round in feeble rings
& find no blossom bye
Then thrum their almost weary wings
Upon the moss & die

Rabbits that find my hills turned oer
Forsake my poor abode
They dread a workhouse like the poor
& nibble on the road

If with a clover bottle now
Spring dares to lift her head
The next day brings the hasty plough
& makes me miserys bed

Ive scarce a nook to call my own
For things that creep or flye
The beetle hiding neath a stone
Does well to hurry bye

& if I could but find a friend
With no deceit to sham
Who'd send me some few sheep to tend
& leave me as I am

To keep my hills from cart & plough
& strife of mongerel men
& as spring found me find me now
I should look up agen

& save his Lordships woods that past
the day of danger dwell
Of all the fields I am the last
that my own face can tell

Yet what with stone pits delving holes
& strife to buy & sell
My name will quickly be the whole
Thats left of swordy well

[*c.* 1822]

EBENEZER ELLIOTT

The Splendid Village

From Part I

Hail, Sister Hills, that from each other hide,
With belts of evergreen, your mutual pride!
Here reigns in placid splendour Madam Grade,
Whose husband nobly made a plum in trade.
And yonder glitters Rapine's bilious slave,
The lucky footman of a palac'd knave; –
Stern foe of learning, genius, press, and pen,
Who lauds all laws that ruin honest men.
Sublime in Satrap-imitating state,
She for her daughter seeks a titled mate;
None other, not an angel, wing'd from Heav'n,
Could woo, or ask to woo, and be forgiv'n.
Too oft, perhaps, she calls her neighbour 'Scrub!'
Yet justly scorns the mean corruption-grub;
For many a 'ruptur'd Ogden' hath he wrong'd,
Long gloating on the captive's chain prolong'd.
He hates and apes her pomp, with upstart haste;
But what in him is pride, in her is taste.
She, queen-like smiles; he, blustering, crams and treats,
And weighs his greatness by the trout he eats.

She never dogg'd a beggar from her lawn,
And he would hang all dogs that will not fawn.
Yet, Clerk of Taxes, Magistrate, and Squire,
Why to be Premier may not he aspire? –
But what is he, that haunts this upstart's door –
Yon fat good fellow, who detests the poor –
Yon mass of meanness, baseness, grease and bone –
Yon jolly soul, that weighs just eighteen stone?
Unmatch'd in quibble, great in If and But,
Sublime in cant, superlative in smut;
He jests, as none but British worthies can,
Laughs at despair, spurns, tramples fallen man;
Condemns misfortune for its wrongs and woe,
And bids his victim thank him for a blow.
Sworn friends are they, Squire Woolpack, and Squire Brush;
One is their creed – 'Impoverish! torture! crush!'
Behold two models, unexcell'd on earth,
Of British wisdom, loyalty, and worth!

★

Broad Beech! thyself a grove! five hundred years
Speak in thy voice, of bygone hopes and fears;
And mournfully – how mournfully! – the breeze
Sighs through thy boughs, and tells of cottages
That, happy once, beneath thy shadow gaz'd
On poor men's fields, which poor men's cattle graz'd!
Now, where three cotters and their children dwelt,
The lawyer's pomp alone is seen and felt;
And the park-entrance of his acres three
Uncrops the ground which fed a family.
What then? All see he is a man of state,
With his three acres, and his park-like gate!
Besides, in time, if times continue dark,

His neighbour's woes may buy his gate a park.
Oh, then, let trade wear chains, that toil may find
No harvests on the barren sea and wind;
Nor glean, at home, the fields of every zone,
Nor make the valleys of all climes his own;
But with the music of his hopeless sigh
Charm the blind worm that feeds on poverty!

*

The village, happy once, is splendid now!
And at the Turkey reigns, with knotted brow,
Stiff as a mile-stone, set up in his bar,
Vice-regal Constable and Bailiff, Marr,
Who nods his 'yes,' and frowns his fatal 'no.'
Woe to the scrimp that ventures near him, woe!
He, she, or it – 'swag'snifle, skink, or trull,'
Shall find a bed, or Wakefield's gaol is full!
Great man, John Marr! He shoots – or who else may?
He knows my Lord, is loyal, and can pay.
The poor all hate him, fear him – all save one;
Broad Jem, the poacher, dreaded is by John.
To draw him drink, objects nor man nor maid;
The froth is brought, Jem winks, and John is paid;
For John, who hates all poachers, likes poor Jem,
While Jem, so kind to others, growls at him;
And when their fierce eyes meet, the tax-made slave
Quakes in his inmost soul, if soul he have,
Thinking of weasand slit by lantern light,
Or slug bang'd through him at the dead of night.
Yet great is he! rich, prudent, tried, and true:
He snores at sermon in his curtain'd pew –
He knows the Steward – he is known afar
To magistrates and bums – great man, John Marr!

*

Churl Jem! why dost thou thrust me from the wall?
I hack no cab, I sham no servant's hall;
Coarse is my coat: – how have I earn'd thy curse?
Suspect'st thou there is money in my purse?
I said, Good day, Sir, and I touch'd my hat:
Art thou, then, vulgar, as the Sage's flat?
Alas! that Sage sees not in thy fierce eyes
Fire-flooded towers, and pride, that shrieks and dies;
The red-foam'd deluge, and the sea-wide tomb;
The arm of vengeance, and the brow of doom;
The grin of millions o'er the shock of all –
A people's wreck, an empire's funeral!

From Part II

Feast of the Village! – yearly held, when June
Sate with the rose, to hear the gold-spink's tune,
And lovers, happy as the warbling bird,
Breath'd raptures sweeter than the songs they heard,
Stealing through lanes, sun-bright with dewy broom,
By fragrant hedge-rows, sheeted o'er with bloom; –
Feast of the happy Village! where art thou?
Pshaw! thou wert vulgar – we are splendid now.
Yet, poor man's pudding! – rich with spicy crumbs,
And tiers of currants, thick as both my thumbs, –
Where art thou, festal pudding of our sires? –
Gone, to feed fat the heirs of thieves and liars; –
Gone, to oppress the wrong'd, the true, the brave,
And, wide and deep, dig Poland's second grave; –
Gone, like the harvest pie, a bullock's load,
Four feet across, with crust six inches broad; –
Gone, like poor England's Satrap-swallow'd store; –
Gone, as her trade will go, to come no more!
Well, let it go, and with it the glad hours

That yearly o'er kind hearts shed cottage flowers.
Nor sisters' daughters now, nor sons of sons,
Shall seek the bridge, where still the river runs,
And bless the roof where busy hands prepar'd
The festal plenty which their fathers shar'd;
When, round their grandsire met, his numerous race
Beheld their children's children in his face;
Saw in his eyes the light of suns gone down,
And hoped they saw in his white locks their own.
No more, no more, beneath his smile serene,
The generations shall in joy convene,
All eager to obey the annual call,
And twang the cord of love that bound them all.

*

Oh, happy, if they knew their bliss, are they
Who, poor themselves, unbounded wealth survey;
Who nor in ships, nor cabs, nor chariots go,
To view the miracles of art below;
But, near their homes, behold august abodes,
That like the temples seem of all the gods!
Nor err they, if they sometimes kneel in pray'r
At shrines like those, for God-like powers are there;
Powers, that on rail-roads base no treasures waste,
Nor build huge mills, that blush like brick at taste,
Where labour fifteen hours, for twice a groat,
The half-angelic heirs of speech and thought;
But pour profusion from a golden hand,
To deck with Grecian forms a Gothic land.
Hence, yeoman, hence! – thy grandsire's land resign;
Yield, peasant, to my lord and power divine!
Thy grange is gone, your cluster'd hovels fall;
Proud domes expand, the park extends its wall;
Then kennels rise, the massive Tuscan grows,

And dogs sublime, like couchant kings, repose!
Lo! 'still all Greek and glorious' art is here!
Behold the pagod of a British Peer!
Admire, ye proud, and clap your hands, ye poor!
The father of this kingling was a boor!
Not Ispahan, nor Stamboul – though their thrones
Make Satraps out of dead men's blood and bones,
And play at death, as God-like power will play –
Can match free Britain's ancients of today.

*

Oh, welcome once again black ocean's foam!
England! Can this be England? – this my home?
This country of the crime without a name,
And men who know nor mercy, hope, nor shame?
Oh, Light! that cheer'st all life, from sky to sky,
As with a hymn, to which the stars reply!
Canst thou behold this land, oh, Holy Light!
And not turn black with horror at the sight?
Fall'n country of my fathers! fall'n and foul!
Thy body still is here, but where the soul?
I look upon a corpse – 'tis putrid clay –
And fiends possess it. Vampires quit your prey!
Or vainly tremble, when the dead arise,
Clarion'd to vengeance by shriek-shaken skies,
And cranch your hearts, and drink your blood for ale!
Then, eat each other – till the banquet fail!
Oh, thou dark tower, that look'st o'er ancient woods
To see the tree of fire put forth its buds!
Baronial keep, whose ruins, ivy-grown,
The time-touch'd ash mistakes for living stone,
Grasping them with his writhen roots, and fast
Binding the present to the faded past!
While, cropp'd with every crime, the tax-plough'd moor,

And foot-paths, stolen from the trampled poor,
And commons, sown with curses loud and deep,
Proclaim a harvest, which the rich shall reap.
Call up the iron men of Runnymeed,
And bid them look on lords, whom peasants feed!
Then – when the worm slinks down, at nature's groan,
And with the shrieking heav'ns, thy dungeons moan
O'er the loud fall of greatness, misery fed,
Let their fierce laugh awake their vassals dead, –
The shaft-fam'd men, whom yet tradition sings,
Who serv'd, but did not feed, the fear'd of kings,
To join the wondering laugh, and wilder yell,
While England flames, 'a garden', and a hell.*

[1833]

* A reference to Goldsmith's *The Deserted Village*: '. . . a garden and a grave', p. 396.

ROMANTICS AND VICTORIANS

The various conflicting strains of eighteenth-century Pastoral and Anti-Pastoral – the cheerful materialism of Thomson; the cultivated retirement of Cowper; the nostalgia of Goldsmith; the realism of Crabbe; the search for an image of nature hostile to the arts of man – all these are brought together in the pastoral poems of Wordsworth. Wordsworth's preoccupation with the landscape of the Lake District is a version of Horace's and of Cowper's retirement; but while they, like him, were in retreat from the money-getting life in towns, the landscape they chose to retire to was cultivated, civilized, and kept before them the natural opulence which supported their idleness. A retreat into the fat arable land of the midland shires would have been no retreat at all for Wordsworth; and his choice of the Lake District is also perhaps to be understood in terms of a taste for the Sublime. But while the amateurs of the Sublime and the Picturesque were tourists, who occasionally visited the wilderness for recreation, but preferred to live in the cultivated south, Wordsworth does inhabit the wilderness himself, and in his poems he populates it with shepherds and yeomen who have achieved a harmony with the sublime landscape that he too wishes to achieve. And because these rustics have somehow remained in close touch with the natural landscape, their language has remained somehow natural, and still expressive of a humanity unrefined and unaffected; so that Wordsworth is persuaded that a version of it might be the proper language of a more naturalistic poetry.

The harmony that Michael, for example, and the leech-gatherer, in 'Resolution and Independence', have achieved with the rough landscape and the elements, has been achieved by work; but by working in co-operation with nature, and not by struggling to subdue her; and in this way Wordsworth goes back to the properly *pastoral* origins of the kind – the herdsman lives by understanding the landscape and the elements, the ploughman by conflict with them. Unlike Thomson, however, and more like Crabbe, Wordsworth is perfectly willing to acknowledge that the work his rustics perform is arduous, and may cause suffering on that account; but, for most, it is rewarded by 'the certainty of honourable gain'. Thus Wordsworth is in many ways a more satisfactory bourgeois moralist than his predecessors, for hard work is an essential element in his version of Pastoral; his idea of natural harmony can make work seem more properly 'congenial' than the 'happy labour' performed by Thomson's labourers; and the arduous nature of work is acknowledged and justified by an appeal to the same idea of harmony with a rough and difficult terrain.

And yet Wordsworth's Pastoral is not without nostalgia, in spite of the fact that his shepherds and yeomen are for the most part happy to inhabit the present – the nostalgia is his, not theirs. It involves, of course, a desire to return to the period of childhood, when Wordsworth felt himself to have been in the same sort of harmony with nature as that enjoyed, for example, by Michael; and this nostalgia is often opposed – in 'Tintern Abbey', in the 'Immortality Ode' – by a determination to see the process of growing older as one by which we develop a deeper understanding of nature and the universe. But there is a wide gap, which Wordsworth acknowledges and cannot cross, between *seeing* 'into the life of things', and being at one with it; this gap is not simply the result of growing up – the rustics remain at one with the landscape at whatever age – and Wordsworth's problem is compounded by his education, class, and the fact of his being a poet. To be a poet is to have (as he sometimes argues) a deeper insight than that of ordinary men; but at times the act of describing things throws a veil across them. To reject the 'artificial' language of eighteenth-century poetry, in favour of the 'real language of men', is only a temporary solution; the real problem becomes the fact of using language at all; and in a number of poems it seems that the whole basis of Wordsworth's Pastoral is demolished by a feeling of harmony with nature as a trance-like state, which can be achieved only by silence, by an annihilation of rational speech and thus arguably of one's very humanity. This is, in one sense, a return to the empty wilderness of the Sublime; but now the only figure in that landscape, the poet, would himself disappear if he could – if he could be like Lucy, without motion, force, or feeling, 'rolled round in earth's diurnal course, with rocks, and stones, and trees'. The aspiration is hopeless, but it destroys the possibility of any harmony with nature achieved on the terms of the habitable landscape of the Pastoral.

The remaining history of the tradition is the history of its slow death; the vitality of the poetry of John Clare, who brings something quite unique to the Pastoral, may seem to be an exception to this statement, but perhaps the most important thing about his poetry is that, by the very nature of its success, it was incapable of influencing the later poetry of rural life. John Clare was the son of an agricultural labourer; Stephen Duck, Robert Bloomfield, and a number of lesser poets, had all written pastoral poetry from a similar background; but however sceptical they had been about the optimism of the eighteenth-century Pastoral, they were all more or less content to accept the main presupposition on which the poetry of the eighteenth century was based – a belief in the existence of a general or abstract nature. To write poetry at all these poets had to learn its proper language, which the aristocratic and the middle-class writer could pick up more automatically; and whether they wanted it to or not, this language would cast the local and individual nature of their experience into the mould of 'general truth'. This generalizing tendency of eighteenth-century poetry had been attacked by Wordsworth, of course, but mainly on the grounds that it was not general enough; and he offers instead a nature which is equally abstract, or equally general, but more inclusive – it finds room for the accidents of nature, as well as for her stereotypes.

After an apprenticeship in the eighteenth-century Pastoral, Clare began to realize that the generalizing tendencies of all the poetry that was available to him were no help to him in understanding his own experience, which was defined by his concrete knowledge of life in his own parish and a few miles beyond; and the insistence that his own experience was purely local, and quite incapable of being generalized in any way, became the entire content of his writings. It was further reinforced as he came to understand the significance of the enclosure of his parish, Helpston; for by the enclosure the place he had known from birth, and thus in a sense the whole of his knowledge, was abolished, and replaced by a regularizing landscape of straight roads and square fields. In the mid-1820s his poems become purely descriptive, and refuse to end with proper, general conclusions; they are written in something like the local dialect of Helpston, for it is only in that language that what Clare has to say can for him be true to his experience; his syntax becomes irregular and idiosyncratic, in a way which is opposed to the orderly and linear ideas of landscape and of general nature that are expressed equally by the square fields and straight roads of his parish after enclosure, and the tradition of eighteenth-century nature-poetry that he had inherited. Only a few of his poems are directly political; but those he wrote between about 1822 and 1832, when he was moved from Helpston, represent a far more radical attack on the presuppositions on which both the pastoral tradition and the agricultural revolution were based, than the poetry of any of his predecessors, including Crabbe.

The poems of John Clare are not to be understood as naïve and innocent affirmations of identity and of the localness of his experience; they are more like self-conscious reconstructions of a way of apprehending experience that even he could not hold on to. The very condition of his understanding the local, concrete nature of his knowledge is a desperate and short-lived hope that his knowledge could survive his exposure to the mainstream of English poetry, the simple fact of his literacy, the enclosure of his parish, and his own increasing ability to travel and to gain a more general knowledge by that means. The Golden Age was a sharper memory for Clare than for anyone else, but it was a memory for him too.

We have not attempted to take this anthology much beyond Clare; we have included several examples of Victorian Pastoral, but for most Victorian poets the countryside became what it had been for Wordsworth, a void, a place to visit in the hope of becoming as invisible as its regular inhabitants; a place in which one recovered from, and prepared for, the massive expenditure of effort demanded by urban life. Such Pastoral as does get written is highly formal and academic, an attempt to preserve an antique form of expression, in the hope that the charming innocence of the pastoral vision would thus be preserved also, despite the fact that nobody could now believe that agriculture was anything but a highly developed industry with an unpleasant history of violent change and deep depression. The essentially formal nature of Arnold's Pastorals is obvious enough, and that of the dialect-poems of Tennyson and Barnes is hardly less so, however excellent they are in their way. The aura of local truth which the Lincolnshire and the Dorset dialects give to the poems of both men is really a way of disguising, while compounding, their artificiality; the dialects try hard to make credible a version of Pastoral which everyone would have realized was too hopelessly nostalgic to be at all serviceable, had it been expressed in the language of the metropolis.

The impossibility of writing a credible version of Pastoral in the Victorian Age and after is illustrated as well as anywhere in Hardy's excellent poem, 'In Time of "The Breaking of Nations"', an exception which does much to prove the rule. In Hardy's novels, the Pastoral coexists awkwardly with his realism, and the tension between them is fairly clearly a result of the impossibility of describing the upheavals in nineteenth-century agricultural history, and their effect on the inhabitants of rural England, in the old terms of a timeless Golden Age and shepherds whose reactions are slow. In this poem, however – and to a degree because it is a poem – history is once again something which happens everywhere but in Wessex, where the weeds will be kept burning, and the old horse who pulls the plough stumbles, but will keep going for ever, half-asleep in his pastoral trance. It is a poem by Hardy at his most nostalgic, trying to see past the unfortunate truths about rural life that he as much as anyone had revealed, and back to a time when it was still possible to look at the country through half-closed eyes. And there is a further nostalgia for us as we read the poem, a nostalgia for Hardy's nostalgia; for there were still horses in 1915 to evoke the pastoral dream.

It would of course have been possible to extend the anthology yet further, to the poetry of the Georgians; to Muir, and to R. S. Thomas, and their several varieties of pessimistic frontier Pastoral; and to other poets still writing today. Indeed, with the current concern with ecology, it is not difficult to anticipate a revival of interest in the Pastoral – Industrial Man looking away from his technological Wasteland to an older and better world, a rural equivalent of the sort of middle-class nostalgia that made the televised version of the *Forsyte Saga* such an enormous success. And the very appearance of this anthology in the Penguin list would be a part of just such a revival. It is not, however, something that can be looked for with anything other than alarm. For today, more than ever before, the pastoral vision simply will not do.

The separation of life in the town and in the country that the Pastoral demands is now almost devoid of any meaning. It is difficult to pretend that the English countryside is now anything more than an extension of the town; that the industrial and technological processes of urban production differ at all significantly from those of the 'Factory-Farm'; that the function of the modern farm-manager is essentially any different from that of his urban counterpart; that the Pastoral has not become in fact just another trip, another Sunday afternoon drive. And if this is true of the setting, it is even more true of its erstwhile shepherds. As the countryside becomes ever more efficiently a dormitory for a managerial and executive *élite* – pricing the traditional inhabitants out of their homes, just as our machinery has priced them out of their jobs – so the last sad remains of the Pastoral are parcelled up and auctioned off in semi-detached lots. The purchasers of such pastoral remains look round in vain for the Arcadian shepherd or shepherdess to reassure them that they, too, are in Arcadia; but for them, much as for Sidney and Pope earlier, the shepherds are invisible, and now for the simplest of reasons – that there are no shepherds left. And so, like Sidney and Pope, the rural executive and his wife must cast themselves in the roles of Damon and Clorinda, but this time without any available vision of reality for them to measure the truth of their imitation against. The Pastoral vision might still have some life elsewhere – in the Third World, or in North America perhaps – where there are still occasional frontiers to confront the regulating effect of urban development; but now and in England, the Pastoral, occasional twitches notwithstanding, is a lifeless form, of service only to decorate the shelves of tasteful cottages, 'modernized to a high standard'.

The rude original pastoral poetry of our country furnishes the first class in the popular pieces called ballads. These consist of the village tale, the dialogue of rustic courtship, the description of natural objects, and the incidents of a rural life. Their language is the language of nature, simple and unadorned; their story is not the wild off-spring of fancy, but the probable adventures of the cottage; and their sentiments are the unstudied expressions of passion and emotions common to all mankind.

[John Aikin, 'Essay on Ballads and Pastoral Songs', 1772]

Not only in professed descriptions of the scenery, but in the frequent allusions to natural objects, which occur, of course, in Pastorals, the Poet must, above all, study variety. He must diversify his face of nature, by presenting to us new images; or otherwise, he will soon become insipid with those known topics of description, which were original, it is true, in the first Poets, who copied them from nature, but which are now worn threadbare by incessant imitation.

[Hugh Blair, 'Pastoral Poetry', 1783]

WILLIAM COWPER

The Task

From Book I

When Winter soaks the fields, and female feet,
Too weak to struggle with tenacious clay,
Or ford the rivulets, are best at home,
The task of new discov'ries falls on me.
At such a season, and with such a charge,
Once went I forth; and found, till then unknown,
A cottage, whither oft we since repair.
'Tis perch'd upon the green-hill top, but close
Environ'd with a ring of branching elms
That overhang the thatch, itself unseen
Peeps at the vale below; so thick beset
With foliage of such dark redundant growth,
I call'd the low-roof'd lodge the *peasant's nest.*
And, hidden as it is, and far remote
From such unpleasing sounds as haunt the ear
In village or in town, the bay of curs
Incessant, clinking hammers, grinding wheels,
And infants clam'rous whether pleas'd or pain'd,
Oft have I wish'd the peaceful covert mine.
Here, I have said, at least I should possess
The poet's treasure, silence, and indulge
The dreams of fancy, tranquil and secure.
Vain thought! the dweller in that still retreat
Dearly obtains the refuge it affords.
Its elevated scite forbids the wretch
To drink sweet waters of the crystal well;
He dips his bowl into the weedy ditch,
And, heavy-laden, brings his bev'rage home,
Far-fetch'd and little worth, nor seldom waits,
Dependant on the baker's punctual call,

To hear his creaking panniers at the door,
Angry and sad, and his last crust consum'd.
So farewell envy of the *peasant's nest!*
If solitude make scant the means of life,
Society for me! – thou seeming sweet,
Be still a pleasing object in my view;
My visit still, but never mine abode.

From Book IV

In such a world; so thorny, and where none
Finds happiness unblighted; or, if found,
Without some thistly sorrow at its side,
It seems the part of wisdom, and no sin
Against the law of love, to measure lots
With less distinguish'd than ourselves; that thus
We may with patience bear our mod'rate ills,
And sympathise with others, suff'ring more.
Ill fares the trav'ller now, and he that stalks
In pond'rous boots beside his reeking team.
The wain goes heavily, impeded sore
By congregated loads adhering close
To the clogg'd wheels; and in its sluggish pace,
Noiseless, appears a moving hill of snow.
The toiling steeds expand the nostril wide,
While ev'ry breath, by respiration strong
Forc'd downward, is consolidated soon
Upon their jutting chests. He, form'd to bear
The pelting brunt of the tempestuous night,
With half-shut eyes, and pucker'd cheeks, and teeth
Presented bare against the storm, plods on.
One hand secures his hat, save when with both
He brandishes his pliant length of whip,
Resounding oft, and never heard in vain.

Oh happy; and, in my account, denied
That sensibility of pain with which
Refinement is endued, thrice happy thou!
Thy frame, robust and hardy, feels indeed
The piercing cold, but feels it unimpair'd.
The learned finger never need explore
Thy vig'rous pulse; and the unhealthful east,
That breathes the spleen, and searches ev'ry bone
Of the infirm, is wholesome air to thee.
Thy days roll on, exempt from household care;
The waggon is thy wife; and the poor beasts,
That drag the dull companion to and fro,
Thine helpless charge, dependent on thy care.
Ah, treat them kindly! rude as thou appear'st,
Yet show that thou hast mercy! which the great,
With needless hurry whirl'd from place to place,
Humane as they would seem, not always show.
Poor, yet industrious, modest, quiet, neat;
Such claim compassion in a night like this,
And have a friend in ev'ry feeling heart.
Warm'd, while it lasts, by labour, all day long
They brave the season, and yet find at eve,
Ill clad and fed but sparely, time to cool.
The frugal housewife trembles when she lights
Her scanty stock of brush-wood, blazing clear,
But dying soon, like all terrestrial joys.
The few small embers left she nurses well;
And, while her infant race, with outspread hands
And crowded knees, sit cow'ring o'er the sparks,
Retires, content to quake, so they be warm'd.
The man feels least, as more inur'd than she
To winter, and the current in his veins
More briskly mov'd by his severer toil;
Yet he, too, finds his own distress in their's.
The taper soon extinguish'd, which I saw

Dangled along at the cold finger's end
Just when the day declin'd, and the brown loaf
Lodg'd on the shelf, half eaten, without sauce
Of sav'ry cheese, or butter, costlier still;
Sleep seems their only refuge: for, alas,
Where penury is felt the thought is chain'd,
And sweet colloquial pleasures are but few!
With all this thrift they thrive not. All the care
Ingenious parsimony takes but just
Saves the small inventory, bed, and stool,
Skillet, and old carv'd chest, from public sale.
They live, and live without extorted alms
From grudging hands; but other boast have none
To sooth their honest pride, that scorns to beg,
Nor comfort else, but in their mutual love.
I praise you much, ye meek and patient pair,
For ye are worthy; choosing rather far
A dry but independent crust, hard earn'd,
And eaten with a sigh, than to endure
The rugged frowns and insolent rebuffs
Of knaves in office, partial in the work
Of distribution; lib'ral of their aid
To clam'rous importunity in rags,
But oft-times deaf to suppliants, who would blush
To wear a tatter'd garb however coarse,
Whom famine cannot reconcile to filth:
These ask with painful shyness, and, refus'd
Because deserving, silently retire!
But be ye of good courage! Time itself
Shall much befriend you. Time shall give increase;
And all your num'rous progeny, well-train'd,
But helpless, in few years shall find their hands,
And labour too. Meanwhile ye shall not want
What, conscious of your virtues, we can spare,
Nor what a wealthier than ourselves may send.

I mean the man, who, when the distant poor
Need help, denies them nothing but his name.
   But poverty, with most who whimper forth
Their long complaints, is self-inflicted woe;
Th' effect of laziness or sottish waste.
Now goes the nightly thief prowling abroad
For plunder; much solicitous how best
He may compensate for a day of sloth . . .

*

   Would I had fall'n upon those happier days
That poets celebrate; those golden times
And those Arcadian scenes, that Maro sings,
And Sidney, warbler of poetic prose.
Nymphs were Dianas then, and swains had hearts
That felt their virtues: innocence, it seems,
From courts dismiss'd, found shelter in the groves;
The footsteps of simplicity, impress'd
Upon the yielding herbage, (so they sing)
Then were not all effac'd: then speech profane,
And manners profligate, were rarely found;
Observ'd as prodigies, and soon reclaim'd.
Vain wish! those days were never; airy dreams
Sat for the picture; and the poet's hand,
Imparting substance to an empty shade,
Impos'd a gay delirium for truth.
Grant it: – I still must envy them an age
That favour'd such a dream; in days like these
Impossible, when virtue is so scarce,
That to suppose a scene where she presides,
Is tramontane, and stumbles all belief.

[1785]

JAMES BEATTIE

From *The Minstrel,* Book I

XI

There lived in Gothic days, as legends tell,
A shepherd swain, a man of low degree;
Whose sires, perchance, in Fairyland might dwell,
Sicilian groves, or vales of Arcady;
But he, I ween, was of the north countrie;
A nation famed for song and beauty's charms;
Zealous, yet modest; innocent, though free;
Patient of toil; serene amidst alarms;
Inflexible in faith; invincible in arms.

XII

The shepherd swain of whom I mention made,
On Scotia's mountains fed his little flock;
The sickle, scythe, or plough he never sway'd:
An honest heart was almost all his stock;
His drink the living water from the rock:
The milky dams supplied his board, and lent
Their kindly fleece to baffle winter's shock;
And he, though oft with dust and sweat besprent,
Did guide and guard their wanderings, wheresoe'er they went.

XIII

From labour health, from health contentment springs:
Contentment opes the source of every joy.
He envied not, he never thought of kings;
Nor from those appetites sustain'd annoy,
That chance may frustrate or indulgence cloy:
Nor Fate his calm and humble hopes beguiled;

He mourn'd no recreant friend nor mistress coy,
For on his vows the blameless Phoebe smiled,
And her alone he loved, and loved her from a child.

XIV

No jealousy their dawn of love o'ercast,
Nor blasted were their wedded days with strife;
Each season look'd delightful as it pass'd,
To the fond husband and the faithful wife.
Beyond the lowly vale of shepherd life
They never roam'd: secure beneath the storm
Which in Ambition's lofty land is rife,
Where peace and love are canker'd by the worm
Of pride, each bud of joy industrious to deform.

XV

The wight, whose tale these artless lines unfold,
Was all the offspring of this humble pair:
His birth no oracle or seer foretold;
No prodigy appear'd in earth or air,
Nor aught that might a strange event declare.
You guess each circumstance of Edwin's birth;
The parent's transport and the parent's care;
The gossip's prayer for wealth and wit and worth;
And one long summer day of indolence and mirth.

XVI

And yet poor Edwin was no vulgar boy:
Deep thought oft seem'd to fix his infant eye;
Dainties he needed not, nor gaude nor toy,
Save one short pipe of rudest minstrelsy:
Silent when glad; affectionate though shy;
And now his look was most demurely sad;
And now he laugh'd aloud, yet none knew why.
The neighbours stared and sigh'd, yet bless'd the lad:
Some deem'd him wondrous wise, and some believed him mad.

XVII

But why should I his childish feats display?
Concourse and noise and toil he ever fled;
Nor cared to mingle in the clamorous fray
Of squabbling imps; but to the forest sped,
Or roam'd at large the lonely mountain's head;
Or where the maze of some bewilder'd stream
To deep untrodden groves his footsteps led;
There would he wander wild, till Phoebus' beam,
Shot from the western cliff, released the weary team.

XVIII

The' exploit of strength, dexterity, or speed
To him nor vanity nor joy could bring.
His heart, from cruel sport estranged, would bleed
To work the woe of any living thing,
By trap or net, by arrow or by sling;
These he detested; those he scorn'd to wield:
He wish'd to be the guardian, not the king,
Tyrant far less, or traitor of the field;
And sure the silvan reign unbloody joy might yield.

XIX

Lo! where the stripling, wrapp'd in wonder, roves
Beneath the precipice o'erhung with pine;
And sees on high, amidst the' encircling groves,
From cliff to cliff the foaming torrents shine:
While waters, woods, and winds in concert join,
And Echo swells the chorus to the skies.
Would Edwin this majestic scene resign
For aught the huntsman's puny craft supplies?
Ah! no: he better knows great Nature's charms to prize.

[1771]

From *The Cotter's Saturday Night*

Let not ambition mock their useful toil,
  Their homely joys, and destiny obscure;
Nor grandeur hear, with a disdainful smile,
  The short but simple annals of the poor.
Gray

My loved, my honoured, much respected friend!
No mercenary bard his homage pays;
With honest pride I scorn each selfish end:
My dearest meed, a friend's esteem and praise:
To you I sing, in simple Scottish lays,
The lowly train in life's sequestered scene;
The native feelings strong, the guileless ways;
What Aiken in a cottage would have been;
Ah! though his worth unknown, far happier there, I ween.

November chill blaws loud wi' angry sugh;
The shortening winter-day is near a close;
The miry beasts retreating frae the pleugh;
The blackening trains o' craws to their repose:
The toil-worn Cotter frae his labour goes,
This night his weekly moil is at an end,
Collects his spades, his mattocks, and his hoes,
Hoping the morn in ease and rest to spend.
And weary, o'er the moor his course does hameward bend.

At length his lonely cot appears in view,
Beneath the shelter of an aged tree;
The expectant wee-things, toddlin, stacher through
To meet their Dad, wi' flichterin[1] noise an' glee. [1] contentious
His wee bit ingle, blinking bonnily,

His clean hearthstane, his thriftie wifie's smile,
The lisping infant prattling on his knee,
Does a' his weary carking cares beguile,
An' makes him quite forget his labour an' his toil.

Belyve[2] the elder bairns come drapping in, [2] by and by
At service out, amang the farmers roun',
Some ca' the pleugh, some herd, some tentie[3] rin [3] careful
A cannie errand to a neebor town:
Their eldest hope, their Jenny, woman grown,
In youthfu' bloom, love sparkling in her e'e,
Comes hame, perhaps, to shew a braw new gown,
Or deposite her sair-won penny-fee,
To help her parents dear, if they in hardship be.

Wi' joy unfeigned brothers and sisters meet,
An' each for other's weelfare kindly spiers[4]: [4] inquires
The social hours, swift-winged, unnoticed fleet;
Each tells the uncos[5] that he sees or hears: [5] news
The parents, partial, eye their hopeful years;
Anticipation forward points the view.
The mother, wi' her needle an' her shears,
Gars[6] auld claes look amaist as weel's the new; [6] makes
The father mixes a' wi' admonition due.

Their masters' an' their mistresses' command,
The younkers a' are warned to obey,
An' mind their labours wi' an eydent[7] hand, [7] diligent
An' ne'er, though out o' sight, to jauk or play:
'An' O! be sure to fear the Lord alway!
An' mind your duty duly, morn an' night!
Lest in temptation's path ye gang astray,
Implore His counsel and assisting might:
They never sought in vain that sought the Lord aright!'

But hark! a rap comes gently to the door;
Jenny, wha kens the meaning o' the same,
Tells how a neebor lad cam' o'er the moor,
To do some errands, and convoy her hame.
The wily mother sees the conscious flame
Sparkle in Jenny's e'e, and flush her cheek;
With heart-struck anxious care, inquires his name,
While Jenny hafilins[8] is afraid to speak: [8] half
Weel pleased the mother hears it's nae wild, worthless rake.

Wi' kindly welcome Jenny brings him ben[9], [9] into the parlour
A strappan youth; he taks the mother's eye;
Blithe Jenny sees the visit's no ill ta'en;
The father cracks of horses, pleughs, and kye[10]: [10] cattle
The youngster's artless heart o'erflows wi' joy.
But blate[11] and laithfu'[12], scarce can weel behave; [11] bashful
The mother, wi' a woman's wiles, can spy [12] sheepish
What makes the youth sae bashfu' an' sae grave;
Weel pleased to think her bairn's respected like the lave[13]. [13] rest

O happy love! where love like this is found!
O heartfelt raptures! bliss beyond compare!
I've paced much this weary mortal round,
And sage experience bids me this declare –
'If Heaven a draught of heavenly pleasure spare,
One cordial in this melancholy vale,
'Tis when a youthful, loving, modest pair,
In other's arms breathe out the tender tale,
Beneath the milk-white thorn that scents the evening gale.'

Is there, in human form, that bears a heart –
A wretch! a villain! lost to love and truth!
That can, with studied, sly, ensnaring art,
Betray sweet Jenny's unsuspecting youth?
Curse on his perjured arts! dissembling smooth!

Are honour, virtue, conscience, all exiled?
Is there no pity, no relenting ruth,
Points to the parents fondling o'er their child?
Then paints the ruined maid, and their distraction wild?

But now the supper crowns their simple board,
The halesome parritch, chief o' Scotia's food:
The soupe their only Hawkie[14] does afford, [14] cow
That 'yont the hallant[15] snugly chows her cood: [15] wall
The dame brings forth in complimental mood,
To grace the lad, her weel-hained kebbuck,[16] fell, [16] well-saved cheese
An' aft he's prest, an' aft he ca's it guid;
The frugal wifie, garrulous, will tell,
How 'twas a towmond[17] auld, sin' lint was i' the bell[18]. [17] twelve-month [18] flax was in blossom

The cheerfu' supper done, wi' serious face,
They round the ingle form a circle wide;
The sire turns o'er, wi' patriarchal grace,
The big ha' Bible, ance his father's pride:
His bonnet rev'rently is laid aside,
His lyart haffets[19] wearing thin an' bare; [19] grey hair
Those strains that once did sweet in Zion glide,
He wales[20] a portion with judicious care; [20] chooses
And 'Let us worship God!' he says, with solemn air.

They chant their artless notes in simple guise;
They tune their hearts, by far the noblest aim:
Perhaps 'Dundee's' wild warbling measures rise,
Or plaintive 'Martyrs', worthy of the name:
Or noble 'Elgin' beets the heavenward flame
The sweetest far of Scotia's holy lays:
Compared with these, Italian trills are tame;
The tickled ears no heartfelt raptures raise;
Nae unison hae they with our Creator's praise.

★

Compared with this, how poor Religion's pride,
In all the pomp of method, and of art,
When men display to congregations wide,
Devotion's every grace, except the heart!
The Power, incensed, the pageant will desert,
The pompous strain, the sacerdotal stole;
But haply, in some cottage far apart,
May hear, well pleased, the language of the soul;
And in his book of life the inmates poor enrol.

Then homeward all take off their several way;
The youngling cottagers retire to rest:
The parent pair their secret homage pay,
And proffer up to Heaven the warm request
That He who stills the raven's clamorous nest,
And decks the lily fair in flowery pride,
Would, in the way his wisdom sees the best,
For them and for their little ones provide;
But chiefly, in their hearts with grace divine preside.

[1786]

WILLIAM BLAKE

Poems written in a copy of 'Poetical Sketches'

Song 1st by a Shepherd

Welcome, stranger, to this place,
Where joy doth sit on every bough,
Paleness flies from every face;
We reap not what we do not sow.

Innocence doth like a rose
Bloom on every maiden's cheek;
Honour twines around her brows,
The jewel health adorns her neck.

Song 2nd by a young Shepherd

When the trees do laugh with our merry wit,
And the green hill laughs with the noise of it,
When the meadows laugh with lively green
And the grasshopper laughs in the merry scene,

When the greenwood laughs with the voice of joy,
And the dimpling stream runs laughing by,
When Edessa, and Lyca, and Emilie,
With their sweet round mouths sing ha, ha, he,

When the painted Birds laugh in the shade,
Where our table with cherries and nuts is spread;
Come live and be merry and join with me
To sing the sweet chorus of ha, ha, he.

Song by an old Shepherd

When silver snow decks Sylvio's clothes
And jewel hangs at shepherd's nose,
We can abide life's pelting storm
That makes our limbs quake, if our hearts be warm.

Whilst Virtue is our walking-staff
And Truth a lantern to our path,
We can abide life's pelting storm
That makes our limbs quake, if our hearts be warm.

Blow, boisterous wind, stern winter frown,
Innocence is a winter's gown;
So clad, we'll abide life's pelting storm
That makes our limbs quake, if our hearts be warm.

[1783]

The Shepherd

From *Songs of Innocence*

How sweet is the Shepherd's sweet lot!
From the morn to the evening he strays;
He shall follow his sheep all the day,
And his tongue shall be filled with praise.

For he hears the lamb's innocent call,
And he hears the ewe's tender reply;
He is watchful while they are in peace,
For they know when their Shepherd is nigh.

[1789]

To a just taste, and unadulterated feelings, the natural beauties of the country, the simple manners, rustic occupations, and rural enjoyments of its inhabitants, brought into view by the medium of a well-contrived dramatic fable, must afford a much higher degree of pleasure, than any chimerical fiction, in which Arcadian nymphs and swains hold intercourse with Pan and his attendant fauns and satyrs.

[Alexander Fraser Tytler, 'Remarks on the Genius and Writings of Allan Ramsay', 1800]

The principal object then which I proposed to myself in these Poems was to make the incidents of common life interesting by tracing in them, truly though not ostentatiously, the primary laws of our nature: chiefly as far as regards the manner in which we associate ideas in a state of excitement. Low and rustic life was generally chosen because in that situation the essential passions of the heart find a better soil in which they can attain their maturity, are less under restraint, and speak a plainer and more emphatic language; because in that situation our elementary feelings exist in a state of greater simplicity and consequently may be more accurately contemplated and more forcibly communicated; because the manners of rural life germinate from those elementary feelings; and from the necessary character of rural occupations are more easily comprehended; and are more durable; and lastly, because in that situation the passions of men are incorporated with the beautiful and permanent forms of nature. The language too of these men is adopted (purified indeed from what appear to be its real defects, from all lasting and rational causes of dislike or disgust) because such men hourly communicate with the best objects from which the best part of language is originally derived; and because, from their rank in society and the sameness and narrow circle of their intercourse, being less under the action of social vanity they convey their feelings and notions in simple and unelaborated expressions.

[William Wordsworth, Preface to *Lyrical Ballads*, 1800]

It is not every man that is likely to be improved by a country life or by country labours. Education, or original sensibility, or both, must pre-exist if the changes, forms and incidents of nature are to prove a sufficient stimulant. And where these are not sufficient, the mind contracts and hardens by want of stimulants, and the man becomes selfish, sensual, gross and hard-hearted. Let the management of the Poor Laws in Liverpool, Manchester or Bristol be compared with the ordinary dispensation of the poor rates in agricultural villages, where the farmers are the overseers and guardians of the poor. If my own experience has not been particularly unfortunate, as well as that of the many respectable country clergymen with whom I have conversed on the subject, the result would engender more than scepticism concerning the desirable influences of low and rustic life in and for itself. Whatever may be concluded on the other side, from the stronger local attachments and enterprising spirit of the Swiss and other mountaineers, applies to a particular mode of pastoral life under forms of property that permit and beget manners truly republican, not to rustic life in general or to the absence of artificial cultivation. On the contrary the mountaineers, whose manners have been so often eulogized, are in general better educated and greater readers than men of equal rank elsewhere. But where this is not the case, as among the peasantry of North Wales, the ancient mountains, with all their terrors and all their glories, are pictures to the blind and music to the deaf.

[Samuel Taylor Coleridge, *Biographia Literaria*, 1817]

The bourgeoisie has subjected the country to the rule of the towns. It has created enormous cities, has greatly increased the urban population as compared with the rural, and has thus rescued a considerable part of the population from the idiocy of rural life. Just as it has made the country dependent on the towns, so it has made barbarian and semi-barbarian countries dependent on the civilized ones, nations of peasants on nations of bourgeois, the East on the West.

[Karl Marx and Friedrich Engels, *The Communist Manifesto*, 1848]

WILLIAM WORDSWORTH

Old Man Travelling

Animal tranquillity and decay.
A Sketch

The little hedge-row birds,
That peck along the road, regard him not.
He travels on, and in his face, his step,
His gait, is one expression; every limb,
His look and bending figure, all bespeak
A man who does not move with pain, but moves
With thought – He is insensibly subdued
To settled quiet: he is one by whom
All effort seems forgotten, one to whom
Long patience has such mild composure given,
That patience now doth seem a thing, of which
He hath no need. He is by nature led
To peace so perfect, that the young behold
With envy, what the old man hardly feels.
– I asked him whither he was bound, and what
The object of his journey; he replied
'Sir ! I am going many miles to take
'A last leave of my son, a mariner,
'Who from a sea-fight has been brought to Falmouth,
'And there is dying in an hospital.'

[1798]

The Last of the Flock

I

In distant countries have I been,
And yet I have not often seen
A healthy man, a man full grown,

Weep in the public roads, alone.
But such a one, on English ground,
And in the broad highway, I met;
Along the broad highway he came,
His cheeks with tears were wet:
Sturdy he seemed, though he was sad;
And in his arms a Lamb he had.

II

He saw me, and he turned aside,
As if he wished himself to hide:
And with his coat did then essay
To wipe those briny tears away.
I followed him, and said, 'My friend,
What ails you? wherefore weep you so?'
– 'Shame on me, Sir! this lusty Lamb,
He makes my tears to flow.
To-day I fetched him from the rock;
He is the last of all my flock.

III

'When I was young, a single man,
And after youthful follies ran,
Though little given to care and thought,
Yet, so it was, an ewe I bought;
And other sheep from her I raised,
As healthy sheep as you might see;
And then I married, and was rich
As I could wish to be;
Of sheep I numbered a full score,
And every year increased my store.

IV

'Year after year my stock it grew;
And from this one, this single ewe,
Full fifty comely sheep I raised,

As fine a flock as ever grazed!
Upon the Quantock hills they fed;
They throve, and we at home did thrive:
– This lusty Lamb of all my store
Is all that is alive;
And now I care not if we die,
And perish all of poverty.

V

'Six Children, Sir! had I to feed;
Hard labour in a time of need!
My pride was tamed, and in our grief
I of the Parish asked relief.
They said, I was a wealthy man;
My sheep upon the uplands fed,
And it was fit that thence I took
Whereof to buy us bread.
"Do this: how can we give to you,"
They cried, "what to the poor is due?"

VI

'I sold a sheep, as they had said,
And bought my little children bread,
And they were healthy with their food;
For me – it never did me good.
A woeful time it was for me,
To see the end of all my gains,
The pretty flock which I had reared
With all my care and pains,
To see it melt like snow away –
For me it was a woeful day.

VII

'Another still! and still another!
A little lamb, and then its mother!
It was a vein that never stopped –

Like blood-drops from my heart they dropped.
Till thirty were not left alive
They dwindled, dwindled, one by one;
And I may say, that many a time
I wished they all were gone –
Reckless of what might come at last
Were but the bitter struggle past.

VIII

'To wicked deeds I was inclined,
And wicked fancies crossed my mind;
And every man I chanced to see,
I thought he knew some ill of me:
No peace, no comfort could I find,
No ease, within doors or without;
And crazily and wearily
I went my work about;
And oft was moved to flee from home,
And hide my head where wild beasts roam.

IX

'Sir! 'twas a precious flock to me,
As dear as my own children be;
For daily with my growing store
I loved my children more and more.
Alas! it was an evil time;
God cursed me in my sore distress;
I prayed, yet every day I thought
I loved my children less;
And every week, and every day,
My flock it seemed to melt away.

X

'They dwindled, Sir, sad sight to see!
From ten to five, from five to three,
A lamb, a wether, and a ewe; –

And then at last from three to two;
And, of my fifty, yesterday
I had but only one:
And here it lies upon my arm,
Alas! and I have none; –
Today I fetched it from the rock;
It is the last of all my flock.'

[1798]

The Reverie of Poor Susan

At the corner of Wood Street, when daylight appears,
Hangs a Thrush that sings loud, it has sung for three years:
Poor Susan has passed by the spot, and has heard
In the silence of morning the song of the Bird.

'Tis a note of enchantment; what ails her? She sees
A mountain ascending, a vision of trees;
Bright volumes of vapour through Lothbury glide,
And a river flows on through the vale of Cheapside.

Green pastures she views in the midst of the dale,
Down which she so often has tripped with her pail;
And a single small cottage, a nest like a dove's,
The one only dwelling on earth that she loves.

She looks, and her heart is in heaven: but they fade,
The mist and the river, the hill and the shade:
The stream will not flow, and the hill will not rise,
And the colours have all passed away from her eyes.

[1800]

'There was a Boy'

There was a Boy; ye knew him well, ye cliffs
And islands of Winander! – many a time,
At evening, when the earliest stars began

To move along the edges of the hills,
Rising or setting, would he stand alone,
Beneath the trees, or by the glimmering lake;
And there, with fingers interwoven, both hands
Pressed closely palm to palm and to his mouth
Uplifted, he, as through an instrument,
Blew mimic hootings to the silent owls,
That they might answer him. – And they would shout
Across the watery vale, and shout again,
Responsive to his call, – with quivering peals,
And long hallooes, and screams, and echoes loud
Redoubled and redoubled; concourse wild
Of jocund din! And, when there came a pause
Of silence such as baffled his best skill:
Then sometimes, in that silence, while he hung
Listening, a gentle shock of mild surprise
Has carried far into his heart the voice
Of mountain-torrents; or the visible scene
Would enter unawares into his mind
With all its solemn imagery, its rocks,
Its woods, and that uncertain heaven received
Into the bosom of the steady lake.

This boy was taken from his mates, and died
In childhood, ere he was full twelve years old.
Pre-eminent in beauty is the vale
Where he was born and bred: the churchyard hangs
Upon a slope above the village-school;
And through that churchyard when my way has led
On summer-evenings, I believe that there
A long half-hour together I have stood
Mute – looking at the grave in which he lies!

[1800]

From *Michael*

Upon the forest-side in Grasmere Vale
There dwelt a Shepherd, Michael was his name;
An old man, stout of heart, and strong of limb.
His bodily frame had been from youth to age
Of an unusual strength: his mind was keen,
Intense, and frugal, apt for all affairs,
And in his shepherd's calling he was prompt
And watchful more than ordinary men.
Hence had he learned the meaning of all winds,
Of blasts of every tone; and oftentimes,
When others heeded not, He heard the South
Make subterraneous music, like the noise
Of bagpipers on distant Highland hills.
The Shepherd, at such warning, of his flock
Bethought him, and he to himself would say,
'The winds are now devising work for me!'
And, truly, at all times, the storm, that drives
The traveller to a shelter, summoned him
Up to the mountains: he had been alone
Amid the heart of many thousand mists,
That came to him, and left him, on the heights.
So lived he till his eightieth year was past.
And grossly that man errs, who should suppose
That the green valleys, and the streams and rocks,
Were things indifferent to the Shepherd's thoughts.
Fields, where with cheerful spirits he had breathed
The common air; hills, which with vigorous step
He had so often climbed; which had impressed
So many incidents upon his mind
Of hardship, skill or courage, joy or fear;
Which, like a book, preserved the memory
Of the dumb animals, whom he had saved,

Had fed or sheltered, linking to such acts
The certainty of honourable gain;
Those fields, those hills – what could they less? had laid
Strong hold on his affections, were to him
A pleasurable feeling of blind love,
The pleasure which there is in life itself.

[1800]

From *The Excursion*, Book I

Among the hills of Athol he was born;
Where, on a small hereditary farm,
An unproductive slip of rugged ground,
His Parents, with their numerous offspring, dwelt;
A virtuous household, though exceeding poor!
Pure livers were they all, austere and grave,
And fearing God; the very children taught
Stern self-respect, a reverence for God's word,
And an habitual piety, maintained
With strictness scarcely known on English ground.

From his sixth year, the Boy of whom I speak,
In summer, tended cattle on the hills;
But, through the inclement and the perilous days
Of long-continuing winter, he repaired,
Equipped with satchel, to a school, that stood
Sole building on a mountain's dreary edge,
Remote from view of city spire, or sound
Of minster clock! From that bleak tenement
He, many an evening, to his distant home
In solitude returning, saw the hills
Grow larger in the darkness; all alone
Beheld the stars come out above his head,

And travelled through the wood, with no one near
To whom he might confess the things he saw.

So the foundations of his mind were laid.
In such communion, not from terror free,
While yet a child, and long before his time,
Had he perceived the presence and the power
Of greatness; and deep feelings had impressed
So vividly great objects that they lay
Upon his mind like substances, whose presence
Perplexed the bodily sense. He had received
A precious gift; for, as he grew in years,
With these impressions would he still compare
All his remembrances, thoughts, shapes, and forms;
And, being still unsatisfied with aught
Of dimmer character, he thence attained
An active power to fasten images
Upon his brain; and on their pictured lines
Intensely brooded, even till they acquired
The liveliness of dreams. Nor did he fail,
While yet a child, with a child's eagerness
Incessantly to turn his ear and eye
On all things which the moving seasons brought
To feed such appetite – nor this alone
Appeased his yearning: – in the after-day
Of boyhood, many an hour in caves forlorn,
And 'mid the hollow depths of naked crags
He sate, and even in their fixed lineaments,
Or from the power of a peculiar eye,
Or by creative feeling overborne,
Or by predominance of thought oppressed,
Even in their fixed and steady lineaments
He traced an ebbing and a flowing mind,
Expression ever varying!
Thus informed,

He had small need of books; for many a tale
Traditionary, round the mountains hung,
And many a legend, peopling the dark woods,
Nourished Imagination in her growth,
And gave the Mind that apprehensive power
By which she is made quick to recognize
The moral properties and scope of things.
But eagerly he read, and read again,
Whate'er the minister's old shelf supplied;
The life and death of martyrs, who sustained,
With will inflexible, those fearful pangs
Triumphantly displayed in records left
Of persecution, and the Covenant – times
Whose echo rings through Scotland to this hour!
And there, by lucky hap, had been preserved
A straggling volume, torn and incomplete,
That left half-told the preternatural tale,
Romance of giants, chronicle of fiends,
Profuse in garniture of wooden cuts
Strange and uncouth; dire faces, figures dire,
Sharp-kneed, sharp-elbowed, and lean-ankled too,
With long and ghostly shanks – forms which once seen
Could never be forgotten!
In his heart,
Where Fear sate thus, a cherished visitant,
Was wanting yet the pure delight of love
By sound diffused, or by the breathing air,
Or by the silent looks of happy things,
Or flowing from the universal face
Of earth and sky. But he had felt the power
Of Nature, and already was prepared,
By his intense conceptions, to receive
Deeply the lesson deep of love which he,
Whom Nature, by whatever means, has taught
To feel intensely, cannot but receive.

Such was the Boy – but for the growing Youth
What soul was his, when, from the naked top
Of some bold headland, he beheld the sun
Rise up, and bathe the world in light! He looked –
Ocean and earth, the solid frame of earth
And ocean's liquid mass, in gladness lay
Beneath him: – Far and wide the clouds were touched,
And in their silent faces could he read
Unutterable love. Sound needed none,
Nor any voice of joy; his spirit drank
The spectacle: sensation, soul, and form,
All melted into him; they swallowed up
His animal being; in them did he live,
And by them did he live; they were his life.
In such access of mind, in such high hour
Of visitation from the living God,
Thought was not; in enjoyment it expired.
No thanks he breathed, he proffered no request;
Rapt into still communion that transcends
The imperfect offices of prayer and praise,
His mind was a thanksgiving to the power
That made him; it was blessedness and love!

A Herdsman on the lonely mountain tops,
Such intercourse was his, and in this sort
Was his existence oftentimes *possessed.*
O then how beautiful, how bright, appeared
The written promise! Early had he learned
To reverence the volume that displays
The mystery, the life which cannot die;
But in the mountains did he *feel* his faith.
All things, responsive to the writing, there
Breathed immortality, revolving life,
And greatness still revolving; infinite:
There littleness was not; the least of things

Seemed infinite; and there his spirit shaped
Her prospects, nor did he believe, – he *saw*.
What wonder if his being thus became
Sublime and comprehensive! Low desires,
Low thoughts had there no place; yet was his heart
Lowly; for he was meek in gratitude,
Oft as he called those ecstasies to mind,
And whence they flowed; and from them he acquired
Wisdom, which works through patience; thence he learned
In oft-recurring hours of sober thought
To look on Nature with a humble heart,
Self-questioned where it did not understand,
And with a superstitious eye of love.

So passed the time; yet to the nearest town
He duly went with what small overplus
His earnings might supply, and brought away
The book that most had tempted his desires
While at the stall he read. Among the hills
He gazed upon that mighty orb of song,
The divine Milton. Lore of different kind,
The annual savings of a toilsome life,
His Schoolmaster supplied; books that explain
The purer elements of truth involved
In lines and numbers, and, by charm severe,
(Especially perceived where nature droops
And feeling is suppressed) preserve the mind
Busy in solitude and poverty.
These occupations oftentimes deceived
The listless hours, while in the hollow vale,
Hollow and green, he lay on the green turf
In pensive idleness. What could he do,
Thus daily thirsting, in that lonesome life,
With blind endeavours? Yet, still uppermost,
Nature was at his heart as if he felt,

Though yet he knew not how, a wasting power
In all things that from her sweet influence
Might tend to wean him. Therefore with her hues,
Her forms, and with the spirit of her forms,
He clothed the nakedness of austere truth.
While yet he lingered in the rudiments
Of science, and among her simplest laws,
His triangles – they were the stars of heaven,
The silent stars! Oft did he take delight
To measure the altitude of some tall crag
That is the eagle's birth-place, or some peak
Familiar with forgotten years, that shows,
Inscribed upon its visionary sides,
The history of many a winter storm,
Or obscure records of the path of fire.

And thus before his eighteenth year was told,
Accumulated feelings pressed his heart
With still increasing weight; he was o'erpowered
By Nature; by the turbulence subdued
Of his own mind; by mystery and hope,
And the first virgin passion of a soul
Communing with the glorious universe.
Full often wished he that the winds might rage
When they were silent: far more fondly now
Than in his earlier season did he love
Tempestuous nights – the conflict and the sounds
That live in darkness. From his intellect
And from the stillness of abstracted thought
He asked repose; and, failing oft to win
The peace required, he scanned the laws of light
Amid the roar of torrents, where they send
From hollow clefts up to the clearer air
A cloud of mist that, smitten by the sun,
Varies its rainbow hues. But vainly thus,

And vainly by all other means, he strove
To mitigate the fever of his heart.

In dreams, in study, and in ardent thought,
Thus was he reared; much wanting to assist
The growth of intellect, yet gaining more,
And every moral feeling of his soul
Strengthened and braced, by breathing in content
The keen, the wholesome, air of poverty,
And drinking from the well of homely life.
– But, from past liberty, and tried restraints,
He now was summoned to select the course
Of humble industry that promised best
To yield him no unworthy maintenance.
Urged by his Mother, he essayed to teach
A village-school – but wandering thoughts were then
A misery to him; and the Youth resigned
A task he was unable to perform.

That stern yet kindly Spirit, who constrains
The Savoyard to quit his naked rocks,
The free-born Swiss to leave his narrow vales,
(Spirit attached to regions mountainous
Like their own stedfast clouds) did now impel
His restless mind to look abroad with hope.
– An irksome drudgery seems it to plod on,
Through hot and dusty ways, or pelting storm,
A vagrant Merchant under a heavy load,
Bent as he moves, and needing frequent rest;
Yet do such travellers find their own delight;
And their hard service, deemed debasing now
Gained merited respect in simpler times;
When squire, and priest, and they who round them dwelt
In rustic sequestration – all dependent
Upon the *Pedlar's* toil – supplied their wants,

Or pleased their fancies, with the wares he brought.
Not ignorant was the Youth that still no few
Of his adventurous countrymen were led
By perseverance in this track of life
To competence and ease: – to him it offered
Attractions manifold; – and this he chose.
– His Parents on the enterprise bestowed
Their farewell benediction, but with hearts
Foreboding evil. From his native hills
He wandered far; much did he see of men,
Their manners, their enjoyments, and pursuits,
Their passions and their feelings; chiefly those
Essential and eternal in the heart,
That, 'mid the simpler forms of rural life,
Exist more simple in their elements,
And speak a plainer language. In the woods,
A lone Enthusiast, and among the fields,
Itinerant in this labour, he had passed
The better portion of his time; and there
Spontaneously had his affections thriven
Amid the bounties of the year, the peace
And liberty of nature; there he kept
In solitude and solitary thought
His mind in a just equipoise of love.
Serene it was, unclouded by the cares
Of ordinary life; unvexed, unwarped
By partial bondage. In his steady course,
No piteous revolutions had he felt,
No wild varieties of joy and grief.
Unoccupied by sorrow of its own,
His heart lay open; and, by nature tuned
And constant disposition of his thoughts
To sympathy with man, he was alive
To all that was enjoyed where'er he went,
And all that was endured; for, in himself

Happy, and quiet in his cheerfulness,
He had no painful pressure from without
That made him turn aside from wretchedness
With coward fears. He could *afford* to suffer
With those whom he saw suffer. Hence it came
That in our best experience he was rich
And in the wisdom of our daily life.
For hence, minutely, in his various rounds,
He had observed the progress and decay
Of many minds, of minds and bodies too;
The history of many families;
How they had prospered; how they were o'erthrown
By passion or mischance, or such misrule
Among the unthinking masters of the earth
As makes the nations groan.
This active course
He followed till provision for his wants
Had been obtained; – the Wanderer then resolved
To pass the remnant of his days, untasked
With needless services, from hardship free.
His calling laid aside, he lived at ease:
But still he loved to pace the public roads
And the wild paths; and, by the summer's warmth
Invited, often would he leave his home
And journey far, revisiting the scenes
That to his memory were most endeared.
– Vigorous in health, of hopeful spirits, undamped
By worldly-mindedness or anxious care;
Observant, studious, thoughtful, and refreshed
By knowledge gathered up from day to day;
Thus had he lived a long and innocent life.

[1814]

When the romantic revival began . . . the doom of such artificial pieces was pronounced. It would be purely fantastic to try to claim for Wordsworth a place among the pastoral poets; his was the influence which, more than any other, was fatal to the Virgilian tradition of piping swains and the artless rural fair. His method of considering rustic life was something quite new, modern, and exact . . . If bucolic drama should ever revive with us, it will need to be strictly realistic and exact.

[Edmund Gosse, 'Essay on English Pastoral Poetry', 1882]

SAMUEL TAYLOR COLERIDGE

Reflections on Having Left a Place of Retirement

Sermoni propriora – *Horace*

Low was our pretty Cot: our tallest Rose
Peep'd at the chamber-window. We could hear
At silent noon, and eve, and early morn,
The Sea's faint murmur. In the open air
Our Myrtles blossom'd; and across the porch
Thick Jasmins twined: the little landscape round
Was green and woody, and refresh'd the eye.
It was a spot which you might aptly call
The Valley of Seclusion! Once I saw
(Hallowing his Sabbath-day by quietness)
A wealthy son of Commerce saunter by,
Bristowa's citizen: methought, it calm'd
His thirst of idle gold, and made him muse
With wiser feelings: for he paus'd, and look'd
With a pleas'd sadness, and gaz'd all around,

Then eyed our Cottage, and gaz'd round again,
And sigh'd, and said, it was a Blesséd Place.
And we *were* bless'd. Oft with patient ear
Long-listening to the viewless sky-lark's note
(Viewless, or haply for a moment seen
Gleaming on sunny wings) in whisper'd tones
I've said to my Belovéd, 'Such, sweet Girl!
The inobtrusive song of Happiness,
Unearthly minstrelsy! then only heard
When the Soul seeks to hear; when all is hush'd,
And the Heart listens!'
But the time, when first
From that low Dell, steep up the stony Mount
I climb'd with perilous toil and reach'd the top,
Oh! what a goodly scene! *Here* the bleak mount,
The bare bleak mountain speckled thin with sheep;
Grey clouds, that shadowing spot the sunny fields;
And river, now with bushy rocks o'er-brow'd,
Now winding bright and full, with naked banks;
And seats, and lawns, the Abbey and the wood,
And cots, and hamlets, and faint city-spire;
The Channel *there*, the Islands and white sails,
Dim coasts, and cloud-like hills, and shoreless Ocean –
It seem'd like Omnipresence! God, methought,
Had built him there a Temple: the whole World
Seem'd *imag'd* in its vast circumference:
No *wish* profan'd my overwhelméd heart.
Blest hour! It was a luxury, – to be!

Ah! quiet Dell! dear Cot, and Mount sublime!
I was constrain'd to quit you. Was it right,
While my unnumber'd brethren toil'd and bled,
That I should dream away the entrusted hours
On rose-leaf beds, pampering the coward heart
With feelings all too delicate for use?

Sweet is the tear that from some Howard's eye
Drops on the cheek of one he lifts from earth:
And he that works me good with unmov'd face,
Does it but half: he chills me while he aids,
My benefactor, not my brother man!
Yet even this, this cold beneficence
Praise, praise it, O my Soul! oft as thou scann'st
The sluggard Pity's vision-weaving tribe!
Who sigh for Wretchedness, yet shun the Wretched,
Nursing in some delicious solitude
Their slothful loves and dainty sympathies!
I therefore go, and join head, heart, and hand,
Active and firm, to fight the bloodless fight
Of Science, Freedom, and the Truth in Christ.

Yet oft when after honourable toil
Rests the tir'd mind, and waking loves to dream,
My spirit shall revisit thee, dear Cot!
Thy Jasmin and thy window-peeping Rose,
And Myrtles fearless of the mild sea-air.
And I shall sigh fond wishes – sweet Abode!
Ah! – had none greater! And that all had such!
It might be so – but the time is not yet.
Speed it, O Father! Let thy Kingdom come!

[1796]

ROBERT SOUTHEY

The Ruined Cottage

Ay, Charles! I knew that this would fix thine eye; . . .
This woodbine wreathing round the broken porch,
Its leaves just withering, yet one autumn flower
Still fresh and fragrant; and yon hollyhock

That through the creeping weeds and nettles tall
Peers taller, lifting, column-like, a stem
Bright with its roseate blossoms. I have seen
Many an old convent reverend in decay,
And many a time have trod the castle courts
And grass-green halls, yet never did they strike
Home to the heart such melancholy thoughts
As this poor cottage. Look! its little hatch
Fleeced with that grey and wintry moss; the roof
Part moulder'd in, the rest o'ergrown with weeds,
House-leek, and long thin grass, and greener moss;
So Nature steals on all the works of man,
Sure conqueror she, reclaiming to herself
His perishable piles.

I led thee here,
Charles, not without design; for this hath been
My favourite walk even since I was a boy;
And I remember, Charles, this ruin here,
The neatest comfortable dwelling-place!
That when I read in those dear books which first
Woke in my heart the love of poesy,
How with the villagers Erminia dwelt,
And Calidore for a fair shepherdess
Forsook his quest to learn the shepherd's lore,
My fancy drew from this the little hut
Where that poor princess wept her hopeless love,
Or where the gentle Calidore at eve
Led Pastorella home. There was not then
A weed where all these nettles overtop
The garden-wall; but sweet-briar, scenting sweet
The morning air; rosemary and marjoram,
All wholesome herbs; and then, that woodbine wreathed
So lavishly around the pillar'd porch
Its fragrant flowers, that when I pass'd this way,
After a truant absence hastening home,

I could not chuse but pass with slacken'd speed
By that delightful fragrance. Sadly changed
Is this poor cottage! and its dwellers, Charles! . . .
Theirs is a simple melancholy tale, . . .
There's scarce a village but can fellow it:
And yet, methinks, it will not weary thee,
And should not be untold.
A widow here
Dwelt with an orphan grandchild: just removed
Above the reach of pinching poverty,
She lived on some small pittance which sufficed,
In better times, the needful calls of life,
Not without comfort. I remember her
Sitting at even in that open doorway,
And spinning in the sun. Methinks I see her
Raising her eyes and dark-rimm'd spectacles
To see the passer-by, yet ceasing not
To twirl her lengthening thread; or in the garden,
On some dry summer evening, walking round
To view her flowers, and pointing as she lean'd
Upon the ivory handle of her stick,
To some carnation whose o'erheavy head
Needed support; while with the watering-pot
Joanna follow'd, and refresh'd and trimm'd
The drooping plant; Joanna, her dear child,
As lovely and as happy then as youth
And innocence could make her.
Charles, it seems
As though I were a boy again, and all
The mediate years with their vicissitudes
A half-forgotten dream. I see the Maid
So comely in her Sunday dress! her hair,
Her bright brown hair, wreathed in contracting curls;
And then her cheek! it was a red and white
That made the delicate hues of art look loathsome.

The countrymen who on their way to church
Were leaning o'er the bridge, loitering to hear
The bell's last summons, and in idleness
Watching the stream below, would all look up
When she pass'd by. And her old Grandam, Charles, . . .
When I have heard some erring infidel
Speak of our faith as of a gloomy creed,
Inspiring superstitious wretchedness,
Her figure has recurr'd; for she did love
The Sabbath-day; and many a time hath cross'd
These fields in rain and through the winter snows,
When I, a graceless boy, and cold of foot,
Wishing the weary service at its end,
Have wonder'd wherefore that good dame came there,
Who, if it pleased her, might have staid beside
A comfortable fire.
                                        One only care
Hung on her aged spirit. For herself,
Her path was plain before her, and the close
Of her long journey near. But then her child
Soon to be left alone in this bad world . . .
That was a thought which many a winter night
Had kept her sleepless: and when prudent love
In something better than a servant's state
Had placed her well at last, it was a pang
Like parting life to part with her dear girl.
   One summer, Charles, when at the holidays
Return'd from school, I visited again
My old accustom'd walks, and found in them
A joy almost like meeting an old friend,
I saw the cottage empty, and the weeds
Already crowding the neglected flowers.
Joanna, by a villain's wiles seduced,
Had play'd the wanton, and that blow had reach'd
Her grandam's heart. She did not suffer long;

Her age was feeble, and this mortal grief
Brought her grey hairs with sorrow to the grave.

I pass this ruin'd dwelling oftentimes,
And think of other days. It wakes in me
A transient sadness; but the feelings, Charles,
Which ever with these recollections rise,
I trust in God they will not pass away.

[1799]

ROBERT BLOOMFIELD

The Farmer's Boy

From *Spring*

Fled now the sullen murmurs of the North,
The splendid raiment of the Spring peeps forth;
Her universal green, and the clear sky,
Delight still more and more the gazing eye.
Wide o'er the fields, in rising moisture strong,
Shoots up the simple flower, or creeps along
The mellow'd soil; imbibing fairer hues,
Or sweets from frequent showers and evening dews;
That summon from their sheds the slumb'ring ploughs,
While health impregnates every breeze that blows.
No wheels support the diving, pointed share;
No groaning ox is doom'd to labour there;
No helpmates teach the docile steed his road;
(Alike unknown the plough-boy and the goad;)
But, unassisted through each toilsome day,
With smiling brow the ploughman cleaves his way,

Draws his fresh parallels, and, wid'ning still,
Treads slow the heavy dale, or climbs the hill:
Strong on the wing his busy followers play,
Where writhing earth-worms meet the' unwelcome day;
Till all is changed, and hill and level down
Assume a livery of a sober brown;
Again disturb'd, when Giles with wearying strides
From ridge to ridge the ponderous harrow guides;
His heels deep sinking every step he goes,
Till dirt adhesive loads his clouted shoes.
Welcome green headland! firm beneath his feet;
Welcome the friendly bank's refreshing seat;
There, warm with toil, his panting horses browse
Their shelt'ring canopy of pendent boughs;
Till Rest delicious chase each transient pain,
And new-born Vigour swell in every vein.
Hour after hour, and day to day succeeds;
Till every clod and deep-drawn furrow spreads
To crumbling mould; a level surface clear,
And strew'd with corn to crown the rising year;
And o'er the whole Giles once transverse again,
In earth's moist bosom buries up the grain.
The work is done; no more to Man is given;
The grateful Farmer trusts the rest to Heaven.
Yet oft with anxious heart he looks around,
And marks the first green blade that breaks the ground;
In fancy sees his trembling oats uprun,
His tufted barley yellow with the sun;
See clouds propitious shed their timely store,
And all his harvest gather'd round his door.

*

His simple errand done, he homeward hies;
Another instantly its place supplies.

The chatt'ring dairy-maid immersed in steam,
Singing and scrubbing midst her milk and cream,
Bawls out, 'Go fetch the Cows!' – he hears no more;
For pigs, and ducks, and turkeys, throng the door,
And sitting hens, for constant war prepared;
A concert strange to that which late he heard.
Straight to the meadow then he whistling goes;
With well-known halloo calls his lazy cows;
Down the rich pasture heedlessly they graze,
Or hear the summon with an idle gaze:
For well they know the cow-yard yields no more
Its tempting fragrance, nor its wintry store.
Reluctance marks their steps, sedate and slow;
The right of conquest all the law they know;
The strong press on, the weak by turns succeed,
And one superior always takes the lead,
Is ever foremost, whereso'er they stray;
Allow'd precedence, undisputed sway:
With jealous pride her station is maintain'd,
For many a broil that post of honour gain'd.
At home the yard affords a grateful scene;
For Spring makes e'en a miry cow-yard clean;
Thence from its chalky bed behold convey'd
The rich manure that drenching Winter made,
Which piled near home, grows green with many a weed,
A promised nutriment for Autumn's seed.
Forth comes the maid, and like the morning smiles;
The mistress too, and follow'd close by Giles.
A friendly tripod forms their humble seat,
With pails bright scour'd, and delicately sweet.
Where shadowing elms obstruct the morning ray,
Begins the work, begins the simple lay;
The full-charged udder yields its willing streams,
While Mary sings some lover's amorous dreams;
And crouching Giles beneath a neighbouring tree

Tugs o'er his pail and chants with equal glee;
Whose hat with tatter'd brim, of nap so bare,
From the cow's side purloins a coat of hair,
A mottled ensign of his harmless trade,
An unambitious, peaceable cockade.
As unambitious too that cheerful aid
The mistress yields beside her rosy maid;
With joy she views her plenteous reeking store,
And bears a brimmer to the dairy door;
Her cows dismiss'd, the luscious mead to roam,
Till eve again recal them loaded home.
And now the Dairy claims her choicest care,
And half her household find employment there:
Slow rolls the churn, its load of clogging cream
At once foregoes its quality and name:
From knotty particles first floating wide
Congealing butter's dash'd from side to side;
Streams of new milk through flowing coolers stray,
And snow-white curd abounds, and wholesome whey.
Due north the' unglaz'd windows, cold and clear,
For warming sunbeams are unwelcome here.
Brisk goes the work beneath each busy hand,
And Giles must trudge, whoever gives command;
A Gibeonite, that serves them all by turns:
He drains the pump, from him the faggot burns;
From him the noisy hogs demand their food;
While at his heels run many a chirping brood,
Or down his path in expectation stand,
With equal claims upon his strewing hand.
Thus wastes the morn, till each with pleasure sees
The bustle o'er, and press'd the new-made cheese.
  Unrivall'd stands thy country cheese, O Giles!
Whose very name alone engenders smiles;
Whose fame abroad by every tongue is spoke,
The well-known butt of many a flinty joke,

That pass like current coin the nation through;
And, ah! Experience proves the satire true.
Provision's grave, thou ever-craving mart,
Dependent, huge metropolis! where Art
Her poring thousands stows in breathless rooms,
Midst pois'nous smokes and steams, and rattling looms;
Where Grandeur revels in unbounded stores;
Restraint, a slighted stranger at their doors!
Thou, like a whirlpool, drain'st the countries round,
Till London market, London price, resound
Through every town, round every passing load,
And dairy produce throngs the eastern road:
Delicious veal, and butter, every hour,
From Essex lowlands, and the banks of Stour;
And further far, where numerous herds repose,
From Orwell's brink, from Waveny, or Ouse.
Hence Suffolk dairy-wives run mad for cream,
And leave their milk with nothing but its name;
Its name derision and reproach pursue,
And strangers tell of 'three times skimm'd sky-blue.'
To cheese converted, what can be its boast?
What, but the common virtues of a post!
If drought o'ertake it faster than the knife,
Most fair it bids for stubborn length of life,
And like the oaken shelf whereon 'tis laid,
Mocks the weak efforts of the bending blade;
Or in the hog-trough rests in perfect spite,
Too big to swallow, and too hard to bite.
Inglorious victory! Ye Cheshire meads,
Or Severn's flow'ry dales, where Plenty treads,
Was your rich milk to suffer wrongs like these,
Farewell your pride! farewell renowned cheese!
The skimmer dread, whose ravages alone
Thus turn the meads' sweet nectar into stone.

From *Summer*

Here once a year Distinction low'rs its crest,
The master, servant, and the merry guest,
Are equal all; and round the happy ring
The reaper's eyes exulting glances fling,
And, warm'd with gratitude, he quits his place,
With sunburnt hands and ale-enliven'd face,
Refills the jug his honour'd host to tend,
To serve at once the master and the friend;
Proud thus to meet his smiles, to share his tale,
His nuts, his conversation, and his ale.

Such were the days, – of days long past I sing,
When Pride gave place to mirth without a sting;
Ere tyrant customs strength sufficient bore
To violate the feelings of the poor;
To leave them distanced in the maddening race,
Where'er refinement shows its hated face:
Nor causeless hated; – 'tis the peasant's curse,
That hourly makes his wretched station worse;
Destroys life's intercourse; the social plan
That rank to rank cements, as man to man:
Wealth flows around him, Fashion lordly reigns;
Yet poverty is his, and mental pains.

Methinks I hear the mourner thus impart
The stifled murmurs of his wounded heart:
'Whence comes this change, ungracious, irksome, cold?
Whence the new grandeur that mine eyes behold?
The widening distance which I daily see,
Has Wealth done this? – then Wealth's a foe to me;
Foe to our rights; that leaves a powerful few
The paths of emulation to pursue: –
For emulation stoops to us no more:

The hope of humble industry is o'er;
The blameless hope, the cheering sweet presage
Of future comforts for declining age.
Can my sons share from this paternal hand
The profits with the labours of the land?
No; though indulgent Heaven its blessing deigns,
Where's the small farm to suit my scanty means?
Content, the poet sings, with us resides;
In lonely cots like mine, the damsel hides;
And will he then in raptured visions tell
That sweet Content with Want can never dwell?
A barley loaf, 'tis true, my table crowns,
That fast diminishing in lusty rounds,
Stops Nature's cravings; yet her sighs will flow
From knowing this, – that once it was not so.
Our annual feast, when earth her plenty yields,
When crown'd with boughs the last load quits the fields,
The aspect still of ancient joy puts on;
The aspect only, with the substance gone:
The self-same horn is still at our command,
But serves none now but the plebeian hand:
For home-brew'd ale, neglected and debased,
Is quite discarded from the realms of taste.
Where unaffected freedom charm'd the soul,
The separate table and the costly bowl,
Cool as the blast that checks the budding Spring,
A mockery of gladness round them fling.
For oft the farmer, ere his heart approves,
Yields up the custom which he dearly loves:
Refinement forces on him like a tide,
Bold innovations down its current ride,
That bear no peace beneath their showy dress,
Nor add one tittle to his happiness.
His guests selected; rank's punctilios known;
What trouble waits upon a casual frown!

Restraint's foul manacles his pleasures maim;
Selected guests selected phrases claim:
Nor reigns that joy, when hand in hand they join,
That good old master felt in shaking mine.
Heaven bless his memory! bless his honour'd name!
(The poor will speak his lasting worthy fame:)
To souls fair-purposed strength and guidance give;
In pity to us still let goodness live:
Let labour have its due! my cot shall be
From chilling want and guilty murmurs free:
Let labour have its due; then peace is mine,
And never, never, shall my heart repine.'

[1800]

JOHN CLARE

The Shepherd's Calendar

From *March*

Muffld in baffles[1] leathern coat and gloves
The hedger toils oft scaring rustling doves
From out the hedgrows who in hunger browze
The chockolate berrys on the ivy boughs
And flocking field fares speckld like the thrush
Picking the red awe from the sweeing bush
That come and go on winters chilling wing
And seem to share no sympathy wi spring
  The stooping ditcher in the water stands
Letting the furrowd lakes from off the lands
Or splashing cleans the pasture brooks of mud

[1] leggings

Where many a wild weed freshens into bud
And sprouting from the bottom purply green
The water cresses neath the wave is seen
Which the old woman gladly drags to land
Wi reaching long rake in her tottering hand
The ploughman mawls[2] along the doughy sloughs
And often stop their songs to clean their ploughs
From teazing twitch that in the spongy soil
Clings round the colter terryfying toil
The sower striding oer his dirty way
Sinks anckle deep in pudgy[3] sloughs and clay
And oer his heavy hopper stoutly leans
Strewing wi swinging arms the pattering beans
Which soon as aprils milder weather gleams
Will shoot up green between the furroed seams
The driving boy glad when his steps can trace
The swelling edding as a resting place
Slings from his clotted shoes the dirt around
And feign woud rest him on the solid ground
And sings when he can meet the parting green
Of rushy balks that bend the lands between
While close behind em struts the nauntling crow
And daws whose heads seem powderd oer wi snow
To seek the worms – and rooks a noisey guest
That on the wind rockd elms prepares her nest
On the fresh furrow often drops to pull
The twitching roots and gathering sticks and wool
Neath trees whose dead twigs litter to the wind
And gaps where stray sheep left their coats behind
While ground larks on a sweeing clump of rushes
Or on the top twigs of the oddling bushes
Chirp their 'cree creeing' note that sounds of spring
And sky larks meet the sun wi flittering wing

[2] drags himself wearily

[3] full of puddles

From *July*

Along the roads in passing crowds
Followd by dust like smoaking clouds
Scotch droves of beast a little breed
In swelterd weary mood proceed
A patient race from scottish hills
To fatten by our pasture rills
Lean wi the wants of mountain soil
But short and stout for travels toil
Wi cockd up horns and curling crown
And dewlap bosom hanging down
Followd by slowly pacing swains
Wild to our rushy flats and plains
At whom the shepherds dog will rise
And shake himself and in supprise
Draw back and waffle in affright
Barking the traveller out of sight
And mowers oer their scythes will bear
Upon their uncooth dress to stare
And shepherds as they trample bye
Leaves oer their hooks a wondering eye
To witness men so oddly clad
In petticoats of banded plad
Wi blankets oer their shoulders slung
To camp at night the fields among
When they for rest on commons stop
And blue cap like a stocking top
Cockt oer their faces summer brown
Wi scarlet tazzeles on the crown
Rude patterns of the thistle flower
Untrickd and open to the shower
And honest faces fresh and free
That breath[e] of mountain liberty

From *August*

Harvest approaches with its bustling day
The wheat tans brown and barley bleaches grey
In yellow garb the oat land intervenes
And tawney glooms the valley thronged with beans
Silent the village grows, wood wandering dreams
Seem not so lovely as its quiet seems
Doors are shut up as on a winters day
And not a child about them lies at play
The dust that winnows neath the breezes feet
Is all that stirs about the silent street
Fancy might think that desert spreading fear
Had whisperd terrors into quiets ear
Or plundering armys past the place had come
And drove the lost inhabitants from home
The fields now claim them where a motley crew
Of old and young their daily tasks pursue
The barleys beard is grey and wheat is brown
And wakens toil betimes to leave the town
The reapers leave their beds before the sun
And gleaners follow when home toils are done
To pick the littered ear the reaper leaves
And glean in open fields among the sheaves

★

The fields are all alive with busy noise
Of labours sounds and insects humming joys
Some oer the glittering sickle sweating stoop
Startling full oft the partridge coveys up
Some oer the rustling scythe go bending on
And shockers follow where their toils have gone
First turning swaths to wither in the sun

Where mice from terrors dangers nimbly run
Leaving their tender young in fears alarm
Lapt up in nests of chimbled[4] grasses warm — [4] nibbled
And oft themselves for safty search in vain
From the rude boy or churlish hearted swain
Who beat their stone chinkd forks about the ground
And spread an instant murder all around
Tho oft the anxious maidens tender prayer
Urges the clown their little lives to spare
Who sighs while trailing the long rake along
At scenes so cruel and forgets her song
And stays wi love his murder aiming hand
Some ted the puffing winnow down the land
And others following roll them up in heaps
While cleanly as a barn door beesome sweeps
The hawling drag wi gathering weeds entwind
And singing rakers end the toils behind

[1827

Winter Fields

O for a pleasant book to cheat the sway
Of winter – where rich mirth with hearty laugh
Listens and rubs his legs on corner seat
For fields are mire and sludge – and badly off
Are those who on their pudgy[1] paths delay — [1] full of puddles
There striding shepherd seeking driest way
Fearing nights wetshod feet and hacking cough
That keeps him waken till the peep of day
Goes shouldering onward and with ready hook
Progs[2] oft to ford the sloughs that nearly meet — [2] prods
Accross the lands – croodling[3] and thin to view — [3] shrinking from the cold
His loath dog follows – stops and quakes and looks

For better roads – till whistled to pursue
Then on with frequent jump he hirkles[4] through

[4] moves in a crouched position.

[*c.* 1830]

JOHN KEATS

From *Endymion*, Book I

Leading the way, young damsels danced along,
Bearing the burden of a shepherd song;
Each having a white wicker over brimm'd
With April's tender younglings: next, well trimm'd,
A crowd of shepherds with as sunburnt looks
As may be read of in Arcadian books;
Such as sat listening round Apollo's pipe,
When the great deity, for earth too ripe,
Let his divinity o'erflowing die
In music, through the vales of Thessaly:
Some idly trail'd their sheep-hooks on the ground,
And some kept up a shrilly mellow sound
With ebon-tipped flutes: close after these,
Now coming from beneath the forest trees,
A venerable priest full soberly,
Begirt with ministring looks: alway his eye
Stedfast upon the matted turf he kept,
And after him his sacred vestments swept.
From his right hand there swung a vase, milk-white,
Of mingled wine, out-sparkling generous light;
And in his left he held a basket full

Of all sweet herbs that searching eye could cull:
Wild thyme, and valley-lillies whiter still
Than Leda's love, and cresses from the rill.
His aged head, crowned with beechen wreath,
Seem'd like a poll of ivy in the teeth
Of winter hoar. Then came another crowd
Of shepherds, lifting in due time aloud
Their share of the ditty. After them appear'd,
Up-followed by a multitude that rear'd
Their voices to the clouds, a fair wrought car,
Easily rolling so as scarce to mar
The freedom of three steeds of dapple brown:
Who stood therein did seem of great renown
Among the throng. His youth was fully blown,
Showing like Ganymede to manhood grown;
And, for those simple times, his garments were
A chieftain king's: beneath his breast, half bare,
Was hung a silver bugle, and between
His nervy knees there lay a boar-spear keen.
A smile was on his countenance; he seem'd,
To common lookers on, like one who dream'd
Of idleness in groves Elysian:
But there were some who feelingly could scan
A lurking trouble in his nether lip,
And see that oftentimes the reins would slip
Through his forgotten hands: then would they sigh,
And think of yellow leaves, of owlets' cry,
Of logs piled solemnly. – Ah, well-a-day,
Why should our young Endymion pine away?

Soon the assembly, in a circle rang'd,
Stood silent round the shrine: each look was chang'd
To sudden veneration: women meek
Beckon'd their sons to silence; while each cheek
Of virgin bloom paled gently for slight fear.

Endymion too, without a forest peer,
Stood, wan, and pale, and with an awed face,
Among his brothers of the mountain chace.
In midst of all, the venerable priest
Eyed them with joy from greatest to the least,
And, after lifting up his aged hands,
Thus spake he: 'Men of Latmos! shepherd bands!
Whose care it is to guard a thousand flocks:
Whether descended from beneath the rocks
That overtop your mountains; whether come
From vallies where the pipe is never dumb;
Or from your swelling downs, where sweet air stirs
Blue hare-bells lightly, and where prickly furze
Buds lavish gold; or ye, whose precious charge
Nibble their fill at ocean's very marge,
Whose mellow reeds are touch'd with sounds forlorn
By the dim echoes of old Triton's horn:
Mothers and wives! who day by day prepare
The scrip, with needments, for the mountain air;
And all ye gentle girls who foster up
Udderless lambs, and in a little cup
Will put choice honey for a favoured youth:
Yea, every one attend! for in good truth
Our vows are wanting to our great god Pan.
Are not our lowing heifers sleeker than
Night swollen mushrooms? Are not our wide plains
Speckled with countless fleeces? Have not rains
Green'd over April's lap? No howling sad
Sickens our fearful ewes; and we have had
Great bounty from Endymion our lord.
The earth is glad: the merry lark has pour'd
His early song against yon breezy sky,
That spreads so clear o'er our solemnity.'

[1818]

Fragment of an Ode to Maia

Mother of Hermes! and still youthful Maia!
    May I sing to thee
As thou wast hymnèd on the shores of Baiae?
    Or may I woo thee
In earlier Sicilian? or thy smiles
Seek as they once were sought, in Grecian isles,
By bards who died content on pleasant sward,
Leaving great verse unto a little clan?
O, give me their old vigour, and unheard
Save of the quiet primrose, and the span
    Of heaven and few ears,
Rounded by thee, my song should die away
    Content as theirs,
Rich in the simple worship of a day.

[1818]

To Autumn

I

Season of mists and mellow fruitfulness,
  Close bosom-friend of the maturing sun;
Conspiring with him how to load and bless
  With fruit the vines that round the thatch-eves run;
To bend with apples the moss'd cottage-trees,
  And fill all fruit with ripeness to the core;
    To swell the gourd, and plump the hazel shells
  With a sweet kernel; to set budding more,
And still more, later flowers for the bees,
Until they think warm days will never cease,
    For Summer has o'er-brimm'd their clammy cells.

II

Who hath not seen thee oft amid thy store?
  Sometimes whoever seeks abroad may find

Thee sitting careless on a granary floor,
  Thy hair soft-lifted by the winnowing wind;
Or on a half-reap'd furrow sound asleep,
  Drows'd with the fume of poppies, while thy hook
    Spares the next swath and all its twined flowers:
And sometimes like a gleaner thou dost keep
  Steady thy laden head across a brook;
  Or by a cyder-press, with patient look,
    Thou watchest the last oozings hours by hours.

III

Where are the songs of Spring? Ay, where are they?
  Think not of them, thou hast thy music too, –
While barred clouds bloom the soft-dying day,
  And touch the stubble-plains with rosy hue;
Then in a wailful choir the small gnats mourn
  Among the river sallows, borne aloft
    Or sinking as the light wind lives or dies;
And full-grown lambs loud bleat from hilly bourn;
  Hedge-crickets sing; and now with treble soft
  The red-breast whistles from a garden-croft;
    And gathering swallows twitter in the skies.

[1820]

PERCY BYSSHE SHELLEY

From *Epipsychidion*

Emily,
A ship is floating in the harbour now,
A wind is hovering o'er the mountain's brow;
There is a path on the sea's azure floor,

No keel has ever ploughed that path before;
The halcyons brood around the foamless isles;
The treacherous Ocean has forsworn its wiles;
The merry mariners are bold and free:
Say, my heart's sister, wilt thou sail with me?
Our bark is as an albatross, whose nest
Is a far Eden of the purple East;
And we between her wings will sit, while Night,
And Day, and Storm, and Calm, pursue their flight,
Our ministers, along the boundless Sea,
Treading each other's heels, unheededly.
It is an isle under Ionian skies,
Beautiful as a wreck of Paradise,
And, for the harbours are not safe and good,
This land would have remained a solitude
But for some pastoral people native there,
Who from the Elysian, clear, and golden air
Draw the last spirit of the age of gold,
Simple and spirited; innocent and bold.
The blue Aegean girds this chosen home,
With ever-changing sound and light and foam,
Kissing the sifted sands, and caverns hoar;
And all the winds wandering along the shore
Undulate with the undulating tide:
There are thick woods where sylvan forms abide;
And many a fountain, rivulet, and pond,
As clear as elemental diamond,
Or serene morning air; and far beyond,
The mossy tracks made by the goats and deer
(Which the rough shepherd treads but once a year)
Pierce into glades, caverns, and bowers, and halls
Built round with ivy, which the waterfalls
Illumining, with sound that never fails
Accompany the noonday nightingales;
And all the place is peopled with sweet airs;

The light clear element which the isle wears
Is heavy with the scent of lemon-flowers,
Which floats like mist laden with unseen showers,
And falls upon the eyelids like faint sleep;
And from the moss violets and jonquils peep,
And dart their arrowy odour through the brain
Till you might faint with that delicious pain.
And every motion, odour, beam, and tone,
With that deep music is in unison:
Which is a soul within the soul – they seem
Like echoes of an antenatal dream. –
It is an isle 'twixt Heaven, Air, Earth, and Sea,
Cradled, and hung in clear tranquillity;
Bright as that wandering Eden Lucifer,
Washed by the soft blue Oceans of young air.
It is a favoured place. Famine or Blight,
Pestilence, War and Earthquake, never light
Upon its mountain-peaks; blind vultures, they
Sail onward far upon their fatal way:
The wingèd storms, chanting their thunder-psalm
To other lands, leave azure chasms of calm
Over this isle, or weep themselves in dew,
From which its fields and woods ever renew
Their green and golden immortality.
And from the sea there rise, and from the sky
There fall, clear exhalations, soft and bright,
Veil after veil, each hiding some delight,
Which Sun or Moon or zephyr draw aside,
Till the isle's beauty, like a naked bride
Glowing at once with love and loveliness,
Blushes and trembles at its own excess:
Yet, like a buried lamp, a Soul no less
Burns in the heart of this delicious isle,
An atom of th' Eternal, whose own smile
Unfolds itself, and may be felt, not seen

O'er the gray rocks, blue waves, and forests green,
Filling their bare and void interstices. –
But the chief marvel of the wilderness
Is a lone dwelling, built by whom or how
None of the rustic island-people know:
'Tis not a tower of strength, though with its height
It overtops the woods; but, for delight,
Some wise and tender Ocean-King, ere crime
Had been invented, in the world's young prime,
Reared it, a wonder of that simple time,
An envy of the isles, a pleasure-house
Made sacred to his sister and his spouse.
It scarce seems now a wreck of human art,
But, as it were Titanic; in the heart
Of Earth having assumed its form, then grown
Out of the mountains, from the living stone,
Lifting itself in caverns light and high:
For all the antique and learnèd imagery
Has been erased, and in the place of it
The ivy and the wild-vine interknit
The volumes of their many-twining stems;
Parasite flowers illume with dewy gems
The lampless halls, and when they fade, the sky
Peeps through their winter-woof of tracery
With moonlight patches, or star atoms keen,
Or fragments of the day's intense serene; –
Working mosaic on their Parian floors.
And, day and night, aloof, from the high towers
And terraces, the Earth and Ocean seem
To sleep in one another's arms, and dream
Of waves, flowers, clouds, woods, rocks, and all that we
Read in their smiles, and call reality.
  This isle and house are mine, and I have vowed
Thee to be lady of the solitude. –
And I have fitted up some chambers there

Looking towards the golden Eastern air,
And level with the living winds, which flow
Like waves about the living waves below. –
I have sent books and music there, and all
Those instruments with which high Spirits call
The future from its cradle, and the past
Out of its grave, and make the present last
In thoughts and joys which sleep, but cannot die,
Folded within their own eternity.
Our simple life wants little, and true taste
Hires not the pale drudge Luxury, to waste
The scene it would adorn, and therefore still,
Nature with all her children haunts the hill.
The ring-dove, in the embowering ivy, yet
Keeps up her love-lament, and the owls flit
Round the evening tower, and the young stars glance
Between the quick bats in their twilight dance;
The spotted deer bask in the fresh moonlight
Before our gate, and the slow, silent night
Is measured by the pants of their calm sleep.
Be this our home in life, and when years heap
Their withered hours, like leaves, on our decay,
Let us become the overhanging day,
The living soul of this Elysian isle,
Conscious, inseparable, one. Meanwhile
We two will rise, and sit, and walk together,
Under the roof of blue Ionian weather,
And wander in the meadows, or ascend
The mossy mountains, where the blue heavens bend
With lightest winds, to touch their paramour;
Or linger, where the pebble-paven shore,
Under the quick, faint kisses of the sea
Trembles and sparkles as with ecstasy, –
Possessing and possessed by all that is
Within that calm circumference of bliss,

And by each other, till to love and live
Be one: – or, at the noontide hour, arrive
Where some old cavern hoar seems yet to keep
The moonlight of the expired night asleep,
Through which the awakened day can never peep;
A veil for our seclusion, close as night's,
Where secure sleep may kill thine innocent lights;
Sleep, the fresh dew of languid love, the rain
Whose drops quench kisses till they burn again.
And we will talk, until thought's melody
Become too sweet for utterance, and it die
In words, to live again in looks, which dart
With thrilling tone into the voiceless heart,
Harmonizing silence without a sound.
Our breath shall intermix, our bosoms bound,
And our veins beat together; and our lips
With other eloquence than words, eclipse
The soul that burns between them, and the wells
Which boil under our being's inmost cells,
The fountains of our deepest life, shall be
Confused in Passion's golden purity,
As mountain-springs under the morning sun.
We shall become the same, we shall be one
Spirit within two frames, oh! wherefore two?
One passion in twin-hearts, which grows and grew,
Till like two meteors of expanding flame,
Those spheres instinct with it become the same,
Touch, mingle, are transfigured; ever still
Burning, yet ever inconsumable:
In one another's substance finding food,
Like flames too pure and light and unimbued
To nourish their bright lives with baser prey,
Which point to Heaven and cannot pass away:
One hope within two wills, one will beneath
Two overshadowing minds, one life, one death,

One Heaven, one Hell, one immortality,
And one annihilation. Woe is me!
The wingèd words on which my soul would pierce
Into the height of Love's rare Universe,
Are chains of lead around its flight of fire –
I pant, I sink, I tremble, I expire!

[1821]

THOMAS HOOD

Agricultural Distress
A Pastoral Report

One Sunday morning – service done –
'Mongst tombstones shining in the sun,
A knot of bumpkins stood to chat
Of that and this, and this and that;
What people said of Polly Hatch –
Which side had won the cricket match;
And who was cotch'd, and who was bowl'd; –
How barley, beans, and 'taters sold –
What men could swallow at a meal –
When Bumpstead Youths would ring a peal –
And who was taken off to jail –
And where they brew'd the strongest ale –
At last this question they address,
'What's Agricultural Distress?'

HODGE:
'For my peart, it's a thought o' mine,
It be the fancy farming line,

Like yonder gemman, – him I mean,
As took the Willa nigh the Green, –
And turn'd his cattle in the wheat;
And gave his porkers hay to eat;
And sent his footman up to town,
To ax the Lonnon gentry down,
To be so kind as make his hay,
Exactly on St Swithin's day; –
With consequences you may guess –
That's Hagricultural Distress.'

DICKON:

'Last Monday morning, Master Blogg
Com'd for to stick our bacon-hog;
But th' hog he cock'd a knowing eye,
As if he twigg'd the reason why,
And dodg'd and dodg'd 'un such a dance,
He didn't give the noose a chance;
So Master Blogg at last lays off,
And shams a rattle at the trough,
When swish! in bolts our bacon-hog
Atwixt the legs o' Master Blogg,
And flops him down in all the muck,
As hadn't been swept up by luck –
Now that, accordin' to my guess,
Be Hagricultural Distress.'

GILES:

'No, that arn't it, I tell 'ee flat;
I'ze bring a worser case nor that!
Last Friday week, I takes a start
To Reading, with our horse and cart;
Well, when I'ze set the 'taters down,
I meet a crony at the Crown;
And what betwixt the ale and Tom,
It's dark afore I starts for home;

So whipping hard, by long and late,
At last we reaches nigh the gate,
And, sure enough, there Master stand,
A lantern flaring in his hand, –
"Why, Giles," says he, "what's that 'un thear?
Yond' chestnut horse bean't my bay mear!
He bean't not worth a leg o' Bess!"
There's Hagricultural Distress!'

COLIN:

'Phoo! phoo! You're nothing near the thing!
You only argy in a ring;
'Cause why? You never cares to look,
Like me, in any larned book;
But schollards know the wrong and right
Of every thing in black and white.

'Well, Farming, that's its common name,
And Agriculture be the same:
So put your Farming first, and next
Distress, and there you have your text.
But here the question comes to press,
What farming be, and what's distress?
Why, farming is to plough and sow,
Weed, harrow, harvest, reap and mow,
Thrash, winnow, sell, – and buy and breed
The proper stock to fat and feed.
Distress is want, and pain, and grief,
And sickness, – things as wants relief;
Thirst, hunger, age, and cold severe,
In short, ax any overseer, –
Well, now, the logic for to chop,
Where's the distress about a crop?
There's no distress in keeping sheep,
I likes to see 'em frisk and leap;

There's no distress in seeing swine
Grow up to pork and bacon fine;
There's no distress in growing wheat
And grass for men or beasts to eat;
And making of lean cattle fat,
There's no distress, of course, in that.
Then what remains? – But one thing more,
And that's the *Farming of the Poor!*'

HODGE, DICKON, GILES, HOB, AND SIMON:
'Yea! – aye! – sure*ly*! – for sartin! – yes! –
That's Hagricultural Distress!'

[1837]

WALTER SAVAGE LANDOR

A Railroad Eclogue

FATHER: What brought thee back, lad?
SON: Father! the same feet
As took me brought me back, I warrant ye.
FATHER: Couldst thou not find the rail?
SON: The deuce himself,
Who can find most things, could not find the rail.
FATHER: Plain as a pike-staff miles and miles it lies.
SON: So they all told me. Pike-staffs in your day
Must have been hugely plainer than just now.
FATHER: What didst thou ask for?
SON: Ask for? Tewkesbury
Thro' Defford opposite to Breedon-hill.
FATHER: Right: and they set ye wrong?
SON: Me wrong? not they;

The best among 'em should not set me wrong,
Nor right, nor anything; I'd tell 'em that. –
FATHER: Herefordshire's short horns and shorter wits
Are known in every quarter of the land,
Those blunt, these blunter. Well! no help for it!
Each might do harm if each had more of each . . .
Yet even in Herefordshire there are some
Not downright dolts . . . before the cidar's broacht,
When all are much alike . . . yet most could tell
A railroad from a parish or a pike.
How thou couldst miss that railroad puzzles me,
Seeing there lies none other round about.
SON: I found the rails along the whole brook-side
Left of that old stone bridge across yon Avon.
FATHER: That is the place.
SON: There was a house hard-by,
And past it ran a furnace upon wheels,
Like a mad bull, tail up in air, and horns
So low ye might not see 'em. On it bumpt,
Roaring, as strait as any arrow flits,
As strait, as fast too, ay, and faster went it,
And, could it keep its wind up and not crack,
Then woe betide the eggs at Tewkesbury
This market-day, and lambs, and sheep! a score
Of pigs might be made flitches in a trice,
Before they well could knuckle.
Father! father!
If they were ourn, thou wouldst not chuckle so,
And shake thy sides, and wipe thy eyes, and rub
Thy breeches-knees, like Sunday shoes, at that rate.
Hows'ever . . .
FATHER: 'Twas the train, lad, 'twas the train.
SON: May-be: I had no business with a train.
'*Go thee by rail*, you told me; *by the rail*
At Defford' . . . and didst make a fool of me.

FATHER: Ay, lad, I did indeed: it was methinks
Some twenty years agone last Martinmas.

[1849]

ALFRED LORD TENNYSON

From *The Princess*

I heard her turn the page; she found a small
Sweet Idyl, and once more, as low, she read:

'Come down, O maid, from yonder mountain height:
What pleasure lives in height (the shepherd sang)
In height and cold, the splendour of the hills?
But cease to move so near the Heavens, and cease
To glide a sunbeam by the blasted Pine,
To sit a star upon the sparkling spire;
And come, for Love is of the valley, come,
For Love is of the valley, come thou down
And find him; by the happy threshold, he,
Or hand in hand with Plenty in the maize,
Or red with spirted purple of the vats,
Or foxlike in the vine; nor cares to walk
With Death and Morning on the silver horns,
Nor wilt thou snare him in the white ravine,
Nor find him dropt upon the firths of ice,
That huddling slant in furrow-cloven falls
To roll the torrent out of dusky doors:
But follow; let the torrent dance thee down
To find him in the valley; let the wild
Lean-headed Eagles yelp alone, and leave
The monstrous ledges there to slope, and spill

Their thousand wreaths of dangling water-smoke,
That like a broken purpose waste in air:
So waste not thou; but come; for all the vales
Await thee; azure pillars of the hearth
Arise to thee; the children call, and I
Thy shepherd pipe, and sweet is every sound,
Sweeter thy voice, but every sound is sweet;
Myriads of rivulets hurrying thro' the lawn,
The moan of doves in immemorial elms,
And murmuring of innumerable bees.'

[1847]

From *In Memoriam*

LXXXIX

Witch-elms that counterchange the floor
  Of this flat lawn with dusk and bright;
  And thou, with all thy breadth and height
Of foliage, towering sycamore;

How often, hither wandering down,
  My Arthur found your shadows fair,
  And shook to all the liberal air
The dust and din and steam of town:

He brought an eye for all he saw;
  He mixt in all our simple sports;
  They pleased him, fresh from brawling courts
And dusty purlieus of the law.

O joy to him in this retreat,
  Immantled in ambrosial dark,
  To drink the cooler air, and mark
The landscape winking thro' the heat.

O sound to rout the brood of cares,
  The sweep of scythe in morning dew,
  The gust that round the garden flew,
And tumbled half the mellowing pears!

O bliss, when all in circle drawn
  About him, heart and ear were fed
  To hear him, as he lay and read
The Tuscan poets on the lawn:

Or in the all-golden afternoon
  A guest, or happy sister, sung,
  Or here she brought the harp and flung
A ballad to the brightening moon:

Nor less it pleased in livelier moods,
  Beyond the bounding hill to stray,
  And break the livelong summer day
With banquet in the distant woods;

Whereat we glanced from theme to theme,
  Discuss'd the books to love or hate,
  Or touch'd the changes of the state,
Or threaded some Socratic dream;

But if I praised the busy town,
  He loved to rail against it still,
  For 'ground in yonder social mill
We rub each other's angles down,

And merge' he said 'in form and gloss
  The picturesque of man and man.'
  We talk'd: the stream beneath us ran,
The wine-flask lying couch'd in moss,

Or cool'd within the glooming wave;
  And last, returning from afar,
  Before the crimson-circled star
Had fall'n into her father's grave,

And brushing ankle-deep in flowers,
  We heard behind the woodbine veil
  The milk that bubbled in the pail,
And buzzings of the honied hours.

[1850]

Northern Farmer
Old Style

I

Wheer 'asta beän saw long and meä liggin' 'ere aloän?
Noorse? thourt nowt o' a noorse: whoy, Doctor's abeän an agoän:
Says that I moänt 'a naw moor äale: but I beänt a fool:
Git ma my äale, fur I beänt a-gawin' to breäk my rule.

II

Doctors, they knaws nowt, fur a says what's nawways true:
Naw soort o' koind o' use to saäy the things that a do.
I've 'ed my point o' äale ivry noight sin' I beän 'ere.
An' I've 'ed my quart ivry market-noight for foorty year.

III

Parson's a beän loikewoise, an' a sittin' 'ere o' my bed.
'The amoighty's a taäkin o' you to 'issén, my friend,' a said,
An' a towd ma my sins, an's toithe were due, an' I gied it in hond;
I done moy duty boy 'um, as I 'a done boy the lond.

IV

Larn'd a ma' beä. I reckons I 'annot sa mooch to larn.
But a cast oop, thot a did, 'bout Bessy Marris's barne.
Thaw a knaws I hallus voäted wi' Squoire an' choorch an' staäte,
An' i' the woost o' toimes I wur niver agin the raäte.

V

An' I hallus coom'd to 's chooch afoor moy Sally wur deäd,
An' 'eard 'um a bummin' awaäy loike a buzzard-clock[1] ower my 'ead,
An' I niver knaw'd whot a meän'd but I thowt a 'ad summut to saäy,
An' I thowt a said whot a owt to 'a said an' I coom'd awaäy.

[1] cock-chafer

VI

Bessy Marris's barne! tha knaws she laäid it to meä.
Mowt 'a beän, mayhap, for she wur a bad un, sheä.
'Siver, I kep 'um, I kep 'um, my lass, tha mun understond;
I done moy duty boy 'um as I 'a done boy the lond.

VII

But Parson a cooms an' a goäs, an' a says it eäsy an' freeä
'The amoighty's a taäkin o' you to 'issén, my friend,' says 'eä.
I weänt saäy men be loiars, thaw summun said it in 'äaste:
But 'e reäds wonn sarmin a weeäk, an' I 'a stubb'd Thurnaby waäste.

VIII

D'ya moind the waäste, my lass? naw, naw, tha was not born then;
Theer wur a boggle in it, I often 'eärd 'um mysen;
Moäst loike a butter-bump,[2] fur I 'eärd 'um about an' about,

[2] bittern

But I stubb'd 'um oop wi' the lot, an' raäved an' rembled 'um out.

IX

Keäper's it wur; fo' they fun 'um theer a-laäid of 'is faäce
Down i' the woild 'enemies[3] afoor I coom'd to the plaäce. [3] anemones
Noäks or Thimbleby – toäner[4] 'ed shot 'um as deäd as a naäil. [4] one or other
Noäks wur 'ang'd for it oop at 'soize – but git ma my aäle.

X

Dubbut looök at the waäste: theer warn't not feeäd for a cow;
Nowt at all but bracken an' fuzz, an' looök at it now –
Warn't worth nowt a haäcre, an' now theer's lots o' feeäd,
Fourscoor yows upon it an' some on it down i' seeäd.[5] [5] clover

XI

Nobbut a bit on it's left, an' I meän'd to 'a stubb'd it at fall,
Done it ta-year I meän'd, an' runn'd plow thruff it an' all,
If godamoighty an' parson 'ud nobbut let ma aloän,
Meä, wi' haäte hoondered haäcre o' Squoire's, an' lond o' my oän.

XII

Do godamoighty knaw what a's doing a-taäkin' o' meä?
I beänt wonn as saws 'ere a beän an' yonder a peä;
An' Squoire 'ull be sa mad an' all – a' dear a' dear!
And I 'a managed for Squoire coom Michaelmas thutty year.

XIII

A mowt 'a taäen owd Joänes, as 'ant not a 'aäpoth o' sense,
Or a mowt 'a taäen young Robins – a niver mended a fence:
But godamoighty a moost taäke meä an' taäke ma now
Wi' aäf the cows to cauve an' Thurnaby hoälms to plow!

XIV

Looök 'ow quoloty smoiles when they seeäs ma a passin' boy,
Says to thessén naw doubt 'what a man a beä sewer-loy!'
Fur they knaws what I beän to Squoire sin fust a coom'd to the 'All:
I done moy duty by Squoire an' I done moy duty boy hall.

XV

Squoire's i' Lunnon, an' summun I reckons 'ull 'a to wroite,
For whoä's to howd the lond ater meä thot muddles ma quoit;
Sartin-sewer I beä, thot a weänt niver give it to Joänes,
Naw, nor a moänt to Robins – a niver rembles the stoäns.

XVI

But summun 'ull come ater meä mayhap wi' 'is kittle o' steäm
Huzzin' an' maäzin' the blessed feälds wi' the Divil's oän teäm.
Sin' I mun doy I mun doy, thaw loife they says is sweet,
But sin' I mun doy I mun doy, for I couldn abeär to see it.

XVII

What atta stannin' theer fur, an' doesn bring ma the aäle?
Doctor's a 'toättler, lass, an a's hallus i' the owd taäle;
I weänt break rules fur Doctor, a knaws naw moor nor a floy;
Git ma my aäle I tell tha' an' if I mun doy I mun doy.

[1864]

Shoreham: Twilight Time

And now the trembling light
Glimmers behind the little hills and corn,
Ling'ring as loth to part; yet part thou must
And though than open day far pleasing more
(Ere yet the fields and pearlèd cups of flowers
    Twinkle in the parting light;)
Thee night shall hide, sweet visionary gleam
That softly lookest though the rising dew;
    Till all like silver bright,
    The faithful witness, pure and white,
    Shall look o'er yonder grassy hill,
    At this village, safe and still.
    All is safe and all is still,
    Save what noise the watch-dog makes
    Or the shrill cock the silence breaks.
    Now and then –
    And now and then –
    Hark! Once again,
    The wether's bell
    To us doth tell
Some little stirring in the fold.
Methinks the ling'ring dying ray
Of twilight time, doth seem more fair,
And lights the soul up more than day
When wide-spread sultry sunshines are:
Yet all is right and all most fair,
For thou, dear God, has formèd all;
Thou deckest every little flower,
Thou girdest every planet ball,
And mark'st when sparrows fall.

[Written before 1835?]

ARTHUR HUGH CLOUGH

From *The Bothie of Tober-na-Vuolich*

Oh, if they knew and considered, unhappy ones! oh, could they see, could
But for a moment discern, how the blood of true gallantry kindles,
How the old knightly religion, the chivalry semi-quixotic
Stirs in the veins of a man at seeing some delicate woman
Serving him, toiling – for him, and the world; some tenderest girl, now
Over-weighted, expectant, of him, is it? who shall, if only
Duly her burden be lightened, not wholly removed from her, mind you,
Lightened if but by the love, the devotion man only can offer,
Grand on her pedestal rise as urn-bearing statue of Hellas; –
Oh, could they feel at such moments how man's heart, as into Eden
Carried anew, seems to see, like the gardener of earth uncorrupted,
Eve from the hand of her Maker advancing, an helpmeet for him,
Eve from his own flesh taken, a spirit restored to his spirit,
Spirit but not spirit only, himself whatever himself is,
Unto the mystery's end sole helpmate meet to be with him; –
Oh, if they saw it and knew it; we soon should see them abandon
Boudoir, toilette, carriage, drawing-room, and ball-room,
Satin for worsted exchange, gros-de-naples for plain linsey-woolsey,
Sandals of silk for clogs, for health lackadaisical fancies!
So, feel women, not dolls; so feel the sap of existence

Circulate up through their roots from the far-away centre of
 all things,
Circulate up from the depths to the bud on the twig that is
 topmost!
Yes, we should see them delighted, delighted ourselves in the
 seeing,
Bending with blue cotton gown skirted-up over striped lin-
 sey-woolsey,
Milking the kine in the field, like Rachel, watering cattle,
Rachel, when at the well the predestined beheld and kissed her,
Or, with pail upon head, like Dora beloved of Alexis,
Comely, with well-poised pail over neck arching soft to the
 shoulders,
Comely in gracefullest act, one arm uplifted to stay it,
Home from the river or pump moving stately and calm to the
 laundry;
Ay, doing household work, as many sweet girls I have looked
 at,
Needful household work, which some one, after all, must do,
Needful, graceful therefore, as washing, cooking, and scour-
 ing,
Or, if you please, with the fork in the garden uprooting
 potatoes.

[1848]

MATTHEW ARNOLD

From *Thyrsis*

A Monody, to commemorate the author's friend, Arthur Hugh Clough, who died at Florence, 1861

How changed is here each spot man makes or fills!
In the two Hinkseys nothing keeps the same;
The village street its haunted mansion lacks,
And from the sign is gone Sibylla's name,
And from the roofs the twisted chimney-stacks –
Are ye too changed, ye hills?
See, 'tis no foot of unfamiliar men
To-night from Oxford up your pathway strays!
Here came I often, often, in old days –
Thyrsis and I; we still had Thyrsis then.

Runs it not here, the track by Childsworth Farm,
Past the high wood, to where the elm-tree crowns
The hill behind whose ridge the sunset flames?
The signal-elm, that looks on Ilsley Downs,
The Vale, the three lone weirs, the youthful Thames? –
This winter-eve is warm,
Humid the air! leafless, yet soft as spring,
The tender purple spray on copse and briers!
And that sweet city with her dreaming spires,
She needs not June for beauty's heightening,

Lovely all times she lies, lovely to-night! –
Only, methinks, some loss of habit's power
Befalls me wandering through this upland dim.
Once pass'd I blindfold here, at any hour;
Now seldom come I, since I came with him.
That single elm-tree bright

Against the west – I miss it! is it gone?
We prized it dearly; while it stood, we said,
Our friend, the Gipsy-Scholar, was not dead;
While the tree lived, he in these fields lived on.

Too rare, too rare, grow now my visits here,
But once I knew each field, each flower, each stick;
And with the country-folk acquaintance made
By barn in threshing-time, by new-built rick.
Here, too, our shepherd-pipes we first assay'd.
Ah me! this many a year
My pipe is lost, my shepherd's holiday!
Needs must I lose them, needs with heavy heart
Into the world and wave of men depart;
But Thyrsis of his own will went away.

It irk'd him to be here, he could not rest.
He loved each simple joy the country yields,
He loved his mates; but yet he could not keep,
For that a shadow lour'd on the fields,
Here with the shepherds and the silly sheep.
Some life of men unblest
He knew, which made him droop, and fill'd his head.
He went; his piping took a troubled sound
Of storms that rage outside our happy ground;
He could not wait their passing, he is dead.

So, some tempestuous morn in early June,
When the year's primal burst of bloom is o'er,
Before the roses and the longest day –
When garden-walks and all the grassy floor
With blossoms red and white of fallen May
And chestnut-flowers are strewn –
So have I heard the cuckoo's parting cry,
From the wet field, through the vext garden-trees,

Come with the volleying rain and tossing breeze:
The bloom is gone, and with the bloom go I!

Too quick despairer, wherefore wilt thou go?
Soon will the high Midsummer pomps come on,
Soon will the musk carnations break and swell,
Soon shall we have gold-dusted snapdragon,
Sweet-William with his homely cottage-smell,
And stocks in fragrant blow;
Roses that down the alleys shine afar,
And open, jasmine-muffled lattices,
And groups under the dreaming garden-trees,
And the full moon, and the white evening-star.

He hearkens not! light comer, he is flown!
What matters it? next year he will return,
And we shall have him in the sweet spring-days,
With whitening hedges, and uncrumpling fern,
And blue-bells trembling by the forest-ways,
And scent of hay new-mown.
But Thyrsis never more we swains shall see;
See him come back, and cut a smoother reed,
And blow a strain the world at last shall heed –
For Time, not Corydon, hath conquer'd thee!

Alack, for Corydon no rival now! –
But when Sicilian shepherds lost a mate,
Some good survivor with his flute would go,
Piping a ditty sad for Bion's fate;
And cross the unpermitted ferry's flow,
And relax Pluto's brow,
And make leap up with joy the beauteous head
Of Proserpine, among whose crowned hair
Are flowers first open'd on Sicilian air,
And flute his friend, like Orpheus, from the dead.

O easy access to the hearer's grace
  When Dorian shepherds sang to Proserpine!
    For she herself had trod Sicilian fields,
  She knew the Dorian water's gush divine,
    She knew each lily white which Enna yields,
      Each rose with blushing face;
  She loved the Dorian pipe, the Dorian strain.
    But ah, of our poor Thames she never heard!
    Her foot the Cumner cowslips never stirr'd;
  And we should tease her with our plaint in vain!

Well! wind-dispersed and vain the words will be,
  Yet, Thyrsis, let me give my grief its hour
    In the old haunt, and find our tree-topp'd hill!
  Who, if not I, for questing here hath power?
    I know the wood which hides the daffodil,
      I know the Fyfield tree,
  I know what white, what purple fritillaries
    The grassy harvest of the river-fields,
    Above by Ensham, down by Sandford, yields,
  And what sedged brooks are Thames's tributaries;

I know these slopes; who knows them if not I? –
  But many a dingle on the loved hill-side,
    With thorns once studded, old, white-blossom'd trees,
  Where thick the cowslips grew, and far descried
    High tower'd the spikes of purple orchises,
      Hath since our day put by
  The coronals of that forgotten time;
    Down each green bank hath gone the ploughboy's team,
    And only in the hidden brookside gleam
  Primroses, orphans of the flowery prime.

Where is the girl, who by the boatman's door,
  Above the locks, above the boating throng,

Unmoor'd our skiff when through the Wytham flats,
Red loosestrife and blond meadow-sweet among
And darting swallows and light water-gnats,
We track'd the shy Thames shore?
Where are the mowers, who, as the tiny swell
Of our boat passing heaved the river-grass,
Stood with suspended scythe to see us pass? –
They all are gone, and thou art gone as well!

[1867]

WILLIAM BARNES

Leädy-Day, An' Ridden House

Aye, back at Leädy-Day, you know,
I come vrom Gullybrook to Stowe;
At Leädy-Day I took my pack
O' rottletraps, an' turn'd my back
Upon the weather-beäten door,
That had a-screen'd, so long avore,
The mwost that theäse zide o' the greäve,
I'd live to have, or die to seäve!
My childern, an' my vier-pleäce,
Where Molly wi' her cheerful feäce,
When I'd a-trod my wat'ry road
Vrom night-bedarken'd vields abrode,
Wi' nimble hands, at evenèn, blest
Wi' vire an' vood my hard-won rest;
The while the little woones did clim',
So sleek-skinn'd, up from lim' to lim',

Till, strugglèn hard an' clingèn tight,
They reach'd at last my feäce's height.
All tryèn which could soonest hold
My mind wi' little teäles they twold.
An' riddèn house is such a caddle[1],
I shan't be over keen vor mwore ō't,
Not yet a while, you mid be sure ō't, –
I'd rather keep to woone wold staddle[2].

[1] muddle

[2] bed (or a frame for hayricks)

Well, zoo, avore the east begun
To redden wi' the comèn zun,
We left the beds our mossy thatch
Wer never mwore to overstratch,
An' borrow'd uncle's wold hoss *Dragon*,
To bring the slowly lumbrèn waggon,
An' when he come, we vell a packèn
The bedsteads, wi' their rwopes an' zackèn;
An' then put up the wold eärm-chair,
An' cwoffer vull ov e'then-ware,
An' vier-dogs, an' copper kittle,
Wi' crocks an' saucepans, big an' little;
An' fryèn-pan, vor aggs to slide
In butter round his hissèn zide,
An' gridire's even bars, to bear
The drippèn steäke above the gleäre
O' brightly-glowèn coals. An' then,
All up o' top o' them ageän
The woaken bwoard, where we did eat
Our croust o' bread or bit o' meat, –
An' when the bwoard wer up, we tied
Upon the reäves[3], along the zide,
The woäken stools, his glossy meätes,
Bwoth when he's beäre, or when the pleätes
Do clatter loud wi' knives, below
Our merry feäces in a row.

[3] a ladder-like framework projecting over the sides of a wagon.

An' put between his lags, turn'd up'ard,
The zalt-box an' the corner cupb'ard.
An' then we laid the wold clock-ceäse,
All dumb, athirt upon his feäce,
Vor we'd a-left, I needen tell ye,
Noo works 'ithin his head or belly.
An' then we put upon the pack
The settle, flat upon his back;
An' after that, a-tied in pairs
In woone another, all the chairs,
An' bits o' lumber wo'th a ride,
An' at the very top a-tied,
The childern's little stools did lie,
Wi' lags a-turn'd towárd the sky:
Zoo there we lwoaded up our scroft[4],
An' tied it vast, an' started off.
An', – as the waggon cooden car all
We had to teäke, – the butter-barrel
An' cheese-wring, wi' his twinèn screw,
An' all the pails an' veäts, an' blue
Wold milk leads, and a vew things mwore,
Wer all a-carr'd the day avore,
And when the mwost ov our wold stuff
Wer brought outside o' thik brown ruf,
I rambled roun' wi' narrow looks,
In fusty holes an' darksome nooks,
To gather all I still mid vind,
O' rags or sticks a-left behind.
An' there the unlatch'd doors did creak,
A-swung by winds, a-streamèn weak
Drough empty rooms, an' meäkèn sad
My heart, where me'th woonce meäde me glad.
Vor when a man do leäve the he'th
An' ruf where vu'st he drew his breath,
Or where he had his bwoyhood's fun,

[4] underwood, or odd left-over bits of firewood

An' things wer woonce a-zaid an' done
That took his mind, do touch his heart
A little bit, I'll answer vor't.
Zoo riddèn house is such a caddle,
That I would rather keep my staddle.

[1844]

The Common A-Took In
Eclogue

THOMAS AN' JOHN

THOMAS:
Good morn t'ye, John. How b'ye? how b'ye?
Zoo you be gwaïn to market, I do zee.
Why, you be quite a-lwoaded wi' your geese.

JOHN:
Ees, Thomas, ees.
Why, I'm a-gettèn rid ov ev'ry goose
An' goslèn I've a-got: an' what is woose,
I fear that I must zell my little cow.

THOMAS:
How zoo, then, John? Why, what's the matter now?
What, can't ye get along? B'ye run a-ground?
An' can't paÿ twenty shillèns vor a pound?
What can't ye put a lwoaf on shelf?

JOHN:
Ees, now;
But I do fear I shan't 'ithout my cow.
No; they do mëan to teäke the moor in, I do hear,
An' 'twill be soon begun upon;
Zoo I must zell my bit o' stock to-year,
Because they woon't have any groun' to run upon.

THOMAS:

Why, what d'ye tell o'? I be very zorry
To hear what they be gwain about;
But yet I s'pose there 'll be a 'lotment vor ye,
When they do come to mark it out.

JOHN:

No; not vor me, I fear. An' if there should,
Why 'twoulden be so handy as 'tis now;
Vor 'tis the common that do do me good,
The run for my vew geese, or vor my cow.

THOMAS:

Ees, that's the job; why 'tis a handy thing
To have a bit o' common, I do know,
To put a little cow upon in Spring,
The while woone's bit ov orcha'd grass do grow.

JOHN:

Aye, that's the thing, you zee. Now I do mow
My bit o' grass, an' meäke a little rick;
An' in the zummer, while do grow,
My cow do run in common vor to pick
A bleäde or two o' grass, if she can vind em,
Vor tother cattle don't leäve much behind em.
Zoo in the evenèn, we do put a lock
O' nice fresh grass avore the wicket;
An' she do come at vive or zix o'clock,
As constant as the zun, to pick it.
An' then, bezides the cow, why we do let
Our geese run out among the emmet[1] hills;
An' then when we do pluck em, we do get
Vor zeäle zome veathers an' zome quills;
An' in the winter we do fat em well,
An' car em to the market vor to zell

[1] ant

To gentlevo'ks, vor we don't oft avvword
To put a goose a-top ov ouer bwoard;
But we do get our feäst, – vor we be eäble
To clap the giblets up a-top o' teäble.

THOMAS:

An' I don't know o' many better things,
Than geese's heads and gizzards, lags an' wings.

JOHN:

An' then, when I ha' nothèn else to do,
Why I can teäke my hook an' gloves, an' goo
To cut a lot o' vuzz and briars
Vor hetèn ovens, or vor lightèn viers.
An' when the childern be too young to eärn
A penny, they can g'out in zunny weather,
An' run about, an' get together
A bag o' cow-dung vor to burn.

THOMAS:

'Tis handy to live near a common;
But I've a-zeed, an' I've a-zaid,
That if a poor man got a bit o' bread,
They'll try to teäke it vrom en.
But I wer twold back tother day,
That they be got into a way
O' lettèn bits o' groun' out to the poor.

JOHN:

Well, I do hope 'tis true, I'm sure;
An 'I do hope that they will do it here,
Or I must goo to workhouse, I do fear.

[1844]

Harry Ploughman

Hard as hurdle arms, with a broth of goldish flue
Breathed round; the rack of ribs; the scooped flank; lank
Rope-over thigh; knee-nave; and barrelled shank –
Head and foot, shoulder and shank –
By a grey eye's heed steered well, one crew, fall to;
Stand at stress. Each limb's barrowy brawn, his thew
That onewhere curded, onewhere sucked or sank –
Soared or sank –,
Though as a beechbole firm, finds his, as at a roll-call, rank
And features, in flesh, what deed he each must do –
His sinew-service where do.

He leans to it, Harry bends, look. Back, elbow, and liquid waist
In him, all quail to the wallowing o' the plough: 's cheek crimsons; curls
Wag or crossbridle, in a wind lifted, windlaced –
See his wind- lilylocks -laced;
Churlsgrace, too, child of Amansstrength, how it hangs or hurls
Them – broad in bluff hide his frowning feet lashed! raced
With, along them, cragiron under and cold furls –
With-a-fountain's shining-shot furls.

[1918]

THOMAS HARDY

In Time of 'The Breaking of Nations'

I

Only a man harrowing clods
  In a slow silent walk
With an old horse that stumbles and nods
  Half asleep as they stalk.

II

Only thin smoke without flame
  From the heaps of couch-grass;
Yet this will go onward the same
  Though Dynasties pass.

III

Yonder a maid and her wight
  Come whispering by:
War's annals will cloud into night
  Ere their story die.

[1915]

WILLIAM BUTLER YEATS

Ancestral Houses

Surely among a rich man's flowering lawns,
Amid the rustle of his planted hills,
Life overflows without ambitious pains;

And rains down life until the basin spills,
And mounts more dizzy high the more it rains
As though to choose whatever shape it wills
And never stoop to a mechanical
Or servile shape, at others' beck and call.

Mere dreams, mere dreams! Yet Homer had not sung
Had he not found it certain beyond dreams
That out of life's own self-delight had sprung
The abounding glittering jet; though now it seems
As if some marvellous empty sea-shell flung
Out of the obscure dark of the rich streams,
And not a fountain, were the symbol which
Shadows the inherited glory of the rich.

Some violent bitter man, some powerful man
Called architect and artist in, that they,
Bitter and violent men, might rear in stone
The sweetness that all longed for night and day,
The gentleness none there had ever known;
But when the master's buried mice can play,
And maybe the great-grandson of that house,
For all its bronze and marble, 's but a mouse.

O what if gardens where the peacock strays
With delicate feet upon old terraces,
Or else all Juno from an urn displays
Before the indifferent garden deities;
O what if levelled lawns and gravelled ways
Where slippered Contemplation finds his ease
And Childhood a delight for every sense,
But take our greatness with our violence?

What if the glory of escutcheoned doors,
And buildings that a haughtier age designed,

The pacing to and fro on polished floors
Amid great chambers and long galleries, lined
With famous portraits of our ancestors;
What if those things the greatest of mankind
Consider most to magnify, or to bless,
But take our greatness with our bitterness?

[1923]

INDEX OF AUTHORS

INDEX OF FIRST LINES AND TITLES

Titles are set entirely in italics